Advanced Placement

ENGLISH

Heather Hilliard
Jessica Egan
John Keefe

XAMonline
Melrose, MA

To obtain permission(s) to use the material from this work for any purpose including workshops or seminars, please submit a written request to:

XAMonline, Inc.
21 Orient Avenue
Melrose, MA 02176
Toll Free: 1-800-301-4647
Email: info@xamonline.com
Web: www.xamonline.com
Fax: 1-617-583-5552

Library of Congress Cataloging-in-Publication Data
Hilliard, Heather

AP English / Heather Hilliard
ISBN: 978-1-60787-632-8

1. Advanced Placement 2. Study Guides 3. English
4. Literature 5. Composition

Disclaimer:
The opinions expressed in this publication are the sole works of XAMonline and were created independently from the College Board, or other testing affiliates. Between the time of publication and printing, specific test standards as well as testing formats and website information may change that are not included in part or in whole within this product. XAMonline develops sample test questions, and they reflect similar content as on real tests; however, they are not former tests. XAMonline assembles content that aligns with test standards but makes no claims nor guarantees candidates a passing score.

Cover photo provided by ©Can Stock Photo Inc./Kurhan;csp4831346; iStock.com/ClaudeLux; iStock.com/jordanchez; iStock.com/stukkey; iStock.com/Ken Brown

Printed in the United States of America
AP English
ISBN: 978-1-60787-632-8

Table of Contents

Section V: Appendices .103

Section VI: Sample Tests .125

Meet the Authors

Heather M. Hilliard

Earning her bachelor's degree in New Orleans and her two masters degrees from the University of Pittsburgh, Heather M. Hilliard serves as an Adjunct Professor for her undergraduate alma mater, Tulane University. From teaching – both at the collegiate level as well as special courses at a leading independent high school – to her corporate endeavors, she has consciously focused aspects of her career and volunteerism on education. She has received several commendations for her achievements, has been inducted into the national honor society for public health and is one of fewer than 1,000 internationally Certified Emergency Managers in the world. She has published on a variety of topics and edited textbooks as well as other fiction and non-fiction work and focuses on strategic communications and improvements for clients – including writing and editing for XAMonline preparation content and tests including Advanced Placement exams, CLEP materials, and the SAT.

Jessica Egan

With a Master's Degree in English Education from Florida State University, Jessica Egan has expertise in the areas of literature, linguistics, and educational psychology. Jessica has worked as an instructional technologist and has experience in teaching secondary English, English as a Second Language (ESL), college-level composition and Adult Basic Education (ABE). She has authored lesson plans, teacher certification materials, and test preparation texts.

John Keefe

John Keefe is an author and editor from Chicago, Illinois. A graduate of Columbia College Chicago, John Keefe has written fiction and non-fiction for publications such as Chicago Literati, Hair Trigger Magazine, and websites like Cracked.com. He is also an actor and playwright.

SECTION I: About the Advanced Placement English Program

Chapter 1: Introduction

The Advanced Placement® program is designed to offer students college credit while still in high school. There are more than 30 AP courses culminating in an intensive final exam given every year in May.

Generally, exams last from two to three hours with limited breaks. Multiple choice questions, if any, typically come before short answer and essay questions. Scores are calculated based on the number of correct answers. Incorrect and unanswered questions do not take away from the overall score.

Successful completion of the course and a passing score on the exam not only demonstrates a student's command of the material, but also gives them a jumpstart on their college careers. AP credit is widely accepted by post-secondary schools, although each school has different guidelines as to what scores they will accept. Typically, a score of three on the five-point scale is considered passing, but some schools seek scores of four or five in order to qualify.

About the Exam

There are two AP English exams in the College Board offerings. There is the AP English Literature and Composition exam and the AP English Language and Composition exam, and we explain the differences in this book. They both align with college-level rhetoric and literary analysis courses, preparing students for argumentative and analytic writing and literary exploration that can be applied throughout the college experience.

This particular exam focuses on rhetorical analysis, argumentation, and synthesis of information drawn from multiple sources. Close reading and critical analysis skills allow students to dive deep into content to examine and break down meaning.

The multiple choice section provides a number of excerpts for students to examine. These selections may include published works of drama, poetry, or prose fiction. Each excerpt typically includes several multiple choice questions relating to its content.

The free-response section provides time for reading the prompt and writing time, for a total of two hours. There are three free-response questions total, which are each graded using a five-point scale. Prompts can ask students to synthesize concepts from three given sources to support a thesis statement, provide an excerpt from a non-fiction text and ask for an analysis of the intended meaning, and provide a topic for students to create an argument around. They can also provide poems and passages from prose fiction for analysis of a given concept or issue. "Open" questions allow students to select a literary work and discuss relevant features in relation to a given concept.

The Curriculum

AP English Literature and Composition is deeply rooted in the advancement of reading and writing skills in preparation for college-level courses. To create an equivalent experience of first year students, those enrolled in AP English courses should expect to focus heavily on expository writing – the Literature and Composition course focuses on literary analysis while the Language and Composition course utilizes rhetoric and reference ability to argue or persuade the reader.

Reading

To achieve a high score on the AP English Literature and Composition exam, students should come prepared to read from a variety of genres and time periods. Skills from previous reading courses will be built upon, including literary analysis of historical and rhetorical references. Previous experiences with literary passages will inform a student's interpretation and analysis of the given work. Close reading skills will greatly benefit the deep analysis of the following reading topics:

- Poetry
- Drama
- Fiction
- Non-fiction
- Literary periods
- Literary genres

Writing

Critical analysis of reading passages will assist students in writing well-constructed answers to free response questions on the AP English exam. Students should practice writing clear and concise messages to convey their perspectives and interpretations. It will be critical to demonstrate knowledge in the following areas:

- Basic elements of rhetoric
- Argumentative writing strategies
- Persuasive writing strategies
- Paraphrasing and proper use of quotations as well as citations
- Summarizing
- Demonstration of revision and editing
- A wide-ranging vocabulary
- Social and historical contexts
- Supporting interpretation of literature
- Proper use of informal and formal writing
- Varied use of sentence structures
- Appropriate use of subordination and coordination
- Logical organization and illustrative detail
- An effective use of rhetoric (including tone, voice, diction, and sentence structure)
- Effective use of time to develop an argument or present an analysis

Exam Structure

Both AP English exams are set up with the same format for sections as well as the same layout and timeframes. Here, we will show the details by using the AP English Literature and Composition as illustration.

The AP English Literature and Composition exam is administered annually in May. The exam is 3 hours, consisting of approximately 55 multiple choice questions and three free-response (short essay) questions. Students are given one hour for the multiple choice questions and two hours for the free-response section.

Part I: Multiple Choice

Question Format	Number of Questions	Time	% of Exam Score
Multiple Choice	52-55	1 hour	45

Multiple choice questions are formulated around American literature, poetry and prose excerpts. Students should focus on being prepared to analyze the following for each of the passages:

- Structure
- Style
- Theme(s)
- Figurative language
- Imagery
- Symbolism
- Tone

Part II: Free-Response

Question Format	Number of Questions	Time	% of Exam Score
Free-response	3	2 hours	55

The free-response portion of the exam prompts students to write short essays that require students to analyze and interpret literary works. Free-responses have a strong focus on literary analysis, and topics can be formulated around prose fiction, poetry, or specific concepts embedded in the given work. In the two hours given, writing assignments include:

- Expository
- Analytical
- Argumentative

Exam Scoring

Each summer, hundreds of college professors, content specialists, and AP English Literature and Composition teachers meet at the annual "AP Reading" to grade the 300,000+ exams that are taken. The multiple choice portion of the test is scored by machine and the free-response section is scored at the AP Reading event.

Free-response questions are weighted and combined with the computer generated score from the multiple choice section. Once both scores have been tallied, they are combined and then scaled. This raw score is then changed into a composite score ranging from 1 – 5. The accuracy of scoring standards is overseen by a highly qualified college-level professor, known as the Chief Reader.

The College Board proposes the following qualifications for each of the potential score:

Exam Grade	Recommendation
5	No recommendation
4	Possibly Qualified
3	Qualified
2	Well Qualified
1	Extremely Well Qualified

The minimum score required for college credit to be granted is a 3. As mentioned, many schools require scores of 4 or 5 in order to grant credit. For comparison, the College Board makes the equivalents of the AP Exam scores as follows:

AP Exam Grade	Letter Grade Equivalent
5	A
4	A-, B+, B
3	B-, C+, C
2	None
1	None

For reference, the 2015 administration of the AP English Literature and Composition exam had this distribution:

Exam Score	Percentage of Students
5	7.6
4	18.2
3	30.5
2	32.7
1	11.1

Based upon these scores, the distribution of students' grades would form a typical bell curve. We go into depth about how you can increase your essay scores in several chapters to help you do your best!

How to Use this Guide

As you move forward through these next pages, you will see a variety of information. The first section is a review of English concepts that you should know. You will see they are broken down by main topic in the Table of Contents. Additionally, you will also find sample multiple choice questions for each topic. While these are not necessarily in the same format you will see on the AP English exam, they will help you to assess your knowledge of the different concepts.

We have arranged this book from the more basic components for review to the more detailed chapters on literary periods and genres, and conclude with chapters that may present new information for you. All of these components – even if they seem "too simple" for an AP review – are keys to success in the multiple choice section and to the free-response compositions for both the AP English Literature and Composition as well as the AP English Language and Composition.

Each chapter in this study guide serves as a mini semester summary for college-level courses, providing critical information that would be necessary to succeed at introductory collegiate courses. In addition to contextual, mechanical, and thematic details, chapters conclude with useful tips for success to help you achieve the highest score possible on your AP exam.

In addition to an inclusive review of content and strategies for success, this book outlines technical components of writing that many schools no longer incorporate into lessons but are essential for strong writing (and high scores). Rubric and enhancing your own writing components will add value to any review session where a student truly uses this to improve his/her writing. These components serve as guides to help you best understand how to approach the exam and succeed in both the multiple choice and written response portions, rather than just providing a quick practice exam. To set yourself up for the best grade possible, all information should be read carefully in order to have a comprehensive review of what is most important on your AP exam.

You will also find seven sample tests at the end of this book. These are designed to give you hands-on experience that simulates the actual exam you will be taking. Each question on these tests has a detailed answer as to why it is correct and why the incorrect answers are wrong. Use this information to help guide your learning. You may also practice by timing yourself as you move through the multiple choice questions and free-response section to best prepare yourself for the day of the exam.

SECTION II: Basic Language Review

Chapter 2: Vocabulary

THE ENGLISH LANGUAGE HAS A MORE EXTENSIVE VOCABULARY THAN ANY OTHER LANGUAGE. English is rich in synonyms, words borrowed from other languages, and newly coined words (neologisms)—many of them introduced by the rapid expansion of technology. It is important to understand that language is in constant flux, and that the English language in particular is constantly evolving with words that are created based on societal trends.

Register (informal and formal language) is a distinction made on the basis of the occasion and the audience. In written English, a formal register would be used for scholarly works, research papers, literary criticisms, professional conference presentations, and other serious works. When the register is formal, longer sentences and exact syntax are used, as is more complex vocabulary. Slang is eschewed, as are common expressions or colloquialisms and contractions. In informal discourse, vocabulary is more casual; slang, colloquialisms, and contractions are used freely. Syntax is more relaxed and sentences are shorter in informal discourse. Informal written communications include magazine articles, popular books, and everyday conversations.

When preparing for the essay portions of the AP English Literature and Composition and/or AP English Language and Composition exams, practicing different tones and incorporating vocabulary will give you an opportunity to familiarize yourself with the proper register. Given your audience (experienced AP teachers), understand that formal language will be used throughout the exam. Avoid all informal discourse. This includes slang and jargon that may not be understood by reviewers that live outside of your geographic region.

A few strategies to understand unfamiliar words and to build vocabulary include the following:

- expand vocabulary through wide reading, listening, and discussing;
- rely on context to determine meanings of words and phrases such as figurative language, idioms, multiple meaning words, and technical vocabulary;
- apply meanings of prefixes, roots, and suffixes in order to comprehend new words;
- research word origins, including Anglo-Saxon, Latin, and Greek words;
- use reference material such as glossary, dictionary, thesaurus, and available technology to determine precise meanings and usage; and
- identify the relation of word meanings in analogies, homonyms, synonyms/antonyms, and connotation/denotation.

Root, Base, and Compound Words

Structural elements within words can be used independently to determine meaning. Often including a historical element, root words commonly stem from Latin or Greek origins. Base words are considered language in the simplest form. Compound words create meaning through the combination of two words that are able to stand alone.

Root words: A root word is a word from which another word is developed. The second word can be said to have its "root" in the first. This structural component lends itself to an illustration of a tree and its roots, which can concretize the meaning for students. Typically, root words cannot stand alone.

Aquatic (aqua = water)
Submerge (sub = under)
Junction (junct = connect)

Base words: Unlike root words, base words are stand-alone linguistic units that cannot be deconstructed or broken down into smaller words. Prefixes and suffixes are connected to base words to create meaning.

Retell (base = tell)
Instructor (base = instruct)
Sampled (base = sample)

Compound words: Compound words occur when two or more base words are connected to form a new word. The meaning of the new word is in some way connected to the meanings of the base words.

Everything (every + thing)
Backpack (back + pack)
Notebook (note + book)

Prefixes and Suffixes

Prefixes are beginning units of meaning that can be added (affixed) to the beginning of a base word or root word. They are also known as bound morphemes, meaning that they cannot stand alone as words.

Prefix	Meaning	Example
Re-	To do again	Reread
Anti-	Against	Anticlimactic
Uni-	One	Unibrow
Mis-	Incorrect	Misunderstood

Suffixes are ending units of meaning that can be affixed to the end of a base word or root word. Suffixes transform the original meanings of base and root words. Like prefixes, they are also known as bound morphemes because they cannot stand alone as words.

Suffix	Meaning	Example
-able	Ability	Likeable
-er	One who	Teacher
-less	Without	Careless
-est	Comparative	Smartest

Inflectional endings are types of suffixes that impart a new meaning to the base word or root word. These endings change the gender, number, tense, or form of the base or root word. Just like other suffixes, these are bound morphemes.

Ending	Original Word	New Word
-s	Road	Roads
-es	Mix	Mixes
-ing	Write	Writes
-ed	Sample	Sampled

Connotation and Denotation

Denotation is the literal meaning of a word, as opposed to its connotative meaning. *Connotation* refers to the implications and associations of a given word, distinct from the denotative or literal meaning. Connotation is used when a subtle tone is preferred. It may stir up a more effective emotional response than if the author had used blunt, denotative diction. For example, "Good night, sweet prince, and flights of angels sing thee to thy rest," a line from Shakespeare's Hamlet, refers to a departure or death; connotatively, it renders the harsh reality of death in gentle terms such as those used in putting a child to sleep.

Informative connotations are definitions agreed upon by the society in which the learner operates. A skunk is "a black and white mammal of the weasel family with a pair of pineal glands which secrete a pungent odor." (denotative) The Merriam-Webster Collegiate Dictionary adds that this odor is also "offensive." The color, species, and glandular characteristics are informative. The interpretation of the odor as offensive is affective (connotative).

Affective connotations refers to the personal feelings a word arouses. A child who has no personal experience with a skunk and its odor will feel differently about the word "skunk" than a child who has smelled the spray of a skunk or been conditioned to associate offensiveness with it. The fact that our society views a skunk as an animal to be avoided will affect the child's interpretation of the word. In fact, it is not necessary for one to have actually seen a skunk (that is, have a denotative understanding) to use the word in either connotative expression. For example, one child might call another child a skunk, connoting an unpleasant reaction (affective use) or, seeing another small black and white animal, call it a skunk based on the definition (informative use).

Figurative Devices

Figurative language allows for the statement of truths that more literal language cannot. Figures of speech add many dimensions of richness to our writing and allow many opportunities for worthwhile analysis. Skillfully used, a figure of speech will help the reader, see more clearly and focus upon particulars. Listing all possible figures of speech is beyond the scope of this list. However, for purposes of building vocabulary, a few are sufficient.

Parallelism: The arrangement of ideas in phrases, sentences, and paragraphs that balance one element with another of equal importance and similar wording. Here is an example from Francis Bacon's *Of Studies:*

"Reading maketh a full man, conference a ready man, and writing an exact man."

Euphemism: The substitution of an agreeable or inoffensive term for one that might offend or suggest something unpleasant. Many euphemisms are used to refer to death to avoid using the word, such as "passed away," "crossed over," or "passed."

Hyperbole: Deliberate exaggeration for dramatic or comic effect. Here is an example from Shakespeare's The Merchant of Venice:

"Why, if two gods should play some heavenly match
And on the wager lay two earthly women,
And Portia one, there must be something else
Pawned with the other, for the poor rude world
Hath not her fellow."

Bathos: A ludicrous attempt to portray pathos—that is, to evoke pity, sympathy, or sorrow. It may result from inappropriately dignifying the commonplace, using elevated language to describe something trivial, or greatly exaggerating pathos.

Oxymoron: A contradiction in terms deliberately employed for effect. It is usually seen in a qualifying adjective whose meaning is contrary to that of the noun it modifies, such as "wise folly."

Irony: Expressing something other than and often opposite of the literal meaning, such as words of praise when blame is intended. In poetry, it is often used as a sophisticated or resigned awareness of contrast between what is and what ought to be and expresses a controlled pathos without sentimentality. It is a form of indirection that avoids overt praise or censure. An early example is the Greek comic character Eiron, a clever underdog who by his wit repeatedly triumphs over the boastful character Alazon.

Malapropism: A verbal blunder in which one word is replaced by another similar in sound but different in meaning. This term comes from Sheridan's Mrs. Malaprop in The Rivals (1775). Thinking of the geography of contiguous countries, she spoke of the "geometry" of "contagious countries."

Other common figurative devices include: simile, metaphor, alliteration, onomatopoeia, personification. These are included in the chapter on poetry for AP English Language and Composition included with this study guide.

Other Syntax Devices

Synonyms and antonyms: A synonym means the same thing as another word and can substitute for it in certain contexts. Diversifying vocabulary in your writing by incorporating synonyms will improve your writing, giving you the best chance for a high score on the written sections for AP exams.

Original word	Synonyms
Smart	Intelligent, bright
Required	Necessary, mandatory
Many	Numerous

An antonym represents a meaning opposite that of a given word.

Original word	Antonym
Optional	Required
Before	After
Complex	Simple

Analogies: An analogy illustrates an idea by means of a more familiar idea that is similar or parallel to it. These are commonly found on AP exams, and studying vocabulary and literary devices will help you in breaking down meaning to find the correct answers. As you read through options for analogies in the multiple choice sections, it's important to keep in mind that you're looking for the most logical answer. Beware of questions that have multiple options that make sense, and try to zero in on the "best" answer. Also, it's best to go with your gut answer while determining the correct option for analogies. Over thinking will lead to second guessing. You could waste valuable test time as you continue to run through the possibilities.

Most commonly, analogies are laid out on AP exams like this:

An apple is to fruit as ____ is to vegetable.

A. Celery
B. Water
C. Organic
D. Hydroponic

The answer is A. Celery.

You may find analogies on AP exams that stem from cause/effect, part of a whole, and characteristics (similar or complete opposite).

Idioms: An idiom is a word or expression that cannot be translated word for word into another language, such as "I am running low on gas." By extension, writers use idioms to convey a way of speaking and writing typical of a group of people. Some idioms are passed down from one generation to the next, but not all. Because language is constantly evolving, some idioms are left behind while new phrases come into use. For example, the saying "burn the midnight oil," meaning working late into the night, has died off. This may have been a common saying around the time oil lamps were used, but technology has evolved to the point this saying would be arbitrary to our current society. Listed below are some common idioms in American English:

- Birthday suit
- Down the drain
- Show off
- At the drop of a hat
- Taste of your own medicine
- Piece of cake
- Keep an eye on it
- Long shot
- Play it by ear
- Raining cats and dogs
- An arm and a leg
- Sick as a dog

Dialect: Dialect, also referred to as regionalism, includes usages that are peculiar to a particular part of a country. A good example is the second-person plural pronoun you. Because the plural is the same as the singular, speakers in various parts of the country have developed their own vocabulary solutions to be sure that they are understood when they are speaking to more than one "you." In the South, "you-all" or "y'all" is common. In the Northeast, one often hears "youse." In some areas of the Midwest, "you'ns" can be heard. Similar to idiomatic expressions, dialect evolves to incorporate societal trends and expands from year to year.

Jargon: Jargon is a specialized vocabulary. It may be the vocabulary peculiar to a particular industry, such as computers, or of a field of interest, such as religion. It may also be the vocabulary of a social group. The jargon of bloggers comprises a whole vocabulary that has even developed its own dictionaries. The speaker must be knowledgeable about and sensitive to the jargon peculiar to the particular audience. That may require some research and some vocabulary development on the speaker's part. For example, technical language is a form of jargon. It is usually specific to an industry, profession, or field of study. Sensitivity to the language familiar to the particular audience is important.

Strategy for Points: Avoiding Vocabulary Errors

- Avoid using the pronunciation of a word, which often results in improper spelling.
- Varying vocabulary is a great way to diversify your writing. Because you will be developing a written response to portray concise, strong, writing, you do not want to take away from your message by using the same words over and over again. Look back over the synonym and antonym section to refresh your memory for substituting and expanding the words used in your written responses. Switching up words, phrases, and methods of emphasizing will give you the best opportunity for

a high score.

- Stick to words that you know. Now is not the time to try to add in a fancy word to make your writing seem college-ready. It is best to use familiar words (in both meaning and usage) than to take a risk and end up losing points because you have used a word incorrectly.
- Use context clues to define words that are unknown. This will assist you when reading multiple choice questions, particularly definitions and analogies, as well as poetry selections that may not be as familiar.
- Flashcards can be a great way to prepare you for unknown words. You may pick up on a root, a common prefix, or suffix that will help you in selecting correct answers on the day of the test.

Chapter 3: Grammar

GRAMMAR IS THE PROPER USAGE OF WORDS AND PHRASES. FOR A TESTS SUCH AS THE AP English Literature and Composition and AP English Language and Composition, it is critical to demonstrate proper use of grammar and avoid errors in usage, spelling, diction, and rhetoric.

Multiple choice questions will test your knowledge of a variety of English grammar rules: parts of speech, syntax, sentence types, sentence structure, sentence combining, phrases and clauses, modifiers, and capitalization.

Writing prompts will give you an opportunity to showcase your knowledge of these rules. Patterns of error in the written sections will immediately result in a lower grade. You will want to be sure to avoid sentence fragments and run-on sentences. Recognition of sentence elements necessary to express a complete thought, proper use of independent and dependent clauses, and proper punctuation will correct such errors. Reviewing the following grammar points will assist in getting higher scores for both multiple choice and essay questions.

Parts of Speech

There are eight parts of speech: nouns, verbs, adjectives, adverbs, pronouns, conjunctions, prepositions, and interjections.

Noun: A person, place or thing. (student, school, textbook)
Verb: An action word. (study, read, run)
Adjective: Describes a verb or noun. (smart, beautiful, colorful)
Adverb: Describes a verb. (quickly, fast, intelligently)
Pronoun: Substitutes for a noun. (he, she, it)
Conjunction: Joins two phrases. (because, but, so)
Preposition: Used before nouns to provide additional details. (before, after, on)
Interjection: Expresses emotion. (Ha!, Hello!, Stop!)

Syntax

Although widely different in many aspects, written and spoken English share a common basic structure or syntax (subject, verb, and object) and the common purpose of fulfilling the need to communicate—but there, the similarities end.

Spoken English follows the basic word order mentioned above (subject, verb, object) as does written English. We would write as we would speak: "I sang a song." It is usually only in poetry or music that that word order or syntax is altered: "Sang I a song."

Types of Sentences

Sentence variety is a great way to demonstrate your knowledge of the various sentence types in the writing portions for the AP English exam.

Sentence Types

Declarative	Makes a statement	I bought a new textbook
Interrogatory	Asks a question	Where did you buy it?
Exclamatory	Expresses strong emotion	I can't believe it!
Imperative	Gives a command	Put it on the table

Clauses are connected word groups that are composed of at least one subject and one verb. (A subject is the doer of an action or the element that is being joined. A verb conveys either the action or the link.)

subject *verb*
Students are waiting for the start of the assembly.

subject *verb*
At the end of the play, students waited for the curtain to come down.

Clauses can be *independent* or *dependent.* Independent clauses can stand alone or can be joined to other clauses, either independent or dependent. Words that can be used to join clauses include the following:

- for
- and
- nor
- but
- or
- yet
- so

Dependent clauses, by definition, contain at least one subject and one verb. However, they cannot stand alone as a complete sentence. They are structurally dependent on an independent clause (the main clause of the sentence). There are two types of dependent clauses: (1) those with a subordinating conjunction and (2) those with a relative pronoun

Coordinating conjunctions include the following:

- although
- when
- if
- unless
- because

Example: Unless a cure is discovered, many more people will die of the disease. (dependent clause with coordinating conjunction [unless] + independent clause)

Relative pronouns include the following:

- who
- whom
- which
- that

Example: The White House has an official website, which contains press releases, news updates, and biographies of the president and vice president. (independent clause + relative pronoun [which] + relative dependent clause)

Sentence Structure

You must recognize simple, compound, complex, and compound-complex sentences. Use dependent (subordinate) and independent clauses correctly to create these sentence structures.

Simple: Joyce wrote a letter.
Compound: Joyce wrote a letter and Dot drew a picture.
Complex: While Joyce wrote a letter, Dot drew a picture.
Compound/complex: When Mother asked the girls to demonstrate their newfound skills, Joyce wrote a letter and Dot drew a picture.

Note: Do not confuse compound sentence elements with compound sentences.

Simple sentence with compound subject: Joyce and Dot wrote letters.
The girl in row three and the boy next to her were passing notes across the aisle.
Simple sentence with compound predicate: Joyce wrote letters and drew pictures.
The captain of the high school debate team graduated with honors and studied broadcast journalism in college.

Simple sentence with compound object of preposition: Coleen graded the students' essays for style and mechanical accuracy.

Parallelism

Recognize parallel structures using phrases (prepositional, gerund, participial, and infinitive) and omissions from sentences that create the lack of parallelism.

Prepositional phrase/single modifier:
Incorrect: Coleen ate the ice cream with enthusiasm and hurriedly.
Correct: Coleen ate the ice cream with enthusiasm and in a hurry.
Correct: Coleen ate the ice cream enthusiastically and hurriedly.

Participial phrase/infinitive phrase:

Incorrect: After hiking for hours and to sweat profusely, Joe sat down to rest and drinking water.

Correct: After hiking for hours and sweating profusely, Joe sat down to rest and drink water.

Recognition of Misplaced and Dangling Modifiers

Dangling phrases are attached to sentence parts in such a way that they create ambiguity and incorrectness of meaning.

Participial phrase:

Incorrect: Hanging from her skirt, Dot tugged at a loose thread.

Correct: Dot tugged at a loose thread hanging from her skirt.

Infinitive phrase:

Incorrect: To improve his behavior, the dean warned Fred.

Correct: The dean warned Fred to improve his behavior.

Prepositional phrase:

Incorrect: On the floor, Father saw the dog eating table scraps.

Correct: Father saw the dog eating table scraps on the floor.

Particular phrases that are not placed near the word they modify often result in misplaced modifiers. Particular phrases that do not relate to the subject being modified result in dangling modifiers.

Error: Weighing the options carefully, a decision was made regarding the punishment of the convicted murderer.

Problem: Who is weighing the options? No one capable of weighing is named in the sentence. Thus, the participle phrase "weighing the options carefully" dangles. This problem can be corrected by adding a subject of the sentence who is capable of doing the action.

Correction: Weighing the options carefully, the judge made a decision regarding the punishment of the convicted murderer.

Error: Returning to my favorite watering hole brought back many fond memories.

Problem: The person who returned is never indicated, and the participle phrase dangles. This problem can be corrected by creating a dependent clause from the modifying phrase.

Correction: When I returned to my favorite watering hole, many fond memories came back to me.

Recognition of Syntactical Redundancy or Omission

These errors occur when superfluous words have been added to a sentence or key words have been omitted from a sentence.

Redundancy

Incorrect: Joyce made sure that when her plane arrived that she retrieved all of her luggage.

Correct: Joyce made sure that when her plane arrived she retrieved all of her luggage.

Incorrect: He was a mere skeleton of his former self.

Correct: He was a skeleton of his former self.

Omission

Incorrect: Dot opened her book, recited her textbook, and answered the teacher's subsequent question.

Correct: Dot opened her book, recited from the textbook, and answered the teacher's subsequent question.

Avoidance of Double Negatives

This error occurs from positioning two negatives that cancel each other out (creates a positive statement).

Incorrect: Dot didn't have no double negatives in her paper. Dot didn't have any double negatives in her paper.

Spelling

Spelling rules are extremely complex, based as they are on rules of phonics and letter doubling, and are replete with exceptions. Even adults who have a good command of written English benefit from using a dictionary. Adolescent students will also benefit from learning how to use a dictionary and thesaurus.

Most plurals of nouns that end in hard consonants or hard consonant sounds followed by a silent e are made by adding s. Some nouns ending in vowels only add s.

fingers, numerals, banks, bugs, riots, homes, gates, radios, bananas

Nouns that end in the soft consonant sounds s, j, x, z, ch, and sh add es. Some nouns ending in o add es.

dresses, waxes, churches, brushes, tomatoes, potatoes

Nouns ending in y preceded by a vowel just add s.

boys, alleys

Nouns ending in y preceded by a consonant change the y to i and add es.

babies, corollaries, frugalities, poppies

Some noun plurals are formed irregularly or are the same as the singular.

sheep, deer, children, leaves, oxen

Some nouns derived from foreign words, especially Latin, may make their plurals in two different ways, one of them anglicized. Sometimes the meanings are the same; other times, the two plurals are used in slightly different contexts. It is always wise to consult the dictionary.

appendices, appendixes
criterion, criteria
indexes, indices
crisis, crises

Make the plurals of closed (solid) compound words in the usual way except for words ending in -ful, which make their plurals on the root word.

timelines, hairpins, cupsful

Make the plurals of open or hyphenated compounds by adding the change in inflection to the word that changes in number.

fathers-in-law, courts-martial, masters of art, doctors of medicine

Make the plurals of letters, numbers, and abbreviations by adding s.

fives and tens, IBMs, 1990s, ps and qs (Note that letters are italicized.)

Capitalization

Capitalize all proper names of persons (including specific organizations or agencies of government); places (countries, states, cities, parks, and specific geographical areas); things (political parties, structures, historical and cultural terms, and calendar and time designations); and religious terms (any deity, revered person or group, or sacred writing).

Percy Bysshe Shelley, Argentina, Mount Rainier National Park,
Grand Canyon, League of Nations, the Sears Tower, Birmingham,
Lyric Theater, Americans, Midwesterners, Democrats, Renaissance,
Boy Scouts of America, Easter, God, Bible, Dead Sea Scrolls, Koran

Capitalize proper adjectives and titles used with proper names.

California Gold Rush, President John Adams, Senator John Glenn

Some words that represent titles and offices are not capitalized unless used with a proper name.

Capitalized	Not capitalized
Congressman McKay	the congressman from Florida
Queen Elizabeth	the queen of England
Commander Alger	the admiral
President George Washington	the president

Strategy for Points: Avoid Common Grammatical Errors

- Allocate 10 minutes to review your written responses before submitting. One last review of your writing could catch grammar mistakes that you made while you were expressing your thoughts.
- Be mindful of the sentence types that you are using. You'll want to diversify your writing and demonstrate your knowledge of a variety of sentence types.
- Pay close attention to your use of commas as you write. It may come naturally to insert a comma whenever you pause, but this can lead to misuse and overuse of commas.
- Review the parts of speech from the start of this chapter and write out several examples that will help you differentiate during the exam.
- Be careful while incorporating words that are often misused. (You're-your; their-they're-there). The final review of your writing will also help in identifying errors that you miss while writing.

Chapter 4: Punctuation

PUNCTUATION CAN HAVE A BIG IMPACT ON THE OVERALL MESSAGE THAT YOU'RE TRYING TO convey, and it's very likely that points will be deducted if punctuation is used incorrectly or omitted within your essay questions. Using improper punctuation in your writing will create incorrect grammar and will confuse the reader of your essay. It can also create inaccurate quotations and names of famous works of literature.

While writing essays and working through multiple choice questions, be mindful of common punctuation mistakes and keep an eye out for catchy scenarios. Embedded in this chapter, there are opportunities to check your understanding of the punctuation points that you have just reviewed. This practice will help you zero in on areas that you may need to review before moving on to the sample tests.

Using Commas

Commas indicate a brief pause. They are used to set off dependent clauses and long introductory word groups, and they can also separate words in a series. Commas are used to set off unimportant material that interrupts the flow of the sentence. They also separate independent clauses joined by conjunctions.

Commas separate two or more coordinate adjectives modifying the same word and three or more nouns, phrases, or clauses in a list:

- Maggie's hair was dull, dirty, and lice-ridden.
- Dickens portrayed the Artful Dodger as skillful pickpocket, loyal follower of Fagin, and defender of Oliver Twist.
- Ellen daydreamed about getting out of the rain, taking a shower, and eating a hot dinner.
- In Elizabethan England, Ben Johnson wrote comedy, Christopher Marlowe wrote tragedies, and William Shakespeare composed both.

Use commas to separate antithetical or complimentary expressions from the rest of the sentence:

- The veterinarian, not his assistant, would perform the delicate surgery.
- The more he knew about her, the less he wished he had known.
- Randy hopes to, and probably will, get an appointment to the United States Naval Academy.

- His thorough, though esoteric, scientific research could not be easily understood by high school students.

Test your knowledge by studying and understanding the following errors:

Error: After I finish my master's thesis I plan to work in Chicago.
Problem: A comma is needed after an introductory dependent word-group containing a subject and verb.
Correction: After I finish my master's thesis, I plan to work in Chicago.

Error: I washed waxed and vacuumed my car today.
Problem: Words in a series should be separated by commas. Although the comma is sometimes considered optional, it is often necessary to clarify the meaning.
Correction: I washed, waxed, and vacuumed my car today.

Error: She was a talented dancer but she is mostly remembered for her singing ability.
Problem: A comma is needed before a conjunction that joins two independent clauses (complete sentences).
Correction: She was a talented dancer but she is mostly remembered for her singing ability.

Using Apostrophes

Apostrophes are used to show either contractions or possession. Contractions show the omission of a letter (wouldn't = would + not. The apostrophe takes the place of the o.) and possession represents ownership (Sam's new car. The apostrophe lets the reader know the new car belongs to Sam).

Test your knowledge on the following errors:

Error: She shouldnt be permitted to smoke cigarettes in the building.
Problem: An apostrophe is needed in a contraction in place of the missing letter.
Correction: She shouldn't be permitted to smoke cigarettes in the building.

Error: The childrens new kindergarten teacher was also a singer.
Problem: An apostrophe is needed to show possession.
Correction: The childrens' new kindergarten teacher was also a singer.
Note: The apostrophe after the s indicates that there are multiple children.

Using Terminal Punctuation in Relation to Quotation Marks

In a quoted statement that is either declarative or imperative, place the period inside the closing quotation marks.

"The airplane crashed on the runway during takeoff."

If the quotation is followed by other words in the sentence, place a comma inside the closing quotations marks and a period at the end of the sentence.

"The airplane crashed on the runway during takeoff," said the announcer.

In most instances in which a quoted title or expression occurs at the end of a sentence, the period is placed before either the single or double quotation marks.

"The middle school readers were unprepared to understand Bryant's poem 'Thanatopsis.'"
Early book-length adventure stories like Don Quixote *and* The Three Musketeers *were known as "picaresque novels."*

In sentences that are interrogatory or exclamatory, the question mark or exclamation point should be positioned outside the closing quotation marks if the quote itself is a statement, a command, or a cited title.

Who decided to lead us in the recitation of the "Pledge of Allegiance"?
Why was she shaking as she recited, "Once upon a midnight dreary . . ."?

In sentences that are declarative but in which the quotation is a question or an exclamation, place the question mark or exclamation point inside the quotation marks.

The hall monitor yelled, "Fire! Fire!"
The hall monitor asked, "Where's the fire?"

Test your knowledge on the following error:

Error: As the man fell to the ground, his daughter yelled, "Someone call 911"!
Problem: Punctuation should always be placed inside quotation marks when it represents a quoted exclamation.
Correction: As the man fell to the ground, his daughter yelled, "Someone call 911!"

Using Periods with Parentheses or Brackets

Place the period inside the parentheses or brackets if they enclose a complete sentence independent of the other sentences around it.

Stephen Crane was a confirmed alcohol and drug addict. (He admitted as much to other journalists in Cuba.)

If the parenthetical expression is a statement inserted within another statement, the period in the enclosure is omitted.

Mark Twain used the character Indian Joe (he also appeared in The Adventures of Tom Sawyer) as a foil for Jim in The Adventures of Huckleberry Finn.

When enclosed matter comes at the end of a sentence requiring quotation marks, place the period outside the parentheses or brackets.

"The secretary of state consulted with the ambassador [Albright]."

Test your knowledge on the following error:

Error: Musician Kurt Cobain died of a drug overdose (making him a part of the 27 club.) in 1994.
Problem: Statements within statements do not receive punctuation. The period within the parentheses is unnecessary.
Correction: Musician Kurt Cobain died of a drug overdose (making him a part of the 27 club) in 1994.

Rare Marks

The following items that are used rarely, but when you use them, you need to use them appropriately. We'll call this "Rare Marks."

Quotations, whether words, phrases, or clauses, should be punctuated according to the rules of the grammatical function they serve in the sentence.

The works of Shakespeare, "the bard of Avon," have been contested as originating with other authors.

"You'll get my money," the old man warned, "when hell freezes over."

Sheila cited the passage that began "Four score and seven years ago . . . ." (Note the ellipsis followed by an enclosed period.)

Old Ironsides" inspired the preservation of the U.S.S. Constitution.

Use quotation marks to enclose the titles of shorter works: songs, short poems, short stories, essays, and chapters of books. (For title of longer works, see "Using italics," below.)

"The Tell-Tale Heart" "Casey at the Bat" "America the Beautiful"

Test your knowledge on the following errors:

Error: Franklin Roosevelt once said, There is nothing to fear but fear itself.
Problem: Double quotation marks are needed to set off the quotation.
Correction: Franklin Roosevelt once said, "There is nothing to fear but fear itself."

Error: In his best-selling novel *The Firm*, published in 1991, author John Grisham probed the sinister doings in a Memphis law firm.
Problem: Double quotation marks are needed to set off the title of an article.
Correction: In his best-selling novel, "The Firm," published in 1991, author John Grisham probed the sinister doings in a Memphis law firm.

Using semicolons: Semicolons are needed to divide two or more closely related independent sentences. They are also needed to separate items in a series containing commas.

Use semicolons to separate independent clauses when the second clause is introduced by a transitional adverb. (These clauses may also be written as separate sentences, preferably by placing the adverb within the second sentence.)

The Elizabethans modified the rhyme scheme of the sonnet; thus, it was called the English sonnet.
or
The Elizabethans modified the rhyme scheme of the sonnet. It thus was called the English sonnet.

Use semicolons to separate items in a series that is long and complex or has internal punctuation.

The Italian Renaissance produced masters in the fine arts: Dante Alighieri, author of the Divine Comedy; Leonardo da Vinci, painter of The Last Supper; and Donatello, sculptor of the Quattro Santi Coronati, the Four Crowned Saints.

The leading scorers in the WNBA were Haizhou Zheng, averaging 23.9 points per game; Lisa Leslie, 22; and Cynthia Cooper, 19.5.

Test your knowledge on the following errors:

Error: I climbed to the top of the mountain, it took me three hours.
Problem: A comma alone cannot separate two independent clauses. Instead a semicolon is needed to separate two related sentences.
Correction: I climbed to the top of the mountain; it took me three hours.

Error: In the movie, asteroids destroyed Dallas, Texas, Kansas City, Missouri, and Boston, Massachusetts.
Problem: Semicolons are needed to separate items in a series that already contains commas.
Correction: In the movie, asteroids destroyed Dallas, Texas; Kansas City, Missouri; and Boston, Massachusetts.

Using colons: Colons are used to introduce lists and to emphasize what follows.

Place a colon at the beginning of a list of items. (Note its use in the sentence about Renaissance Italians under "Using semicolons," above.)

The teacher directed us to compare Faulkner's three symbolic novels: Absalom, Absalom!; As I Lay Dying; and Light in August.

Do not use a colon if the list is preceded by a verb.

Three of Faulkner's symbolic novels are Absalom, Absalom!; As I Lay Dying, and Light in August.

Test your knowledge on the following error:

Error: Essays will receive the following grades, A for excellent, B for good, C for average, and D for unsatisfactory.
Problem: A colon is needed to emphasize the information or a list that follows.
Correction: Essays will receive the following grades: A for excellent, B for good, C for average, and D for unsatisfactory.

Using Dashes: Place "en" dashes (short dashes) to denote sudden breaks in thought.

Some periods in literature – the Romantic Age, for example – spanned different time periods in different countries.

Use "em" dashes (long dashes) instead of commas if commas are used elsewhere in the sentence for amplification or explanation.

The Fireside Poets included three Brahmans—James Russell Lowell, Henry Wadsworth Longfellow, Oliver Wendell Holmes—and John Greenleaf Whittier.

Test your knowledge on the following error:

Error: There are many works of art that combine historical and structural elements – Frida Kahlo's "Blue House," for example.
Problem: En dashes should be used for sudden breaks of thought. This break in thought should be placed in the center of the sentence instead of at the end. Placing it at the end makes it an afterthought.
Correction: There are many works of art – Frida Kahlo's Blue House, for example – that combine historical and structural elements.

Using italics: Use italics to style the titles of long works of literature, names of periodical publications, musical scores, works of art, movies, and television and radio programs.

Idylls of the King	*Hiawatha*	*The Sound and the Fury*
Mary Poppins	*Newsweek*	*Nutcracker Suite*

(Note: When unable to write in italics, you should underline where italics would be appropriate.)

Test your knowledge on the following error:

Error: The historically non-profit *National Geographic* magazine was sold to 21st Century Fox for $725 million dollars.
Problem: The title of the magazine should be italicized, which is National Geographic. The

word magazine is not a proper noun or part of the title, so it shouldn't be capitalized or italicized.

Correction: The historically non-profit *National Geographic* magazine was sold to 21st Century Fox for $725 million dollars.

Strategy for Points: Identify and Avoid Punctuation Errors

- Leave yourself some time to review your writing one last time for punctuation. You may go through the written responses to zero in on grammatical mistakes first and then give it a final review specific to punctuation mistakes and omissions.
- Be mindful of the punctuation that you are using. You do not want to add something for the sake of diversifying your punctuation if you are not 100% sure how to use it correctly. It's better to avoid taking risks and ensure your punctuation has been used accurately.
- Pay close attention to your use of apostrophes. It may come naturally to insert an apostrophe as you are writing, but you should review them before submitting to ensure the word required an apostrophe. For example, the word may have simply needed to be pluralized (automobiles) vs. made possessive (automobile's).
- Review the proper uses for quotation marks from the start of this chapter and write out several examples that will help you differentiate during the exam.
- Be careful while incorporating famous works of literature. You'll want to ensure you are spelling them correctly and writing them out correctly (for example, italicized) so that points are not deducted for improper format.

SECTION III: Essential Literary Review

Chapter 5: Literary Periods

THROUGHOUT HISTORY, THE POLITICS OF EACH CULTURE ARE REFLECTED IN ITS LITERATURE. Developments in technology, philosophy, and language can be charted through familiarity with each culture's body of work. The AP English Literature and Composition test has a focus on English language literature, specifically that of the United States and the British Isles, but an understanding of major developments in world literature is also essential. By knowing the major works, authors, and themes of each literary period, you can demonstrate a fuller understanding of the literary canon that shaped the world we live in today.

This chapter can act as a refresher to each literary period throughout world literature, but it's also important to do more in-depth research of specific literary works as you study for the AP test. An understanding of the historical context of these works is also important.

American Literature

The earliest literature to come out of North America was produced by the various indigenous tribes that inhabited the continent before European settlers appeared. These stories were almost always oral tellings, passed down from generation to generation, dealing with themes such as the interconnectedness of nature and a reverence for family and tradition. After European colonization began, Native American stories took on a somber tone as they lamented the destruction of their people and culture.

The **Colonial Period** of American literature, by contrast, was written down instead of told orally, and was deeply Christian and neoclassical in style. In the 1630s, the first printing presses were built by colonists in the New World, and they created writings that borrowed heavily from the British literary canon. Colonists were often taught proper English grammar and spelling, and their works depicted the struggles of early colonial life, always with an emphasis on order, family, and religion. William Bradford's Mayflower Compact recounted the daily hardships of colonization during the harsh winter in Massachusetts, whereas Anne Bradstreet explored colonial daily life through poetry. Captain John Smith is sometimes considered the first author of the New World due to his journals recalling his earliest days on the new continent.

Values at this time were distinctly Puritan, emphasizing the church as the center of all daily life. Indeed, much of the writing produced at this time was intended simply to be read aloud during sermons. It wasn't until the **Revolutionary Period** in the mid-1700s that works of a more political nature began to appear.

In 1775, Thomas Paine, a philosopher and activist, wrote a pamphlet that would become the top-selling piece of American literature of all time. *Common Sense* was an incendiary piece of writing, detailing in clear, simple prose the need for rebellion against British rule. The pamphlet's fierce rhetoric stirred the hearts of the colonial upper class, and its concise style meant it could be read aloud in taverns and town squares so that even the illiterate could hear Paine's words. John Adams would later say, "Without the pen of the author of *Common Sense*, the sword of Washington would have been raised in vain." *Common Sense* epitomized this period of American literature, emphasizing freedom from Britain and the need to forge a new identity as Americans.

Among the educated elite, enlightenment was the watchword of the day. Enlightenment thinkers criticized the religious and political dogma they had been raised with, insisting that a new social order based on reason was necessary to modernize the human race. Some enlightenment thinkers, like Benjamin Franklin, explored new concepts of morality outside of Puritanism – Franklin's *Poor Richard's Almanack* was a collection of wit and wisdom that detailed Franklin's concepts of common virtue in an entertaining style. Many of Franklin's aphorisms from this book ("A penny saved is a penny earned") survive to this day.

The Revolutionary Period also produced stirring oration – Patrick Henry's "Speech to the Virginia House of Burgesses" produced the timeless quotation "Give me liberty or give me death!" This directness was a necessary component of Revolutionary writing, as it needed to be accessible to even the uneducated and illiterate citizens the upper class wished to recruit.

Even the Declaration of Independence exhibits characteristics of good Revolutionary literature. Written by Thomas Jefferson, it offers neoclassical style, direct prose, and plenty of irresistible quotations that deliver a unified political message.

The 1800s saw the rise of the **Romantic Period** in American literature. Romanticism was considered very liberal and radical for its time, a reaction to the Industrial Revolution and the increasing scientific rationalization of nature. Romanticism focused on intense emotions, such as awe, horror, love, lust, and depression, and found artistic beauty in the wonders of nature. American Romanticists also lionized their own exploits – the trials against the Indians, Manifest Destiny, and the triumphs of Revolutionary heroes like George Washington. Later critics would characterize Romanticism as naïve, but the influence of the movement on world literature was indelible.

Washington Irving was an early American Romantic, creating folk tales like "The Legend of Sleepy Hollow" and "Rip Van Winkle," which largely rejected British influence in favor of a new American consciousness. The Romantic Period also saw a rise in poetry intended to be read as cozy fireside entertainment. "Fireside Poets" such as James Russell Lowell, Oliver Wendell Holmes, and John Greenleaf Whittier wrote of scenarios familiar to Americans at the time, such as the harshness and beauty of New England winters. Henry Wadsworth Longfellow wrote longer poetic epics like *The Song of Hiawatha* and *The Courtship of Miles Standish* which could thrill as well as educate.

Another prominent American Romantic author is Edgar Allan Poe. Among the first authors to make his living solely by writing, Poe's influence has been felt around the world.

With short stories like "Murders in the Rue Morgue," Poe invented the genre of detective fiction, and works like "The Cask of Amontillado" pioneered in the genre of horror. His works explored topics of depression and family strife, drawing heavily upon his own struggles. He had a major influence on other genres like science fiction and mystery, and he is considered one of the all-time masters of the short story, helping to establish it as a major literary form.

Meanwhile, Nathaniel Hawthorne offered some of the first true criticisms of the Puritan lifestyle that had been so prominent in Colonial times. *The Scarlet Letter* is considered his masterwork, depicting the public shaming and ostracization of Hester Prynne, a Puritan woman accused of adultery. Though a fundamentally Romantic book, it eschews much of the wide-eyed naiveté common to the movement, focusing more on the grim realities of human nature.

This political bent in Romantic literature was pushed further by the "Transcendentalists" – Henry David Thoreau and Ralph Waldo Emerson created this subgenre of Romanticism which sought beauty in the simplicity of nature and freedom from the struggles of society. Both authors were intensely political and anti-government, this being reflected in the works *Walden* and the anti-authoritarian screed "On the Duty of Civil Disobedience." In *Walden*, Thoreau painted an attractive portrait of his time living simply in the bounty of nature. The book mixes social commentary, satire, and observations of the natural world to great effect.

But perhaps the single most prominent work of American Romantic literature is Herman Melville's *Moby Dick*. The timeless story pits mad Captain Ahab against the whale that took his leg, casting their struggle as a battle between man and nature, or perhaps man against the very universe itself. Melville explores a heightened dialect in the book, harkening back to the works of Shakespeare or the ancient Greeks, which rejects realism in favor of operatic emotion. Though unappreciated in its time, the story is now considered among the best novels ever produced by an American.

As the Romantic Period faded in the 1850s with the American Civil War, a new **Realist Period** began to take hold. Americans felt Romantic writings no longer reflected the grim realities of life during wartime and began producing simpler, more grounded literature, replete with imagery and often expressing cynicism and dissatisfaction.

Walt Whitman was among the early Realist pioneers. His poetry made use of simple images and was very prose-like. He's considered the "Father of Free Verse" for his influential style, which shirked much of the established rules of poetry of the time. Emily Dickinson is also sometimes considered a Realist. A reclusive woman, Dickinson's body of work is deeply introspective, focusing on intense sensory input and attention to detail that reflects her apprehension of the outside world.

But no one captured the sentiment of post-Civil War America quite like Mark Twain. The pen name of Samuel Longhorn Clemens, Twain is considered by many to be America's first great humorist, penning works of staggering wit that oozed nostalgia, appealing to both young readers and old. His works explore the American South during the Reconstruction period, drawing on his own childhood and adventures as a river boat worker for inspiration. His works, like *The Adventures of Huckleberry Finn*, also explore racial themes and are considered controversial to this day.

Other authors of note include Stephen Crane, whose book, *The Red Badge of Courage*, offered a realistic depiction of a soldier's life during the Civil War. He also wrote *Maggie: A Girl of the Streets,* a cynical tale of a poor woman who turns to prostitution. Upton Sinclair's work is similarly unromantic, with books like *The Jungle* exposing the deplorable working conditions of Chicago meat packers. Sinclair was considered a major agitator in his time. He also wrote *Oil!*, which criticized the greed of American oilmen and proved extremely controversial due to its depiction of a sexual encounter in a motel.

Twentieth Century literature is very diverse due to the rise of mass media, and can be divided into the realms of fiction, poetry, and drama. Among the greatest American dramatists is Eugene O'Neill, who won an unprecedented four Pulitzer Prizes ford drama for his works. Deeply personal, O'Neill's works reflect his own struggles with depression, alcoholism, and family dysfunction that bordered on abuse. His masterpiece is *A Long Day's Journey Into Night*, a semi-autobiographical tale of a family being slowly torn apart by substance abuse and their own incompatible egos. Tennessee Williams is another giant of American drama, penning classics like *Cat On a Hot Tin Roof* and *A Streetcar Named Desire*, which deal with issues of sexuality, gender, and mental illness. Both dramatists evoked the Realist style from decades earlier, creating terse and sometimes pessimistic deconstructions of modern American life through the lenses of volatile families and failed careers.

In poetry, the 20th century produced such great names as T.S. Eliot, Hart Crane, Robert Frost, and Wallace Stevens. Other popular poets include Maya Angelou and Langston Hughes. Angelou was a civil rights activist who wrote poetry and memoirs on themes of racism and gender, with the autobiographical *I Know Why the Caged Bird Sings* detailing her growth from an insecure and abused young woman into an independent firebrand. Hughes, likewise, wrote detailed accounts of the African-American experience. He was a leading figure in the Harlem Renaissance, a movement in the 1920s that gave voice to black writers in New York City, many of whom would go on to become quite influential. Frost's poems are more traditional, detailing the beauty of the natural world he experienced growing up in rural New England. His poem "The Road Less Traveled" is among the most well-known and acclaimed work of our time.

But prose fiction has always had the largest reach and greatest influence, and many 20th century American authors have written works that continue to change the world. In 1925, F. Scott Fitzgerald published *The Great Gatsby*, considered by many to be among the greatest American novels. The book follows wealthy, newly rich Jay Gatsby as viewed through the eyes of his friend and confidante Nick Carraway. Gatsby tries in vain to leverage his vast wealth and influence and win the woman of his dreams. The book exposes the vacuity of the wealth and material gains that so many Americans strive for.

John Steinbeck explored the struggles of the economically deprived. Steinbeck's *The Grapes of Wrath* follows the Joad family during the Great Depression as they try time and again to carve out a better future for themselves, being twarted at every turn by greedy opportunists and exploitative businessmen. Steinbeck wrote in a very colloquial dialect that made his works extremely popular.

Hemingway developed a new style involving simple words and short declarative sentences that emphasized action and image rather than introspection. He wrote philosophical tales of fate like *The Old Man and the Sea* and wartime narratives like *A Farewell to Arms* and *For Whom the Bell Tolls.*

And lastly, William Faulkner explored sometimes grotesque scenarios involving characters in the American South. Faulkner's work described the lingering effects of slavery and the erosion of traditional Southern institutions in an absurdist and experimental style. *As I Lay Dying* and *The Sound and the Fury* are considered his masterpieces.

Since the beginning, American literature has focused largely on issues of class, race, religion, and the struggle for independence, be it from oppressive institutions, economic inequality, or bigotry. The so-called "pioneer spirit" can still be found in contemporary American iconography. The cowboys and superheroes that Americans enjoy reflect a fierce belief in the power of the individual and the need to struggle against life's unfairness. Much world literature focuses on groups, on collectives or movements, but it is not uncommon for American stories to focus on one character only and tell a more universal tale through that character's experiences. From the earliest pioneer tales to modern stories of the empty promises of the American Dream, the United States has proved itself a powerhouse in the world of literature.

British Literature

The myriad varieties of literature found throughout the world are too numerous to explore in any one book, but for the purposes of AP study, some of the most significant literary accomplishments can be summarized. Remember, there is no substitute for in-depth research. Read reviews, summaries, criticisms, or the works themselves to get a fuller understanding of the power these stories have held in whatever culture they have their roots. The most significant direct influence on American literature comes from our neighbors across the Atlantic in the British Isles. During the Anglo-Saxon period between the 8th and 11th centuries, the English language was still coming into its own as a unique dialect separate from Latin or German. Among the earliest works in the English language is *Beowulf*, an epic poem describing the exploits of its titular hero as he attempts to slay the monstrous creature, Grendel. *Beowulf*'s author is not known. The story likely originated as an oral telling that distorted real historical events into the realm of myth.

The medieval period lasted until the 15th century and introduced many other stories that have become an essential part of British consciousness. Thomas Malory's *La Morte D'Arthur* recounts one of the first Arthurian legends, describing the exploits of King Arthur, Guinevere, Sir Lancelot, and the rest of the Knights of the Round Table, thus making an indelible mark on world literature. But Geoffrey Chaucer's *Canterbury Tales* is the true apex of Medieval British literature. This work, which follows a group of pilgrims engaged in a storytelling contest as they travel to a famous shrine, featured an unprecedented mastery of common language and a large cast of characters from all walks of life. Chaucer introduced many new words and phrases into the English language. His view of English life as seen through the eyes of worldly lower class laborers has proven invaluable to historians ever since.

Of course, no mention of British literature is complete without Shakespeare and his contemporaries who worked during the **Renaissance Era** of the 14th through 17th

centuries. Considered by many to be the greatest writer in the English language, William Shakespeare produced thirty-nine plays – ranging from broad comedies to heartfelt tragedies and bloody historical tellings – and over one hundred sonnets. Shakespeare was a master of iambic pentameter, a poetical meter in which each line five iambs or "feet," each containing a stressed and unstressed syllable. This style of verse was said to mimic the beating of the human heart, and it lent Shakespeare's prose a lively energy that has proved attractive to actors and readers for centuries. Shakespeare was a great wit and an incredible craftsman of language. No other author has contributed more words to the English language than Shakespeare. His contemporaries, such as Christopher Marlowe and John Webster, also experimented with new forms of vernacular storytelling.

In the 17th century, British literature largely focused on religious concerns. John Milton, a staunch Puritan, gave *Paradise Lost* to the world. This epic poem details the fall of the archangel Lucifer from heaven and his rebellion against God. The work proved so influential that it is sometimes mistaken for Biblical canon. John Bunyan's *The Pilgrim's Progress* is also staunchly religious, telling of a man's journey towards heaven after death. For many years, the book was second only to the Bible in terms of sales. John Donne's poetry, meanwhile, was more personal and introspective. Common turns of phrase like "for whom the bell tolls" and "no man is an island" come from his works.

18th century British literature became even more intensely political following the revival of the monarchy under Charles II. **Neoclassical** writing was the rule at this time, as British citizens sought to reconnect with their past. Notable authors include Alexander Pope, a poet who dabbled in a variety of neoclassical forms, and Robert Burns, a Scotsman who explored common Scottish brogue in his poems such as "To A Mouse." But William Blake came to be viewed as the preeminent voice of this generation. A notably progressive thinker with decidedly anti-church politics, Blake fought for the dissolution of gender roles and more critical views of religion. He was also a poet of mystical insight. He was a contemporary of Thomas Paine, and the two shared many views popular amongst Enlightenment figures at this time.

The works of Blake help usher in an era of **Romanticism** in British literature in the 1800s. The "first generation" of Romantics included William Wordsworth and Samuel Taylor Coleridge, who collaborated to publish *Lyrical Ballads*, a collection of experimental poems like "Rime of the Ancient Mariner" that epitomized the Romantic style. The poems in this collection also illustrated Wordsworth's philosophical belief that men are inherently good but can be corrupted by society.

The Second Generation of Romantics includes John Keats, Lord Byron, and Percy Bysshe Shelley, who wrote sonnets and narrative poems. Byron's *Don Juan* is a masterpiece of British satire, and his autobiographical *Childe Harold's Pilgrimage* is exceedingly self-deprecating. Shelley's works feature remarkable sensory detail. His poem "Ozymandias" describes a traveler who discovers a monument to a forgotten pharoah whose grand empire has crumbled to dust. Keats' works display maturity far beyond his years, as the poet died at the early age of 25.

The Romantic era also saw the rise of the some of the first prominent female authors in British history, creating a feminist perspective that was often missing from literature until that point. Jane Austen is the most popular author from this time, and her works, such as *Pride & Prejudice* and *Mansfield Park*, embody realistic characters and social commentary that have endured in popularity even to the present day. Charlotte and Emily Brontë were sisters and professional rivals, who wrote *Jane Eyre* and *Wuthering Heights* respectively, two grand Romantic novels focusing on duplicity and unrequited love amongst the landed gentry of England. All of these authors struggled against societal expectations of women during this time, and many critics were less than generous with their reviews, leading another prominent author of this time, Mary Ann Evans, to write under the alias of George Eliot to get a fairer appraisal of her work.

The rise of print media in the 1800s created a diverse range of literature in Britain, ranging from the sharply **satirical** to the proudly **adventurous**. Great satirists like Oscar Wilde skewered the manners and customs of the upper class to a greater degree than ever before, earning scorn from censors and traditionalists while keeping readers enraptured. It was also a great time for young adult literature. Robert Louis Stevenson's *Treasure Island* wove an action-packed tale of high adventure that appealed to young readers. Still other authors focused their attention on social commentary, such as Rudyard Kipling, who created many fables and parables that taught valuable lessons in works such as *The Jungle Book*. Charles Dickens's works were more critical, deconstructing Victorian values of greed and decadence, focusing attention on the downtrodden orphans and lower class laborers who suffered during the Industrial Revolution. He also wrote immensely popular stories such as *A Christmas Carol*, which helped re-popularize the Christmas holiday and has never once been out of publication since its first printing.

This experimentation and variety has continued in the 20th century, in which Britain has firmly established itself as a major force in world literature. Irish authors James Joyce and Samuel Beckett pioneered **Modernist** literature, which remixed and recontextualized existing dramatic forms in absurd, experimental new ways. Beckett's *Waiting for Godot* is among the most influential plays ever written, examining the tragedy and comedy of the human condition via two clownish vagabonds contemplating their own inability to accomplish anything of note. The play is a landmark work of Absurdist and Post-Modern theater, two experimental styles that pushed the limits of what audiences could expect from the stage.

Joyce's *Ulysses* is considered by many critics to be among the greatest novels in the English language. It experiments and invents in nearly every literary style, using the dreamlike stream-of-consciousness narrative of a man's madcap journey through Dublin on a single day.

The works of George Orwell are more political. A former police officer in English-occupied Burma, Orwell wrote works that are fiercely anti-fascist, providing stark warnings about the dangers of totalitarianism. His science-fiction/dystopian novel *1984* is considered his masterpiece, telling the tale of a common man's struggle against a brutally conformist society led by the mysterious dictator, "Big Brother."

British literature has flitted between proud lionization of their own accomplishments and self-deprecating laughter at their failings. Traditions of satire and wordplay run deep in English writings, from the comedies of Shakespeare with their puns and double entendres, to the biting, controversial ironies of Oscar Wilde. Still other authors have sought to elevate institutions of British life, such as religion or the monarchy. British writings owe a strong debt to the works of the ancient Greeks, whose tragedies and philosophical writings inspired countless English-language works. The body of work produced by this small island nations continues to grow and develop, further establishing its place as a force to be reckoned with in world media.

World Literature

The AP English test focuses largely on American and British writings, but a familiarity with other figures of world literature is also useful.

Among the most important authors from the rest of the European continent, **ancient Greek** dramatists such as Sophocles, Euripedes, and Aeschylus wrote many tragedies that have formed the backbone of much of Western literature. Greek tragedies focus largely on the failings of the main character, on their pride (or "hubris") that causes them to subvert the natural order of things and earn the ire of the gods. These things eventually lead to their downfall (a "catharsis" or cleansing). Most of their plays contain a mythic or religious component, and many end with direct intervention from the gods themselves (termed a "deus ex machina," a sudden ending where a godlike figure appears and re-establishes order). Important Greek tragedies include *Oedipus Rex, Medea*, and *Antigone.*

The epics of Homer are also noteworthy, standing, as they do, at the very head of the Western tradition. Two works are attributed to Homer, *The Iliad* and *The Odyssey*, epic poems that describe the exploits of Greek warriors and their struggles against each other and the gods themselves. Homer is the first great European author, and his influence cannot be overstated.

French literature has also proven very influential to American writers. Victor Hugo is considered to be one of the most important French authors, penning heartbreaking novels like *The Hunchback of Notre Dame* and *Les Miserables.* These two books explore the suffering of outcasts and the lower class, in a manner similar to that Charles Dickens across the English Channel. The works of Alexandre Dumas are more pulpy and readable, often classified as swashbucklers or tales of high adventure. Dumas' works include *The Three Musketeers* and *The Count of Monte Cristo,* focusing on tales of revenge, rebellion, and complex love triangles. His works have been translated into over 100 languages and have formed the basis for countless adaptations into film and theater.

One of the most important writers from the **Slavic** nations (he wrote, however, in German) would have to be Franz Kafka. Though largely unnoticed during his lifetime, Kafka is now considered one of the most influential figures in 20th century literature, writing accounts of depression, anxiety, and isolation that blended the realistic and surreal. He was among the first authors to criticize bureaucratic institutions, with works like *The Trial* and *In the Penal Colony*, which feature characters being tormented by shadowy government figures for reasons that are never fully explained. He also delved into more fantastical subject matter with works like *The Metamorphosis*, a tale of a traveling salesman who awakens one day to find he has been transformed into a massive bug. The term "Kafkaesque" is common in literary criticism today, describing situations in which a main character is being persecuted for unclear reasons and has no clear method of escaping his terrible situation.

Russian literary greats include Leo Tolstoy, who described Napolean's capture of the city of Moscow in *War and Peace*, and Fyodor Dostoyevski, who wrote *The Brothers Karamazov*, a philosophical depiction of the dissolving relationship between three brothers and their father that eventually culminates in murder. Tolstoy wrote *Anna Karenina*, a prime example of Realist fiction that follows the exploits of its titular heroine as she pursues a doomed affair with a wealthy count. The 20th century gave Vladimir Nabokov to the world, the controversial author of such works as *Lolita*, which describes the relationship between a literarily-minded pedophile and his stepdaughter. Nabokov's works are replete with sensory detail and are sharply ironic, offering many cutting observations about the American culture that Nabokov gradually assimilated into.

Anton Chekov is considered Russia's prime dramatist, giving the world plays like *Uncle Vanya* and *The Cherry Orchard* that stretched the limits of actors' abilities and paved new ground for concepts like subtext and psychological realism in theater.

These works form much of the basis for the Western canon of literature. One can study them for a lifetime and not scratch the surface of the stories available. For the purposes of the AP exam, however, and a functional understanding of Western literature, a good comprehension of the primary titles and authors will suffice.

Strategy for Points: Literary Periods

- If nothing else, understand the following literary periods – Colonial, Revolutionary, Romantic, Realist, and Contemporary or 20th Century. Most of these periods contain numerous sub-movements as well.
- If nothing else, understand the following literary periods – Colonial, Revolutionary, Romantic, Realist, and Contemporary or 20th Century. Most of these periods contain numerous sub-movements as well.
- Know how these movements affected and were affected by major events in American history. The Colonial era inspired literature that was religious and orderly, the Revolution created an era of political agitation. Romanticism harkened back to simpler times before industry and reason removed much of the wonder from life, and Realism reminded us of the grim realities of the Civil War. Literature is always a reflection of the time period that creates it.
- Familiarize yourself with the works of the major names in American literature, such as Hemingway, Faulkner, Poe, Melville, Fitzgerald, or Twain. Even if the test does not require you to analyze these authors directly, a familiarity with their work will prove useful for comparisons, and it will demonstrate your broader knowledge of literary history.
- It's not enough to merely state that a work belongs in a certain literary period. You must demonstrate why, often with explicit references to the text.

- Most great works of literature are considered to have pioneered in some respect, to have shirked what came before and created something innovative and new. Knowing what literary period preceded a work can help you make your case as to why the piece is a work of genius.

Chapter 6: Prose

UNLIKE POETRY (COVERED IN THE NEXT CHAPTER), PROSE DOES NOT CONTAIN METRICAL structure. While it follows the normal grammatical rules for the language, prose includes a more literal, natural way of speaking. It's straightforward and does not follow a rhyme scheme.

At the start of Section II of this study guide, you learned:

- Thomas Paine wrote *Common Sense*, a pamphlet in 1175 that would go on to become the top-selling piece of American literature of all time. The piece included simple prose, encouraging and promoting rebellion against British rule.
- While poets have produced a number of famous pieces, prose fiction has always had the most significant global influence.
- Famous prose works of note include:
  Jane Austen – *Pride & Prejudice* (1813)
  Charlotte Brontë – *Jane Eyre* (1847)
  Emily Brontë – *Wuthering Heights* (1847)
  Robert Louis Stevenson – *Treasure Island* (1883)
  Rudyard Kipling – *The Jungle Book* (1894)
  James Joyce – *Ulysses* (1922)
  F. Scott Fitzgerald – *The Great Gatsby* (1925)
  William Faulkner *The Sound and the Fury* (1929); *As I Lay Dying* (1930)
  John Steinbeck – *The Grapes of Wrath* (1939)
  Ernest Hemingway – *For Whom the Bell Tolls* (1926); *A Farewell to Arms* (1929); *The Old Man and the Sea* (1952)

It is very likely that an excerpt from a famous work of prose will be included in the written portions of your AP exam. By familiarizing yourself with the differences between poetry and prose and the various styles of each, you will set yourself up for the best probability of a high score on your writing sections. You should also take some time to review the most famous works of prose and the literary periods in which they were written, many of which you will have read during your AP course. There is a list in Appendix C for your review of popularly chosen authors and works. Being familiar with the context from the time period and the author's background will be instrumental in creating strong support for your responses.

Poetry Versus Prose

Poetry follows a structure with metric or rhyme scheme, while prose does not have a standard style of writing. In addition, poetry often leads the reader to read between the lines, while prose invites a much more literal approach. There is minimal critical thinking involved when it comes to reading a piece of prose. You are simply reading a story. You usually do not have to continuously question the author's intention or the intended meaning of the piece.

Poetry	Prose
Written in verse	Written in narrative form
Contains poetic meter	Contains paragraphs
Reader determines author's intention	Includes a setting, characters, plot, and a point of view
Metaphorical	Literal

If you were to write a piece in both poetry and prose formats and put them beside one another, they would represent the same idea using extremely different formats. Take a look at the two examples below, Emily Dickinson's famous poem "*The Carriage*," and "*Life*" by Charlotte Brontë.

Example 1: *The Carriage* Poetry

Because I could not stop for Death –
He kindly stopped for me –
The Carriage held but just Ourselves –
And Immortality.

We slowly drove – He knew no haste
And I had put away
My labor and my leisure too,
For His Civility –

We passed the School, where Children strove
At Recess – in the Ring –
We passed the Fields of Gazing Grain –
We passed the Setting Sun –

Or rather – He passed us –
The Dews drew quivering and chill –
For only Gossamer, my Gown –
My Tippet – only Tulle –
We paused before a House that seemed

A Swelling of the Ground –
The Roof was scarcely visible –
The Cornice – in the Ground –

Since then – 'tis Centuries – and yet
Feels shorter than the Day
I first surmised the Horses' Heads
Were toward Eternity –

—*Emily Dickinson*

Prose version

As I look back on my life, I cannot help but think about lost opportunity and what it will be like when I leave this world. (She dies and is buried in a cemetery where she will stay for eternity.)

Example 2: *Life* Poetry

Life, believe, is not a dream
So dark as sages say;
Oft a little morning rain
Foretells a pleasant day.
Sometimes there are clouds of gloom,
But these are transient all;
If the shower will make the roses bloom,
O why lament its fall?

Rapidly, merrily,
Life's sunny hours flit by,
Gratefully, cheerily,
Enjoy them as they fly!

What though Death at times steps in
And calls our Best away?
What though sorrow seems to win,
O'er hope, a heavy sway?
Yet hope again elastic springs,
Unconquered, though she fell;
Still buoyant are her golden wings,
Still strong to bear us well.

Manfully, fearlessly,
The day of trial bear,
For gloriously, victoriously,
Can courage quell despair!

—*Charlotte Brontë*

Prose version

I think it's critical to understand that even if you're having a bad day, your outlook and attitude can help you be happy. Everyone should strive to live life in the moment and enjoy the good times because time passes by faster than you'd expect.

Prose Categories

Fictional prose: The most common example of fictional prose is a novel. Using a narrative form of writing, fictional prose has been used to tell tales of adventure, erotica, and mystery. Other examples include romance and short story.

Nonfiction prose: Nonfiction prose is based on facts, but it may also include fictional elements. It is used to be informative and persuasive, yet it does not include any scientific evidence to support its claims. Examples include: journal entry, biography, and essay.

Heroic prose: Also written in the narrative form, heroic prose has a dramatic style that allows for the works to be recited or performed. The most common form of heroic prose is the legend.

Rhymed prose: The difference between prose and poetry is not always clear. Rhymed prose is written with rhymes that are not metrical and is considered to be an artistic, skilled form of writing across the world. Examples include Rayok in Russian culture, Saj' from Arabic culture, and Fu from Chinese culture.

Prose poetry: Prose poetry can be considered a combination, or fusion, of both poetry and prose. It uses extreme imagery, yet does not include the typical metrical structure or rhyme scheme found in a poem.

Types of Prose

Allegory: A story in verse or prose with characters representing virtues and vices. An allegory has two meanings: symbolic and literal. John Bunyan's The Pilgrim's Progress is the most renowned of this genre.

Epistle: A letter that was not always intended for public distribution, but due to the fame of the sender and/or recipient, becomes widely known. Paul wrote epistles that were later placed in the Bible.

Essay: Typically a relatively short prose work focusing on a topic, propounding a definite point of view and using an authoritative tone. Great essayists include Carlyle, Lamb, DeQuincy, Emerson, and Montaigne (who is credited with defining this genre).

Legend: A traditional narrative or collection of related narratives, popularly regarded as historically factual but actually a mixture of fact and fiction. The tales of King Arthur or Robin Hood could be described as legends.

Novel: The longest form of fictional prose containing a variety of characters, settings, local color, and regionalism. Most novels have complex plots, expanded descriptions, and attention to detail. Some of the great novelists include Jane Austen, the Brontë sisters, Twain, Tolstoy, Hugo, Hardy, Dickens, Hawthorne, Forster, and Flaubert.

Romance: A highly imaginative tale set in a fantastical realm dealing with the conflicts between heroes, villains, and/or monsters. "The Knight's Tale" from Chaucer's Canterbury Tales, Sir Gawain and the Green Knight, and Keats' "The Eve of St. Agnes" are representatives.

Short story: Typically a terse narrative, with less development and background about characters; may include description, author's point of view, and tone. Poe emphasized that a successful short story should create one focused impact. Some great short story writers are Hemingway, Faulkner, Twain, Joyce, Shirley Jackson, Flannery O'Connor, Guy de Maupassant, Saki, Edgar Allen Poe, and Pushkin.

Analyzing Prose

The analysis of prose, similar to the analysis of poetry, calls attention to structural elements so as to discern meaning, purpose, and themes. The author's intentions are gleaned through the elements he or she uses and how they are used. Because your written response questions will most likely include either poetry or prose within the prompt, it's critical to deeply analyze all structural elements (plot, characters, setting, and point of view). This will assist you in supporting your own claims and will give you the best opportunity for a high score on the writing portion.

Plot:

The plot is the sequence of events (it may or may not be chronological) that the author chooses to represent the story to be told-both the underlying story and the externals of the occurrences the author relates. An author may use "flashbacks" to tell the back story (or what went before the current events begin). Often, authors begin their stories *in medias res*, or in the middle of things, and, over time, supply the details of what has gone before to provide a clearer picture to the reader of all the relevant events.

Sometimes authors tell parallel stories in order to make their points. For example, in Leo Tolstoy's classic *Anna Karenina*, the unhappy extramarital affair of Anna Karenina and Count Vronsky is contrasted with the happy marriage of Lev and Kitty through the use of alternating chapters devoted to each couple. The plot consists of the progress of each couple: Anna and Count Vronsky into deeper neurosis, obsession, and emotional pain, and Lev and Kitty into deeper and more meaningful partnership through growing emotional intimacy, parenthood, and caring for members of their extended family.

In good novels, each part of the plot is necessary and has a purpose. For example, in *Anna Karenina*, a chapter is devoted to a horse race in which Count Vronsky participates. This might seem like mere entertainment, but, in fact, Count Vronsky is riding his favorite mare, and, in a moment of carelessness in taking a jump, puts the whole weight of his body on the mare's back, breaking it. The horse must be shot. Vronsky loved and admired the mare, but being overcome by a desire to win, he kills the very thing he loves. Similarly, Anna descends into obsession and jealousy as their affair isolates her from society and separates her from her child. Ultimately she kills herself. The chapter symbolizes the destructive effect that Vronsky's love, coupled with inordinate desire, has upon what and whom he loves.

Other authors use repetitious plot lines to reveal the larger story over time. For example, in Joseph Heller's tragic-comedy *Catch-22*, the novel repeatedly returns to a horrific incident in an airplane while it was flying a combat mission. Each time the protagonist, Yossarian, recalls the incident, more detail is revealed. The reader knows from the beginning that this incident is key to why Yossarian wants to be discharged from the army, but it is not until the full details of the gruesome incidents are revealed late in the book that the reader knows why the incident has driven Yossarian almost mad. Interspersed with comedic and ironic episodes, the book's climax (the full revealing of the incident) remains powerfully with the reader, showing the absurdity, insanity, and inhumanity of war. The comic device of Catch-22, a fictitious army rule from which the title is derived, makes this point in a funny way: Catch-22 states that a soldier cannot be discharged from the army unless he is crazy; yet, if he wants to be discharged from the army, he is not crazy. This rule seems to embody the insanity, absurdity, and inhumanity of war.

Characters:

Characters usually represent or embody an idea or ideal acting in the world. For example, in the *Harry Potter* series, Harry Potter's goodness, courage and unselfishness as well as his capacity for friendship and love make him a powerful opponent to Voldemort, whose selfishness, cruelty, and isolation make him the leader of the evil forces in the epic battle of good versus evil. Memorable characters are many-sided: Harry is not only brave, strong, and true, he is vulnerable and sympathetic; orphaned as a child, bespectacled, and often misunderstood by his peers, Harry is not a stereotypical hero.

Charles Dickens's *Oliver Twist* illustrates the principle of goodness, oppressed and unrecognized, unleashed in a troubled world. Oliver encounters a great deal of evil, which he refuses to cooperate with, and also a great deal of good in people who have sympathy for his plight. In contrast to the gentle, kindly, and selfless Maylies who take Oliver in, recognizing his goodness, are the evil Bill Sykes and Fagin—thieves and murderers—who are willing to sell and hurt others for their own gain. When Nancy, a thief in league with Sykes and Fagin, essentially "sells" herself to help Oliver, she represents redemption from evil through sacrifice.

Setting:

The setting of a work of fiction adds a great deal to the story. Historical fiction relies firmly on an established time and place: *Johnny Tremain* takes place in revolutionary Boston. The story could not take place anywhere else or at any other time. Ray Bradbury's *The Most Dangerous Game* requires an isolated, uninhabited island for its plot.

Settings are sometimes changed in a work to represent different periods of a person's life or to compare and contrast life in the city or life in the country.

Point of View:

The point of view is the perspective of the person who is the focus of the work of fiction: a story told in the first person is from the point of view of the narrator. In more modern works, works told in the third person usually concentrate on the point of view of one character or else the changes in point of view are clearly delineated, as in *Cold Mountain* by Charles Frazier, who names each chapter after the person whose point of view is being shown. Sudden, unexplained shifts in point of view—i.e., going into the thoughts of one character after another within a short space of time—are a sign of amateurish writing.

Strategy for Points: Prose

- Review the poetry, prose, and literary periods chapters. Understanding the context and time period will assist you in identifying pieces in multiple choice questions and connecting the author's intention with your written responses.
- When reviewing a prompt, pay close attention to the point of view in the work that is being used. This will help you in describing the author's intended message.
- Analyze pieces for rhyme scheme and rhythm when trying to determine if it's poetry or prose. Familiarize yourself with the "poetry vs. prose" section at the start of this chapter.
- Cite specific examples from prose pieces to support your claims in your written responses. (And don't forget to use quotations while citing.)
- Utilize the list of famous works of prose at the start of this chapter to build your familiarity with prose pieces that are most likely to appear on the AP test.

Chapter 7: Poetry

POETRY USES WORDS AND RHYTHM TO CONVEY IMAGE AND EMOTION. POETRY IS OFTEN less explicit than prose, relying on implication and suggestion rather than overt statement of fact. Poetry is not always concerned with "realism," often shirking basic tenets of grammar and syntax for better artistic effect. There are few true "answers" in poetry, as poems are often interpreted in a variety of ways, but certain conclusions can be drawn from a close reading of the text. This is an essential skill for the AP English Literature and Composition exam, which focuses largely on poetic forms, styles, movements, and nomenclature.

For the AP English Literature and Composition exam, you will be required to interpret certain poetic works. You will be asked to answer such questions as these: What was the author trying to accomplish? How did he achieve his goal? What poetic devices did they employ in this pursuit and how effective were they? If you can answer these questions while demonstrating knowledge of the mechanics and style of poetry, you will succeed at AP English Literature and Composition.

Poetic Terminology

• *Rhyme*: Indicates a repeated end sound of lines or words within a poem. Rhymes usually occur at the ends of lines, though they can also be internal.

Example:

"Because I could not stop for Death
He kindly stopped for me
The Carriage held but just Ourselves
And Immortality."

– *Emily Dickinson,* "Because I could not stop for Death."

"Me" and "Immortality" rhyme in this poem, lending a sense of finality to the last line and giving it a pleasing rhythm.

• *Rhyme scheme*: The pattern of rhymes in each line of a poem. Rhyme schemes are usually indicated with letters. Some poets follow strict rhyme schemes, some shirk them entirely, but most employ repetitive rhyme schemes when aesthetically appropriate and then subvert them for stronger effect.

Example:

"A wonderful bird is the pelican;

His beak can hold more than his belly-can.
He can hold in his beak
Enough food for a week,
Though I'm damned if I know how the hell-he-can!"
— Dixon Lanier Merritt

This is an example of a limerick—a short, humorous poem employing a five line rhyme scheme. Limericks always follow an AABBA rhyme scheme. The first two lines rhyme, the next two shorter lines have a different rhyme, and the fifth line calls back to the original rhyme. Limerick structure is intentionally simplistic, highlighting the absurdity of the subject matter and allowing the poet to focus more on wordplay. The B rhymes of the third and fourth lines build anticipation for the final reveal on the fifth line, where the author can reveal a witty subversion.

• *Slant Rhyme*: A slant rhyme is also known as a "near rhyme," "half rhyme" or "lazy rhyme." Slant rhymes sometimes have the same vowel sounds but different consonants, or the reverse. Slant rhymes are sometimes considered childish or uncreative, but many poets of have made use of them in order to avoid clichés, to create disharmony in a piece, or to draw unusual connections between words.

Example:

"When have I last looked on
The round green eyes and the long wavering bodies
Of the dark leopards of the moon?
All the wild witches, those most noble ladies"
— W. B. Yeats, "Lines Written in Dejection"

"On" and "moon" are slant rhymes, as are "bodies" and "ladies." This could be said to suggest the author's discordant, dejected state of mind. Perhaps in a happier poem these rhymes would be clearer and more musical. But not here.

• *Stanza*: A group of lines, offset by punctuation or spacing, forming a metrical unit or verse in a poem.

Example:

"Do not go gentle into that good night,
Old age should burn and rave at close of day;
Rage, rage against the dying of the light.

Though wise men at their end know dark is right,
Because their words had forked no lightning they
Do not go gentle into that good night."
— Dylan Thomas, "Do not go gentle into that good night."

Each short stanza contains three lines and ends with either "do not go gentle into that good night" or "rage, rage against the dying of the light." This end rhyme repeats throughout the entire poem, ensuring that each stanza delivers the essential message in a profound and affecting way.

Meter: The basic rhythmic structure of a poem, the "music" of it. Some poetic forms prescribe their own metrical structure, but other poets invented or modified their own.

Example:

"Shall I compare thee to a summer's day?
Thou art more lovely and more temperate /
Rough winds do shake the darling buds of May,
And summer's lease hath all too short a date."
— William Shakespeare, "Sonnet 18."

Almost any poem could be said to have some form of meter, but Shakespeare's "iambic pentameter" is among the most famous styles. This metrical style is divided into "iambs," five of them per line, each containing a stressed and unstressed syllable. The pattern could be described as "ba-BUM, ba-BUM, ba-BUM," not unlike the beating of a heart. This metrical rhythm permeates Shakespeare's work, proving very attractive to actors who appreciate the clear, emphatic delivery.

Alliteration: The use of repeated sounds at the start of words in quick succession. Alliteration is often used to draw attention to specific words or sounds, to lend emphasis to specific aspects of the poem. It can also be used to provide an entertaining and engaging voice to a poem.

Example:

"One short sleepe past, wee wake eternally,
And death shall be no more; death, thou shalt die."
— John Donne, "Death Be Not Proud."

In this poem, the alliterative W and D sounds draw parallels between their respective words, and create a vocal punctuation for the line. A D sound begins the last line and a D sound ends it, creating a sense of urgency, of continuity and finality in the line.

Assonance: Similar to alliteration, except that the repeated sounds are contained within certain words.

Example:

"And miles to go before I sleep
And miles to go before I sleep."

The repeated O sounds create a sense of speed and urgency. The sound carries us through the line, creating contrast with the E sound in "sleep," where both the narrator and reader finally rest.

Enjambment: An enjambed line flows into the next line without a break. No punctuation divides one line from the next. The line simply continues.

Example:

"April is the cruellest month, breeding
Lilacs out of the dead land, mixing
Memory and desire, stirring
Dull roots with spring rain."
— T. S. Eliot, "The Waste Land."

Eliot's use of enjambment in "The Waste Land" creates a sense of suspense in the poem. The action of breeding, mixing, and stirring are lent equal or superior importance to the actual subject, *April*. The enjambment also creates a slant rhyme as well, with each line ending on an "-ing" until we arrive at "rain."

Free Verse: Poetry that avoids an identifiable meter or rhyme scheme could be said to be "free." The style became more popular amongst avant-garde, modern, and post-modern poets. It was comparatively rare in classical poetry.

Example:

i carry your heart with me (i carry it in
my heart) i am never without it (anywhere
i go you go, my dear; and whatever is done
by only me is your doing, my darling)
— e e cummings, "i carry your heart with me."

Cummings' style shirked literary conventions, creating poems that challenged traditional assumptions about form and aesthetic appeal through his use of strange capitalization, heavy enjambment, and free verse. Cummings' poems sometimes defy clear explanation, but some critics suggest he wrote in this manner to evoke a childish, earnest state of mind.

Metaphor: An indirect comparison between two things, denoting one object or action in place of another to suggest a comparison between them. This is distinct from a simile, which directly compares two things using words such as "like" or "as."

Example:

"I'm a riddle in nine syllables,
An elephant, a ponderous house,
A melon strolling on two tendrils.
red fruit, ivory, fine timbers!"
— Sylvia Plath, "Metaphors."

Appropriately enough, Sylvia Plath's "Metaphors" contains several playful metaphors used to describe her pregnancy. Plath uses herself as a subject, comparing her pregnant state to an elephant, a melon, and in several ways to a shelter for the life growing inside her. At first the metaphors seem self-deprecating and humorous, but later in the poem, where she calls herself a "means, a stage" and mentions how she's "boarded the train there's no getting off," the metaphors take on darker connotation as they reflect her dehumanization and resigned acceptance that she's become merely an incubator for the child she now carries.

Sonnet: A poetic form that originated in Italy, consisting of fourteen lines which follow a clear alternating rhyme scheme. Conventions of sonnets have shifted through the centuries, and the form has proved popular in England, Italy, and France.

Example:

Do not stand at my grave and weep:
I am not there; I do not sleep.
I am a thousand winds that blow,
I am the diamond glints on snow,
I am the sun on ripened grain,
I am the gentle autumn rain.
When you awaken in the morning's hush
I am the swift uplifting rush
Of quiet birds in circling flight.
I am the soft starshine at night.
Do not stand at my grave and cry:
I am not there; I did not die.

— Mary Elizabeth Frye, "Do not stand at my grave and weep."

This sonnet showcases much of what is attractive about the form to poets. The simple rhyme scheme is unpretentious and readable, and the poem's format lends itself well to repetition. The repeated "I am's" create a soothing rhythm, sort of a lullaby quality.

The subject matter is bittersweet, as with many sonnets that have explored romance, mortality, or spirituality. The first and last two lines mirror each other, suggesting change and finality. The poem's subject matter insists we not fear the end, and this is reflected in the sonnet's form.

Imagery: Any sequence of words that refers to a sensory experience can be considered imagery. Rather than merely describing the visual aspect of something, imagery often relies on taste, touch, smell, or sound to draw a fuller portrait of the subject.

Example:

"Whirl up, sea—
Whirl your pointed pines,
Splash your great pines
On our rocks,
Hurl your green over us—
Cover us with your pools of fir."
— Hilda Doolittle, "O read."

Doolittle's poem neatly encapsulates a style known as *Imagism*, a short-lived movement in the early 20th century that sought to reduce poetic language to its barest components. Each line, each word in this poem reveals something new. Doolittle likens a forest to a sea (or perhaps a sea to a forest), encouraging us to imagine green trees like torrential waves, evoking sound, color, and texture to maintain this dual metaphor. The poem is unique in that there is no "correct" image. Both the sea and the forest are equally valid interpretations of this poem, drawn together by their shared sensory features.

Onomatopoeia: A "sound effect," a word that imitates that actual sound it describes. "Buzz" or "hiss" both sound like the actions of buzzing or hissing.

Example:

"I chatter over stony ways,
In little sharps and trebles,
I bubble into eddying bays,
I babble on the pebbles."
— Alfred, Lord Tennyson, "The Brook."

The onomatopoeia in Tennyson's "The Brook" evokes the sounds of its subject. The assonant B and T sounds suggest the burbling of a river, water running over rocks.

Personification: When human qualities are applied to a non-human entity, such as an animal, an emotion, an object, or something more esoteric.

Example:

"Let the rain kiss you
Let the rain beat upon your head with silver liquid drops
Let the rain sing you a lullaby"
— Langston Hughes, "April Rain Song."

In this poem, Hughes suggests that the rain has the human ability to kiss and to sing. Rather than merely describing pleasant, "realistic" aspects of rain, he personifies it as a friendly, motherly figure to better describe his feelings towards rain.

Couplet: A pair of rhyming lines with the same meter. A "heroic couplet" is a couplet in iambic pentameter that is "self-contained" and not enjambed. Shakespeare often ended his sonnets with a heroic couplet, allowing the piece to build towards a climactic, self-contained final rhyme that delivered the sonnet's chief message.

Example:

"Sol thro' white Curtains shot a tim'rous Ray,
And op'd those Eyes that must eclipse the Day;
Now Lapdogs give themselves the rowzing Shake,
And sleepless Lovers, just at Twelve, awake:"
— Alexander Pope, "Rape of the Lock."

Pope's "Rape of the Lock" is a satirical narrative poem written entirely in heroic couplets. The subject matter of the piece, regarding a baron's attempts to gain a lock of a woman's hair, is silly and banal. Thus, the constant use of triumphant, heroic couplets renders the whole thing a bizarre parody.

Narrative poem: Appropriately enough, a narrative poem is a poem that tells a story. It can make use of narrators, characters, plot, setting, and other literary devices, though they often contain more poetic features, such as rhyme, meter, and metaphor. An "epic poem" is a type of narrative poem that's usually lengthy and recounts heroic deeds and mythology.

Example:

"By the shore of Gitche Gumee,
By the shining Big-Sea-Water,
At the doorway of his wigwam,
In the pleasant Summer morning,
Hiawatha stood and waited."
— Henry Wadsworth Longfellow, "The Song of Hiawatha"

Longfellow's epic poem, "The Song of Hiawatha," recalls the mythologized exploits of the titular Native American hero. Hiawatha is based on a few historical persons, but as with much epic poetry, his exploits are expanded into something superhuman.

When setting out to interpret a poem, authorial intention is a good starting point. What message was the author intending to convey with the piece? Read it through a few times, and pause to consider words or references you don't understand. Start with the easy solution, not every poem is a labyrinth of mysterious interpretations. Consider the fact that, in an enduring poem, nothing happens by accident. Each line, each word was selected very carefully by the poet for a specific effect. This will allow you to go deeper off of your original assessment of the poem, and to infer the meaning of unclear references and unusual devices.

Example Analysis

Let's try one. The following is one of the most read poems in the English canon, "Ozymandias" by Percy Bysshe Shelley. Read it through, and see what your initial reactions are. Try reading it out loud as well. Some poems are better understand when heard.

I met a traveller from an antique land
Who said: "Two vast and trunkless legs of stone

Stand in the desert . . . Near them, on the sand,
Half sunk, a shattered visage lies, whose frown,
And wrinkled lip, and sneer of cold command,
Tell that its sculptor well those passions read
Which yet survive, stamped on these lifeless things,
The hand that mocked them, and the heart that fed:
And on the pedestal these words appear:
'My name is Ozymandias, king of kings:
Look on my works, ye Mighty, and despair!'
Nothing beside remains. Round the decay
Of that colossal wreck, boundless and bare
The lone and level sands stretch far away."

First, let's summarize the literal basics. What is the "story" of this poem? What is the "plot," the actual event being described? Our narrator is unnamed, and the story is told by him second hand, a tale he recalls hearing from some traveler from an "antique land." The traveler describes a two pillars of stone he found in the endless desert, and next to them lay a shattered stone face, well-carved but slowly eroding away. Beside the face is a pedestal telling of some "king of kings," Ozymandias, who declares his "works" would cause even the mighty to despair. What "works" this describes is not clear to the traveler, for they seem to have crumbled to dust during endless centuries, leaving only sand as far as the eye can see.

On a surface level, this is a simple tale of a stranger remembering a statue he found in the desert. Why is this important? Why did Shelley find this necessary to recount?

To answer this, we need to look past what is literally stated to find what is implied. We can infer that some grander structure was once mounted on the pedestal, a monument perhaps. The face and pillars, at the very least, likely towered above the desert sometime in the past, depicting their fearsome subject for all to see. Surely this Ozymandias must have been wealthy to erect such a sculpture, and it is telling that he wished to be depicted with a commanding sneer. The face was carved by some sculptor who either feared or greatly revered his subject. Ozymandias fancied himself a conqueror, one who would inspire awe in all who saw his monument.

But it did not last. The monument is crumbling, the desert around it is bare. Even this traveler from his "antique land" knows nothing of great Ozymandias except what he reads on some plinth in the desert. Why did Ozymandias fade from memory? Who can say? Whatever great and terrible things Ozymandias accomplished, it was not enough to save him or his memory from the ravages of time.

The pedestal thus becomes sadly ironic. Whereas once the mighty may have despaired upon seeing a fearsome monument that dwarfed them, today they will despair upon seeing that even the "king of kings," Ozymandias, has been forgotten for all time. Shelley is trying to teach us that even the mightiest of men can die and be forgotten. Time waits for no man.

What poetic devices are on display here? The poem is a sonnet, though not a typical one. There is a rhyme scheme but it is far less pronounced than in most sonnets – it makes frequent use of slant rhymes, such as "stone" and "frown" or "fear" and "despair," and the enjambment of the piece alters its flow, preventing "sing-song" rhymes from appearing. It contains no heroic couplet. The poem also features iambic pentameter, though it is less pronounced than in works such as Shakespeare's. Each line contains five iambs of two syllables each, with exactly one exception: line 10, "my name is Ozymandias," breaks the ten syllable pattern, offering eleven syllables instead. Perhaps this is Shelley's way of drawing attention to that line and to Ozymandias himself. Truly, Ozymandias was so great that even this sonnet form could not contain him.

The poem also makes sparing using of alliteration, particularly in the last two lines with "boundless and bare" and "lone and level sands stretch." This seems to be Shelley's substitute for the heroic couplet. Rather than offering a two-line rhyme to announce the poem's final thought, he builds more subtly with alliterative turns of phrase that offset the final words "far away." This is the note he leaves us on. There is nothing in the desert but sand, lone and level, boundless and bare. This is what history remembers and this is what he offers as his final word on the subject. It is also worth noting that the poem is told second hand – even the narrator is hearing about this from some nameless traveler from a nameless land. He's simply repeating what he heard. The great Ozymandias has been reduced to a half-remembered plaque in some forgotten desert that our raconteur.

That's a heavy message for such a short poem, and it is Shelley's mastery of poetic forms that allow him to deliver it so forcefully. An AP English Literature and Composition exam will likely require you to interpret a poem along a more specific guideline, such as how it might reflect the styles and forms of a specific movement of poetry. But if you can demonstrate a strong core knowledge of poetic style, you will have little trouble passing the exam.

Strategy for Points : Poetry

- Poetry is not about finding the "correct" answer. Many poems have multiple interpretations, while others are less obscure. Your personal interpretation must be supported by the text. As long as it is not contradicted, you're in the clear.
- You must understand the names and functions of poetic devices. Simply deciding the poem uses alliteration is not enough. Where is the alliteration, why was it used, and what effect does it have on the reader? Be ready to support your idea with specific examples.
- Many poems make references that are unfamiliar to the modern reader. A good understanding of historical references is useful, but not essential. Simply understanding the role of such references in the context of the poem will serve you well enough. A case in point is the name "Ozymandias" from the above example. This another name for Rameses II, a ruler of ancient Egypt. Knowing this can enhance your understanding of the poem, but it is not necessary. You need only understand that Ozymandias was a powerful ruler who faded from memory.

- Understand that nothing in a poem happens by accident. Everything, even the most oblique stream-of-consciousness phrase, is used by the poet for a specific effect.
- It is also important to understand how poems fit into broader literary movements. Imagism, post-modernism, avant-garde, classical, romantic, all offer unique takes on poetic styles and forms. See the "Literary Periods" chapter for a more in-depth look at developments in Western poetry.

Chapter 8: Drama

DRAMA IS THE PRIMARY EXPRESSION OF NARRATIVE IN PERFORMANCE. ANY TYPE OF creative display involving performers and an audience could be said to have its roots in drama. In Greek, the word ***drama*** means "action," derived from the verb form *drao*, meaning "to do" or "to act." More specifically, "drama" often refers to a composition in verse or prose, delivered to a live audience, involving characters and a conflict of some sort. Thus, things that are not true drama, such as poems, songs, or real-life situations that contain elements of conflict and high emotion are often said to be dramatic. Drama is also a unique art form in that is, by necessity, collaborative. An author needs only a pen and paper to write a story, but a drama requires multiple voices, such as actors, authors, and directors of some kind, to deliver the performance, as well as an audience to receive it. Drama is a fundamental understanding of storytelling that stretches back to the earliest works in the western canon.

Ancient Greek Drama

The first Western dramatists to record their works were the Greeks, and it is from their experiments that much of our modern dramatic structures are derived. It was the understanding of Greek dramatists like Sophocles, Aeschylus, and Euripides, that drama was governed by the laws of comedy and tragedy, represented by the famous grinning and weeping masks. The Greeks saw a clear delineation between comedy and tragedy, deciding that essentially, a comedy could be defined as a drama with a happy ending whereas a tragedy would have a sad one. This terminology continued up through the Renaissance, where even the works of Shakespeare and Marlowe can be clearly separated into comedies and tragedies. Comedies, to the Greeks, were life-affirming romps, often containing satire, clowning, and jokes involving scatological references and innuendo.

Tragedies, on the other hand, were serious business. The "Greek Tragedy" is considered the most enduring gift of the ancient Greeks to world culture. The most famous of these is the *Oedipus The King*, Sophocles' masterpiece, describing the rise and fall of the mighty Oedipus, doomed by fate to slay his father and marry his mother. A common trope in Greek tragedy is the prophecy, delivering the will of the gods to the hero via an oracle, which the hero ignores or seeks to defy more often than not. This reveals the hero's ***hamartia***, his fatal flaw that brings about his downfall. For Oedipus, this is ***hubris***, a great pride that sets him above the will of the gods and thus incurs their wrath. In the play, Oedipus was a brilliant man, able to solve the Sphinx's riddle and become king of Thebes, but even his vaunted intellect could not save him from his prophecy. In a fit of blind rage, King Oedipus slays a traveler he meets on the road, later revealed to be his father, Laius. He also unwittingly took his mother, Jocasta, to bride, who bore him four children before their true relationship was uncovered. In true tragic form, the play ends with a ***catharsis***, a cleansing act brought on by extreme emotion: Jocasta hangs herself due to shame, and Oedipus, upon finding the body, takes the pins from her dress and plunges them into his eyes.

These concepts, as outlined by the Greeks, would go on to define Western drama for millennia, even as drama declined in relevance over the centuries as European languages evolved and borders were drawn. Most performance in Europe up to the Middle Ages was strictly religious in nature. Drama amongst the working classes amounted to little more than campfire stories and folk songs, whereas the church performed live re-enactments, feeling they could be a useful imparting Biblical tales to the illiterate masses. High drama for the purposes of entertainment or art was little known. This changed in the 16th century with the rise of vernacular English, and the flowering of literary giants like Christopher Marlowe, John Webster, and William Shakespeare.

British Dramatists

Considered perhaps the greatest and most influential author in the English language, **William Shakespeare** wrote 39 plays, 154 sonnets, and two long-form poems, displaying a mastery of language that has a larger influence on the Western canon of drama than that of any other figure. He invented or popularized roughly 1700 words that are in common use to this day (only Geoffrey Chaucer can claim to have created nearly as many), and displayed a stunning skill in utilizing the tropes and forms common in Greek tragedy.

Like the Greeks, Shakespeare divided his works into comedies and tragedies, with a few historical plays belonging to neither category. Shakespeare's tragedies exhibit many Greek forms: in the tragedy of *Macbeth*, for instance, the plot is set in motion by supernatural forces, though Shakespeare substitutes three meddlesome witches for an oracle. Macbeth, the protagonist, possesses the *hamartia* of ambition. He seeks to become king of Scotland and is driven to commit many terrible crimes in this pursuit. In the end, this destroys him, as the honorable MacDuff avenges the deaths of his family by beheading Macbeth in single combat, thus bringing peace and order back to the realm, albeit at a terrible cost. The comedies of Shakespeare, likewise, are light-hearted romps involving romance, wordplay, physical comedy, and numerous innuendos.

Shakespeare dabbled in satire and social commentary, but his works are still fundamentally religious and pro-status quo. More often than not, order is restored through royal decree or divine intervention. Conflicts have a tendency to resolve themselves or peter out entirely, as is the case in *Much Ado About Nothing*, where the villainous Don John is captured by unnamed soldiers with no help from the main characters. This kind of abrupt conclusion harkens back to another term coined by the ancient Greeks: the ***deus ex machina***, a sudden conclusion brought on by forces not previously established in the play. In Greek plays, it was not uncommon for the action to be resolved by the appearance of a god on stage. Zeus may appear, brandishing thunderbolts, to destroy the wicked, punish the prideful, and restore the natural order of things, before disappearing just as suddenly. Even the Greeks considered the *deus ex machina* to be a hallmark of lazy writing, Aristotle being one of the trope's most famous critics, but the plot device endured in the works of Shakespeare, sometimes as tongue-in-cheek parody and other times as an earnest expression of the belief that godly order will naturally assert itself, even in bizarre or dangerous situations.

Stylistically, Shakespeare's works reveal an astounding command of the English language of his time. Though he invented many words and phrases that became common to English speakers, his dialogue was intentionally heightened for dramatic effect. Shakespeare wrote in **blank verse**, a type of poetic style involving regular metrical lines with only occasional rhymes. Each line in blank verse has the same poetic meter, consisting of equal syllables on each line. More specifically, Shakespeare's style of blank verse made use of the **iambic pentameter**, a style developed by Shakespeare's contemporary Christopher Marlowe. This line uses ten syllables per line divided into five "feet" consisting of a stressed and unstressed syllable. This creates sort of a galloping or heartbeat cadence for each line, a buh-BUM buh-BUM buh-BUM rhythm that has proved attractive to actors for centuries. The limitations imposed by iambic pentameter are numerous, but Shakespeare mastered the form, creating dialogue that was heightened enough to be dramatic yet witty and ribald enough to be understood and enjoyed by the common listener.

The styles of Renaissance artists like Shakespeare and Marlowe, as well as the Greeks who inspired them, provided much inspiration for English and American dramatists in the centuries to come. The first professional theater company to perform in America, the Lewis Hallam troupe, staged Shakespeare's *The Merchant of Venice* in Williamsburg, Virginia in 1752. Their run in the colonies was a mild success, though theater companies struggled to find an audience in more conservative areas where Puritan communities considered theater to be, at best, a frivolous distraction and at worst, blasphemy. It was not until after the Revolutionary War, where the populace had been inspired by the fiery orations of leaders like Patrick Henry ("Give me liberty or give me death!") and the lean, aggressive prose of authors like Thomas Paine, that American drama would find its own identity.

American Dramatists

William Dunlap is considered the father of American theater. A painter, historian, and artist, Dunlap produced over sixty plays in his career, many of them being translations of German or French works. He displayed a broad knowledge of politics and a fierce loyalty to the newly minted American identity. His most famous works include *Andre,* a tragedy that dramatizes the trial of Major John Andre, a British soldier who was hanged as a spy for his support of Benedict Arnold, and *The Italian Father*, a comedy which borrowed heavily from the works of English dramatist Thomas Dekker.

In the 19th century, American theater was largely melodramatic. American authors mimicked the style of the classical greats who inspired them, creating broad and operatic pieces dealing with issues of class, race, and the American dream. *Uncle Tom's Cabin* was by far the most popular American play of the 1800s. Due to sparsely-enforced copyright laws and the immense popularity of **Harriet Beecher Stowe's** source novel, many "Tom shows" were performed throughout the United States and England, incorporating elements of heightened soap opera and blackface minstrelsy. Though the novel is staunchly anti-slavery, it resorts heavily to stereotypes, and theaters portrayed these with varying degrees of sensitivity and clownishness. It was not uncommon at this time for white actors to portray black characters, complete with darkened faces and exaggerated African-American dialects, and the various "Tom shows" and minstrel shows this spawned dominated the American theatrical scene for some time. These shows often validated the racist attitudes of Americans instead of challenging them, and they became symbolic of the American South's troubled history with race.

The 20th century saw a flowering of American theater. The Civil War, the Depression, and the rise of mechanization and industry left many Americans nostalgic for simpler times and confused about the modern world they lived in. The early quarter of the century was dominated by vaudeville revues featuring circus acts, burlesque, music, and fast-paced comedy. After Later, American drama would finally discover its own voice in the works of Eugene O'Neill, Tennessee Williams, and Arthur Miller, each of whom would explore distinctly American themes relating to family, individuality, sexuality, and the failings of a capitalist system.

Eugene O'Neill was born into a family with deep ties to the theater. His father, James O'Neill, was considered one of the greatest actors of his generation, at least until he squandered his career playing in a successful production of *The Count of Monte Cristo* for a full six thousand performances, causing many critics to label him a sell-out. The family James built with his wife, Mary Ellen Quinlan, was rife with dysfunction, alcohol abuse, and emotional manipulation.

Eugene dropped out of school at a young age and spent several years at sea, struggling with alcoholism and depression. He became a popular fixture in Greenwich village's literary scene before writing his first play, *Beyond the Horizon*, in 1920. The play would win the young author a Pulitzer Prize for Drama. O'Neill won three more of the prizes over his vaunted career, an unprecedented accomplishment for any author.

Other great works by O'Neill include *Strange Interlude, Anna Christie, The Hairy Ape*, and his masterpiece, *Long Day's Journey Into Night,* which depicts in brutal detail the emotional manipulation and substance abuse that turned his childhood into a living hell. O'Neill was among the first authors to explore American vernacular as a legitimate dialect of the theater. His works often dealt with alcoholism and masculinity, and his plays often featured characters who lived on the fringes of society, such as prostitutes, addicts, and homeless people. O'Neill was also the first author to write a major play starring an African-American in a serious role: *The Emperor Jones,* which was influential in the black literary community despite resorting to stereotypes to get its message across. O'Neill died in 1953 after years of declining health.

Like his contemporary, **Tennessee Williams** struggled with various addictions and depression throughout his life, channeling these struggles into his plays. Williams was also a closeted homosexual. This revelation, an open secret during much of Williams' career but not formally acknowledged until after his death, has caused many critics to re-evaluate Williams' works from a new perspective. The machismo and violence of many of his male characters, such as the brutish Stanley Kowalski from *A Streetcar Named Desire*, represents a stern commentary by Williams on the strict gender roles that had caused him to hide his sexuality for much of his life. Williams was also very close with his sister, Rose, who was diagnosed with schizophrenia at a young age and spent much of her life in institutions. Williams used her as an inspiration for many similar characters, such as the disabled Laura in *The Glass Menagerie* and even in *Streetcar's* Blanche Dubois, who suffers a mental breakdown at the end of the play after being preyed upon by the overly masculine Stanley.

Williams other works deal with the identity of the American South and the notion of the "fading Southern belle," an upper class woman struggling with new realities after her money runs out and her looks begin to go. This trope is explored in some of Williams' best works, such as *Cat on a Hot Tin Roof, Orpheus Descending,* and *The Glass Menagerie,* in which the mother, Amanda, wishes to recapture her glamorous youth by living vicariously through Laura, whose illness prevents her from socializing. Williams was also instrumental in advancing the careers of great talents like director Elia Kazan, and actors Kate Hepburn and Marlon Brando, the latter of whom originated the role of Stanley Kowalski, considered by many to be one of the great stage performances of all time.

Arthur Miller's output was largely concerned with the social upheaval of the 1950s. He was forced to testify in front of Senator Joseph McCarthy's House Unamerican Activities committee to ascertain his supposed communist sympathies, and he became a controversial voice during the period known as the Red Scare. This formed the basis for his classic play, *The Crucible*, which explores the paranoia of the time by transplanting it back to the Salem witch trials. His other great works include *All My Sons*, a tragic play centering around a family business and WWII, and *Death of a Salesman*, which follows fading businessman Willy Loman as he slides into obscurity and purposelessness. Miller's works were harshly critical of some American values, prompting Sen. McCarthy's to attack Miller's reputation. Miller's career survived the hearings, though he did "out" several of his contemporaries as communist sympathizers.

Modern American Drama

In the latter half of the 20th century, American theater became a dominant cultural force, even as the popularity of the art form was eclipsed by film. The Civil Rights movement of the 1960s inspired many new plays dealing with issues of race, such as Lorraine Hansberry's *A Raisin in the Sun*, which followed the struggles of a black family in Chicago. The play won a Pulitzer Prize, making Hansberry the first African-American to win the award. Her works were heavily influenced by the Harlem Renaissance of the 1920s, a movement amongst black intellectuals such as Langston Hughes and Zora Neale Hurston to forge a new African-American identity in the United States through artistic and political action in the Harlem neighborhood of New York.

In recent years, American drama has proven to be experimental and uncompromising, displaying a facility with both naturalistic and heightened dialogue as well as finding strong humanity in characters from all walks of life. Dominant theatrical voices since the 1950s include David Mamet (*Glengarry Glen Ross, Speed-The-Plow*), Neil Simon (*Lost in Yonkers, The Odd Couple*), Henry David Hwang (*M. Butterfly*), and Tony Kushner (*Angels in America*). American drama continues to explore themes of sexuality, race, class, and gender as they affect all walks of life.

Strategy for Points: Drama

- Know the fundamental aspects of drama: the role of *hamartia, hubris*, and *catharsis* as they appear in classical works, as well as more contemporary dramas. These forms appear in nearly all western drama in some form or another.
- Theater has always been closely tied to the culture that creates it. Try to connect theatrical works to the social issues of its time. The works of Williams and O'Neill are concerned with money, important to a generation that survived the Great Depression. The works of Hansberry and Hurston deal with race, just as the civil rights movement came into its own.
- Understand the styles of classical artists like Shakespeare and Marlowe. Familiarize yourself with iambic pentameter, blank verse, and the relationship between poetic language and dialogue they created.
- Many authors drew from elements of their own life. For instance, Williams explored issues of mental illness and strict gender roles, whereas O'Neill dramatized his own struggles with alcohol and family dysfunction.
- Be prepared to analyze text directly. You must offer quotations to support your point.

SECTION IV: Effective Reading and Writing Review

Chapter 9: Analysis

WHILE YOU ARE VERY WELL AWARE AT THIS POINT OF A VARIETY OF LITERARY GENRES AND authors, over the past few years you may have considered the volume of materials you've read as more important than what you were reading – or why you were reading it. When you are reading for comprehension, there are generally three types of ways to approach material in a test setting: problem solving, comprehension, or critical reasoning.

While each of these are related, it's not so much why you are being asked a question, but what is the goal of the question. It's likely that you are familiar with at least some of the passages used in the multiple choice section of the exam if you have read a lot of literature over the past four years, but your applied cognitive skills – how well you use what you know – as well as testing what you actually know, is just as important as having done your homework before getting to this exam.

For the practice exams and on the actual test day, you need to employ strategic reading tactics and critical reading to get the highest score; speed alone will lower your points. Critical reading involves dissecting the text to see the structure of the information presented and classify how things are said – if you were using critical thinking, as you would when completing classwork, you would be trying to validate or repudiate what the author says. Here, in Section I of the AP English Literature and Composition, you need to just take what the author says as true for multiple choice. You may not like it, but it's how you get more points in multiple choice – you get to use all the critical thinking you want for Section II and free-response essays and compositions!

Modes of Each Text (or Passage)

The various pieces that you are asked to read do three things – the text states something, the text describes something, and the text means something. You need to use the various components of this guide and your lessons in English to determine what an author means by looking at the words chosen, the tone used, and any bias the author may readily present. When you break down all the words to what you need for a thorough analysis, you can handle all the reading passages and multiple choice questions very well. Analysis is what to look for in the passages for the multiple choice selections – remember, it's not about finding the deeper meaning of the literary passage. This test doesn't have time to get into all of that!

Types of Passages

It's fairly easy to spot **problem solving** selections, as they literally solve a problem. You could be given a passage that explains how a science project was conducted, or the techniques used to file through samples from an archeological site. There is usually a chronological progress to these passages, and you need to pay attention to the order in which information is presented in addition to what facts or numerical descriptions apply to which steps in a process. These passages tend to lure people towards thinking they can rapidly answer the questions following the selection, but will focus on descriptive words to get you to "just pick" and not think.

Reading comprehension passages typically have several complex paragraphs, especially in the AP English Language and Literature Exam, Section I. Just by looking at the passage, without any additional investigation, you should be able to determine that it is about comprehension. This means that while the testers do not intend to trick you, they likely will try to pick something that deals with a character's state of mind or an interaction between people that has an "unknown" aspect that isn't covered in much detail so that all students taking the test are being judged on comprehension – NOT what they memorized through class work.

When given **critical reasoning** options, these are typically shorter passages that will use persuasive arguments to reach an unstated conclusion. Most often, one of the questions will include "what was the author trying to convey" type of selection. In critical reasoning, you need to determine what the author is trying to state or prove, and it helps to figure out what assumption is made during the passage.

Types of Questions

Regardless of the type of passage provided, there are several kinds of questions to evaluate your reading skills when under time constraints.

The first kind of question is **inference** – by the passage suggesting ideas or presenting information that perhaps can be linked to a "position" or a belief held by a character or author, you need to determine what the author was trying to persuade you to believe. These multiple choice questions nearly always have an absolute wrong answer – a closely-worded option to the best answer, but uses words opposite of the structure in the passage or by throwing in an "absolute" – never, always, not, et cetera. It could also have an option that is way off topic from the main idea in the passage. You can go back to the paragraph in the passage to select the right answer, but read carefully so you don't pick the absolute wrong one.

The second way they test materials presented and your **knowledge** of what was presented in the passage. By giving details and facts in a passage, perhaps a very descriptive passage of the organization of a room from a character's viewpoint, the test coordinators can overwhelm you with lots of different kinds of information. This frequently happens in passages with a lot of numbers or many items of the same kind in a passage, and the multiple choice answer options will 0give numbers that are close to each other – and again, there will be at least one option that is the opposite of what you should answer and like one that is totally contrived, not to be found anywhere in the passage at all. These do not only deal with numbers, but those are the simplest to identify as they look to see if you can decipher the content of the passage.

Also, questions may be written to test your ability to induce or reason through an **assumption** begun by an author. This includes **cause-and-effect** scenarios, where the question asks "if" and the answer options present "then" finishing options based on the facts presented in the passage. Another way to look at this is making a **prediction** based on what the author presented. A possible question could ask what is likely to happen next between two characters – and you need to select the best answer based on the information given in the passage. You will have to use reasoning to answer the assumption sort of questions and ensure you follow the path established by the author of the passage, not just what you think would be the correct way to solve a problem.

Similar to assumption and inference is **sequential analysis** – but the difference here, and it is a slight difference but one you should be able to recognize – is when a set of instructions is given, results are posted yet the question reviews a slightly different set of information following the same set of instructions. You need to be able to follow through ordered steps to get to the right answer. This could be dance steps described in Victorian era, a servant's daily chores, or any number of options in literary examples. The point is that you need to follow the instructions of the author and not select the answer that you think sounds best or makes the most sense according to what you are accustomed to doing.

There are also some seemingly simpler questions on the exam in the multiple choice section that may cause you to miss points because they seem so easy that you don't really pay attention to them. These **story line** questions make you slow down and answer what you actually read, not what your mind thinks you read. You will be in a hurry on the exam, but remember you really do have enough time to answer all the questions thoughtfully. When faced with story detail questions, go back and find the exact point in question – the multiple choice answers will have four options that read very similar to one another and then the one odd-ball that is not like anything you read previously.

Other Important Aspects of Analysis

Knowing the ways passages are constructed as well as how questions are written are not the only things tested on the first section of the AP English Literature and Composition exam. The other areas of this guide have incorporated literary periods, vocabulary, details on various genres – and these will all be tested throughout the various multiple choice questions on Section I of the exam.

Strategy for Points: Analysis

- Every multiple choice question includes one "trap" – you can determine which kind of trap depending on the style of the question.
- You cannot answer questions in multiple choice based on your previous classwork or what you think you know – your experience can hurt you in multiple choice. You must answer passages based only on what's presented in front of you. All of the questions can be answered by the information presented.

- Story line questions are frequently thought by test-takers to be the easiest and these are questions usually missed because they rely on memory instead of taking a few extra – and well rewarded – seconds to check the story facts and select the right answer.
- Bias from an author can provoke an emotional response from you, but don't let it distract you from your goal of answering the questions accurately.
- Some instructors recommend "test taking approaches" such as read the passage's questions (not the answer options) before you actually read the passage, so you can pre-sort the information as you read it according to the questions that will follow. This may allow you to erase or eliminate the trap answer choices because if you know the question first, you can be specific about your attention as you read the passage. However, you need to know whatever is the best work method for you – now is not the time to change your good habits just because you think your score will improve. In all likelihood, making a change close to a test will add stress and possibly even bring down your score.

Chapter 10: Organization in Your Compositions

WHEN YOU ARE WRITING YOU ARE TRYING TO CONVEY A MESSAGE TO THE READER AND persuade him to see your point of view. The AP essays are most often designed for you to write a persuasive supportive-style argument, where you lead off with your idea and then support it. There are certain points you need to be sure are understood, and there is a proper order to help in the delivery of your information. All the facts or quotes that you can muster, even when they are true and correctly used, cannot help you make your points if they aren't well organized.

Throughout the middle section of this AP study guide, individual chapters review important topics that must you must understand and utilize throughout a good essay: correct punctuation, appropriate grammar, sophisticated vocabulary, and solid syntax. There is no "right time" to apply these tools; they must be used all of the time. If you are weak in any of these areas and your writing is filled with mistakes, your score is automatically lowered.

The *content* of your essay also contributes significantly to your grade. It is important to use the conventional structure to receive the highest grade. High scores are granted only to essays that make the most sense (we pointed out earlier that only 18% of all participants earn a "5," the top score). There is a pattern that should be followed. This is NOT the time to attempt to highlight your individuality by venturing off into another pattern. Rather than fight the organizational structure, use the content within your essay and the standard structure to illustrate your points using strong critical thinking and good organization.

Make an Outline: Your Map for the Essay

As you begin to develop the message that you want the reader to understand, it is best to create an outline (or "mind map," if that's a more comfortable term for you). Any time there is a limited time frame to finish writing, the few minutes spent organizing your thoughts are very beneficial, saving time as you translate thoughts to full sentences. Most people need to write an outline (or type it out) and not rely on what they can track in their head.

To create an outline, brainstorm things about the book, author or subject matter first. These are the three areas that AP essays are usually going to ask you to consider. You may ask yourself "what questions does this raise for me?" and write the answers down in a list. Perhaps there are obvious messages conveyed in the text, and you should put those on the list. Don't forget to include any large topics or themes of the book, such as gender issues, good versus evil, or the individual versus society. Again, these are all favorites on exams.

Essentially, this is all you need to do for the short time you have to write an AP essay. You have created a list of important topics. As you write the essay, you may list these first on a page that is not to be scored, then draw lines or symbols to get related ideas next to one another and place them in appropriate order. Finally, don't forget to look back at your outline. This now serves as a checklist to help you maintain the "integrity" of the essay — listing the topics you need to cover and the order in which you need to do it, so it helps readers understand your thought (especially when they are reading and grading hundreds of essays).

With the time constrictions of the AP essay, it is strongly recommended that you create an outline and map your important points in order to make sure a) that they support your main idea, b) that you can write a clear paragraph around that thought and c) that your ideas don't drift (meaning your paper has a different main idea than the one you first thought you had). Short notes allow you to organize what you know and then write out complete, thoughtful sentences rather than to spend lots of time rewriting at the end. This process is the best way to form a persuasive argument. When you have taken a few minutes to draft the outline, when you reach the concluding portion, it is fairly easy to determine if you have indeed identified the correct thesis or if you should change it. This is much simpler to do before you get deep into writing.

Short Well-Organized Essays

The structure of an essay, regardless of length, is fairly straightforward. A clear structure is critical in an AP essay. Beginning with a thesis paragraph, you relay the main idea of your essay and introduce what you will be discussing. The next several paragraphs of your essay support your main idea, using examples from various books that give credence to your main idea. However, if you have a very strong thesis statement, you may sometimes use the compare-and-contrast organizational style that gives "counterpoints" at the end of your supporting paragraphs to show that you recognize opposing arguments but show their shortcomings. Lastly, you need to share a concluding statement in the last paragraph (which does not mean you just restate the first paragraph), bring your ideas together, and give resolution to your analysis.

Introduction and main idea or "thesis" of your essay:

The traditional essays — and the ones that score the highest — state the main idea early in the first paragraph. It is this topic paragraph that answers a question or expresses the writer's position, lays an argument, and presents brief highlights of how the writer plans to support that argument. This first paragraph makes a claim (statement) and shows how your composition will support it. Typically, this paragraph should be only five or six sentences long.

The most common introductory sentences (usually two at the beginning of the paragraph) begin to set the tone and topic for a reader. When you begin outlining what you want to say, typically one of the first things you put into your notes is this main idea. "Frankenstein was not a monster, but rather a representation of the ills in society" is an example of a strong main idea that could be supported by passages in Mary Shelley's book as well as other writings of that time. It clearly and plainly states what the reader will learn in the paper.

As you continue listing thoughts in your outline regarding your thesis, additional components for the essay start to shine. You can pull together a few themes that are clear, strongly supported with quotes or examples, and show the reader specifically how you are justified in making your main claim of the essay. These ideas support the thesis, and make up the next three sentences in your introduction paragraph.

Using the idea that Frankenstein is a representation of societal ills, your next three sentences would be generalizations of how you intend to support your thesis. During the outline, you may see that you have five, six or even seven points you want to make, which is an appropriate volume for the time frame of the AP essay. It's not about how much you write, but how well you write it. Bundle these points into three categories, and generalize them for the introductory paragraph. In this illustration with Frankenstein, you could coordinate supporting ideas using boundaries, grotesqueness and secrecy/shame as the main ways you can show society's problems reflected in the novel.

The best introductory paragraphs avoid three mistakes. First, they don't restate the question either directly or paraphrased. You need to consider the question and formulate your answer in a manner that simply answers the question, as incorporation of the AP essay statement (or the college professor's assignment or your boss' question) will show you haven't given much thought to the assignment, even if that's untrue. Next, don't write about how you thought about the assignment or how you came to decide what you would write. That's all background that feeds the paper, but is NOT the paper. For the final mistake to avoid, don't start your paper with what someone else has said — including the author, a dictionary, a character in the book, et cetera. This is about what you have considered and present, so it should start with your own main idea in your own words.

Remember, if you haven't captured the reader's attention in this first paragraph (or "hooked" them, as teachers like to say), they will not want to read further and that yields a lower grade for an AP essay. In your first five sentences, be certain you have presented an interesting idea and have provoked the reader to think about your main idea in a new way. You could also highlight support for a less appealing idea as these tactics will get the scorer to read your content with interest and score your essay higher than they would a more boring paper.

Body: Persuasive-Supportive Style:

A high percentage of successful AP essays are constructed in the persuasive-supportive style framework. This is a relatively easy method by which to make a point in a limited period of time. People are accustomed to reading lists of three. When considering that studies have shown repeatedly that a person must hear a message before they believe it, this three-fold format makes sense. Each of the three support ideas has two sub-supporting prongs that uphold or illustrate the supporting idea. That makes six points to support your main idea.

And again, this is where the outline is so important. When listing the ways you can prove your main idea, you should make sure you have six or seven specific examples to support it. As previously mentioned, you then generalize this list of examples into three categories, placing two into each "bundle" of support. This gives you three paragraphs in order to support your introductory thesis paragraph, and each of these support paragraphs has two examples to support the topic of each paragraph as listed in your outline. Each paragraph should go back to your thesis and "question the question" you are answering, to ensure you are presenting arguments that support your main idea (and not just restating it).

Notice that the body of the paper will not include is a summary of what you've read, what the book has said, or what critics have stated about the topic. The reader — in this case, the AP grader (who is almost always a teacher or professor) — has likely read the book more than once, and won't need you to restate it. In fact, when you include summaries during an AP exam, you are reducing the time you have for thoughtful analysis. If you don't have time to incorporate solid commentary, your grade will drop. So stick with the outline, and you'll see another way it helps keep you on task during a timed writing event.

When reviewing your notes on each generalized item and the two examples that support each of the three ideas, you should feel that one of the generalizations is your strongest argument (that it is the most certain, that it is the most logical, that it gives your essay a bang). This strongest generalization with the best points should be your third in the series of three.

In music, composers build the momentum of a piece of music to a crescendo just before a finale. This is how you should consider yourself and your writing. The composer (the writer, you) uses phrases and parts to bring a melody (your main idea) to a crescendo (the best of the three generalizations with the strongest examples) that nails your point just before your finale (conclusion and finish).

We will continue to use the Frankenstein example, where our generalization of societal ills incorporated the supportive categories of boundaries, grotesqueness and secrecy/shame. Under each of these, you would list the two points that helped you create these categories:

Point 1 — Boundaries
  Subpoint A: isolation or alienation from society
  Subpoint B: perspectives alter viewpoint(s)/interpretation

Point 2 — Grotesqueness
  Subpoint C: delusions of personal grandeur and lack of self-reflexion
  Subpoint D: personal assumptions based on appearance

Point 3 — Secrecy/shame
  Subpoint E: shame of rejection, which leads to revenge
  Subpoint F: madness compels Victor to create his own reality

Use your knowledge of the book and the subpoints to determine the strongest one (the one you can write about the most easily and with the most confidence). You should shift the order of the list so that this identified strong point now is the last grouping. You may even reorder the subpoints within the point, to help ensure that the final subpoint in each paragraph is the strongest. While your list may appear differently, your list may now appear as follows:

Point 1 — Grotesqueness
Subpoint A: delusions of personal grandeur and lack of self-reflexion
Subpoint B: personal assumptions based on appearance

Point 2 — Boundaries
Subpoint C: perspectives alter viewpoint(s)/interpretation
Subpoint D: isolation or alienation from society

Point 3 – Secrecy/shame
Subpoint E: madness compels Victor to create his own reality
Subpoint F: shame of rejection, which leads to revenge

If this persuasive support is the style that you've chosen (and most students should use this style for the AP essays), you can then go to the outline for creating the conclusion paragraph before you begin to write. However, if the question posed by the AP would be better addressed by showing how the phrase is not true, then the next style may be appropriate (but use it sparingly for AP responses).

Body: Persuasive Compare-and-Contrast Style:

A compare-and-contrast argument is an alternative that, in rare instances for the AP essay, allows you to provide the alternative point of view, shows a reduction in potential bias, and when done properly, builds to support the original thesis assertion. However, it is really not suggested for the AP essay unless absolutely necessary, since more time is generally needed to construct a solid composition in this style. But, so you will know how it works should you need to employ this tactic, we are including it for you here.

This structure can be written in point/counterpoint fashion or all pro then all con (block all of one side of the argument and then block all of the other side of the argument), thus ensuring that the strongest arguments, just as before, are incorporated at the end of the composition. This means that another decision must be made before you can start writing — and it all comes from reviewing the ideas you "mapped" earlier for your outline.

If you find that you are comparing two people and how they performed their jobs — authors, politicians, characters or whomever — the block method is probably best suited for that persuasion. You take the points for each, but list Author A with all of her qualities on the topics (remember, it's best to stick to three) and then provide Author B with all of his qualities on the *same points*. In this way, you block the points one, two, and three for each of the persons, and your transitions explain the differences in the second person's outline by using such phrases as "compared to Author A, Author B said…" or "unlike Author A, Author B thought it important to focus on…" to relate the blocks to each other.

When you are very organized and knowledgeable on a topic, you may decide to use the point/counterpoint method. Taking your six subpoints and again arranging them in an order that builds toward your strongest argument, you then review them and pair two sides of the argument to develop these discussions. This involves taking both sides without showing blatant favor to one side or the other. The way you show your "favoritism" is how you are going to make a supportive decision by presenting one "side" stronger, and that's the side with which you finish the six points. That point leads directly into your conclusion when you link it to your final statements.

Persuasive arguments always engage a reader to follow your train of thought to reach a conclusion, but these two methods take much more energy, focus and commitment on your part as the writer. The block method in this particular style results in a composition that appears "A, A and A whereas B, B and B lead to the conclusion that [A or B] was…" and the effort must be focused on showing the differences on these pieces and how or why one is preferred over the other. The point/counterpoint method needs you to keep the reader engaged and wanting to read further as the "argument ball" goes back and forth. The final "shot" is the one that cinches support for your main idea. Once your support pieces are completed, you move to the final step of the essay.

Conclusion Section (Just One Paragraph):

The final piece of a story is always the most memorable — for good or bad. You want to make sure that your conclusion is NOT a mirror image of your opening with only a few word changes. Rather, you want to state your thesis slightly modified, building upon the facts and subpoints used. It's strongest when you are able to state your thesis in another manner, summarizing quickly and giving the reader something positive to consider for the future.

To restate the main idea of our Frankenstein paragraph, we can adjust it to reflect the generalized supportive points. For example, we may wrap the conclusion around the main sentence for this paragraph as "The monster was a manifestation of personal flaws — shame, alienation, outrageous ego — and Shelley compelled the reader to reflect on how environment/nature shapes the development of a person and society's acceptance of things that are different."

This statement takes the reader back to what was included in the body, but in a different phrasing and actually gives the action item of how to read the story without asking a question. (It is considered very informal and should not be done in most any academic writing — you are answering a question inherently in the essay so don't dummy-it-down by stating it.) A strong conclusion practically begs the reader to ask himself or herself if he/she was smart enough to think of it in the way that you just presented.

You score more points when you answer tough questions and give effective supportive excerpts of examples during the body. You are leading the reader to a conclusion not only about the topic you've chosen, but also leading the reader to ask if he or she has ever considered it like this before reading your essay. Your final paragraph should be a graceful closure to a well-organized presentation of the evidence that supported your main idea.

As you write the critical finishing review of the body of your essay, you need to make sure the whole paragraph (because in this AP essay, it will be only one paragraph. Later in college or professional writing, it will likely be more) clearly makes the reader feel like the discussion or presentation of your argument is completed. You can't have a dangling idea at the end of a great argument and expect to earn the highest score.

The conclusion is what the readers — graders — will remember. It is the last thing they see before giving you a score. Make it count. Restate in a different way why your argument was oriented the way you chose, wrap up the ideas, and complete the ending thought so that it clearly shows the reader that you had enough time to finish saying everything. That's another way the AP exam may catch you off guard. — people drop off effort in the conclusion, so it counts for a significant weight of points (because they can tell if you rushed through it).

Special Notes on Organization of Supporting Information

There will be times when a question to which you are required to write a response is presented, and the organization of your response may have unique needs. You will be able to determine this from the phrasing of the question or statement you need to address. All of these possibilities still need the strong foundation (punctuation, grammar, vocabulary and syntax) and thoughtful clear discussion around your thesis response to the question. But how you provide the supporting ideas may vary.

For instance, if you need to provide instructions, there is a chronological order that needs to be followed. You cannot ice a cake before you bake it; nor can you easily or successfully discuss the Boston Tea Party without revealing aspects of the origin or impetus for the fighting. Rarely in a sophisticated essay should the support paragraphs be presented in a stepwise manner (as in literally "first, second and third") to give the reader baby-steps in understanding your points.

Similarly, and this is used in fiction quite frequently, there may be events that indeed happened in a certain order because there is a pinnacle event — one that culminates the reader's experience in a grand climatic moment. Murder mysteries typically are written in chronological order, but give special consideration to the actual event that is the reason for the book. This may be incorporated into the persuasive support style, but must fall under the persuasive points listed previously and then used to order the separate points.

Conversely, popular criminal investigation television shows do not order events by timelines. The fictional detectives have to piece together the mystery backwards after they stumble upon the crime. But this is actually a third way, through historical analysis. It is almost a reverse chronology in presenting the supporting facts of the main idea (such as the 'title' of that episode or the type of crime being investigated). Timing of events is still important, but review of data and information has to be researched in order to determine their correct order.

These three styles are not necessarily appropriate for AP essays. They take more time to develop than you will be given in the writing section of the exam. These methods may be used on college papers, so you should be aware that while the organization mechanism remains intact, there are various styles for supporting the main idea that may be more appropriate in other situations.

Similarly inappropriate for AP essays is building support for a position that isn't stated until the last paragraph. It is strongly recommended that you do not try to use this more formal and difficult style for AP essays or even college entrance essays. It takes much practice and a great deal of time to organize, research, phrase, and conclude using this style since the conclusion is actually the thesis and requires great finesse. It requires the reader to have the energy and patience to realize by sentence five that you intend to change the typical format.

Keep your chances highest for the best score. Practice using the formats that have proven successful for years and you will be successful in this exam.

The Three Essay "Prompts"

The AP English exams provides three prompts in Section II. You will need to answer each of them; you cannot choose to complete two of the three as your grade will significantly drop. The organization listed in this chapter should be used for all three prompts, though you can vary the style slightly because the three prompts may be very different.

The reason we have included the previous chapters is because each one helps improve your score not only for Section I, but also in Section II. The three prompts for AP English Literature and Composition exam— poetry, prose and "free response" — all use vocabulary skills to build sophisticated and clear replies to the prompts. (For prompts in the AP English Language and Composition, see Chapter 12.) Every essay needs to incorporate correct grammar, punctuation, syntax, and more for the highest store. Poetry focuses on technique and the meaning of a poem (or phrase in a poem). The prose question provides a fiction passage where you then review literary techniques used to deliver a message. In free response, you will use your own selection of a play or novel to explain how a literary concept or other community issue is handled by an author.

As mentioned previously, do not summarize the story or poem because the essays are intended to highlight your ability to analyze the technique or message. It's also not appropriate to use the personal pronoun "I" to state what you think or feel (you are writing it; it's obviously "I"). Using conflicts between characters, lines in a poem, the treatment of language in a work of prose are all ways you can reference the plot without giving a belabored "book review." Make sure you address the main point of each prompt in the time allotted – this is also about making sure you have good time management skills (two hours for three questions, giving 55% of your score) as well as excellent writing ability.

Strategy for Points: Writing Essays

- Just because it's true doesn't mean it has to go into your essay. More "stuff" doesn't give you a higher grade. Only clear and direct support for your main idea will raise your grade.
- Organizing in the traditional format for this AP exam may seem "boring" or "safe" — but consider your target audience: graders of hundreds of essays. If you help them fly through your essay with standard organization points, it will raise your grade.
- Fancy writing doesn't elevate your grade. Solid sentences with flawless foundation (punctuation, grammar, vocabulary and syntax) are the best ways to get the top score.
- Make sure you transition between thoughts and paragraphs smoothly, so your ideas flow from one another (instead of bouncing) for the highest possible score.
- As you read each paragraph, continue asking yourself "so what" or "how does this support my thesis" to make sure everything relates to your main point, so you can earn the top score.

Chapter 11: Editing Your Own Writing

FAR TOO OFTEN, ENGLISH COURSES FOCUS ON GENERATING CONTENT AND NOT ON REFINING it. Too many aspiring writers have become obsessed with making a deadline rather than crafting a piece that convinces and enthralls. The AP English exams are intended to measure one's affinity for the English language and the thinkers who have helped shape it. The test itself does not have an editing portion, but understanding how to redraft, review, and critique one's own work will serve you well when you are presented with an essay question or a piece of literature you must analyze. Remember, other eyes will read your piece come grading time. It behooves you to know how they will look at it.

Most writing teachers insist that editing your work as you write it is a poor habit. First drafts, even of pieces that go on to become great works of literature, are often shockingly sloppy. Existing early drafts of the works of Kafka, Hemingway, and many other writers of the first rank are nearly blacked out by jagged corrective lines and exes. This is a natural part of the writing process. Some teachers even insist that considerations like grammar and spelling should be set aside while you churn out your first copy. Don't be afraid to be "wrong" with your first draft. It's called a "rough draft" for a reason.

So, once you've gotten it all on the page, it's time, as the saying goes, "to murder your darlings." Every writer becomes deeply attached to his prose. Chopping it to bits with a red pen just feels wrong. Unfortunately, if it has to go, it has to go. Be brutal. Cut out everything that does not serve the piece, no matter how pretty.

But how to know what to cut? One reliable method of identifying wooden phrasing and unrefined points is to read your text out loud. Information entering through the ears passes through a different part of the brain than information that enters solely through the eyes. You're literally discovering the piece from a new perspective. So practice your public speaking. Go line by line through the piece, or at least the sections you're not sure of, and talk it out. For bonus efficacy, consider printing out the piece and holding the physical copy in your hand while you do this. Seeing it as a manuscript instead of glowing letters on a screen gives you some emotional distance from the thing. Ask yourself, what parts sound best out loud? What parts do you stumble over? Oftentimes, this will reveal awkward sections that your eyes thought were just fine.

This is also a good place to do some basic copyediting. Underline misspelled words, cross out superfluous passages, and feel free to scribble arrows and notes to your heart's content. The page will not look pretty when you're done. This is a good sign. There are a few less obvious issues you should cut or remedy in the editing phase.

Redundancy and Superfluous Detail

Redundancy is the hallmark of mediocre writing. Good writing exists on the edge of discovery, always pushing through new details, new arguments. To repeat oneself is to insult the reader's attention span and cause the piece to drag as a result. Repetition can be a useful rhetorical device, but always be conscious of using it.

Superfluous detail is a similar issue. Authors are chronic over-explainers, eager to paint each scene with microscopic precision. Come editing time, any section or phrase that repeats information the reader has already been told must go. Even embellishing descriptive words must be removed if they're communicating repetitive detail. For instance: "John ran quickly down the hall."

There's no need for "quickly" in that sentence. "Ran" already implies "quickly." Is it possible for John to "run slowly" down a hall? "John ran down the hall" flows much better.

This strikes at another calling card of immature writing: the adverb. Far too much writing is cluttered by unnecessary modifiers like "shouted loudly" or "shone brightly." The odd adverb will not ruin your piece, but any word ending in -ly should be among the first on the chopping block when you're in editing mode. Be sparing.

Passive Voice

The passive voice dogs persuasive writing. As a writer, your job is to convince. Whether you're arguing why hot dogs are better than burgers or describing a character's beautiful hair, you must always speak with the authority of one who knows.

The passive voice ruins this. Too many authors couch their arguments in passive voice, burying attractive direct statements in layers of conjunctions and general pronouns. Case in point: "The committee will be meeting at 4:30."

This sounds wishy-washy. If the committee is meeting at 4:30, then say so. "The committee will meet at 4:30" is leaner and quicker to the point.

Similarly, there is no need to pepper your work with prevarications like "I believe" or "in my opinion" or "seems to be" or "it appears as if." If we're reading your work, we know this is your opinion. That's the reason we're here. Be emphatic and the audience will respond.

Excessive Punctuation

This is an issue that goes beyond incorrect grammar. Plenty of punctuation is used correctly from a technical standpoint while still hampering the piece's readability. Commas are the worst offender. Older works are replete with commas, partially because authors used to get paid by the word and thus they took their time explaining everything in great detail to maximize a paycheck. Today, we favor slimmer writing. For example: "This machine could, in theory, break down heavy plastics, and thus, reuse the base particles in creating newer, stronger kinds of materials."

The commas make it crawl. We can purge "in theory" from the sentence entirely, or insert it at the front with only one comma to separate it instead of two. "In theory, this machine could break down heavy plastics…" is already much better.

The comma after "plastics" is more justified as it separates two clauses in the sentence, but the one after "thus" isn't needed. If we remove that one, then suddenly the comma after "newer" reads better. Our complete sentence becomes "In theory, this machine could break down heavy plastics, and thus reuse the base particles in creating newer, stronger kinds of materials." Both sentences are grammatically correct, but the second one is a much better read.

A final note about commas – the serial comma (or Oxford comma) remains controversial amongst editors and writers, with no clear consensus on its usefulness or aesthetic appeal. Most American style guides, such as Strunk & White or The MLA Style Manual, suggest using a serial comma whenever possible. To them, "carrots, peas, and grapes" (with the serial comma before "and") is superior to "carrots, peas and grapes" (with no serial comma). Canadian or British style guides often recommend against using the serial comma, and thus confusion abounds. What is certain is that you must be consistent. If you're using a serial comma, stick with it through the whole piece.

Here are a few more notes on common punctuation flaws:

- Ellipses require only three dots ("…"). No more are required, even if you're indicating a longer pause.
- One exclamation point is plenty. Those writing dialogue sometimes get away with two ("I'm so mad right now!!"), but there's rarely any need for it.
- The same applies for question marks. More than one is unnecessary.
- Semicolons are tricky to master, and many authors simply do without. Kurt Vonnegut famously quipped that even after decades of writing best sellers, he still couldn't understand the value of a semicolon over a comma or a period.
- Quotation marks denote something that has been said, word for word. You should not put paraphrased statements in quotation marks. Be careful with this. Newspapers have been sued for adding a single word to a direct quotation.

And lastly, remember that there's only so much any author can do on his own. There's a reason we pay editors all that cash. Editing is a time-consuming process, far from an exact science. Errors of grammar and spelling can be removed with the push of a button, but creating a piece that entertains and informs requires a human touch. Give the piece your full attention for as long as you can, but understand, at some point you simply must put new eyes to it. There's no point in writing if no one gets to read it.

Strategy for Points: Proofreading Essays

- Put it all on the page for your first draft. Considerations like grammar, spelling, and punctuation can come later, during the editing phase.
- Avoid over-explaining. Trust the audience to follow what you're trying to say.
- Always write with authority. Argue your point, describe what you see. Saying "in my opinion" only hinders your argument and patronizes your audience.
- Consider printing out a physical copy and making changes on the page. This lets you see what you've altered.
- Be spare. If a word, paragraph, or punctuation mark doesn't serve your needs, it has to be removed, no matter how pretty it might be.

Chapter 12: Differences Between AP English Language and AP English Literature

THE COLLEGE BOARD, CREATORS OF THE AP EXAMS, PROVIDE THE FOLLOWING INformation in various locations concerning the distinctions between the two AP English exams:

- Students choosing AP English Language and Composition should be interested in studying and writing various kinds of analytic or persuasive essays. Doing so is meant to help develop critical literacy and facilitate informed citizenship. Effective use of rhetoric, including controlling tone, establishing and maintaining voice, and achieving appropriate emphasis through diction and sentence structure is critical for success. Multiple choice questions are based on reading comprehension of non-fiction passages. Free response (essay) topics consist of three that must be answered, one from each type: synthesis, non-fiction rhetorical analysis, and argument.
- Students choosing AP English Literature and Composition should be interested in studying literature of various periods and genres and using this wide reading knowledge to discuss literary topics. This part of the exam focuses on a work's structure, style and themes as well as such smaller-scale elements as the use of figurative language, imagery, symbolism and tone. Absorbing the richness of meaning in works from the 16th to the 21st centuries is important in order to analyze how that meaning is embodied in literary form, and is the basis for the multiple choice questions. Again, free response (essay) topics consist of three that must be answered, one from each type: poem analysis, prose analysis, and a concept or issue of literary interest.

Both of the exams look at an author's content, the student's ability to analyze it, and the production of strong, persuasive arguments. The language exam tests the ability of a student to take information (with at least one essay question being non-fiction) that may be new to them and rapidly form an argument using the materials provided. The literature exam looks at the genre and conventions of certain authors or historic periods, so that the student should have a good understanding of influential events and underlying social and cultural values that likely influenced the author.

The multiple choice sections both test your ability to read accurately. The topics of the passages for the questions may be slightly different — language (non-fiction, more recently published written works, and perhaps some controversial themes from recent events) versus literature (prose of famous authors, poetry, and some drama is included). There are more extensive differences in the essay section. Both tests present approximately four short passages about different topics and test your ability to infer meaning and understand the formal features of the text.

Essentially, the type of information presented on the exams is the differentiator. In both exams, you are provided three prompts in Section II, and this Section comprises 55% of the total score. You will need to answer each of the questions asked; you cannot choose to complete two of the three as your score will significantly drop. The organization used for all three prompts in the two tests should be the same as discussed for AP English Literature and Composition, though you can vary the style slightly because the three prompts may be very different. This test — the AP English Language and Composition Exam — requires the essay portion to have students use non-fiction references with appropriate citation formatting. Does that help clarify?

Points are given for consistency in citation and appropriateness.

In the AP English Language and Composition exam, the following three types of prompts must be answered in two hours and fifteen minutes, remembering good grammar, punctuation, syntax and general composition is still evaluated in addition to the following criteria (counting for 55% of the overall exam score):

- The three prompts — **synthesis, rhetorical analysis** and **argument** — all look at the writer's ability to review provided content for the first two prompts or free knowledge in the last prompt. The student must comprehend and present an analysis based on the information presented. The synthesis section gives six or seven texts, graphs, articles or other information (even cartoons) about a particular topic and asks the student to pick three in support of the main idea they develop. The rhetorical analysis section focuses on a non-fiction text (typically a speech from a historical figure, excerpt of a letter, or other time-sensitive piece). Test takers must use vocabulary skills and knowledge of writer's language and structure to determine the meaning of the given text. The argument portion is a free-response. The student must "agree, disagree, or provide qualification" for a given statement which will typically focus on a controversial topic (such as social, political, racial, religious or class viewpoints).

In the AP English Literature and Composition, the following three types of question must be answered in two hours (counting for 55% of the overall exam score):

The three prompts — **poetry, prose** and **"literary merit"** — all use vocabulary skills to build sophisticated and clear replies to the prompts. Every essay needs to incorporate correct grammar, punctuation, and syntax to achieve the highest store. Poetry focuses on poetic technique and the meaning of a poem (or phrase in a poem). The prose question provides a fiction passage (typically classical literature written in English but may come from African, Australian, Canadian, Indian or West Indian authors; works in translation, such as Greek tragedies. Russian or Latin American fiction may be included as sources). You will be asked to review the literary techniques used to deliver a message. In the free response section, you will use your own selection of a play or novel to explain how a literary concept or other community issue is handled by an author.

The "set of three" for support of your main idea when creating the structure of your essay holds true from the AP English Literature and Composition helpful hints and chapters in the previous manual. Fifteen extra minutes are given for AP English Language and Composition to allow you to read the provided documents for the first question as well as the single passage in the second prompt. The strategy used for essays previously hold true — outlines, importance of introduction and main idea as well as conclusion are all supported by the support in the body of three solid themes or ides. Here, when using non-fiction documents, you must use citations from the provided materials in order to get the highest score. This makes it easier in a way than the literature essay, as it is provided directly to you rather than having you recall what you have read in the past (with the exception of the third prompt).

In keeping with the "same but different" theme, the essay section of each AP English exam tests slightly different topics. While demonstrating understanding and control of standard written English, syllogistic maturity, and control over various reading and writing processes is tested by both exams, there are some differences that make certain learning objectives have been met in the pre-college teaching environment:

Students taking the AP English Language and Composition exam, among other things, should be able to:

- analyze and interpret samples of purposeful writing, identifying and explaining an author's use of rhetorical strategies (including what the author is saying, how the author is saying it, and why the author is saying it).
- analyze images and other multi-modal texts for rhetorical features.
- use effective rhetorical strategies and techniques when writing.
- write for a variety of purposes and readers.
- respond to different writing tasks according to their unique rhetorical and composition demands, and translate rhetorical assessment into a plan for writing.
- create and sustain original arguments based on information synthesized from readings, research, and/or personal observation and experience.
- incorporate sources and demonstrate understanding of the conventions of citing primary and secondary sources.

Students choosing AP English Literature and Composition should be interested in studying the literature of various periods and genres and using this wide reading to discuss literary topics. They should be able to:

- demonstrate a level of maturity and sophistication in their writing.
- use a wide-range of vocabulary with denotative accuracy and connotative resourcefulness.
- incorporate a variety of sentence structures, including appropriate use of subordinate and coordinate constructions.
- employ a balance of generalization with specific illustrative detail.
- achieve emphasis through parallelism and antithesis.

In this AP English Language and Composition essay format, the rhetorical approach to answering an essay can indeed use the persuasive compare-and-contrast style that was earlier discouraged for literature essay responses. Rhetorical forms include not only compare-and-contrast but also cause-and-effect, assertion/justification, and definition/classification/example. Any of these four are appropriate to employ as mechanisms to deliver the best style and length essay response to the language prompts.

A first-look at rhetoric (in the next chapter) is important before you use these methods in responding to prompts on the sample tests.

Chapter 13: What Is Rhetoric and What are Rhetorical Techniques?

WHILE MANY OF THE COMPONENTS REMAIN THE SAME AS IN THE AP ENGLISH LITERATURE and Composition segments of the exam, there is a greater focus in the multiple choice section for rhetoric in the "other" English exam, AP English Language and Composition. Many people throw general language around, and you have probably even said yourself, "Is that a rhetorical question?" However, most people don't understand rhetoric — and if you make the assumption that you do, your test score on this exam will likely suffer.

So, let's review some of the essential foundations of rhetoric and the techniques used in the AP English Language and Composition exam.

What is Rhetoric?

Rhetoric is a way to describe a manner of speaking or writing that is meant to generate a substantial effect on its audience. Some people say a person uses rhetoric well when they claim "she has a way with words" or perhaps state "he makes a good argument. " The word may also refer to the study of the way someone speaks or presents words. But for this exam, rhetoric refers to the way an image is created through word choice, emphasis, and the intent to influence beliefs. These things count when you are reading passages in the multiple choice section as well as passages for your essay prompts.

Be cautious, as rhetoric is not just a philosophy being presented, a means of persuasion, or merely speaking well. Rather, it is the intention behind the statements and selection of the words used — not just what's said.

What Are Rhetorical Techniques?

The techniques used in rhetoric are the same things students have been told for years that good essays will answer — who, what, how — as well as the way information is delivered, the actual content, and the method used to convey the message. Two main rhetorical techniques, or devices, are *tropes* and s*chemes*.

Tropes are figures of speech that provide an unexpected twist in the meaning of words, and are used when there is a change in words that embellishes or energizes a phrase. The four most frequently used tropes (and the most essential ones) are metaphor, metonymy, synecdoche, and irony. We define these for you below, so you will have a quick reference list. Schemes are the pattern and format of words.

A trope is also sometimes called a "figure of thought" where as when the pattern changes for schemes, it may be called "figure of speech. "

How is Rhetoric Created or Used?

There are different ways that people use words to get a point across, to persuade listeners to believe in what they are saying. These ways include the pace or speed of their delivery, the tone of voice of the speaker (or author) and the interaction with body language as the words are spoken. You can see that rhetoric likely does not work very well on the phone (where other distractions can pull a listener away from a speaker's delivery and there is no way to see the body language); similarly, to be understood well in writing, the author must be very accomplished indeed.

The way to achieve good writing and speaking is through a rhetorical device. It's how the speaker persuades the listener to understand and convert to a different perspective. The primary purpose is for the listener to believe in the argument, though side effects (of emotional response or reaction) are likely to occur depending on the method used by the speaker.

Some Important Philosophers Who Used Rhetoric

Since this is an English exam and not one in philosophy, these particular individuals won't likely be asked about on the AP exam, but you will possibly understand English devices better when you understand their views. The great ancient orators employed rhetoric successfully to speak on any topic, persuading listeners even when the speaker was not extraordinarily informed on a particular subject. Frequently rhetoric was used in politics. It is important to remember that rhetoric is important for communication in any field;

These four orators were rhetorical geniuses (no pun intended):

Confucius

A Chinese philosopher who focused on eloquence of speech and economy of words, Confucius was a very sophisticated user of rhetoric. Though his is one of the earliest examples of a recognizable historical name, some think that rhetoric dates back even further to ancient Mesopotamia and Egypt — several thousand years before Confucius.

Plato

Plato used criticism against the "art" of rhetoric to show its usefulness in expanding deceit rather than expounding and exposing truths. Plato considered rhetoric as lowly flattery and flowery language, not as an educated and sophisticated debate tactic. He considered Sophists (wandering lecturers) to use rhetoric in their efforts to attract followers — in a non-positive light.

Aristotle

Although a student of Plato, Aristotle believed in the positive attributes of rhetoric and explained there were three genres available for people to use as the best method to persuade listeners in any given situation. However, he also firmly believed that rhetoric was the domain of politicians and not "just anyone" could use it to their own ends (another "opposite" of his teacher's ideas).

Aristotelian analysis consists of genres as well as methods. According to the philosopher, there are three genres, or paths, rhetoric takes in speaking or writing: **deliberative** (debating about future options and which decision to make), **forensic** (as television lingo would suggest, the truth of evidence presented), and **epideictic** (the emotional appeal to an audience). Quick tip: depending on your essay prompts, you may use one or all three of these on your exam answer in the essay section.

Aristotle also defined the three methods by which rhetoric could be used: **pathos** (presenting using emotions to persuade following through to a conclusion), **ethos** (believability of a speaker based on what could be described as points of ethics), and **logos** (the "l" stood for logic, such as inductive or deductive reasoning, to prove a point). Another quick tip: you should concentration on using logic for your essay replies.

Cicero

A Roman, Cicero is considered one of the greatest orators in history. He was able not only to utilize rhetoric in his speeches but also in his letters and documents. He used nearly all rhetorical devices and all of the rhetorical canons as he developed speeches to persuade his audiences. More information on the canons comes later in this chapter.

The conflict between Plato and Aristotle — everyone can employ rhetoric versus only politicians can use rhetoric — has led to a contemporary divergence of thought and analysis. Neo-sophistic views align with Plato, that anyone can use rhetoric to make a point (whereas "original" Sophists were those learned men who went from town to town educating the townspeople by lecturing in large assemblies). Conversely, Neo-Aristotelians believe only political purposes and those in that sphere can truly use rhetoric.

In very modern times, debate clubs are a way to try to train college students (and now high school students as well) in the "art" of rhetoric — and speaking groups also were opportunities for group discussion and cultured interactions between learned people. While there are additional recent philosophies and leaders of thought on "who can use rhetoric," the only ones with which you likely need to be familiar are the ancient Greeks. Names of other historical yet more modern rhetorical experts include Francis Bacon, Thomas Hobbes, and John Quincy Adams among many others.

What Are Examples of Rhetorical Devices?

Devices or different "mechanisms" are used to convey ideas, and they are very important in successful rhetoric. Here is a partial list of rhetorical devices in alphabetical order, including the most common (the most likely to be used or asked in definitions on the AP exam). You need to know the definitions as well as be able to identify/create examples and to help you on the multiple choice section. If you understand these — and don't just memorize them — you will be able to consider the provided answers faster in context with the reading selection, ruling out one if not two answers immediately, then you will be able to select the most appropriate answer from the ones remaining.

Some of these are called "sonic" because they depend on sound and they are marked by (s) to help you distinguish them. Others classified as "imagery" because they conjure visions and they are marked by (i) for ease in identification. A few more are listed in your AP Literature and Composition study guide, so review those as well.

Adynaton — a ridiculous over-exaggeration, much more than "just" hyperbole; "when donkey's fly" was a quote from an old television show when a waitress didn't believe something would happen

Alliteration (s) — repetitive initial consonant sounds, usually with an overtone of humor or nonsense; she sells sea shells by the sea shore. *Assonance* (s) would be the same, though with vowel sounds.

Allusion — a reference to an event, literary work or person; "he's as fast as The Flash"

Antanagoge — places a criticism and compliment together

Antonomasia — using an epithet or nickname instead of a person's true name; "The Lionheart"

Epithet (i) — using an adjective or adjective phrase to describe. This can be metaphorical or transferred (adjective modifying something it normally doesn't); "lazy road" and "blind mouths", respectively

Euphemism — replacing a harsh plain phrase with a less offensive one; "her elevator doesn't go to the top"

Hypocatastasis (i) — labelling far beyond metaphor or simile; "that snake"

Irony — saying something contrary to make a point — but in rhetoric, it's most often used a device of humor to reduce an option for a course of action; Abraham Lincoln said about an adversary that he "died down deeper into the sea of knowledge and came up drier than any other man he knew. "

Metaphor (i) — compares two things without "as" or "like"; "she is a lion "

Metonymy — when a similar word is substituted for the actual or typical word or when you describe something or a person by describing what's around the item being depicted; like "redneck" to describe someone who lives in a rural area (in a negative way)

Onomatopoeia (s) — words that sound like what they describe; "bang"

Oxymoron — a two word paradox; "near miss"

Simile (i) — compares one object to another with "like" or "as" "strong as the sun"

Synecdoche — when parts are used to name a whole (can be a subvariant of metonymy; "a new set of wheels" to describe a new car

When Are Rhetorical Canons Used?

Cicero (mentioned above) was very effective in persuading listeners to accept his point of view by using various rhetorical canons. These styles, or categories, provide a template of the author's argument. There are other styles, but on the AP exam, the following are the five predominant canons that examples will use for structure or that The College Board may use in the multiple choice question/answer options. You'll also be able to see it mirrors the way we showed you to organize your essays.

- Invention — a derivative of Aristotle's logos, this is when the author finds (or "invents") something to say and bases the point on logic. It may include an "if… then" technique to explain cause and effect or compare different aspects to reach the desired conclusion. This is generally a brainstorming phase, where the author must consider the audience, the facts are available to use in the presentation, the best Aristotelian method to present those facts, and the time he has to deliver the argument.
- Arrangement — in this process, Cicero uses all of the tools from Aristotle, beginning with an introduction using ethos; the next sections of facts, divisions,

proofs, refutations, and pathos. (This is very similar to how we explained handling compositions and essays in the AP English Literature and Composition portion of this book. Not all literature test takers opt to take the AP Language test, so they may not read about rhetoric.)

- Style — the style in which something is said. Style is very intentional in rhetoric and one should remember that the style used gives clues to the author's meaning. Style includes grammar, consideration of audience, address of appeal, decorum (appropriateness and "situation"), and ornamental language. Style is more than pathos — it incorporates ethos as well, or persuasion effect.
- Memory — Cicero often had to improvise and interact with his audience, and thus this style was intended to continue the direction of the speech but give sensitivity to "input" (verbal or other visual cues) from an audience. This is a psychological component of the rhetoric in addition to the formality of a speech, especially since the most effective speeches in ancient times were totally memorized. (In fact, ancient orators were scorned if they used notes; memorization was a must.)
- Delivery — Very important, though frequently not considered as important as word choice, is how something was said. This is what Cicero termed delivery. As you may have experienced yourself, the way a teacher presents a topic can get you engaged . . . or not. Delivery can significantly alter the way something is interpreted, thus pathos is integral to successful delivery. Today, people are very skeptical of someone who has a speech memorized and polished — they almost prefer a little authenticity and "humanness" in a composition, though if it is too rough the speaker will get criticized for that, too!

By identifying the various facets of rhetoric in the multiple choice section and then using the tools of successful experts in rhetoric within your essay responses, you will be able to achieve your highest possible score.

Strategy for Points: Rhetorical Devices

- Remember that rhetoric is an author or speaker attempting to persuade a reader or listener to his/her point of view.
- You don't need to know all of the words for rhetorical devices — some lists have more than 160 options! Remember the main definitions as multiple choice questions frequently are given with a statement and you must select the correct device.
- It is a good idea to know the difference between sonic and imagery — it will likely come in handy during your composition section (though you will not be able to look back at the multiple choice section). Use these devices at appropriate times.
- Understanding the differences in Aristotle's mechanisms for using rhetoric will help in reading comprehension, to know when there is a play on words, or which of the three efforts is being utilized by the author (or speaker) and why.
- The AP Language and Composition asks more questions about reading comprehension and devices of literature and rhetoric; the AP Literature and Composition asks more questions about the types of literature and differences in eras.

Chapter 14: Advanced Technical Support, Research, and Evidence Citation

It's all well and good when you write well, paying attention to all of the technical requirements of good writing. It's even better when you understand how to employ the different rhetorical devices.

There is a way to make your essays stronger for this test. The synthesis prompt will have six or seven sources that must be read and incorporated into the essay. The more seamless the inclusion of these provided resources, the higher the grade will be.

Why Include Citations?

Knowing that you need to craft a well-structured essay with care and not shove irrelevant statements in just to "meet the citation" component of the first essay, careful consideration of why you are including the information is your first consideration. It should not be "include four citations just to get a better score." The readers are very knowledgeable and will be able to tell immediately if you choose this strategy.

Resources Have Clues

All resources tell you something about the prompt given in the exam. However, there are other easy things to see in anything provided in the test. In the AP English Language and Composition exam in particular, one prompt will have items you need to read and use in your response — but you can still use citations in the AP English Literature and Composition essay section if you recall things from particular books or authors that strengthen your points. Instead of just rushing off to include all the resources included with the AP English Literature and Composition prompt, you should read the resources after the prompt with a few things in mind — perhaps even circling them as you read, so you can quickly refer to them when you make a rough outline.

- Topic of citation, or the main idea
- Original publication date
- Original publication source
- Author

There will likely be a few other clues, too, in at least one or two of the attachments for this prompt:

- Are footnotes or endnotes included?
- What are the dates, sources, or authors in any citations within each reference?
- Is there a bibliography with any of the material?

With these additional hints, you can incorporate the pieces that are right for your composition rather than the whole "kitchen sink."

In fact, if you don't include references smoothly, you will likely have points taken from your otherwise well-written essay. You need to show that you can support your ideas with those provided in the resources in the prompt.

What Do Top Scores Show?

Using rhetoric as speaker or author that support and convey your ideas to the reader (the graders in the AP exam), you are completing the rhetoric triangle. This is what's included in the best essays year after year. Those who do well in the essay portion do so because they understand rhetoric and how to interpret reference material. They do exceedingly well in the multiple choice section, too, because they use their knowledge to rapidly understand the passages and accurately answer the questions that follow.

Reviewing all of the skills that are necessary in the best student's exams scores shows several things:

- Students have **learned** — not just memorized — the rhetorical devices as well as techniques, so that they swiftly interpret reading passages, digest the key factors about the non-fiction passages by using the citations, eliminate poor answers, and know their definitions.
- It is easier for the high-achieving students to **review** the questions that they may not be able to answer immediately and make an appropriate **inquiry** (review) back to the reading passage or reference information to narrow answers down to two options if they cannot immediately determine the best answer.
- When answering the three free-response prompts, it is clear that the top performing students are able to **think** about the resource material provided, synthesize a solid idea, and **communicate** their own idea by using the reference material or the ideas in the passage provided. This is achieved in all three of the prompts: synthesis, non-fiction analysis, and argument.

How to Organize with Citations

There are three ways to organize your essays for the responses on Section II of the AP English Literature and Composition exam. First, you may create a "report" on topics, like you would do in a research paper (similar to a summary of facts). Alternatively, you may be "exploratory," describing how you were working the process to find answers (though you may not actually arrive at an answer). Either of these is suitable for a longer-duration opportunity than what's permissible in a two hour and fifteen minute section of an exam where you must answer three prompts completely.

A more interesting essay — a realistic one to write in the time allowed as well as for readers grading your efforts — is a "positional" essay. In such an essay you take one of the facts and support an argument with the other materials available to you. As you discuss a new idea, or infuse an idea noted in a document included in your exam packet, you need to thoughtfully include the citation's idea and reference.

As you frame your outline, and note where you want to use particular quotes (you can do this by symbols back on the resource material and putting it directly in the outline), consider these ways to use as much appropriate material as possible:

- Frame the idea or direct quote with a soft introduction, such as "In the December 2015 article from Archeology entitled "Dietary Changes in Iroquois Indians, the author notes...." Use the information you found in the article as a direct citation.
- Organize a paragraph that supports your main thesis. Put your ideas first and then give a generalized reference to a similar idea from one of the reference sources. You may describe a political process and at the end of that paragraph, related it to the documentation by a phrase such as "Similar ideas were presented by the satirical cartoonist in the sample from Washington Today, though were not as detailed as described here. "
- Join thoughts that disagree with your own by using a transition sentence to explain where the dissent emerges and from what source. If you are discussing historical art research, for instance, provide your own review of other information and then contrast it with the expert report that provides the opposite interpretation: "While the conclusions of the historian, Richard Spear, in his book Il Domenichino published in 1982 regarding the particular portrait are valid and supported by multiple accounts, the science of the infrared technology in Dr. Glasgow's report dated September 1996 do not align with the various other less-scientific techniques presented and should be explored further. "

You will still need to follow a standardized citation format. Whichever you've been trained to use — American Psychological Association (APA), Chicago Manual of Style or other version, Modern Language Association (MLA) — stick to the same one through each essay's composition. It's best to use the same format for all three answers, too.

Refresher of Citation Formats

This is just a very quick review of the format you will use foe citations at the end of your composition, in each of the three predominant styles. For more in-depth information, look to specific guides published by these three entities.

APA: Author's last name, first name (Last edited date). Title of reference. If the College Board provides a web article, you also will need to include "Retrieved from http:// address" without a period at the end. If there are multiple authors, all are listed by last name followed by first name.

Chicago: List the first author by first name. Additional authors, if any, are listed first name last name. Then give the title (Publishing location: Publisher, year), and page numbers. If you are using a web reference, you then add the address followed by a period.

MLA: First author's last name, first name; second author's first name last name; and then third author's first name last name. Title. Reference location. Day, month, year. If you are using a web reference, you then add it. Note day, month, year accessed. Don't include the word "accessed."

Strategy for Points: Citations

- You need to ensure smooth transitions when including direct quotes or thoughts from the reference material provided. Don't just dump quotes into the text in the hopes of getting a higher score.
- Use one of the main types of citation methodologies, and use the same one throughout the responses. This includes the appropriate citation list at the end of your essay (with the appropriate punctuation).
- Even when there is more than one author, in the APA style for citation you always list last name first for all contributors. When you include a web address in the citation, there is no period at the end.
- Chicago style lists names first then last, and uses only one period at the very end — either of page numbers or web address.
- When there is more than one author, in the MLA style of citation you list only the first contributor by last name followed by first name; all subsequent contributors are listed first name last name. There is always a period at the end of the citation, whether a web address is included or not.

SECTION V:
Appendices

Appendix A: Hints for Taking the Test

Part I – Multiple Choice Questions (60 minutes)

Multiple choice questions can be tricky. It is often possible to eliminate one or two of the answers right away, but then get stuck with more than one option that seems like a good fit. While multiple options may seem to be correct, it's important to consider that only one can be considered best. On the AP English exam, there is no penalty for incorrect answers. You simply gain points for the number of correct answers. Be sure to record an answer for every question, even if it is a guess.

It is also important to know what the question is asking of you. Similar to selecting the "best" option, College Board is notorious for saying things like, "All of the following are examples, EXCEPT…" or, "Which of these is NOT…" These words can change the entire meaning of the sentence. Be on alert for qualifiers like this.

You will be using a Number 2 pencil to bubble in your answers on an answer sheet. If you need to erase an answer, be sure to do so completely.

Remember your timing. Sure, 55 questions in 60 minutes may seem reasonable, but many questions are tied to longer passages that require close reading and analysis. Keep a record of your time throughout the exam to ensure you stay on track. Questions that take longer than three minutes should be skipped and returned to when you have finished answering all other questions. If you find yourself running out of time, guess on the last few answers. Again, you are not penalized for incorrect answers, so your score will not be negatively impacted by guessing.

Part II – Free-Response (120 minutes)

The free response questions are usually the items that give students the most difficulty. This is not because they do not they know the answers. The problem usually results from not organizing one's thoughts sufficiently and then getting them down on paper fast enough. There are three free-response questions total, so you should expect to devote approximately 40 minutes to each. You may split this 40 minutes up to allow for 10 minutes of planning and organizing your thoughts on scrap paper and then 30 minutes of writing. Be sure to write down any key terms that will be important to incorporate during this planning time.

As in the multiple choice section, you do not lose credit for presenting incorrect information. However, you do lose time. Other things the readers take off minimal points off for include: spelling, grammar, and penmanship. Obviously, if a reader is unable to determine what is was you wrote, they cannot grade it, but they do their best to interpret a student's "chicken scratch." One thing you'll want to be certain of is writing in essay form (tell a story). Do NOT simply list important concepts in an outline.

Also like the multiple choice questions, the free response questions have key terms to which you should pay particular attention. These terms include "Compare,' "Contrast," Describe,' and their favorite, "Analyze." Pay particular attention to these terms and be sure to do what they ask. You do not want to say one thing in the first paragraph and then say the complete opposite in the second paragraph. If you do this, you will not get any credit, even if one of them is correct. This is because the reader does not know if you knew which was correct or just took a guess and got lucky.

Finally, the biggest piece of advice for answering the free response questions is time management works. Write what the question asks you to write and then move on. This will be the fastest 120 minutes you have ever seen and you have a lot of writing to do, so writing brief, but detailed, essays is essential to obtaining the highest score possible.

Appendix B: Example Rubrics for Grading Essays

Many complaints of college students involve not understanding the differences between the grading practices of various professors. As writing is subjective, often the confusion is centered around what the student perceives as style or opinion, but it is much more than that when the composition is broken into key points.

In order to assist in the development of writing, not just for this AP English exam but also for reports and future professional use, it is helpful to understand various aspects of a "good essay" as well as the most important features in a strong composition that help give an edge to your writing. This appendix gives examples of what college and university professors consider important when grading papers. The reason for this focus is that this is an advanced placement review, and the writing submitted needs to be of a higher caliber than "just" high school writing. The writing should be of the quality to get the highest score possible in order to place out of introductory composition as the first level English.

Regardless of the total number of "points," there are components that are required in all good writing. Punctuation, syntax, grammar (and word choice), and organization (inclusive of transitions between paragraphs) are extremely important. If a reader — or grader — gets tripped up by poor use of these main areas of writing, the grade is likely to decrease rapidly.

The following are some example rubrics used by colleges and professors to determine the best writing. Note that there are different styles of charts: some rubrics give general score for what important factors are present or missing, while others provide overall specific point breakdown for each topic in order to achieve various letter grades.

The main fact you can gather for your writing strategy is to make sure you hit all the important points in the top grade category of any rubric for the best essays possible.

Example A) "Best Writing" to "Needs Improvement" Writing Rubric

This rubric is used by topic (listed in the first column) and then marked which rating is received (last three columns). "Syntax/Grammar" and "Content" weigh more than "Writing," which weighs more than "Citation." Though it's not a strictly listed as 35% / 35%/ 20% / 10%, it is fair to consider that that approximate percentage scheme is the weight used when scoring a composition.

	Highest Possible Score	Acceptable Submission	Needs Improvement
Syntax and grammar	No punctuation errors, no word choice or spelling errors, all subject/verb agreement appropriate	Some punctuation errors OR some spelling errors or word choice errors; all other components on this area correct	Punctuation errors and spelling as well as word choice errors; generally a messy submission riddled with simple errors
Content	Clear and insightful thesis, transitions are smooth between paragraphs and fact presentation, cohesive complex arguments, thoughtful and sophisticated discussion, all information supports main idea, reader could easily see this published in a reputable journal	Transitions may be a bit rough if all other aspects in this category are coherent; otherwise, some information too simplistic or writer tries too hard to sound sophisticated, may have awkwardness in writing as trying to force information to support topic	Content is not organized, supporting paragraphs do not flow well and do not provide direct support for the main idea; Main idea is unclear or is in the final paragraph rather than introductory section
Writing and format	No definition errors, smooth paragraphs, applications of theory are correct, first paragraph gives clear main idea/thesis, uses complex analysis in clear manner, conclusion brings smooth closure	Some words used inconsistently or explanation has insufficient clarity (or is wrong); main idea still needs to be clear and a fairly complex presentation of idea, non-compelling information presented	Words used inconsistently, main idea not presented clearly or in first paragraph, supporting ideas not actually supporting the main idea/thesis of essay; conclusion merely restates introduction
Citations	No citation errors in format, no omissions of citations, layout correct for long quotes, appropriate and consistent format for style, any headings or pagination formats correct	Some citation errors such as long quote format incorrect OR end citations are wrong format but consistent between all listings	Many citation errors OR negligent in listing citations; Also includes using inconsistent format for citations; May have no pagination or incorrect headers

B) Composition Rubric: This rubric isolates topics (ten, listed in the first column) and then grades via columns based on the description that reflects the composition best. There are a total of 50 points available at maximum, and 20 at lowest - which, when multiplied by two, can be equated to standard letter-grade equivalents. Every component is as important as any other topic (even distribution).

	5	4	3	2
Subject Knowledge	Demonstrates full knowledge of topic, presents thoughtfully	Obvious understanding present but may have a few errors	Confusion with facts, chrono-logy or relevance of material	Inappropriate information not relevant to topic
Organization	Logical sequences	Fairly organized, with one or two stray thoughts	Haphazard organization	No thoughtful pattern
Content presentation	Feelings presented in a non-personal manner	At most there is one strong personal feeling presented (zero targeted)	Topic only is apparent in last paragraph	Main idea is never presented
Main topic identification	First paragraph includes clear direction	Main topic a bit muddled but can be recognized as essay progresses	Topic only is apparent in last paragraph	Support is not or cited, no clear relevance to main topic statement(s)
Main Topic Support	Subsequent paras give solid facts in orderly fashion directly relating tomain idea	Most paragraphs give support, though one or two drift off topic	Half of the essay or less gives factual support to the main topic	Support is not factual or cited, no clear relevance to main topic statement(s)
Spelling	Perfect	Very few errors	Moderate errors	Very poor spelling
Punctuation	Perfect	Few errors	Inconsistant	Ongoing errors
Sentence Mechanics	Sophisticated syntax, varying sentence construction	Sophisticated syntax but truncated (short) sentences	Simple words and simply structured sentences, but still correctly written	Poor structure, fragments, dangling prepositions,
Precision	Word choice is appropriate, nonrepetitive	Word choice is appropriate, but repetitive transition words	Word choice has some wrong words (as though auto correct)	Word choice uses inappropriate language
Proof reading	Obvious time spent, cohesive, error-free	Time spent, but one or two errors	Several errors on a few topics, but still makes sense	Rushed and incoherent offering

C) *Point Score Rubric*: Some professors and instructors are more comfortable using a rubric that lessens interpretation flexibility. When each topic is given a precise point value, it reduces variations or considerations of longevity improvements. Rarely used at a collegiate level, a similar rubric may be used when grading AP exam essays because so many compositions are reviewed.

	Below Expectation	**Meets Expectation**	**Exceeds Expectation**	**Far Exceeds Expectation**	**Points**
Introduction	Does not present main topic or subtopics — no thesis given	Presents some topics but no main idea is clearly stated	Clear main idea and support points presented	Strong and defined main thesis with distinct define	15
Sequence	Little evidence, disorganized presentation, information not related to main idea	Most information relates to main idea but not clearly organized	Clear main idea and support points presented	Strong and defined main thesis with distinct defined support ideas	15
Support	Little evidence, disorganized presentation, information not related to main idea	Most information relates to main idea but not clearly organized	Information defined between topic and subtopic, transitions logical but may be unclear	Strong facts and support for topic, integrates clear support and progress of ideas	15
Conclusion	No cohesive summary, no real conclusion and essay just "stops"	Minimal linkage back to main idea, gives review of composition	Clear review and direct links to main idea and supporting facts	Direct conclusion, specific analysis supports thesis	20
Mechanics	Writing errors significantly detract	Few grammar and spelling errors	Rare grammar and spelling errors	Writing flows well, good syntax, word selection	20
Style	Personal pronouns and informal writing	Informal syntax and includes unclear sentences	Academic and/or professional writing style, fairly clear	Writing flows well, good syntax and word selection	20
References	No citations or errors in the ones presented	References presented incorrect format	Too few references OR appropriate references with few errors	References in correct format, accurate and good volume	15

Each AP essay is scored on a scale of 0-9, with nine being the highest score possible. High scores are given for doing everything correctly, just like the applicable columns in the above tables illustrate. Because each question is oriented on a separate topic (a poetry prompt, a prose prompt and the free response prompt), each is scored slightly differently. However, by using the rubrics provided here, you will have a better understanding of strong writing versus weaker submissions. Make sure you are doing everything in the top column, and practice!

The scores or the three essays are added together, so you can earn as low as a zero or as high as a twenty-seven. That's why you need to manage time efficiently and answer all three questions. What the creators of the test do with that score is complex, and the reported Section II results in a calculated "can't figure out my average essay grade" answer. This contributes to your final score of a one through five for the final score of your test. Hopefully, this book has helped you earn a five so you needed worry about all of that math!

Strategy for Points: Checklists and How You Get Points

- Manage your time wisely. Three questions with 120 minutes means 40 minutes for each question. This is enough time to map an outline, write, and proofread.
- The most important part of each essay in terms of content is the introduction and the second most important is the conclusion. Spend time on these for each essay.
- Keep your sentences short and clean. Make sure your writing is legible. If they can't read it, they will grade lower.
- Review the areas that you know you can strengthen. The basics are the most important, so punctuation, syntax and grammar need to be great. Don't write like you text!
- Practice makes perfect, even in writing. It's hard to "grade" yourself, but perhaps a parent or your teacher could grade what you write for these practice tests.

Appendix C: Key Authors and Works

Past Authors, Books and Poems

The following authors are those frequently referenced in multiple choice questions or as suggestions for the free-form question in the AP English Literature and Composition. We have added the years they were alive and placed them in chronological order. For a good "mental workout," match each one to the correct literary era (as well as genre for an extra challenge) and see how many you get correct.

Do not use this list as a "checkoff" to make sure you have read them all. Instead, use this to remind yourself of the plot and characters of the ones you have read, and the underlying messages author by the author. If you find a main topic (such as honesty or conflict resolution) isn't on your "have read" list, pick one or two to read and thoroughly understand so that you may appropriately use it in an essay.

Poets referenced in the past and recommended (chronological by birth)
Geoffrey Chaucer (1343-1400)
William Shakespeare (1564-1616)
John Donne (1572-1631)
Ben Jonson (1572-1637)
George Herbert (1593-1633)
John Milton (1608-1674)
Anne Bradstreet (1612-1672)
Andrew Marvell (1621-1678)
Alexander Pope (1688-1744)
Samuel Taylor Coleridge (1772-1834)
William Blake (1757-1827)
William Wordsworth (1770-1850)
George Gordon, Lord Byron (1788-1824)
Percy Bysshe Shelley (1792-1822)
John Keats (1795-1821)
Edgar Allan Poe (1809-1849)
Alfred, Lord Tennyson (1809-1892)
Robert Browning (1812-1889)
Emily Dickinson (1830-1886)
Gerard Manley Hopkins (1844-1889)
William Butler Yeats (1865-1939)
Paul Laurence Dunbar (1872-1906)
William Carlos Williams (1883-1963)
Marianne Moore (1887-1972)
T. S. Eliot (1888-1965)
Robert Frost (1874-1963)
H. D. (Hilda Doolittle) (1886-1961)
Langston Hughes (1902-1967)
W. H. Auden (1907-1973)
Elizabeth Bishop (1911-1979)
Wallace Stevens (1914-1955)
Robert Lowell (1917-1977)
Walt Whitman (1919-1892)
Richard Wilbur (1921-)
Philip Larkin (1922-1985)
Anne Sexton (1928-1974)
Adrienne Rich (1929-2012)
Edward Kamau Brathwaite (1930-)
Derek Walcott (1930-)
Sylvia Plath (1932-1963)
Lucille Clifton (1936-2010)
Seamus Heaney (1939-2013)
Billy Collins (1941-)

Leslie Marmon Silko (1948-)
Rita Dove (1951-)
Joy Harjo (1951-)
Garrett Hongo (1951-)
Lorna Dee Cervantes (1954-)
Cathy Song (1955-)
Gwendolyn Brooks (1971-2000)

Dramatic authors with works frequently cited (chronological by birth)
Aeschylus (425-456 BC)
Sophocles (496-406 BC)
Ben Jonson (1532-1637)
William Shakespeare (1564-1616)
Moliere (1622-1673)
William Congreve (1670-1729)
Henrik Ibsen (1828-1906)
Oscar Wilde (1854-1900)
George Bernard Shaw (1856-1950)
Anton Chekhov (1860-1904)
Luigi Pirandello (1867-1936)
Sean O'Casey (1880-1964)
Eugene O'Neill (1888-1953)
Lillian Hellman (1905-1984)
Samuel Beckett (1906-1989)
Tennessee Williams (1911-1983)
Arthur Miller (1915-2005)
Edward Albee (1928 -)
Lorraine Hansberry (1930-1965)
Harold Pinter (1930-2008)
Athol Fugard (1932 -)
Amiri Baraka (1934-2014)
Tom Stoppard (1937 -)
Caryl Churchill (1938 -)
Luis Valdez (1940 -)
Sam Shepard (1943 -)
August Wilson (1945-2005)
David Mamet (1947 -)
Marsha Norman (1947 -)
David Henry Hwang (1957 -)
Suzan-Lori Parks (1963 -)

Expository Prose (chronological by birth)
Joseph Addison (1672-1719)
Samuel Johnson (1709-1784)
James Boswell (1740-1795)
Charles Lamb (1775-1834)
William Hazlitt (1778-1830)
Thomas Macaulay (1800-1859)
Ralph Waldo Emerson (1803-1882)
John Stuart Mill (1806-1873)
Henry David Thoreau (1817-1862)
Frederick Douglass (1818-1895)
Matthew Arnold (1822-1888)
James Baldwin (1834-1887)
W. E. B. Du Bois (1868-1963)
Virginia Woolf (1882-1941)
E. B. White (1899-1985)
Jesus Colon (1901-1974)
George Orwell (1903-1950)
Mary McCarthy (1912-1989)
Lewis Thomas (1913-1993)
Joan Didion (1934 -)
Edward Said (1935-2003)
Gloria Anzaldua (1942-2004)
Richard Rodriguez (1944 -)
bell hooks (1952 -)
Michael Pollan (1955 -)

Prose (Fiction), Novels and Short Stories (chronological by birth)
Daniel Defoe (1660-1731)
Jonathan Swift (1667-1745)
Henry Fielding (1707-1754)
Jane Austen (1775-1817)
Nathaniel Hawthorne (1804-1864)
Charles Dickens (1812-1870)
Charlotte Bronte (1816-1855)
Emily Bronte (1818-1848)
George Eliot (1819-1880)
Fyodor Dostoevsky (1821-1881)
Mark Twain (1835-1910)
Thomas Hardy (1840-1928)
Henry James (1843-1916)
Joseph Conrad (1857-1924)
Edith Wharton (1862-1937)
E. M. Forster (1879-1970)
James Joyce (1882-1941)
D. H. Lawrence (1885-1930)
Virginia Woolf (1882-1941)
Katherine Anne Porter (1890-1980)

Zora Neale Hurston (1891-1960)
F. Scott Fitzgerald (1896-1940)
William Faulkner (1897-1962)
Ernest Hemingway (1899-1961)
Vladimir Nabokov (1899-1970)
Evelyn Waugh (1903-1966)
Richard Wright (1908-1960)
Eudora Welty (1909-2001)
Ralph Ellison (1914-1994)
Bernard Malamud (1914-1986)
Saul Bellow (1915-2005)
James Baldwin (1924-1987)
Flannery O'Connor (1925-1964)
Margaret Laurence (1926-1987)
Gabriel Garcia Marquez(1927-2014)
Chinua Achebe (1930-2013)
John Updike (1932-2009)
Joy Kogawa (1935 -)
Rudolfo Anaya (1937 -)
Anita Desai (1937 -)
Margaret Atwood (1939 -)
Maxine Hong Kingson (1940 -)
Bharati Mukherjee (1940 -)
John Edgar Wideman (1941 -)
Isabel Allende (1942 -)
Marilynne Robinson (1943 -)
Alice Walker (1944 -)
Edward P. Jones (1951 -)
Orhan Pamuk (1952 -)
Louise Erdrich (1954 -)
Kazuo Ishiguro (1954 -)
Ha Jin (1956 -)
Chang-rae Lee (1965 -)
Sherman Alexie (1966 -)
Jhumpa Lahiri (1967 -)
Edwidge Danticat (1969 -)

Additional authors referenced less frequently, alphabetically
Albert Camus
Miguel de Cervantes
Kate Chopin
Ralph Ellison
Khaled Hosseini
Cormac McCarthy
Ian McEwan
Toni Morrison
Chaim Potok
J. D. Salinger
John Paul Sartre
Upton Sinclair
John Steinbeck
Leo Tolstoy

Top works (prose) referenced in the past forty-five years
Invisible Man
Wuthering Heights
Great Expectations
Heart of Darkness
King Lear
Crime and Punishment
Jane Eyre
The Adventures of Huckleberry Finn
Moby Dick
Portrait of the Artist as a Young Man
The Scarlett Letter
Their Eyes Were Watching God
The Awakening
Catch-22

Top Shakespearian works (drama)
King Lear
Othello
The Tempest
Merchant of Venice
Macbeth
Hamlet
Julius Caesar
Romeo and Juliet
As You Like It
Winter's Tale
Twelfth Night

Appendix D: Past Five Years of All Essay Questions

Actual Past Essay Prompts, 2015-2010

These are actual prompts from the AP English Literature and Composition exams. You can use these to practice your writing using the tips given in this book before you take a full practice exam. Practice outlining and good writing. If you aren't familiar with the books or authors mentioned in these past AP essay questions, look them up - and look up others of the same literary period or genre. That will help you prepare for upcoming tests.

In addition, look at the third question for each year - sometimes books are repeated in these lists. There is a wide variety of titles, but certain literary periods remain constant. Note how many you have read on each list - and if there is a title that appears several times that you have not read, you may want to read it in preparation, considering the question(s) asked for the AP essay prompt.

Remember, no matter what order the three prompts are presented, you may answer them in any order that you choose. Feel free to answer your most comfortable question first, which will help put you in the mindset of writing good essays and alleviate some anxiety about writing a solid essay. You know the topic, so go for it first.

You will have two hours to answer all three questions, and the score is used as 55% of your AP exam grade. The first question in each grouping provides an except or whole poem provided during the actual exams that may be used in answering the question. To practice with the specific passage if you cannot locate it online, you may go to the College Board's site and download each year's references (http://apcentral.collegeboard.com/apc/members/exam/exam_information/2002.html). Likewise, specific prose passages are used for each second question and may be obtained on the same website. You can also go onto the College Board website to see examples of past AP English Language and Composition questions if you are planning to take that exam.

2015

- In a poem by Caribbean writer Derek Walcott, *XIV* from MIDSUMMER, the speaker recalls a childhood experience of visiting an elderly woman storyteller. Discuss the speaker's recollection and analyze how Walcott uses poetic devices to convey the significance of the experience.
- The first six paragraphs from the opening of *The Beet Queen*, a 1986 novel by Louise Erdrich depicts the impact of the environment on the two children. Analyze how

literary devices, tone, imagery, selection of detail, and/or point of view are used to convey the author's message.

- In literary works, cruelty often function as a crucial motivation or a major social or political factor. Select a novel, play, or epic poem in which acts of cruelty are important to the theme. Then write a well-developed essay analyzing how cruelty functions in the work as a whole and what the cruelty reveals about the perpetrator and/or victim. You may select a work from the list below or another work of equal literary merit. Do not merely summarize the plot.

Beloved
A Bend in the River
Billy Budd
Black Boy
Catch-22
Cat's Eye
The Crucible
Frankenstein
A Gesture Life
Great Expectations
Heart of Darkness
Invisible Man
The Kite Runner
The Last of the Mohicans
Lord of the Flies
Mansfield Park
Medea
The Merchant of Venice
Night
The Odyssey
Oliver Twist
One Flew Over the Cuckoo's Nest
Othello
The Red Badge of Courage
The Scarlet Letter
Sister Carrie
Sophie's Choice
Tess of the d'Urbervilles
To Kill a Mockingbird
Who's Afraid o Virginia Woolf?
Wuthering Heights

2014

- The poem, *For That He Looked Not Upon Her*, is by the sixteenth-century English poet George Gascoigne. Read the poem carefully. Then write an essay in which you analyze how the complex attitude o the speaker is developed through such devices as form, diction, and imagery.
- After reading a passage from the beginning of the novel *The Known World* by Edward P. Jones, analyze how the author reveals the character of Moses. In your analysis, you may wish to consider such literary elements as point-of-view, select of detail, and imagery.
- It has been often said that what we value can be determined only by what we sacrifice. Consider how this statement applies to a character from a novel or play. Select a character that has deliberately sacrificed, surrendered, or forfeited something in a way that highlights that character's values. Then write a well-organized essay in which you analyze how the particular sacrifice illuminates the character's values and provides a deeper understanding of the meaning of the work as a whole. You may choose a novel or play from the list below or one of comparable literary merit. Do not merely summarize the plot.

The Age of Innocence
Antigone
The Awakening
Beloved
The Crucible
Death of a Salesman
Ethan Frome
King Lear
Linden Hills
The Memory Keeper's Daughter
Much Ado About Nothing
Noah's Compass
Oryx and Crake
Othello
The Poisonwood Bible
The Portrait of a Lady
A Prayer for Owen Meany
A Raisin in the Sun
The Scarlett Letter
A Streetcar Named Desire
A Tale of Two Cities
Tess of the d/Urbervilles
Their Eyes Were Watching God
Things Fall Apart
A Thousand Acres
The Women of Brewster Place

2013

- The poem, *The Black Walnut Tree* (published in the book *Twelve Moons*, is written by Mary Oliver. Write a well-organized essay in which you analyze how Oliver conveys the relationship between the tree and family through the use of figurative language and other poetic technique.
- A passage from *The Rainbow* (1915) by D. H. Lawrence, focuses on the lives of the Brangwens, a farming family who lived in rural England during the late nineteenth century. Analyze how Lawrence employs literary devices to characterize the woman and capture her situation.
- A bildungsroman, or coming-of-age novel, recounts the psychological or moral development of its protagonist from youth to maturity, when this character recognizes his or her place in the world. Select a single pivotal moment in the psychological or moral development of the protagonist of a bildungsroman. Then write a well-organized essay that analyzes how that single moment shapes the meaning of the work as a whole. You may choose a novel or play from the list below or one of comparable literary merit. Do not merely summarize the plot.

The Adventures of Augie March
Adventures of Huckleberry Finn
All the Pretty Horses
Atonement
Black Boy
Breath, Eyes, Memory
Brown Girl, Brownstones
The Catcher in the Rye
Cat's Eye
The Chosen
The Cider House Rules
The Color Purple
David Copperfield
The God of Small Things
The Grapes of Wrath
Great Expectations
The House on Mango Street
Invisible Man
Jane Eyre
Jasmine
The Joy Luck Club
The Joys of Motherhood
The Namesake
A Portrait of the Artist as a Young Man

Purple Hibiscus
The Secret Life of Bees
A Separate Peace
Siddhartha
Song of Solomon
The Sorrows of Young Werther
The Sound and the Fury
The Story Edgar Sawtelle
Their Eyes Were Watching God
A Thousand Splendid Suns
To Kill a Mockingbird
A Tree Grows in Brooklyn
The Woman Warrior

2012

- The poem, *Thou Blind Man's Mark*, by Sir Philip Sidney (1554-1586), has the speaker address the subject of desire. Analyze how poetic devices help convey the speaker's complex attitude toward desire.
- Carefully read an excerpt from the novel *Under the Feet of Jesus* by Helena Maria Viramontes, where early in the novel Estrella finds Perfecto's red tool chest and Perfecto names the various tools and explains their uses. Analyze the developments of Estrella's character, considering such literary elements as selection of detail, figurative language, and tone.
- "And, after all, our surroundings influence our lives and characters as much as fate, destiny, or any supernatural agency." Pauline Hopkins, *Contending Forces.* Choose a novel or play in which cultural, physical, or geographical surroundings shape psychological or moral traits in a character. Analyze how surroundings affect this character and illuminate the meaning of the work as a whole. You may choose a novel or play from the list below or one of comparable literary merit. Do not merely summarize the plot.

Absalom, Absalom!
The Age of Innocence
Another Country
Brideshead Revisited
Ceremony
The Color Purple
Daisy Miller
Death of a Salesman
The Glass Menagerie
The Grapes of Wrath
Great Expectations
Heart of Darkness
Invisible Man
King Lear
Maggie: A Girl of the Streets
M. Butterfly
A Midsummer Night's Dream
My Antonia
Native Son
No Exit
One Flew Over the Cuckoo's Nest
One Hundred Years of Solitude
Oryx and Crake
A Passage to India
The Piano Lesson
The Plague
The Poisonwood Bible
Pride and Prejudice
A Raisin in the Sun
Snow Falling on Cedars
Sula
The Sun Also Rises
Tess of the D/Urbervilles
Waiting for Godot
When the Emperor Was Divine
The Women of Brewster Place
Wuthering Heights

2011

- The poem, *A Story,* by the contemporary poet Li-Young Lee in his book *The City in Which I Love You*, has a complex relationship of the father and the son. Analyze how the poet conveys this through the use of literary devices such as point of view and structure.
- A passage from the novel *Middlemarch* by George Eliot the pen name of Mary Ann Evans (1819-1880), describes when Rosamond and Tertius Lydgate, a recently married couple, confront financial difficulties. Analyze how Eliot portrays these two characters and their complex relationship as husband and wife, considering such literary devices as narrative perspective and selection of detail.
- In a novel by William Stryon, a father tells his son that life "is a search for justice." Chose a character from a novel or play who responds in some significant way to justice or injustice. Analyze the character's understanding of justice, the degree to which the character's search for justice is successful, and the significance of this search for the work as a whole. You may choose a novel or play from the list below or one of comparable literary merit. Do not merely summarize the plot.

All the King's Men
All the Pretty Horses
Antigone
Atonement
Beloved
The Blind Assassin
The Bonesetter's Daughter
Crime and Punishment
A Gathering of Old Men
The God of Small Things
The Grapes of Wrath
Invisible Man
King Lear
A Lesson Before Dying
Light in August
Medea
The Merchant of Venice
Murder in the Cathedral
Native Son
No Country for Old Men
Oedipus Rex
The Poisonwood Bible
Rosencrantz and Guildenstern Are Dead
Set This House on Fire
The Story of Edgar Sawtelle
The Stranger
Things Fall Apart
A Thousand Acres
A Thousand Splendid Suns
To Kill a Mockingbird
The Trial

2011: Form B

- The poem, "*AN ECHO SONNET to an Empty Page*," by Robert Pack, illustrates a relationship between form and meaning. Analyze how the literary techniques used in this poem contribute to its meaning.
- The opening of the novel *Kiss of the Fur Queen* (1998) by the Cree novelist and playwright Tomson Highway, describe the end of a race. Analyze how Highway uses literary devices to dramatize Okimasis' experience.

- In *The Writing of Fiction* (1925), novelist Edith Wharton states the following:

"At every stage in the process of his tale the novelist must rely on what may be called the *illuminating incident* to reveal and emphasize the inner meaning of each situation. Illuminating incidents are the magic casements of fiction, its vistas in infinity."

Choose a novel or play that you have studied and write a well-organized essay in which you describe and "illuminating" episode or moment and explain how it functions as a "casement," a window that opens onto the meaning of life of the work as a whole. You may choose a novel or play from the list below or one of comparable literary merit. Do not merely summarize the plot.

Adventures of Huckleberry Finn
As I Lay Dying
The Awakening
Beloved
Catch-22
The Catcher in the Rye
Dr. Faustus
Emma
The Good Soldier
Heart of Darkness
M. Butterfly
Major Barbara
The Mayor of Casterbridge
Mrs. Dalloway
Native Son
Oedipus Rex
Othello
Passing
A Portrait of the Artist as a Young Man
The Portrait of a Lady
Pride and Prejudice
The Remains of the Day
The Scarlet Letter
A Soldier's Play
A Streetcar Named Desire
Surfacing
Their Eyes Were Watching God
Twelfth Night
Who's Afraid of Virginia Woolf?
Who Has Seen the Wind

2010

- The poem, *The Century Quilt (for Sarah Mary Taylor, Quilter)* is from *Mama's Promises*, by Marilyn Nelson Waniek. Analyze how Waniek employees literary techniques to develop the complex meanings that the speaker attributes to The Century Quilt. You may wish to consider such elements as structure, imagery, and tone.
- In a passage from Maria Edgeworth's 1801 novel, *Belinda*, the narrator provides a description of Clarence Hervey, one of the suitors of the novel's protagonist, Belinda Portman. Mrs. Stanhope, Melinda's aunt, hopes to improve her niece's social prospects and therefore has arranged to have Belinda stay with the fashionable Lady Delacour. Analyze Clarence Hervey's complex character as Edgeworth develops it through such literary techniques as tone, point of view, and language.
- Palestinian American literary theorist and cultural critic Edward Said has written that "Exile is strangely compelling to think about but terrible to experience. It is the unsealable rift forced between a human being and a native place, between the self and its true home: its essential sadness can never be surmounted." Said has also said that exile can bemuse "a potent, even enriching" experience. Select a novel, play, or epic in which a character experiences such a rift and becomes cut off from

"home," whether that home is the character's birthplace, family, homeland, or other special place and analyze how the character's experience with exile is both alienating and enriching, and how this experience illuminates the meaning of the work as a whole. You may choose a novel or play from the list below or one of comparable literary merit. Do not merely summarize the plot.

The American
Angle of Repose
Another Country
As You Like It
Brave New World
Crime and Punishment
Doctor Zhivago
Heart of Darkeness
Invisible Man
Jane Eyre
Jasmine
Jude the Obscure
King Lear
The Little Foxes
Madame Bovary
The Mayor of Casterbridge
My Antonia
Obasan
The Odyssey
One Day in the Life of Ivan Denisovich
The Other
Paradise Lost
The Poisonwood Bible
A Portrait of the Artist as a Young Man
The Road
Robinson Crusoe
Rozencrantz and Guildenstern Are Dead
Sister Carrie
Sister of My Heart
Snow Falling on Cedars
The Tempest
Things Fall Apart
The Women of Brewster Place
Wuthering Heights

2010 : Form B

- Two poems are concerned with a young man at the age of twenty-one traditionally the age of adulthood: *To Sir John Lade, on His Coming of Age* (*'A Short Song of Congratulation'*) by Samuel Johnson (1709-1784) and *When I Was One-and-Twenty* by A. E. Housman (1859-1936). Compare and contrast the poems, analyzing the poetic techniques, such as point of view and tone, that each writer uses to make his point about coming of age.
- Consider a passage from the story "Cherry Bomb" by Maxine Clair. Analyze how Clair uses literary techniques to characterize the adult narrator's memories of her fifth-grade summer world.
- Sonsyrea Tate's statement, "You can leave home all you want, but home will never leave you" suggests that "home" may be conceived o as a dwelling, a place, or a state of mind. It may have positive of negative associations, but in either case, it may have a considerable influence on an individual. Chose a novel or play in which a central character leaves home yet find that home remains significant. Analyze the importance of "home" to this character and the reasons for its continuing influence. You may choose a novel or play from the list below or one of comparable literary merit. Do not merely summarize the plot.

Absalom, Absalom!
All the Pretty Horses
Beloved
Bleak House
Candide
The Cherry Orchard
The Country of the Pointed Firs
Fences
A Free Life: A Novel
The Glass Menagerie
The God of Small Things
Going After Cacciato
The Grapes of Wrath
Great Expectations
The Great Gatsby
Home to Harlem
A House for Mr. Biswas
The House of Mirth
The House on Mango Street

The Inheritance o Loss
Invisible Man
Jane Eyre
The Little Foxes
Look Homeward, Angel
The Namesake
Never Let Me Go
The Piano Lesson
The Poisonwood Bible
A Portrait of the Artist as a Young Man
The Road
Song of Solomon
A Streetcar Named Desire
Sula
Their Eyes Were Watching God
Things Fall Apart
Wise Blood
The Women of Brewster Place
Wuthering Heights

SECTION VI: Sample Tests

Sample Test One

Section I

Multiple Choice Questions.
Time: 60 minutes.
Percent of total grade on the exam: 45 percent.

Instructions: This section of the exam consists of selections from literary works and questions on their content, form, and style. After reading each passage and poem, choose the best answer to each question and then fill in the corresponding oval on the answer sheet.

Questions 1-8. Read the following passage carefully before you decide on your answers to the questions.

THE BROAD-BACKED hippopotamus
Rests on his belly in the mud;
Although he seems so firm to us
He is merely flesh and blood.
Flesh and blood is weak and frail,
Susceptible to nervous shock;
While the True Church can never fail
For it is based upon a rock.

The hippo's feeble steps may err
In compassing material ends,
While the True Church need never stir
To gather in its dividends.

The potamus can never reach
The mango on the mango-tree;
But fruits of pomegranate and peach
Refresh the Church from over sea.

At mating time the hippos voice
Betrays inflexions hoarse and odd,
But every week we hear rejoice
The Church, at being one with God.

The hippopotamus's day
Is passed in sleep; at night he hunts;
God works in a mysterious way;
The Church can sleep and feed at once.

I saw the potamus take wing
Ascending from the damp savannas,
And quiring angels round him sing
The praise of God, in loud hosannas.
Blood of the Lamb shall wash him clean
And him shall heavenly arms enfold,
Among the saints he shall be seen
Performing on a harp of gold.
He shall be washed as white as snow,
By all the martyrd virgins kist,
While the True Church remains below
Wrapt in the old miasmal mist.

1. **Who is the author of this poem?**

   A. William Faulkner

   B. T.S. Eliot

   C. William Blake

   D. C.S. Lewis

   E. William Shakespeare

2. **What is the rhyme scheme in the second stanza?**

   A. ABAB

   B. ABCD

   C. ABCA

   D. ADDA

   E. None of the above

3. What literary device is used in this passage?

A. Alliteration

B. Allegory

C. Analogy

D. Anecdote

E. Anagram

4. What does the hippo represent?

A. The devil

B. Sinners

C. Animals

D. Heaven

E. Good luck

5. What does the mud represent?

A. Sin

B. Dirt

C. Home

D. Comfort

E. All of the above

6. What does "take wing" symbolize in the following line?
"I saw the potamus take wing"

A. Hunting a bird

B. Flying in a plane

C. Laying down on its side

D. Going to heaven

E. None of the above

7. **What word does the author emphasize with repetition?**

A. Church

B. Hippo

C. Hippopotamus

D. God

E. Mud

8. **Which of the following best describes "He shall be washed as white as snow"?**

A. He will be washed by angels in heaven.

B. He will no longer rest in the mud

C. His sins will be forgiven.

D. His skin will be bleached.

E. He will become pure.

Questions 9-16. Read the following selection and answer the questions below, selecting the best choice of the options presented.

Two roads diverged in a yellow wood,
And sorry I could not travel both
And be one traveler, long I stood
And looked down one as far as I could
To where it bent in the undergrowth;

Then took the other, as just as fair,
And having perhaps the better claim,
Because it was grassy and wanted wear;
Though as for that the passing there
Had worn them really about the same,

And both that morning equally lay
In leaves no step had trodden black.
Oh, I kept the first for another day!
Yet knowing how way leads on to way,
I doubted if I should ever come back.

I shall be telling this with a sigh
Somewhere ages and ages hence:
Two roads diverged in a wood, and I—

I took the one less traveled by,
And that has made all the difference.

9. Who wrote this poem?

A. Robert Frost

B. Emily Dickinson

C. John Keats

D. William Wadsworth

E. Emily Bronte

10. When the author uses the phrase "wanted wear" in the third stanza, what does that mean?

A. It looked just as fair as the other path.

B. It was not as inviting.

C. The path didn't go the same way as the other one.

D. The path was less traveled than the other one.

E. You cannot determine what the author means.

11. The author says that he "took the one less traveled by"; what does that mean?

A. The other path looked like it was used more.

B. He did the right thing when others chose the wrong one.

C. He took the one on the left.

D. He took the one on the right.

E. It cannot be determined what the author meant by this short selection.

12. What is another way the author states his path was the "one less traveled by"?

A. "both that morning equally lay"

B. "no step had trodden black"

C. "Somewhere ages and ages hence"

D. "bent in the undergrowth"

E. "having perhaps the better claim"

13. What does the author imply since he took the path less traveled?

A. He has run into fewer people that try to bully him into doing what they want.

B. Life is tougher getting to see the light.

C. He was sorry he didn't chose to go the more well-trod path.

D. He didn't make as much money as the people that took the other path.

E. His life is better for choosing to go his own path.

14. What is the rhyme scheme?

A. ABBAB

B. ABABA

C. ABAAC

D. ABCAB

E. ABAAB

15. Taking the road less traveled by made all the difference because ________.

A. the decision shaped his life

B. it was a good hike

C. the character was able to find peace

D. he created a new path on the road

E. he will always be able to go back to walk on the more traveled path if he chooses to

16. What literary device is used in this poem?

A. Personification

B. Propaganda

C. Paradox

D. Parallelism

E. Pentameter

Questions 17-24. Read the following selection and answer the questions below, selecting the best choice of the options presented.

Fever 103°

Pure? What does it mean?
The tongues of hell
Are dull, dull as the triple

Tongues of dull, fat Cerberus
Who wheezes at the gate. Incapable
Of licking clean

The aguey tendon, the sin, the sin.
The tinder cries.
The indelible smell

Of a snuffed candle!
Love, love, the low smokes roll
From me like Isadora's scarves, I'm in a fright

One scarf will catch and anchor in thewheel,
Such yellow sullen smokes
Make their own element. They will not rise,

But trundle round the globe
Choking the aged and the meek,
The weak

Hothouse baby in its crib,
The ghastly orchid
Hanging its hanging garden in the air,

Devilish leopard!
Radiation turned it white
And killed it in an hour.

Greasing the bodies of adulterers
Like Hiroshima ash and eating in.
The sin. The sin.

17. Who is the author of this poem?

A. Margaret Atwood

B. Emily Dickinson

C. Sylvia Plath

D. Maya Angelou

E. Alice Walker

18. What imagery does "the tongues" create?

A. Flames

B. Gates

C. Sins

D. Lies

E. None of the above

19. Who is Cerberus?

A. A man entering the underworld

B. The guard of the underworld

C. The maid of the underworld

D. An angel

E. The devil

20. What does *aguey* mean?

A. Sinful

B. Torn

C. Deceitful

D. Beautiful

E. Burning

21. **The word *trundle* is significant because ____.**

A. It represents moving very slowly.

B. It is a roll out bed, used for camping.

C. it is not dark nor light.

D. it represents being instinctive.

E. None of the above.

22. **What literary device is used in this poem?**

A. Repetition

B. Onomatopoeia

C. Alliteration

D. Flashback

E. Flash forward

23. **Which of the following best describes the setting?**

A. Utopia

B. Dystopia

C. Promised land

D. Eden

E. Erotic

24. **Why is the title substantial?**

A. You can sweat out sins with a fever

B. It's the temperature in the underworld

C. This level of a fever would kill you

D. This is the temperature of fire

E. All of the above

Questions 25-32. Read the following selection and answer the questions below, selecting the best choice of the options presented.

"I went to work the next day, turning, so to speak, my back on that station. In that way only it seemed to me I could keep my hold on the redeeming facts of life. Still, one must look about sometimes; and then I saw this station, these men strolling aimlessly about in the sunshine of the yard. I asked myself sometimes what it all meant. They wandered here and there with their absurd long staves in their hands, like a lot of faithless pilgrims bewitched inside a rotten fence. The word 'ivory' rang in the air, was whispered, was sighed. You would think they were praying to it. A taint of imbecile rapacity blew through it all, like a whiff from some corpse. By Jove! I've never seen anything so unreal in my life. And outside, the silent wilderness surrounding this cleared speck on the earth struck me as something great and invincible, like evil or truth, waiting patiently for the passing away of this fantastic invasion.

—*Heart of Darkness*

25. Who wrote this novel?

A. Joseph Conrad

B. James Joyce

C. Jane Austen

D. Charlotte Brontë

E. Charles Dickens

26. What does the following line represent?
"I saw this station, these men strolling aimlessly about in the sunshine of the yard."

A. Soldiers enjoying their day

B. Men being unaware of the negativ,ity that surrounds them

C. Positivity is infectious

D. The station is a happy place

E. Embracing the weather before a storm hits

27. What does the word *staves* mean?

A. Machete

B. Axe

C. Gun

D. Bomb

E. Wooden club

28. What does the ivory represent?

A. Death

B. Prosperity

C. Jewelry

D. Trade

E. None of the above

29. What literary device is used when describing the ivory?

A. Alliteration

B. Allegory

C. Simile

D. Personification

E. Repetition

30. What does *rapacity* represent?

A. Greed

B. Rapid movement

C. Intelligent

D. Affluent

E. Generous

31. What literary device is used in this passage?

"And outside, the silent wilderness surrounding this cleared speck on the earth struck me as something great and invincible, like evil or truth, waiting patiently for the passing away of this fantastic invasion."

A. Simile

B. Metaphor

C. Illusion

D. Personification

E. Onomatopoeia

32. Which style of writing is represented in this novel?

A. Biographical

B. Autobiographical

C. Expository

D. Persuasive

E. None of the above

Questions 33-40. Read the following selection and answer the questions below, selecting the best choice of the options presented.

"Where, in Heaven's name, could anyone even be alone in Calcutta? What hanky-panky business, in my mother's words, could go on? Everyone knew the rules and the rules stated caste and community narrowed the range of intimate contact."

—*Desirable Daughters* by Bharati Mukherjee

33. Where is Calcutta?

A. Indonesia

B. China

C. New Zealand

D. Jamaica

E. India

34. Why is it abnormal for someone to be alone in Calcutta?

A. Everyone travels with their spouses

B. It's a very busy city

C. The city is very dangerous

D. It's sarcastic because it's such a rural place

E. None of the above

35. What is *hanky-panky* business?

A. Dancing

B. Illegal trade

C. Corruption

D. A romantic kiss

E. Sexual activity

36. What does the word *caste* mean?

A. Division of the classes

B. Enclosed

C. Oppression

D. Sin

E. Sexualized

37. What form of speech is *in heaven's name*?

A. Analogy

B. Definition

C. Idiom

D. Quotation

E. Allegory

38. What is the author implying in this passage?

A. Sexual abuse

B. Adultery

C. Secret lovers

D. Pregnancy

E. All of the above

39. This novel represents _____.

A. Feminism

B. Nature

C. Misogyny

D. City life

E. None of the above

40. How could community narrow the range of intimate contact?

A. Arranged marriage is common

B. Rural areas limit physical contact

C. People do not associate with others outside of their class

D. Communities are not tight-knit

E. Men and women attend same-sex schools

Questions 41-47. Read the following selection and answer the questions below, selecting the best choice of the options presented.

"Finished, it's finished, nearly finished, it must be nearly finished. Grain upon grain, one by one, and one day, suddenly, there's a heap, a little heap, the impossible heap. I can't be punished any more. I'll go now to my kitchen, ten feet by ten feet by ten feet, and wait for him to whistle me. Nice dimensions, nice proportions, I'll lean on the table, and look at the wall, and wait for him to whistle me."

—*Endgame*

41. Who wrote this play?

A. Anton Chekov

B. William Shakespeare

C. Lillian Hellman

D. Athol Fugard

E. Samuel Beckett

42. What literary device is used throughout this passage?

A. Simile

B. Metaphor

C. Euphemism

D. Flashback

E. Repetition

43. What does the *impossible heap* represent?

A. Life's greatest hurdles

B. A pile of grain so tall it cannot be moved

C. Death

D. A mountain

E. Heaven

44. The whistle symbolizes _____.

A. A referee

B. The character's father

C. Death

D. An angel

E. All of the above

45. What is an endgame?

A. The final play in a game, such as chess

B. The end of a negotiation

C. A wish

D. The final approval for a lease

E. None of the above

46. What is the author trying to portray in this selection?

A. An old man

B. A prisoner

C. A farmer

D. A mill worker

E. A plantation

47. What best describes this selection?

A. Epic

B. Foreshadowing

C. Cliffhanger

D. Flashback

E. Irony

Questions 48-55. Read the following selection and answer the questions below, selecting the best choice of the options presented.

"If people bring so much courage to this world the world has to kill them to break them, so of course it kills them. The world breaks every one and afterward many are strong at the broken places. But those that will not break it kills. It kills the very good and the very gentle and the very brave impartially. If you are none of these you can be sure it will kill you too but there will be no special hurry."

—*A Farewell to Arms*

48. Who wrote this novel?

A. Henry David Thoreau

B. Ernest Hemingway

C. F. Scott Fitzgerald

D. Harper Lee

E. J.R.R. Tolkien

49. What is the theme of this novel?

A. Innocence

B. War

C. Love

D. Death

E. Grief

50. What does the title symbolize?

A. An amputation caused during war

B. Being discharged

C. Saying goodbye to the arms of someone you love

D. Saying goodbye to weaponry and warfare

E. C & D

51. Which literary device is used to describe war?

A. Personification

B. Alliteration

C. Simile

D. Metaphor

E. Idiom

52. What best describes the author's intention in the following line?
"It kills the very good and the very gentle and the very brave impartially."

A. Everyone will die sooner or later

B. Murderers target nice people

C. The good, gentle and brave are easier to kill

D. The good, gentle and brave die protecting others

E. War kills everyone, it doesn't have a bias

53. How does the world *break* people?

A. It creates challenging times

B. It represents being shot and not dying

C. It causes extreme wounds, mentally and physically

D. People can have broken bones

E. Physical objects and precious belongings can be broken

54. Which of the following best represents this passage?

A. Sarcasm

B. Resentment

C. Irony

D. Sympathy

E. Affectionate

55. Which literary period is this from?

A. Romanticism

B. Renaissance

C. The Enlightenment

D. Existentialism

E. Modernism

Free Response Essay Sample Questions

Section II

Time: 120 minutes

Percent of total grade on the exam: 55 percent.

Question 1.

(Suggested time—40 minutes. This question counts as one-third of the total essay sec-tion score.)

In the following speech from Shakespeare's play King Lear, the king is considering his downfall into madness; thus, he turns to the fool to rationalize the situation. Read the speech carefully. They write a well-organized essay in which you analyze how Shakespeare uses elements such as allusion, figurative language, and tone to convey the king's complex response to his situations evolving in his court.

Lear: What! art mad? A man may see how this world goes with no eyes. Look with thine ears: see how yond justice rails upon bond simple thief. Hark, in thine ear: change places, and, handy-dandy, which is the justice, which is the thief? Thou has seen a farmer's dog bark at a beggar?

Glou: Ay, Sir.

Lear: An the creature run from the cur? There thou might's behold
The great image of Authority:
A dog's obey'd in office.
Thou rascal beadle, hold they bloody hand!
Why doest thou lash that whore? Strip thine own back;
Thou hotly lusts to use her in that kind
For which thou whipp'st her.. The usurer hangs the cozen-er.
Thorough tatter'd clothes small vices do appear;
Robes and furr'd gowns hide all. Plat4e sin with gold,
And the strong lance of justice hurtles breaks;
Arm it in rags, a pigmy' straw does pierce it.
None does offend, none, I say, none; I'll able 'em:
Take that of me, my friend, who have the power
To seal th' accuser's lips. Get thee glass eyes;
And, like a scurvy politician, seem
To see the things thou dost not. Now, now, now, now;
Pull off my boots; harder, harder; so.

Question 2.

(Suggested time—40 minutes. This question counts as one-third of the total essay sec-tion score.)

The following passage is from The Scarlett Letter. Read the passage carefully. Then write a well-organized essay in which you analyze how literary devices dramatize the experiences of characters. Do not summarize the plot.

> The door of the jail being flung ope from within, there appeared, in the first place, like a black shadow emerging into sunshine, the grim and grisly presence of the town-beadle, with a sword by his side an his staff of office in his hand. This personage prefigured and represented in his aspect the whole dismal severity of the Puritanic code of law, which it was his business to administer in its final and closest application to the offender. Stretching forth the official staff in hi left hand, he laid his right upon the shoulder of a young woman, whom he thus drew forward; until, on the threshold of the prison-door, she repelled him by an action marked with natural dignity and once of character, and stepped into the open air as if by her own free will. She bore in her arms a child, a baby of some three months old, who wind and turned aside its little face rom the two vivid light of day; because its existence, heretofore, had brought it ac-quainted only with the grey twilight of a dungeon, or other darksome apartment of the prison.
>
> When the young woman - the mother of this child - stood fully revealed before the crow, it seemed to be her first impulse to clasp the infant closely to her bosom; not so much by an impulse of motherly affection, as that she might thereby conceal a cer-tain token, which was wrought or fastened into her dress. In a moment, however, wise-ly judging that one token of her shame would but poorly serve to hide another, she took the baby on her arm, and, with a burning blush, and ye3t a haughty smile, and a glance that would not b abashed, looked around at her townspeople and neighbours. On the breast of her gown, in fine red cloth, surrounded with an elaborate embroidery and fantastic flourishes of gold thread, appeared the letter A. It was so artistically done, and with so much fertility and gorgeous luxuriance of fancy, that it had all the effect of a last and fitting decoration to the apparel which she wore; and which was of a splen-dour in accordance with the taste of the age, but greatly beyond what was allowed by the sumptuary regulations of the colony.

Question 3.

(Suggested time—40 minutes. This question counts as one-third of the total essay sec-tion score.)

Many works of literature, particularly in 20th century American novels, deal with civil rights issues and how social justice is achieved outside of the legislative process. Public agitation of issues, such as micro-aggressions or violent protests, may shape stories. Choose a novel or play that focuses on a contemporary issue, explaining how the literary devices contribute to the development of the author's theme. Do not merely summarize the plot.

Sample Test One: ANSWER KEY

Question Number	Correct Answer	Your Answer
1.	B	
2.	A	
3.	B	
4.	B	
5.	A	
6.	D	
7.	A	
8.	C	
9.	A	
10.	D	
11.	A	
12.	B	
13.	E	
14.	E	
15.	A	
16.	D	
17.	C	
18.	A	
19.	B	
20.	E	
21.	A	
22.	A	
23.	B	
24.	A	
25.	A	
26.	B	
27.	E	
28.	B	

Question Number	Correct Answer	Your Answer
29.	B	
30.	A	
31.	A	
32.	D	
33.	E	
34.	B	
35.	E	
36.	A	
37.	C	
38.	A	
39.	A	
40.	C	
41.	E	
42.	E	
43.	C	
44.	C	
45.	A	
46.	B	
47.	B	
48.	B	
49.	B	
50.	E	
51.	A	
52.	E	
53.	C	
54.	B	
55.	E	

Answer Key and Rationale

If there are words that are options for answers that you do not know, now is the time to look them up and prepare yourself for the exam! Many answer options includes words or phrases used in literary discussions, and some may not be familiar. It is possible they will be on the actual exam, so you should familiarize yourself with them now.

Questions 1-8. Read the following passage carefully before you decide on your answers to the questions.

THE BROAD-BACKED hippopotamus
Rests on his belly in the mud;
Although he seems so firm to us
He is merely flesh and blood.
Flesh and blood is weak and frail,
Susceptible to nervous shock;
While the True Church can never fail
For it is based upon a rock.

The hippo's feeble steps may err
In compassing material ends,
While the True Church need never stir
To gather in its dividends.

The potamus can never reach
The mango on the mango-tree;
But fruits of pomegranate and peach
Refresh the Church from over sea.

At mating time the hippos voice
Betrays inflexions hoarse and odd,
But every week we hear rejoice
The Church, at being one with God.

The hippopotamus's day
Is passed in sleep; at night he hunts;
God works in a mysterious way;
The Church can sleep and feed at once.

I saw the potamus take wing
Ascending from the damp savannas,
And quiring angels round him sing
The praise of God, in loud hosannas.
Blood of the Lamb shall wash him clean
And him shall heavenly arms enfold,
Among the saints he shall be seen
Performing on a harp of gold.

He shall be washed as white as snow,
By all the martyrd virgins kist,
While the True Church remains below
Wrapt in the old miasmal mist.

1. Who is the author of this poem?

A. William Faulkner

B. T.S. Eliot

C. William Blake

D. C.S. Lewis

E. William Shakespeare

The correct answer is B.

T.S. Eliot is the author of this poem.

2. What is the rhyme scheme in the second stanza?

A. ABAB

B. ABCD

C. ABCA

D. ADDA

E. None of the above

The correct answer is A.

The rhyme scheme in the second stanza follows ABAB. The first and third lines rhyme, and the second and fourth lines rhyme.

3. What literary device is used in this passage?

A. Alliteration

B. Allegory

C. Analogy

D. Anecdote

E. Anagram

The correct answer is B.

An allegory is a literary device that includes hidden meaning in a poem or short story. Because the hippo represents sinners in this poem, B is the best answer.

4. What does the hippo represent?

A. The devil

B. Sinners

C. Animals

D. Heaven

E. Good luck

The correct answer is B.

The hippo represents sinners in this poem. Given the religious context of the poem, sinners is the most appropriate answer.

5. What does the mud represent?

A. Sin

B. Dirt

C. Home

D. Comfort

E. All of the above

The correct answer is A.

Because the hippo represents sinners, the mud represents sin. The hippo may be dirty (B), and could feel at home (C) or comforted by the mud (D), but this does not parallel the symbolism within the writing.

6. What does "take wing" symbolize in the following line?
"I saw the potamus take wing"

A. Hunting a bird

B. Flying in a plane

C. Laying down on its side

D. Going to heaven

E. None of the above

The correct answer is D.

Taking wing is a representation of going to the heavens in the sky. Flying a plane and laying on its side are obviously incorrect and it's easy to narrow down to (A) and (D). The literal interpretation, (A), is incorrect and does not represent the symbolism embedded in the writing.

7. What word does the author emphasize with repetition?

A. Church

B. Hippo

C. Hippopotamus

D. God

E. Mud

The correct answer is A.

The only word that is emphasized in this poem with repetition is church; therefore, (A) is the most appropriate answer.

8. Which of the following best describes "He shall be washed as white as snow"?

A. He will be washed by angels in heaven.

B. He will no longer rest in the mud

C. His sins will be forgiven.

D. His skin will be bleached.

E. He will become pure.

The correct answer is C.

Washing is a representation of cleansing one of their sins. The symbolism in this quote represents the forgiveness of sins. (C) is the correct answer for this question.

Questions 9-16. Read the following selection and answer the questions below, selecting the best choice of the options presented.

Two roads diverged in a yellow wood,
And sorry I could not travel both
And be one traveler, long I stood
And looked down one as far as I could
To where it bent in the undergrowth;

Then took the other, as just as fair,
And having perhaps the better claim,
Because it was grassy and wanted wear;
Though as for that the passing there
Had worn them really about the same,

And both that morning equally lay
In leaves no step had trodden black.

Oh, I kept the first for another day!
Yet knowing how way leads on to way,
I doubted if I should ever come back.

I shall be telling this with a sigh
Somewhere ages and ages hence:
Two roads diverged in a wood, and I—
I took the one less traveled by,
And that has made all the difference.

9. Who wrote this poem?

A. Robert Frost

B. Emily Dickinson

C. John Keats

D. William Wadsworth

E. Emily Bronte

The correct answer is A.

Robert Frost is the author of this poem.

10. When the author uses the phrase "wanted wear" in the third stanza, what does that mean?

A. It looked just as fair as the other path.

B. It was not as inviting.

C. The path didn't go the same way as the other one.

D. The path was less traveled than the other one.

E. You cannot determine what the author means.

The correct answer is D.

One path had obviously been walked on, or "worn" more than the other. By stating that one of the paths "wanted wear," the author is implying that this path had not been trav-eled on often. Therefore, (D) is the best answer.

11. The author says that he "took the one less traveled by"; what does that mean?

A. The other path looked like it was used more.

B. He did the right thing when others chose the wrong one.

C. He took the one on the left.

D. He took the one on the right.

E. It cannot be determined what the author meant by this short selection.

The correct answer is A.

Just as we learned in the previous question, one of the paths had been walked on far more frequently. The author took the one "less traveled by," meaning it had a minimal path already carved out. This makes A the best answer.

12. What is another way the author states his path was the "one less traveled by"?

A. "both that morning equally lay"

B. "no step had trodden black"

C. "Somewhere ages and ages hence"

D. "bent in the undergrowth"

E. "having perhaps the better claim"

The correct answer is B.

(B) is the only reference to travel, as the author suggests with a step.

13. What does the author imply since he took the path less traveled?

A. He has run into fewer people that try to bully him into doing what they want.

B. Life is tougher getting to see the light.

C. He was sorry he didn't chose to go the more well-trod path.

D. He didn't make as much money as the people that took the other path.

E. His life is better for choosing to go his own path.

The correct answer is E.

The author implies that he has had a better life due to the decisions that he's made on his own. He believes his life is better for choosing to go his own path.

14. What is the rhyme scheme?

A. ABBAB

B. ABABA

C. ABAAC

D. ABCAB

E. ABAAB

The correct answer is E.

This poem follows the ABAAB rhyme scheme.

15. Taking the road less traveled by made all the difference because ________.

A. the decision shaped his life

B. it was a good hike

C. the character was able to find peace

D. he created a new path on the road

E. he will always be able to go back to walk on the more traveled path if he chooses to

The correct answer is A.

Going on the other path would have led to a different life for this character. The best answer is (A) because choosing the road less traveled by has been a decision that has shaped his life. While (B), (C), (D), and (E) may have partial truths, A is the best answer for this question.

16. What literary device is used in this poem?

A. Personification

B. Propaganda

C. Paradox

D. Parallelism

E. Pentameter

The correct answer is D.

Because we know the path represents roads the author has taken in life, it's easy to determine that parallelism is the literary device used in this poem.

Questions 17-24. Read the following selection and answer the questions below, selecting the best choice of the options presented.

Fever 103°

Pure? What does it mean?
The tongues of hell
Are dull, dull as the triple

Tongues of dull, fat Cerberus
Who wheezes at the gate. Incapable
Of licking clean

The aguey tendon, the sin, the sin.
The tinder cries.
The indelible smell

Of a snuffed candle!
Love, love, the low smokes roll
From me like Isadora's scarves, I'm in a fright

One scarf will catch and anchor in thewheel,
Such yellow sullen smokes
Make their own element. They will not rise,

But trundle round the globe
Choking the aged and the meek,
The weak

Hothouse baby in its crib,
The ghastly orchid
Hanging its hanging garden in the air,

Devilish leopard!
Radiation turned it white
And killed it in an hour.

Greasing the bodies of adulterers
Like Hiroshima ash and eating in.
The sin. The sin.

17. Who is the author of this poem?

A. Margaret Atwood

B. Emily Dickinson

C. Sylvia Plath

D. Maya Angelou

E. Alice Walker

The correct answer is C.

Sylvia Plath wrote this poem.

18. What imagery does "the tongues" create?

A. Flames

B. Gates

C. Sins

D. Lies

E. None of the above

The correct answer is A.

There is a strong connection to the afterlife in this poem, and the tongues create im-agery of flames. (A) is the best answer for this question.

19. Who is Cerberus?

A. A man entering the underworld

B. The guard of the underworld

C. The maid of the underworld

D. An angel

E. The devil

The correct answer is B.

(A), (C), and (D) are easy to eliminate because they are general and there are no refer-ences to point to them being correct. (E) can be eliminated because the description would have been much more detailed and powerful if Cerberus was the devil. Because he is the guard of the underworld, (B) is the correct answer.

20. What does *aguey* mean?

A. Sinful

B. Torn

C. Deceitful

D. Beautiful

E. Burning

The correct answer is E.

Keeping the theme with the temperature in the title and the descriptions of the hellish afterlife, this should be an easy question. E is the obvious answer.

21. The word *trundle* is significant because ____.

A. It represents moving very slowly.

B. It is a roll out bed, used for camping.

C. it is not dark nor light.

D. it represents being instinctive.

E. None of the above.

The correct answer is A.

Trundle is the word for a bed that is used for camping, but it also represents moving very slowly. In the context of this piece, trundle represents traveling around the world very slowly. (C) and (D) are easy to mark off as incorrect for this question.

22. What literary device is used in this poem?

A. Repetition

B. Onomatopoeia

C. Alliteration

D. Flashback

E. Flash forward

The correct answer is A.

This is an obvious answer. "The sin." is repeated several times.

23. Which of the following best describes the setting?

A. Utopia

B. Dystopia

C. Promised land

D. Eden

E. Erotic

The correct answer is B.

Unlike utopia, where everything is perceived to be beautiful and happy, dystopia is the complete opposite. It represents a very negative, unpleasant environment. Because the poem represents a hell-like environment, it's easy to eliminate (C) and (D). There are no sexual references, so (E) can also be eliminated. This leaves (B) as the best answer.

24. Why is the title substantial?

A. You can sweat out sins with a fever

B. It's the temperature in the underworld

C. This level of a fever would kill you

D. This is the temperature of fire

E. All of the above

The correct answer is A.

While it's assumed that the underworld is a hot place, we are not aware of the exact temperature; therefore, (B) can be eliminated. The temperature of fire is much higher, and can reach as high as 1500 degrees. This level of a fever would be dangerous, but not necessarily deadly. This leaves (A) as the best answer, as it represents a cleanse of sins by sweating them out with a fever.

Questions 25-32. Read the following selection and answer the questions below, selecting the best choice of the options presented.

"I went to work the next day, turning, so to speak, my back on that station. In that way only it seemed to me I could keep my hold on the redeeming facts of life. Still, one must look about sometimes; and then I saw this station, these men strolling aimlessly about in the sunshine of the yard. I asked myself sometimes what it all meant. They wandered here and there with their absurd long staves in their hands, like a lot of faithless pilgrims bewitched inside a rotten fence. The word 'ivory' rang in the air, was whispered, was sighed. You would think they were praying to it. A taint of imbecile rapacity blew through it all, like a whiff from some corpse. By Jove! I've never seen anything so unreal in my life. And outside, the silent wilderness surrounding this cleared speck on the earth struck me as something great and invincible, like evil or truth, waiting patiently for the passing away of this fantastic invasion.

—*Heart of Darkness*

25. Who wrote this novel?

A. Joseph Conrad

B. James Joyce

C. Jane Austen

D. Charlotte Brontë

E. Charles Dickens

The correct answer is A.

Joseph Conrad is the author of *Heart of Darkness.*

26. What does the following line represent?
"I saw this station, these men strolling aimlessly about in the sunshine of the yard."

A. Soldiers enjoying their day

B. Men being unaware of the negativ,ity that surrounds them

C. Positivity is infectious

D. The station is a happy place

E. Embracing the weather before a storm hits

The correct answer is B.

The sunshine represents happiness and the fact that they are strolling around aimlessly implies they are unaware of their surroundings. Given the representation of this symbolism, (B) is the best option for this question.

27. What does the word *staves* mean?

A. Machete

B. Axe

C. Gun

D. Bomb

E. Wooden club

The correct answer is E.

Because of the invasion mentioned, it can be determined that the characters are walk-ing around with staves in order to protect themselves. Although each of the options for this question are weapons, (E) is the correct answer. It's a word that is most common to the time period in which this book was written.

28. What does the ivory represent?

A. Death

B. Prosperity

C. Jewelry

D. Trade

E. None of the above

The correct answer is B.

Ivory has historically been very valuable. While it can be viewed as representing trade, (D) is incorrect because this piece includes symbolism. (B) is the best answer because ivory best represents prosperity. (A) and (C) are easy to knock out as incorrect options.

29. What literary device is used when describing the ivory?

A. Alliteration

B. Allegory

C. Simile

D. Personification

E. Repetition

The correct answer is B.

An allegory represents a piece of writing with hidden meaning or significant hidden symbolism. This is the only option that makes sense for this question.

30. What does *rapacity* represent?

A. Greed

B. Rapid movement

C. Intelligent

D. Affluent

E. Generous

The correct answer is A.

Rapacity represents greed; therefore, (A) is the correct answer.

31. What literary device is used in this passage?

"And outside, the silent wilderness surrounding this cleared speck on the earth struck me as something great and invincible, like evil or truth, waiting patiently for the passing away of this fantastic invasion."

A. Simile

B. Metaphor

C. Illusion

D. Personification

E. Onomatopoeia

The correct answer is A.

A simile is a comparison or description that uses "like" or "as." Because this passage uses "like evil or truth" to describe the wilderness, A is the best answer.

32. Which style of writing is represented in this novel?

A. Biographical

B. Autobiographical

C. Expository

D. Persuasive

E. None of the above

The correct answer is D.

The story being told is fiction, so (A) and (B) can be eliminated from the start. (C) is incorrect because the writing does not intend to give information. The writing is intended to persuade the reader, leaving (D) as the best answer.

Questions 33-40. Read the following selection and answer the questions below, selecting the best choice of the options presented.

"Where, in Heaven's name, could anyone even be alone in Calcutta? What hanky-panky business, in my mother's words, could go on? Everyone knew the rules and the rules stated caste and community narrowed the range of intimate contact."

—*Desirable Daughters* by Bharati Mukherjee

33. Where is Calcutta?

A. Indonesia

B. China

C. New Zealand

D. Jamaica

E. India

The correct answer is E.

Calcutta is a large city located in India.

34. Why is it abnormal for someone to be alone in Calcutta?

A. Everyone travels with their spouses

B. It's a very busy city

C. The city is very dangerous

D. It's sarcastic because it's such a rural place

E. None of the above

The correct answer is B.

Because Calcutta is such an urban area, it's unlikely that anyone would ever be alone. (B) is the only option of the five that make sense for this question.

35. What is *hanky-panky* business?

A. Dancing

B. Illegal trade

C. Corruption

D. A romantic kiss

E. Sexual activity

The correct answer is E.

Hanky-panky is a slang phrase that describes sexual activity. Therefore, (E) is the correct answer.

36. What does the word *caste* mean?

A. Division of the classes

B. Enclosed

C. Oppression

D. Sin

E. Sexualized

The correct answer is A.

The "rules stated caste" is an indication that everyone in society is expected to follow the rules of obeying the class divisions. Therefore, (A) is the best answer.

37. What form of speech is *in heaven's name*?

A. Analogy

B. Definition

C. Idiom

D. Quotation

E. Allegory

The correct answer is C.

An idiom is a figure of speech that often does not represent literal meaning. The saying in heaven's name does not truly represent the name of heaven, it is a saying that rep-resents emotion in a statement. This makes (C) the best answer.

38. What is the author implying in this passage?

A. Sexual abuse

B. Adultery

C. Secret lovers

D. Pregnancy

E. All of the above

The correct answer is A.

The story questions how two could be left alone in such a large city, implying there was a potential case of sexual abuse. (A) is the correct answer.

39. This novel represents _____.

A. Feminism

B. Nature

C. Misogyny

D. City life

E. None of the above

The correct answer is A.

This is a representation of standing up for women's rights and supporting a feminist future. It's straightforward to see that (A) is the correct answer.

40. How could community narrow the range of intimate contact?

A. Arranged marriage is common

B. Rural areas limit physical contact

C. People do not associate with others outside of their class

D. Communities are not tight-knit

E. Men and women attend same-sex schools

The correct answer is C.

We already know that communities stick to their own class systems. Narrowing the range of intimate contact represents following this rule and avoiding any association with others outside of their class. This makes (C) the best answer.

Questions 41-47. Read the following selection and answer the questions below, selecting the best choice of the options presented.

"Finished, it's finished, nearly finished, it must be nearly finished. Grain upon grain, one by one, and one day, suddenly, there's a heap, a little heap, the impossible heap. I can't be punished any more. I'll go now to my kitchen, ten feet by ten feet by ten feet, and wait for him to whistle me. Nice dimensions, nice proportions, I'll lean on the table, and look at the wall, and wait for him to whistle me."

—*Endgame*

41. Who wrote this play?

A. Anton Chekov

B. William Shakespeare

C. Lillian Hellman

D. Athol Fugard

E. Samuel Beckett

The correct answer is E.

Samuel Beckett is the author of *Endgame.*

42. What literary device is used throughout this passage?

A. Simile

B. Metaphor

C. Euphemism

D. Flashback

E. Repetition

The correct answer is E.

Starting with the first line, repetition is an obvious literary device in this passage. Because nearly every statement includes repetition, (E) is the best answer for this question.

43. What does the *impossible heap* represent

A. Life's greatest hurdles

B. A pile of grain so tall it cannot be moved

C. Death

D. A mountain

E. Heaven

The correct answer is C.

The impossible heap represents death. (B) is a literal interpretation of the setting, along with (D). The symbolism throughout the selection lets the reader know that the end is near. There is no reference to life's hurdles or heaven, leaving (C) as the best answer.

44. The whistle symbolizes _____.

A. A referee

B. The character's father

C. Death

D. An angel

E. All of the above

The correct answer is C.

Again, this selection is setting up a scene of the end of someone's life. (A) can quickly be eliminated, as there is no reference to sports. (B) would create a more positive, less drastic waiting period. Therefore, (C) is the correct answer.

45. What is an endgame?

A. The final play in a game, such as chess

B. The end of a negotiation

C. A wish

D. The final approval for a lease

E. None of the above

The correct answer is A.

Because we know this passage represents the end of someone's life, the title is an obvious connection. An endgame represents the final play in a game, which is the best connection for this question.

46. What is the author trying to portray in this selection?

A. An old man

B. A prisoner

C. A farmer

D. A mill worker

E. A plantation

The correct answer is B.

The passage does not incorporate any positive or happy references, therefore (A) can be eliminated. The character is not angry, and there are no implications that he/she is hungry, so (C) and (D) can be eliminated as well. The character is anxious and question-ing their punishment, which makes (B) the correct answer.

47. What best describes this selection?

A. Epic

B. Foreshadowing

C. Cliffhanger

D. Flashback

E. Irony

The correct answer is B.

The selection gives an idea of what's coming in the character's life, so (B) is the best answer. It is not climactic (C), and it does not look back throughout their life (D). The passage is not ironic (E) and is not considered to be an epic (A).

Questions 48-55. Read the following selection and answer the questions below, selecting the best choice of the options presented.

"If people bring so much courage to this world the world has to kill them to break them, so of course it kills them. The world breaks every one and afterward many are strong at the broken places. But those that will not break it kills. It kills the very good and the very gentle and the very brave impartially. If you are none of these you can be sure it will kill you too but there will be no special hurry."

—*A Farewell to Arms*

48. Who wrote this novel?

A. Henry David Thoreau

B. Ernest Hemingway

C. F. Scott Fitzgerald

D. Harper Lee

E. J.R.R. Tolkien

The correct answer is B.

A Farewell to Arms was written by Ernest Hemmingway.

49. What is the theme of this novel?

A. Innocence

B. War

C. Love

D. Death

E. Grief

The correct answer is B.

Arms represents guns, making the connection of the theme and the title of the book very obvious. While love, death, and grief may be involved in the book, war is the theme.

50. What does the title symbolize?

A. An amputation caused during war

B. Being discharged

C. Saying goodbye to the arms of someone you love

D. Saying goodbye to weaponry and warfare

E. C & D

The correct answer is E.

The word arms represents war, and the title symbolizes saying goodbye to warfare, weaponry, and love. (A) and (B) are literal translations and do not include symbolism.

51. Which literary device is used to describe war?

A. Personification

B. Alliteration

C. Simile

D. Metaphor

E. Idiom

The correct answer is A.

Personification is used to describe the war, particularly in the statement "it will kill you."

52. What best describes the author's intention in the following line?
"It kills the very good and the very gentle and the very brave impartially."

A. Everyone will die sooner or later

B. Murderers target nice people

C. The good, gentle and brave are easier to kill

D. The good, gentle and brave die protecting others

E. War kills everyone, it doesn't have a bias

The correct answer is E.

While it's true that everyone will die sooner or later (A), and the good, gentle and brave die protecting others (D), the author's intention was to show that there is no bias when it comes to death during war. (B) and (C) are easy to eliminate, leaving (E) as the best answer.

53. How does the world *break* people?

A. It creates challenging times

B. It represents being shot and not dying

C. It causes extreme wounds, mentally and physically

D. People can have broken bones

E. Physical objects and precious belongings can be broken

The correct answer is C.

The war leaves soldiers with many wounds, both mentally and physically. (C) is the best answer because it covers both of these scenarios.

54. Which of the following best represents this passage?

A. Sarcasm

B. Resentment

C. Irony

D. Sympathy

E. Affectionate

The correct answer is B.

The author is resentful in his tone throughout this passage, so (B) is the best answer of these options.

55. Which literary period is this from?

A. Romanticism

B. Renaissance

C. The Enlightenment

D. Existentialism

E. Modernism

The correct answer is E.

Because it was written in the 19th century, this passage is from the Modernism period. The reference to war should be an obvious reference to this era, making it easy to eliminate A-D.

Sample Test Two

Section I

Multiple Choice Questions.
Time: 60 minutes.
Percent of total grade on the exam: 45 percent.

Instructions: This section of the exam consists of selections from literary works and questions on their content, form, and style. After reading each passage and poem, choose the best answer to each question and then fill in the corresponding oval on the answer sheet.

Questions 1-8. Read the following passage carefully before you decide on your answers to the questions.

O for a Muse of fire, that would ascend
The brightest heaven of invention,
A kingdom for a stage, princes to act
And monarchs to behold the swelling scene!
Then should the warlike Harry, like himself,
Assume the port of Mars; and at his heels,
Leash'd in like hounds, should famine sword and fire
Crouch for employment. But pardon, and gentles all,
The flat unraised spirits that have dared
On this unworthy scaffold to bring forth
So great an object: can this cockpit hold
The vasty fields of France? or may we cram
Within this wooden O the very casques
That did affright the air at Agincourt?
O, pardon! since a crooked figure may
Attest in little place a million;
And let us, ciphers to this great account,
On your imaginary forces work.
Suppose within the girdle of these walls
Are now confined two mighty monarchies,
Whose high upreared and abutting fronts
The perilous narrow ocean parts asunder:
Piece out our imperfections with your thoughts;
Into a thousand parts divide one man,
And make imaginary puissance;
Think when we talk of horses, that you see them
Printing their proud hoofs i' the receiving earth;
For 'tis your thoughts that now must deck our kings,
Carry them here and there; jumping o'er times,
Turning the accomplishment of many years
Into an hour-glass: for the which supply,

Admit me Chorus to this history;
Who prologue-like your humble patience pray,
Gently to hear, kindly to judge, our play.

1. The first four lines could best be described as...

A. A warning of violence to come.

B. A celebration of military victory.

C. An exultation of creative vision.

D. A lamentation of the inadequacy of mortals.

E. A plea for patience from the audience.

2. What can the reader infer from lines 5-8?

A. Harry was a man who inspired awe and fear.

B. Harry was a god.

C. Harry will soon rule over all people.

D. Harry is the villain of the play.

E. Harry was a sailor.

3. What is meant by the line "since a crooked figure may attest in little place a million"?

A. Small men can enact great change if they fulfill their potential.

B. A hand written number can evoke a massive value.

C. Trials can be overcome through perseverance.

D. Some tests are insurmountable to any man.

E. There are mysteries we cannot solve.

4. What does the narrator wish for the audience to do in lines 20-28?

A. Draw upon their own experiences at the theater.

B. Imagine the horror and glory of war.

C. Pretend the physical aspects of the theater reflect things far greater than can be shown onstage.

D. Appreciate history, both the good and bad aspects.

E. Understand their own smallness in the face of this epic tale.

5. What is the narrator's attitude towards the audience?

A. Egocentric disdain

B. Haughty dismissal

C. Meek terror

D. Wide-eyed fascination

E. Humble entreating

6. What is the "unworthy scaffold"?

A. A run-down building

B. A poorhouse

C. The barracks

D. The stage itself

E. A church

7. The narrator wishes to

A. Deceive the audience with propaganda.

B. Relay a tale too great for the stage to contain.

C. Repent for the sins committed by his people.

D. Slander the memory of a great leader.

E. Absolve himself of any guilt he may be feeling.

8. Who are the "ciphers to this great account"?

A. Soldiers

B. Actors

C. Women

D. Scholars

E. Royalty

Questions 9-16. Read the following passage carefully before you decide on your answers to the questions.

A child said, What is the grass? fetching it to me with full hands;
How could I answer the child?. . . .I do not know what it is any more than he.

I guess it must be the flag of my disposition, out of hopeful green stuff woven.

Or I guess it is the handkerchief of the Lord,
A scented gift and remembrancer designedly dropped,
Bearing the owner's name someway in the corners, that we may see and remark, and say Whose?

Or I guess the grass is itself a child. . . .the produced babe of the vegetation.

Or I guess it is a uniform hieroglyphic,
And it means, Sprouting alike in broad zones and narrow zones,
Growing among black folks as among white,
Kanuck, Tuckahoe, Congressman, Cuff, I give them the same, I receive them the same.

And now it seems to me the beautiful uncut hair of graves.

Tenderly will I use you curling grass,
It may be you transpire from the breasts of young men,
It may be if I had known them I would have loved them;
It may be you are from old people and from women, and
from offspring taken soon out of their mother's laps,
And here you are the mother's laps.

This grass is very dark to be from the white heads of old mothers,
Darker than the colorless beards of old men,
Dark to come from under the faint red roofs of mouths.

O I perceive after all so many uttering tongues!
And I perceive they do not come from the roofs of mouths for nothing.

I wish I could translate the hints about the dead young men and women,
And the hints about old men and mothers, and the offspring taken soon out of their laps.

What do you think has become of the young and old men?
What do you think has become of the women and children?

They are alive and well somewhere;
The smallest sprouts show there is really no death,
And if ever there was it led forward life, and does not wait at the end to arrest it,
And ceased the moment life appeared.

All goes onward and outward. . . .and nothing collapses,
And to die is different from what any one supposed, and luckier.

9. What best describes the tone of this poem?

A. Melancholic

B. Stream-of-consciousness

C. Bittersweet

D. Exuberant

E. Regretful

10. Why does the author decide death is lucky?

A. Death leads to new life, as evidenced by the grass.

B. People are immortal in the afterlife.

C. Children bring hope for the future, ever growing stronger.

D. Life is meaningless, and people are no worse off in death than cut grass.

E. Man's cruelty makes life not worth living.

11. What does the speaker mean by "tenderly I will use you curling grass"?

A. He will attempt to nurture a better generation.

B. He will ponder the implications and meanings of the grass.

C. He has no easy answers, the question is too complex to examine.

D. When he dies, he will become grass.

E. The grass connects him to all beings.

12. What can we infer from the first stanza in context?

A. The speaker is dim and uneducated.

B. The speaker has no mind for philosophy.

C. The child is cleverer than he appears.

D. The question is too complex for a simple answer.

E. The grass is a strange variety not seen in this location.

13. Who does the speaker decide is "the mother's laps"?

A. The child

B. Humanity

C. Himself

D. The grass

E. The dead

14. What is meant by lines 7-10?

A. The Lord works in mysterious ways.

B. The grass is an object, inanimate as a handkerchief.

C. The Lord created the grass, and it bears his signature.

D. There is no need for God with such natural beauty around us.

E. The answers to these questions float before us, like a handkerchief on the wind.

15. What can we infer that the author believes from stanza 5?

A. He is a mild racist.

B. All of humanity is fundamentally the same.

C. We are all united in death

D. Disharmony can be overcome through change.

E. Social class is a fact of life.

16. In context, what does the author mean by "I wish I could translate the hints about the dead young men and women"?

A. He wishes he could discern things about the people from the grass they became.

B. He wants to think no more of depressing matters like death.

C. He wishes he could speak to the dead to better understand what awaits him.

D. He wants to cure the suffering in the world.

E. He feels it is unnatural that mothers must lose their children.

Questions 17-24. Read the following passage carefully before you decide on your answers to the questions.

These pictures were in watercolors. The first represented clouds low and livid, rolling over a swollen sea: all the distance was in eclipse; so, too, was the foreground; or rather, the nearest billows, for there was no land. One gleam of light lifted into relief a half-submerged mast, on which sat a cormorant, dark and large, with wings flecked with foam; its beak held a gold bracelet set with gems, that I had touched with as brilliant tints as my palette could yield, and as glittering distinctness as my pencil could impart. Sinking below the bird and mast, a drowned corpse glanced through the green water; a fair arm was the only limb clearly visible, whence the bracelet had been washed or torn.

The second picture contained for foreground only the dim peak of a hill, with grass and some leaves slanting as if by a breeze. Beyond and above spread an expanse of sky, dark blue as at twilight: rising into the sky was a woman's shape to the bust, portrayed in tints as dusk and soft as I could combine. The dim forehead was crowned with a star; the lineaments below were seen as through the suffusion of vapour; the eyes shone dark and wild; the hair streamed shadowy, like a beamless cloud torn by storm or by electric travail. On the neck lay a pale reflection like moonlight; the same faint lustre touched the train of thin clouds from which rose and bowed this vision of the Evening Star.

The third showed the pinnacle of an iceberg piercing a polar winter sky: a muster of northern lights reared their dim lances, close serried, along the horizon. Throwing these into distance, rose, in the foreground, a head,--a colossal head, inclined towards the iceberg, and resting against it. Two thin hands, joined under the forehead, and supporting it, drew up before the lower features a sable veil, a brow quite bloodless, white as bone, and an eye hollow and fixed, blank of meaning but for the glassiness of despair, alone were visible. Above the temples, amidst wreathed turban folds of black drapery, vague in its character and consistency as cloud, gleamed a ring of white flame, gemmed with sparkles of a more lurid tinge. This pale crescent was "the likeness of a kingly crown;" what it diademed was "the shape which shape had none."

"Were you happy when you painted these pictures?" asked Mr. Rochester presently.

"I was absorbed, sir: yes, and I was happy. To paint them, in short, was to enjoy one of the keenest pleasures I have ever known."

"That is not saying much. Your pleasures, by your own account, have been few; but I daresay you did exist in a kind of artist's dreamland while you blent and arranged these strange tints. Did you sit at them long each day?"

"I had nothing else to do, because it was the vacation, and I sat at them from morning till noon, and from noon till night: the length of the midsummer days favoured my inclination to apply."

"And you felt self-satisfied with the result of your ardent labours?"

"Far from it. I was tormented by the contrast between my idea and my handiwork: in each case I had imagined something which I was quite powerless to realise."

"Not quite: you have secured the shadow of your thought; but no more, probably. You had not enough of the artist's skill and science to give it full being: yet the drawings are, for a school- girl, peculiar. As to the thoughts, they are elfish. These eyes in the Evening Star you must have seen in a dream. How could you make them look so clear, and yet not at all brilliant? for the planet above quells their rays. And what meaning is that in their solemn depth? And who taught you to paint wind. There is a high gale in that sky, and on this hill-top. Where did you see Latmos? For that is Latmos. There! put the drawings away!"

I had scarce tied the strings of the portfolio, when, looking at his watch, he said abruptly -

"It is nine o'clock: what are you about, Miss Eyre, to let Adele sit up so long? Take her to bed."

Adele went to kiss him before quitting the room: he endured the caress, but scarcely seemed to relish it more than Pilot would have done, nor so much.

"I wish you all good-night, now," said he, making a movement of the hand towards the door, in token that he was tired of our company, and wished to dismiss us. Mrs. Fairfax folded up her knitting: I took my portfolio: we curtseyed to him, received a frigid bow in return, and so withdrew.

17. What best describes Mr. Rochester's objective in the previous scene?

A. To break Jane down by insulting her art.

B. To determine her romantic interests and possibly woo her.

C. To discover more about her personality through her work.

D. To find something he can use against her family.

E. To establish his dominance over her and her household.

18. What is meant by the line "but scarcely seemed to relish it more than Pilot would have done"?

A. He despises the young Adele.

B. He dislikes such an expression of familiarity.

C. He is a sacrilegious man.

D. His depression prevents him from enjoying intimacy.

E. He is an antagonist.

19. Mr. Rochester feels Jane's paintings are...

A. Naïve and unskilled, but showing potential.

B. A frivolous waste of time.

C. Unique, perhaps disturbingly so.

D. Blasphemous, though well-made.

E. Extraordinary, though he struggles to express his admiration.

20. What is meant by the term "diademed" in this passage:
This pale crescent was "the likeness of a kingly crown;" what it diademed was "the shape which shape had none."

A. Illuminated

B. Exposed

C. Pierced

D. Crowned

E. Blended

21. The primary effect of the imagery in the description of Jane's second painting is to:

A. Emphasize the painting's religious themes

B. Explore its ethereal, supernatural quality

C. Determine its ill-formed concepts and amateurish execution

D. Characterize Jane as a hopeless romantic

E. Place the painting as an interpretation of Mr. Rochester

22. What is the primary subject of the first painting?

A. A bird holding a piece of jewelry

B. A Naval skirmish in full swing

C. A horrific murder and robbery

D. An abstract image of a woman shrouded in clouds

E. A religious ceremony

23. Inferring from the text, Jane must be Adele's...

A. Mother

B. Sister

C. Caretaker

D. Employer

E. Maid

24. What is Jane's attitude towards her paintings?

A. Loathing

B. Embarrassment

C. Pride

D. Dissatisfaction

E. Indifference

Questions 25-32. Read the following passage carefully before you decide on your answers to the questions.

"You've just told me some high spots in your memories. Want to hear mine? They're all connected with the sea.

Here's one. When I was on the Squarehead square rigger, bound for Buenos Aires. Full moon in the trades. The old hooker driving 14 knots. I lay on the bowsprit, facing astern, with the water foaming into spume under me. Every mast with sail white in the moonlight - towering high above me. I became drunk with the beauty and singing rhythm of it - and for a second I lost myself, actually lost my life. I was set free! I dissolved into the sea, became white sails and flying spray - became beauty and rhythm, became moonlight and the ship and the high dim-starred sky. I belonged, without past or future, within peace and unity and a wild joy, within something greater than my own life, or the life of man, to Life itself! To God if you want to put it that way.

Then another time, on the American line, when I was lookout in the crow's nest on the dawn watch. A calm sea that time. Only a lazy ground swell and a slow drousy roll of the ship. The passengers asleep and none of the crew in sight. No sound of man. Black smoke pouring from the funnels behind and beneath me. Dreaming, not keeping lookout, feeling alone, and above, and apart, watching the dawn creep like a painted dream over the sky and sea which slept together.

Then the moment of ecstatic freedom came. The peace, the end of the quest, the last harbor, the joy of belonging to a fulfillment beyond men's lousy, greedy fears and hopes and dreams! And several other times in my life, when I was swimming far out, or lying alone on the beach, I have had the same experience. Became the sun, the hot sand, green seaweed anchored to a rock, swaying in the tide. Like a saint's vision of beatitude. Like the veil of things as they seem drawn back by an unseen hand. For a second you see - and seeing the secret, are the secret. For a second there is meaning! Then the hand lets the veil fall and you are alone, lost in the fog again, stumbling on toward no where, for no good reason!

it was a great mistake, my being born a man. I would have been much more successful as a seagull or fish. As it is, I will always be a stranger who never feels at home, who does not want and is not really wanted, who can never belong, who must always be a little in love with death."

25. What adjective best describes Edmund's tone in this piece?

A. Disaffected

B. Morose

C. Longing

D. Celebratory

E. Inspired

26. This piece can best be described as…

A. A poem

B. A dramatic monologue

C. Prose fiction

D. An ode

E. A dirge

27. What are the two primary contrasts of this piece?

A. The sea with the land; drunkenness with sobriety.

B. Depression and joy; sailing with being "anchored".

C. The wild sea with the calm sea; ecstasy with numbness.

D. Edmund with his father; freedom with responsibility.

E. Humanity with nature; godlessness with holiness.

28. The author conveys the sea using what primary technique?

A. Analogy

B. Assonance

C. Simile

D. Personification

E. Imagery

29. The phrase "like a saint's vision of beatitude" serves to reinforce what idea?

A. Edmund's desire to die.

B. Edmund finds spirituality in nature.

C. Edmund wishes to sail again.

D. Edmund wishes to repent

E. Edmund dislikes religion.

30. In the first paragraph, the author characterizes this piece as a…

A. Story-within-a-story

B. Memory

C. Soliloquy

D. Ballad

E. Fabrication

31. Where does the primary shift in tone occur in this piece?

A. Paragraph two, "I became drunk with the beauty…"

B. Paragraph three, "The another time, on the American line…"

C. Paragraph four, "Then that moment of ecstatic freedom came!"

D. Paragraph four, "Then the hand lets the veil fall…"

E. Paragraph five, "I will always be a stranger…"

32. What natural image does the author use to contrast the sea and its feelings of freedom?

A. Black smoke

B. Fog

C. Spray

D. Seagull

E. Waves

Questions 33-40. Read the following passage carefully before you decide on your answers to the questions.

In a village of La Mancha, the name of which I have no desire to call to mind, there lived not long since one of those gentlemen that keep a lance in the lance-rack, an old buckler, a lean hack, and a greyhound for coursing. An olla of rather more beef than mutton, a salad on most nights, scraps on Saturdays, lentils on Fridays, and a pigeon or so extra on Sundays, made away with three-quarters of his incom(E). The rest of it went in a doublet of fine cloth and velvet breeches and shoes to match for holidays, while on week-days he made a brave figure in his best homespun. He had in his house a housekeeper past forty, a niece under twenty, and a lad for the field and market-place, who used to saddle the hack as well as handle the bill-hook. The age of this gentleman of ours was bordering on fifty; he was of a hardy habit, spare, gaunt-featured, a very early riser and a great sportsman. They will have it his surname was Quixada or Quesada (for here there is some difference of opinion among the authors who write on the subject), although from reasonable conjectures it seems plain that he was called Quexana. This, however, is of but little importance to our tale; it will be enough not to stray a hair's breadth from the truth in the telling of it.

You must know, then, that the above-named gentleman whenever he was at leisure (which was mostly all the year round) gave himself up to reading books of chivalry with such ardour and avidity that he almost entirely neglected the pursuit of his field-sports, and even the management of his property; and to such a pitch did his eagerness and infatuation go that he sold many an acre of tillage land to buy books of chivalry to read, and brought home as many of them as he could get. But of all there were none he liked so well as those of the famous Feliciano de Silva's composition, for their lucidity of style and complicated conceits were as pearls in his sight, particularly when in his reading he came upon courtships and cartels, where he often found passages like "the reason of the unreason with which my reason is afflicted so weakens my reason that with reason I murmur at your beauty;" or again, "the high heavens, that of your divinity divinely fortify you with the stars, render you deserving of the desert your greatness deserves." Over conceits of this sort the poor gentleman lost his wits, and used to lie awake striving to understand them and worm the meaning out of them; what Aristotle himself could not have made out or extracted had he come to life again for that special purpose. He was not at all easy about the wounds which Don Belianis gave and took, because it seemed to him that, great as were the surgeons who had cured him, he must have had his face and body covered all over with seams and scars. He commended, however, the author's way of ending his book with the promise of that interminable adventure, and many a time was he tempted to take up his pen and finish it properly as is there proposed, which no doubt he would have done, and made a successful piece of work of it too, had not greater and more absorbing thoughts prevented him.

33. **The author's tone in this piece can best be described as...**

A. Heroic

B. Comedic

C. Florid

D. Epic

E. Mysterious

34. **The line "were as pearls to his sight" is an example of a...**

A. Metaphor

B. Analogy

C. Simile

D. Allegory

E. Conceit

35. **Our main character's attitude towards reading can best be described as...**

A. Lackadaisical

B. Unusual

C. Illiterate

D. Obsessive

E. Joyous

36. **The passage "the high heavens, that of your divinity divinely fortify you with the stars, render you deserving of the desert your greatness deserves" contains several examples what poetic device?**

A. Alliteration

B. Onomatopoeia

C. Diction

D. Resonance

E. Enjambment

37. According to the text, who is Count Belianis?

A. A historical champion

B. A fictional character

C. A competing nobleman

D. A romantic rival

E. A dead family member

38. The passage "it will be enough not to stray a hair's breadth from the truth in the telling of it" characterizes the previous passage as...

A. Essential

B. Metaphorical

C. Unimportant

D. Esoteric

E. Bland

39. What are the two defining traits of the main character described above?

A. Laziness and obsessiveness

B. Ignorance and piousness

C. Diligence and valor

D. Prideful and vain

E. Curious and kindhearted

40. The final sentence of this excerpt is an example of...

A. Satire

B. Foreshadowing

C. Interstitial

D. Subtext

E. Premonition

Questions 41-48. Read the following passage carefully before you decide on your answers to the questions.

Every light in the hall was ablaze; every lamp turned as high as it could be without smoking the chimney or threatening explosion. The lamps were fixed at intervals against the wall, encircling the whole room. Some one had gathered orange and lemon branches, and with these fashioned graceful festoons between. The dark green of the branches stood out and glistened against the white muslin curtains which draped the windows, and which puffed, floated, and flapped at the capricious will of a stiff breeze that swept up from the Gulf.

It was Saturday night a few weeks after the intimate conversation held between Robert and Madame Ratignolle on their way from the beach. An unusual number of husbands, fathers, and friends had come down to stay over Sunday; and they were being suitably entertained by their families, with the material help of Madame Lebrun. The dining tables had all been removed to one end of the hall, and the chairs ranged about in rows and in clusters. Each little family group had had its say and exchanged its domestic gossip earlier in the evening. There was now an apparent disposition to relax; to widen the circle of confidences and give a more general tone to the conversation.

Many of the children had been permitted to sit up beyond their usual bedtime. A small band of them were lying on their stomachs on the floor looking at the colored sheets of the comic papers which Mr. Pontellier had brought down. The little Pontellier boys were permitting them to do so, and making their authority felt.

Music, dancing, and a recitation or two were the entertainments furnished, or rather, offered. But there was nothing systematic about the programme, no appearance of prearrangement nor even premeditation.

At an early hour in the evening the Farival twins were prevailed upon to play the piano. They were girls of fourteen, always clad in the Virgin's colors, blue and white, having been dedicated to the Blessed Virgin at their baptism. They played a duet from "Zampa," and at the earnest solicitation of every one present followed it with the overture to "The Poet and the Peasant."

"Allez vous-en! Sapristi!" shrieked the parrot outside the door. He was the only being present who possessed sufficient candor to admit that he was not listening to these gracious performances for the first time that summer. Old Monsieur Farival, grandfather of the twins, grew indignant over the interruption, and insisted upon having the bird removed and consigned to regions of darkness. Victor Lebrun objected; and his decrees were as immutable as those of Fate. The parrot fortunately offered no further interruption to the entertainment, the whole venom of his nature apparently having been cherished up and hurled against the twins in that one impetuous outburst.

41. This passage "*and his decrees were as immutable as those of Fate*" characterizes its subject, how?

A. He will not be denied

B. He is an angry man

C. He is the eldest in the family

D. He strikes fear into those around him

E. He is easily ignored

42. "Music, dancing, and a recitation or two were the entertainments furnished, or rather, offered." This unusual passage speaks to the proceeding's...

A. Modest entertainment

B. Banality and blandness

C. Informality and spontaneity

D. Inexpensiveness and triteness

E. Luster and joyousness

43. The term "prevailed upon" in paragraph five characterizes the Farival twins as...

A. Talented

B. Reluctant

C. Timid

D. Eager

E. Popular

44. In context, the line "the whole venom of his nature apparently having been cherished up and hurled against the twins in that one impetuous outburst" (paragraph six) can best be paraphrased as...

A. He calmed immediately after being chastised

B. He spent all of his pent-up rage in one interjection

C. He naturally felt himself sickened by these proceedings

D. He exposed his deep feelings for them all in out exclamation

E. He hated the twins

Sample Test Two

45. **What aspect of imagery consistently appears in this excerpt?**

A. Odor

B. Sound

C. Tactile sensation

D. Color

E. Emotion

46. **"With the material help of Madame Lebrun" (paragraph two) implies what in context?**

A. Madame Lebrun barely helped

B. Madame Lebrun assisted in constructing the stage

C. Madame Lebrun provided many of the physical necessities

D. Madame Lebrun aided as best she could

E. Madame Lebrun provided only reluctant support

47. **The gathering depicted in the excerpt can best be described as...**

A. Bland

B. Ineffective

C. Low-key

D. Snobbish

E. Enjoyable

48. **Paragraph five implies the primary characteristic of the Farival twins is their…**

A. Beauty

B. Skill

C. Oddness

D. Chicness

E. Purity

Questions 49-55. Read the following passage carefully before you decide on your answers to the questions.

O wild West Wind, thou breath of Autumn's being,
Thou, from whose unseen presence the leaves dead
Are driven, like ghosts from an enchanter fleeing,

Yellow, and black, and pale, and hectic red,
Pestilence-stricken multitudes: O thou,
Who chariotest to their dark wintry bed

The winged seeds, where they lie cold and low,
Each like a corpse within its grave, until
Thine azure sister of the Spring shall blow

Her clarion o'er the dreaming earth, and fill
(Driving sweet buds like flocks to feed in air)
With living hues and odors plain and hill:

Wild Spirit, which art moving everywhere;
Destroyer and preserver; hear, oh, hear!

Thou on whose stream, 'mid the steep sky's commotion,
Loose clouds like earth's decaying leaves are shed,
Shook from the tangled boughs of Heaven and Ocean,

Angels of rain and lightning: there are spread
On the blue surface of thine aery surge,
Like the bright hair uplifted from the head

Of some fierce Maenad, even from the dim verge
Of the horizon to the zenith's height,
The locks of the approaching storm. Thou dirge

Of the dying year, to which this closing night
Will be the dome of a vast sepulchre,
Vaulted with all thy congregated might

Of vapors, from whose solid atmosphere
Black rain, and fire, and hail will burst: oh, hear!

49. The first line of this poem exhibits what poetic devices?

I. Alliteration

II. Personification

III. Onomatopoeia

A. Only I

B. Only II

C. Only III

D. I and II

E. I, II, and III

50. What best describes the final stanza of this selection?

A. Slant rhyme

B. Heroic couplet

C. Hyperbole

D. Irony

E. Blank verse

51. "Wild Spirit, which art moving everywhere; Destroyer and preserver; hear, oh, hear!" This passage displays a...

A. Enjambment

B. Slant rhyme

C. Simile

D. Iamb

E. Allegory

52. This poem is written in what style?

A. Vers libre

B. Heroic couplet

C. Epic saga

D. Imagist soliloquy

E. Iambic pentameter

53. What in the poem is compared to "Angels of rain and lightning"?

A. The wind

B. Maenads

C. Clouds

D. Human souls

E. Autumn

54. "Of the dying year, to which this closing night/ Will be the dome of a vast sepulchre,/ Vaulted with all thy congregated might"
This passage exhibits…

A. A metaphor

B. An allegory

C. A comparison

D. A consonance

E. An allusion

55. How many stanzas does this poem contain?

A. Four

B. Five

C. Eight

D. Ten

E. Twelve

Free Response Essay Sample Questions

Section II

Time: 120 minutes

Percent of total grade on the exam: 55 percent.

Question 1.

(Suggested time—40 minutes. This question counts as one-third of the total essay section score.)

Read the following excerpt from Homer's *The Odyssey*. Paying particular attention to the author's tone, analyze how the topic of the passage frames the subject of love, over and money. Compose a thoughtful essay highlighting the use of literary devices achieve's the author's goals. Do not merely summarize the plot.

She spake, and fastened underneath her feet
The fair, ambrosial golden sandals worn
To bear her over ocean like the wind,
And o'er the boundless land. In hand she took,
Well tipped with trenchant brass, the mighty spear,
Heavy and huge and strong, with which she bears
Whole phalanges of heroes to the earth,
When she, the daughter of a mighty sire,
Is angered. From the Olympian heights she plunged,
And stood among the men of Ithaca,
Just as the porch and threshold of their chief,
Ulysses. In her hand she bore the spear,
And seemed the stranger Mentes, he who led
The Taphians. There before the gate she found
The haughty suitors. Some beguiled the time
With draughts, while sitting on the hides of beeves
Which they had slaughtered. Heralds were with them,
And busy menials: some who in the bowls
Tempered the wine with water, some who cleansed
The tables with light sponges, and who set
The banquet forth and carved the meats for all.

Question 2.

(Suggested time—40 minutes. This question counts as one-third of the total essay section score.)

Read the following passage from Huckleberry Finn. Education in literature can have a variety of outcomes for characters. Analyze how the author describes in the passage the way the protagonist was educated and discuss in an essay how this affected the character. Do not summarize the plot.

> Her sister, Miss Watson, a tolerable slim old maid, with goggles on, had just come to live with her, and took a set at me now with a spelling-book. She worked me middling hard for about an hour, and then the widow made her ease up. I couldn't stood it much longer. Then for an hour it was deadly dull, and I was fidgety. Miss Watson would say, "Don't put your feet up there, Huckleberry - set up straight;" and pretty soon she would say, "Don't gap and stretch like that, Huckleberry - why don't you try to behave?" Then she told me all about the bad place, and I said I wished I was there. She got mad then, abut I didn't mean no harm. All I wanted was to go somewheres; all I wanted was a change, I warn't particular. She said it as wicked to say what I said; said she wouldn't say it for the whole world; she was going to live so as to go to the good place. Well, I couldn't see no advantage in going where she was going, so I made up my mind I wouldn't try for it. But I never said so, because it would only make trouble, and wouldn't do no good.

Question 3.

(Suggested time—40 minutes. This question counts as one-third of the total essay section score.)

Choose a character from a novel or play who responds in some significant way to a life-changing incident. Then write a well-developed essay in which you analyze the way that incident was used by the author to make a change in either the character's life or the community that surrounds the character, describe the way the event influences justice or injustice being served.

Sample Test Two: ANSWER KEY

Question Number	Correct Answer	Your Answer
1.	C	
2.	A	
3.	B	
4.	C	
5.	E	
6.	D	
7.	B	
8.	B	
9.	C	
10.	A	
11.	B	
12.	D	
13.	D	
14.	C	
15.	B	
16.	A	
17.	C	
18.	B	
19.	A	
20.	D	
21.	B	
22.	A	
23.	C	
24.	D	
25.	C	
26.	B	
27.	C	
28.	E	

Question Number	Correct Answer	Your Answer
29.	B	
30.	B	
31.	D	
32.	B	
33.	B	
34.	C	
35.	D	
36.	A	
37.	B	
38.	C	
39.	A	
40.	B	
41.	A	
42.	C	
43.	B	
44.	B	
45.	E	
46.	C	
47.	E	
48.	E	
49.	D	
50.	B	
51.	B	
52.	E	
53.	C	
54.	A	
55.	D	

Answer Key and Rationale

Questions 1-8. Read the following passage carefully before you decide on your answers to the questions.

O for a Muse of fire, that would ascend
The brightest heaven of invention,
A kingdom for a stage, princes to act
And monarchs to behold the swelling scene!
Then should the warlike Harry, like himself,
Assume the port of Mars; and at his heels,
Leash'd in like hounds, should famine sword and fire
Crouch for employment. But pardon, and gentles all,
The flat unraised spirits that have dared
On this unworthy scaffold to bring forth
So great an object: can this cockpit hold
The vasty fields of France? or may we cram
Within this wooden O the very casques
That did affright the air at Agincourt?
O, pardon! since a crooked figure may
Attest in little place a million;
And let us, ciphers to this great account,
On your imaginary forces work.
Suppose within the girdle of these walls
Are now confined two mighty monarchies,
Whose high upreared and abutting fronts
The perilous narrow ocean parts asunder:
Piece out our imperfections with your thoughts;
Into a thousand parts divide one man,
And make imaginary puissance;
Think when we talk of horses, that you see them
Printing their proud hoofs i' the receiving earth;
For 'tis your thoughts that now must deck our kings,
Carry them here and there; jumping o'er times,
Turning the accomplishment of many years
Into an hour-glass: for the which supply,
Admit me Chorus to this history;
Who prologue-like your humble patience pray,
Gently to hear, kindly to judge, our play.

1. The first four lines could best be described as...

A. A warning of violence to come.

B. A celebration of military victory.

C. An exultation of creative vision.

D. A lamentation of the inadequacy of mortals.

E. A plea for patience from the audience.

The correct answer is C.

The "Muse of fire" is understood to be figurative, referencing the "muse" of inspiration that will allow the speaker to spin his tale. The entire monologue centers around the author explaining the limitations of his storytelling capabilities, so (C) is the safest answer.

2. What can the reader infer from lines 5-8?

A. Harry was a man who inspired awe and fear.

B. Harry was a god.

C. Harry will soon rule over all people.

D. Harry is the villain of the play.

E. Harry was a sailor.

The correct answer is A.

Lines 5 through 8 exult Harry's fearsome figure, comparing Harry to the war god Mars and explaining how even the concepts of famine, sword and fire must bow to him like obedient dogs. The other answers require assumptions not present in the text, (A) is the safest answer.

3. What is meant by the line "since a crooked figure may attest in little place a million"?

A. Small men can enact great change if they fulfill their potential.

B. A hand written number can evoke a massive value.

C. Trials can be overcome through perseverance.

D. Some tests are insurmountable to any man.

E. There are mysteries we cannot solve.

The correct answer is B.

"Crooked figure" refers to a number. The speaker is explaining that even a small, handwritten numeral can be understood to evoke a huge number, and so can their play be understood to represent a titanic struggle.

4. What does the narrator wish for the audience to do in lines 20-28?

A. Draw upon their own experiences at the theater.

B. Imagine the horror and glory of war.

C. Pretend the physical aspects of the theater reflect things far greater than can be shown onstage.

D. Appreciate history, both the good and bad aspects.

E. Understand their own smallness in the face of this epic tale.

The correct answer is C.

With lines such as "into a thousand parts divide one man", the author is requesting that the audience use their imaginations to fill in the gaps of their tale. (C) is the best answer.

5. What is the narrator's attitude towards the audience?

A. Egocentric disdain

B. Haughty dismissal

C. Meek terror

D. Wide-eyed fascination

E. Humble entreating

The correct answer is E.

E is the best answer. The raconteur even uses the word "humble" towards the end of the piece. He does not wish to talk down to the audience in any way.

6. What is the "unworthy scaffold"?

A. A run-down building

B. A poorhouse

C. The barracks

D. The stage itself

E. A church

The correct answer is D.

The "flat, unraised spirits" are the actors, and their "unworthy scaffold" is the stage upon which they are performing.

7. **The narrator wishes to**

A. Deceive the audience with propaganda.

B. Relay a tale too great for the stage to contain.

C. Repent for the sins committed by his people.

D. Slander the memory of a great leader.

E. Absolve himself of any guilt he may be feeling.

The correct answer is B.

The answer is (B). The speaker states many times that, though this tale is grander than we can comprehend, he wishes to make his best effort at telling it.

8. **Who are the "ciphers to this great account"?**

A. Soldiers

B. Actors

C. Women

D. Scholars

E. Royalty

The correct answer is B.

The speaker refers to the ciphers as "us". This line also connects with the "crooked figure" line, as the "figure" he refers to is the numeral for one million, and since "cipher" means "zero", the actors likewise are zeros in the figure evoking a far greater value.

Questions 9-16. Read the following passage carefully before you decide on your answers to the questions.

A child said, What is the grass? fetching it to me with full hands;
How could I answer the child?. . . .I do not know what it is any more than he.

I guess it must be the flag of my disposition, out of hopeful green stuff woven.

Or I guess it is the handkerchief of the Lord,
A scented gift and remembrancer designedly dropped,
Bearing the owner's name someway in the corners, that we may see and remark, and say Whose?

Or I guess the grass is itself a child. . . .the produced babe of the vegetation.

Or I guess it is a uniform hieroglyphic,
And it means, Sprouting alike in broad zones and narrow zones,
Growing among black folks as among white,
Kanuck, Tuckahoe, Congressman, Cuff, I give them the same, I receive them the same.

And now it seems to me the beautiful uncut hair of graves.

Tenderly will I use you curling grass,
It may be you transpire from the breasts of young men,
It may be if I had known them I would have loved them;
It may be you are from old people and from women, and
from offspring taken soon out of their mother's laps,
And here you are the mother's laps.

This grass is very dark to be from the white heads of old mothers,
Darker than the colorless beards of old men,
Dark to come from under the faint red roofs of mouths.

O I perceive after all so many uttering tongues!
And I perceive they do not come from the roofs of mouths for nothing.

I wish I could translate the hints about the dead young men and women,
And the hints about old men and mothers, and the offspring taken soon out of their laps.

What do you think has become of the young and old men?
What do you think has become of the women and children?

They are alive and well somewhere;
The smallest sprouts show there is really no death,
And if ever there was it led forward life, and does not wait at the end to arrest it,
And ceased the moment life appeared.

All goes onward and outward. . . .and nothing collapses,
And to die is different from what any one supposed, and luckier.

9. **What best describes the tone of this poem?**

   A. Melancholic

   B. Stream-of-consciousness

   C. Bittersweet

   D. Exuberant

   E. Regretful

   The correct answer is C.

   The poem discusses topics relating to innocence and joy for life, counterbalanced by musings on the inevitability of death. Though ultimately positive in message, it could not be characterized as exuberant (D), nor does its acceptance of death suggest any regret (E) or melancholy (A). The style is not stream-of-consciousness.

10. **Why does the author decide death is lucky?**

   A. Death leads to new life, as evidenced by the grass.

   B. People are immortal in the afterlife.

   C. Children bring hope for the future, ever growing stronger.

   D. Life is meaningless, and people are no worse off in death than cut grass.

   E. Man's cruelty makes life not worth living.

   The correct answer is A.

   The author makes no reference to the afterlife (B), and is not preoccupied with the future (C). (D) and (E) likewise do not apply, the poem exhibits no such pessimism.

11. **What does the speaker mean by "tenderly I will use you curling grass"?**

   A. He will attempt to nurture a better generation.

   B. He will ponder the implications and meanings of the grass.

   C. He has no easy answers, the question is too complex to examine.

   D. When he dies, he will become grass.

   E. The grass connects him to all beings.

   The correct answer is B.

   The author makes this statement and then proceeds to explore the implications of grass for life, death, and divinity. He does not give up, as referenced by answer (C), nor does he make any firm statements about any future generations (A). He does understand he will become grass like all things (D) and (E) but these notions are not connected to the quote in the question.

12. What can we infer from the first stanza in context?

A. The speaker is dim and uneducated.

B. The speaker has no mind for philosophy.

C. The child is cleverer than he appears.

D. The question is too complex for a simple answer.

E. The grass is a strange variety not seen in this location.

The correct answer is D.

As the poem features an author philosophically overthinking the question about grass, (A) and (B) do not apply. The child also does not exhibit undue cleverness by asking such a typical question (C). The author also makes no mention of this particular grass being unique (E). (D) is the correct answer.

13. Who does the speaker decide is "the mother's laps"?

A. The child

B. Humanity

C. Himself

D. The grass

E. The dead

The correct answer is D.

The author is referring to grass when he makes this statement.

14. What is meant by lines 7-10?

A. The Lord works in mysterious ways.

B. The grass is an object, inanimate as a handkerchief.

C. The Lord created the grass, and it bears his signature.

D. There is no need for God with such natural beauty around us.

E. The answers to these questions float before us, like a handkerchief on the wind.

The correct answer is C.

The author spins a metaphor about God leaving his signature in the grass in much the same way a dropped handkerchief might feature its owner's initials. The author characterizes the grass as alive, so (B) is inaccurate, and A is a vagary the inquisitive author would not be satisfied with. (D) is inaccurate as the author sees God IN the natural beauty.

15. What can we infer that the author believes from stanza 5?

A. He is a mild racist.

B. All of humanity is fundamentally the same.

C. We are all united in death

D. Disharmony can be overcome through change.

E. Social class is a fact of life.

The correct answer is B.

The author is suggesting that we all come from the same source and all return to the same dirt. It could be considered a political statement, but from the poem itself we cannot infer enough for the other answers to be appropriate.

16. In context, what does the author mean by "I wish I could translate the hints about the dead young men and women"?

A. He wishes he could discern things about the people from the grass they became.

B. He wants to think no more of depressing matters like death.

C. He wishes he could speak to the dead to better understand what awaits him.

D. He wants to cure the suffering in the world.

E. He feels it is unnatural that mothers must lose their children.

The correct answer is A.

(B) is inaccurate as the author is delving into the subject of death headlong. (C) is close but still inaccurate, he does not ask what awaits him in the afterlife. (D) is untrue, he makes no mention of curing suffering, and (E) is also inaccurate, as he suggests that all of these occurrences are in fact completely natural, albeit sad.

Questions 17-24. Read the following passage carefully before you decide on your answers to the questions.

These pictures were in watercolors. The first represented clouds low and livid, rolling over a swollen sea: all the distance was in eclipse; so, too, was the foreground; or rather, the nearest billows, for there was no land. One gleam of light lifted into relief a half-submerged mast, on which sat a cormorant, dark and large, with wings flecked with foam; its beak held a gold bracelet set with gems, that I had touched with as brilliant tints as my palette could yield, and as glittering distinctness as my pencil could impart. Sinking below the bird and mast, a drowned corpse glanced through the green water; a fair arm was the only limb clearly visible, whence the bracelet had been washed or torn.

The second picture contained for foreground only the dim peak of a hill, with grass and some leaves slanting as if by a breeze. Beyond and above spread an expanse of sky, dark blue as at twilight: rising into the sky was a woman's shape to the bust, portrayed in tints as dusk and soft as I could combine. The dim forehead was crowned with a star; the lineaments below were seen as through the suffusion of vapour; the eyes shone dark and wild; the hair streamed shadowy, like a beamless cloud torn by storm or by electric travail. On the neck lay a pale reflection like moonlight; the same faint lustre touched the train of thin clouds from which rose and bowed this vision of the Evening Star.

The third showed the pinnacle of an iceberg piercing a polar winter sky: a muster of northern lights reared their dim lances, close serried, along the horizon. Throwing these into distance, rose, in the foreground, a head,--a colossal head, inclined towards the iceberg, and resting against it. Two thin hands, joined under the forehead, and supporting it, drew up before the lower features a sable veil, a brow quite bloodless, white as bone, and an eye hollow and fixed, blank of meaning but for the glassiness of despair, alone were visible. Above the temples, amidst wreathed turban folds of black drapery, vague in its character and consistency as cloud, gleamed a ring of white flame, gemmed with sparkles of a more lurid tinge. This pale crescent was "the likeness of a kingly crown;" what it diademed was "the shape which shape had none."

"Were you happy when you painted these pictures?" asked Mr. Rochester presently.

"I was absorbed, sir: yes, and I was happy. To paint them, in short, was to enjoy one of the keenest pleasures I have ever known."

"That is not saying much. Your pleasures, by your own account, have been few; but I daresay you did exist in a kind of artist's dreamland while you blent and arranged these strange tints. Did you sit at them long each day?"

"I had nothing else to do, because it was the vacation, and I sat at them from morning till noon, and from noon till night: the length of the midsummer days favoured my inclination to apply."

"And you felt self-satisfied with the result of your ardent labours?"

"Far from it. I was tormented by the contrast between my idea and my handiwork: in each case I had imagined something which I was quite powerless to realise."

"Not quite: you have secured the shadow of your thought; but no more, probably. You had not enough of the artist's skill and science to give it full being: yet the drawings are, for a school-girl, peculiar. As to the thoughts, they are elfish. These eyes in the Evening Star you must have seen in a dream. How could you make them look so clear, and yet not at all brilliant? for the planet above quells their rays. And what meaning is that in their solemn depth? And who taught you to paint wind. There is a high gale in that sky, and on this hill-top. Where did you see Latmos? For that is Latmos. There! put the drawings away!"

I had scarce tied the strings of the portfolio, when, looking at his watch, he said abruptly -

"It is nine o'clock: what are you about, Miss Eyre, to let Adele sit up so long? Take her to bed."

Adele went to kiss him before quitting the room: he endured the caress, but scarcely seemed to relish it more than Pilot would have done, nor so much.

"I wish you all good-night, now," said he, making a movement of the hand towards the door, in token that he was tired of our company, and wished to dismiss us. Mrs. Fairfax folded up her knitting: I took my portfolio: we curtseyed to him, received a frigid bow in return, and so withdrew.

17. **What best describes Mr. Rochester's objective in the previous scene?**

A. To break Jane down by insulting her art.

B. To determine her romantic interests and possibly woo her.

C. To discover more about her personality through her work.

D. To find something he can use against her family.

E. To establish his dominance over her and her household.

The correct answer is C.

Rochester is terse with Jane, but he does not directly insult her work. He makes no motion towards romantic interest (B), and (D) and (E) are inaccurate as Rochester is already very dominant in this context and has no need to exert force over the family.

18. **What is meant by the line "but scarcely seemed to relish it more than Pilot would have done"?**

A. He despises the young Adele.

B. He dislikes such an expression of familiarity.

C. He is a sacrilegious man.

D. His depression prevents him from enjoying intimacy.

E. He is an antagonist.

The correct answer is B.

"Despise" (A) is too strong a word, he has tolerated Adele's presence for the entire scene, indeed, a moment earlier he exhibits concern for her being up so late. We don't have enough information to ascertain (D) or (E)'s accuracy, and though Pilot is a biblical reference, we learn nothing from this comparison about his sacrilege (C).

19. **Mr. Rochester feels Jane's paintings are…**

A. Naïve and unskilled, but showing potential.

B. A frivolous waste of time.

C. Unique, perhaps disturbingly so.

D. Blasphemous, though well-made.

E. Extraordinary, though he struggles to express his admiration.

The correct answer is A.

Even grumpy Mr. Rochester allows that the paintings display some talent, though not much. The answer is (A).

20. **What is meant by the term "diademed" in this passage:**
This pale crescent was "the likeness of a kingly crown;" what it diademed was "the shape which shape had none."

A. Illuminated

B. Exposed

C. Pierced

D. Crowned

E. Blended

The correct answer is D.

A diadem is a circlet worn by royalty. In verb form, this supports the royal aspects of the image.

21. **The primary effect of the imagery in the description of Jane's second painting is to:**

A. Emphasize the painting's religious themes

B. Explore its ethereal, supernatural quality

C. Determine its ill-formed concepts and amateurish execution

D. Characterize Jane as a hopeless romantic

E. Place the painting as an interpretation of Mr. Rochester

The correct answer is B.

The picture is described as dreamlike, replete with clouds and moonbeams. It is described in great detail, so (C) would not apply, and (D) is too great an assumption to draw from a single painting. (E) would not apply, the painting is of a cloudy woman, nor would (A), as there are no clear religious motifs in the painting.

22. **What is the primary subject of the first painting?**

A. A bird holding a piece of jewelry

B. A Naval skirmish in full swing

C. A horrific murder and robbery

D. An abstract image of a woman shrouded in clouds

E. A religious ceremony

The correct answer is A.

A bird is clearly identified as the prominent foreground image of the picture. Though it seems to feature a sunken ship, we see no Naval battle (B), and it features a corpse, but no indications of murder or robbery (C). (D) refers to the second painting, not the first, and there is no religious ceremony in this picture.

23. Inferring from the text, Jane must be Adele's...

A. Mother

B. Sister

C. Caretaker

D. Employer

E. Maid

The correct answer is C.

Rochester clearly suggests Jane is responsible for Adele's well-being by letting her stay up so late. We have no proof of the other answers, so (C) is the safest.

24. What is Jane's attitude towards her paintings?

A. Loathing

B. Embarrassment

C. Pride

D. Dissatisfaction

E. Indifference

The correct answer is D.

Jane clearly says she was "tormented" by her inability to capture the full idea of each painting. Though she enjoyed painting them, she is not proud of them (C), nor is she embarrassed by them (B) as she speaks freely about their creation. Loathing (A) is too strong a term, and she is anything but indifferent towards her paintings (E).

Questions 25-32. Read the following passage carefully before you decide on your answers to the questions.

"You've just told me some high spots in your memories. Want to hear mine? They're all connected with the sea.

Here's one. When I was on the Squarehead square rigger, bound for Buenos Aires. Full moon in the trades. The old hooker driving 14 knots. I lay on the bowsprit, facing astern, with the water foaming into spume under me. Every mast with sail white in the moonlight - towering high above me. I became drunk with the beauty and singing rhythm of it - and for a second I lost myself, actually lost my life. I was set free! I dissolved into the sea, became white sails and flying spray - became beauty and rhythm, became moonlight and the ship and the high dim-starred sky. I belonged, without past or future, within peace and unity and a wild joy, within something greater than my own life, or the life of man, to Life itself! To God if you want to put it that way.

Then another time, on the American line, when I was lookout in the crow's nest on the dawn watch. A calm sea that time. Only a lazy ground swell and a slow drousy roll of the ship. The passengers asleep and none of the crew in sight. No sound of man. Black smoke pouring from the funnels behind and beneath me. Dreaming, not keeping lookout, feeling alone, and above, and apart, watching the dawn creep like a painted dream over the sky and sea which slept together.

Then the moment of ecstatic freedom came. The peace, the end of the quest, the last harbor, the joy of belonging to a fulfillment beyond men's lousy, greedy fears and hopes and dreams! And several other times in my life, when I was swimming far out, or lying alone on the beach, I have had the same experience. Became the sun, the hot sand, green seaweed anchored to a rock, swaying in the tide. Like a saint's vision of beatitude. Like the veil of things as they seem drawn back by an unseen hand. For a second you see - and seeing the secret, are the secret. For a second there is meaning! Then the hand lets the veil fall and you are alone, lost in the fog again, stumbling on toward no where, for no good reason!

it was a great mistake, my being born a man. I would have been much more successful as a seagull or fish. As it is, I will always be a stranger who never feels at home, who does not want and is not really wanted, who can never belong, who must always be a little in love with death."

25. What adjective best describes Edmund's tone in this piece?

A. Disaffected

B. Morose

C. Longing

D. Celebratory

E. Inspired

The correct answer is C.

This monologue is a memory piece describing Edmund's happiest days. "Longing" best describes this tone.

26. This piece can best be described as...

A. A poem

B. A dramatic monologue

C. Prose fiction

D. An ode

E. A dirge

The correct answer is B.

The piece is a monologue from Eugene O'Neill's "Long Day's Journey Into Night". It contains few poetic elements, and is not a prose piece, as it's written in first person and does not break this form.

27. What are the two primary contrasts of this piece?

A. The sea with the land; drunkenness with sobriety.

B. Depression and joy; sailing with being "anchored".

C. The wild sea with the calm sea; ecstasy with numbness.

D. Edmund with his father; freedom with responsibility.

E. Humanity with nature; godlessness with holiness.

The correct answer is C.

Edmund uses the sea to characterize his own emotional ups and downs. (C) is the best answer.

28. The author conveys the sea using what primary technique?

A. Analogy

B. Assonance

C. Simile

D. Personification

E. Imagery

The correct answer is E.

Edmund does not describe the sea with an analogy, nor with any specific poetic devices beyond imagery. He describes how it looks, sounds, and how that makes him feel.

29. The phrase "like a saint's vision of beatitude" serves to reinforce what idea?

A. Edmund's desire to die.

B. Edmund finds spirituality in nature.

C. Edmund wishes to sail again.

D. Edmund wishes to repent

E. Edmund dislikes religion.

The correct answer is B.

"Beatitudes" are saintly blessings. In this sentence, Edmund is describing how he finds such things only in nature, specifically the sea.

30. In the first paragraph, the author characterizes this piece as a...

A. Story-within-a-story

B. Memory

C. Soliloquy

D. Ballad

E. Fabrication

The correct answer is B.

Right off the bat, Edmund characterizes this piece as a memory tale.

31. Where does the primary shift in tone occur in this piece?

A. Paragraph two, "I became drunk with the beauty..."

B. Paragraph three, "The another time, on the American line..."

C. Paragraph four, "Then that moment of ecstatic freedom came!"

D. Paragraph four, "Then the hand lets the veil fall..."

E. Paragraph five, "I will always be a stranger..."

The correct answer is D.

"The hand lets the veil fall" is the "climax" of this piece. Until that point, Edmund's story is happy, building up to pure ecstasy. With that line, the piece becomes somber and regretful.

32. What natural image does the author use to contrast the sea and its feelings of freedom?

A. Black smoke

B. Fog

C. Spray

D. Seagull

E. Waves

The correct answer is B.

Edmund describes the fog as his counter to the sea. The sea makes him feel alive and open, the fog makes him feel numb and depressed.

Questions 33-40. Read the following passage carefully before you decide on your answers to the questions.

In a village of La Mancha, the name of which I have no desire to call to mind, there lived not long since one of those gentlemen that keep a lance in the lance-rack, an old buckler, a lean hack, and a greyhound for coursing. An olla of rather more beef than mutton, a salad on most nights, scraps on Saturdays, lentils on Fridays, and a pigeon or so extra on Sundays, made away with three-quarters of his income. The rest of it went in a doublet of fine cloth and velvet breeches and shoes to match for holidays, while on week-days he made a brave figure in his best homespun. He had in his house a housekeeper past forty, a niece under twenty, and a lad for the field and market-place, who used to saddle the hack as well as handle the bill-hook. The age of this gentleman of ours was bordering on fifty; he was of a hardy habit, spare, gaunt-featured, a very early riser and a great sportsman. They will have it his surname was Quixada or Quesada (for here there is some difference of opinion among the authors who write on the subject), although from reasonable conjectures it seems plain that he was called Quexana. This, however, is of but little importance to our tale; it will be enough not to stray a hair's breadth from the truth in the telling of it.

You must know, then, that the above-named gentleman whenever he was at leisure (which was mostly all the year round) gave himself up to reading books of chivalry with such ardour and avidity that he almost entirely neglected the pursuit of his field-sports, and even the management of his property; and to such a pitch did his eagerness and infatuation go that he sold many an acre of tillage land to buy books of chivalry to read, and brought home as many of them as he could get. But of all there were none he liked so well as those of the famous Feliciano de Silva's composition, for their lucidity of style and complicated conceits were as pearls in his sight, particularly when in his reading he came upon courtships and cartels, where he often found passages like "the reason of the unreason with which my reason is afflicted so weakens my reason that with reason I murmur at your beauty;" or again, "the high heavens, that of your divinity divinely fortify you with the stars, render you deserving of the desert your greatness deserves." Over conceits of this sort the poor gentleman lost his wits, and used to lie awake striving to understand them and worm the meaning out of them; what Aristotle himself could not have made out or extracted had he come to life again for that special purpose. He was not at all easy about the wounds which Don Belianis gave and took, because it seemed to him that, great as were the surgeons who had cured him, he must have had his face and body covered all over with seams and scars. He commended, however, the author's way of ending his book with the promise of that interminable adventure, and many a time was he tempted to take up his pen and finish it properly as is there proposed, which no doubt he would have done, and made a successful piece of work of it too, had not greater and more absorbing thoughts prevented him.

33. The author's tone in this piece can best be described as...

A. Heroic

B. Comedic

C. Florid

D. Epic

E. Mysterious

The correct answer is B.

The passage contains several wry commentaries and witty asides to the audience which characterize the piece as comedic in tone, such as the author's insistence that he does not wish to remember specific names. The actions of the person described, likewise, are absurd, as he spends his time not working, spending his money on ridiculous finery, and reading unrealistic novels.

34. The line "were as pearls to his sight" is an example of a...

A. Metaphor

B. Analogy

C. Simile

D. Allegory

E. Conceit

The correct answer is C.

The hardest false answer to eliminate here is (B), "Analogy." The difficulty arises because an analogy is also a comparison between unlike things, but it generally is more elaborate, drawing more than one point of comparison. These points may themselves be in the form of similes or metaphors. The question directs your attention to a single phrase, in which the books of the de Silva are described as pleasing Don Quixote the way a pearl would please his eye. A single phrase couldn't convey an entire analogy any more than it could an elaborate allegory, and the presence of "as" indicated that this is a simile, not a metaphor.

35. **Our main character's attitude towards reading can best be described as…**

A. Lackadaisical

B. Unusual

C. Illiterate

D. Obsessive

E. Joyous

The correct answer is D.

The author explains the main character reads with "ardour and avidity" such that he neglects other household chores. (A), (B), and (C) do not apply, and though he certainly could be said to enjoy reading, the piece clearly characterizes this behavior as obsessive and not joyous (E).

36. **The passage "the high heavens, that of your divinity divinely fortify you with the stars, render you deserving of the desert your greatness deserves" contains several examples what poetic device?**

A. Alliteration

B. Onomatopoeia

C. Diction

D. Resonance

E. Enjambment

The correct answer is A.

The answer (D), "Resonance," is intended to be tricky – you could make an argument that the passage exemplifies the combination of a rich variety of sounds, but the question asks about several examples of a particular device. The best answer to the question as it is written is "alliteration," because several discrete examples of alliteration can be found in the passage "Enjambment" is only meaningful in the context of lines of verse; since this passage is from a novel written in prose, it canbe safely eliminated.

37. According to the text, who is Count Belianis?

A. A historical champion

B. A fictional character

C. A competing nobleman

D. A romantic rival

E. A dead family member

The correct answer is B.

The piece mentions Belianis as being a character created by Feliciano de Silva, one who is often harmed in the course of his adventures and is likely covered in scars.

38. The passage "it will be enough not to stray a hair's breadth from the truth in the telling of it" characterizes the previous passage as...

A. Essential

B. Metaphorical

C. Unimportant

D. Esoteric

E. Bland

The correct answer is C.

The quoted passage is one of the author's wry asides. A moment earlier he was describing the surname of the main character, but he cannot recall the correct name, explaining that it doesn't matter anyway.

39. What are the two defining traits of the main character described above?

A. Laziness and obsessiveness

B. Ignorance and piousness

C. Diligence and valor

D. Prideful and vain

E. Curious and kindhearted

The correct answer is A.

The character is said to rarely work nor even to play outside, hiring servants to take care of him. Yet he reads obsessively, even to the point of it affecting his mental health. He exhibits no piousness, so (B) is inaccurate, nor does he exhibit pride, diligence, or kindheartedness. Indeed, he seems rather aloof and disconnected.

40. The final sentence of this excerpt is an example of...

A. Satire

B. Foreshadowing

C. Interstitial

D. Subtext

E. Premonition

The correct answer is B.

The main character finds pleasure in how the author always ends with the promise of a new adventure, suggesting he will go on one himself. The entire selection could be considered satirical, but the last sentence in particular holds no special satirical value, so A is inaccurate. The sentence is not an interstitial (C) nor does it hold subtextual value (D). Since we do not know where the story goes from here, we cannot say for certain if this is a premonition (E).

Questions 41-48. Read the following passage carefully before you decide on your answers to the questions.

Every light in the hall was ablaze; every lamp turned as high as it could be without smoking the chimney or threatening explosion. The lamps were fixed at intervals against the wall, encircling the whole room. Some one had gathered orange and lemon branches, and with these fashioned graceful festoons between. The dark green of the branches stood out and glistened against the white muslin curtains which draped the windows, and which puffed, floated, and flapped at the capricious will of a stiff breeze that swept up from the Gulf.

It was Saturday night a few weeks after the intimate conversation held between Robert and Madame Ratignolle on their way from the beach. An unusual number of husbands, fathers, and friends had come down to stay over Sunday; and they were being suitably entertained by their families, with the material help of Madame Lebrun. The dining tables had all been removed to one end of the hall, and the chairs ranged about in rows and in clusters. Each little family group had had its say and exchanged its domestic gossip earlier in the evening. There was now an apparent disposition to relax; to widen the circle of confidences and give a more general tone to the conversation.

Many of the children had been permitted to sit up beyond their usual bedtime. A small band of them were lying on their stomachs on the floor looking at the colored sheets of the comic papers which Mr. Pontellier had brought down. The little Pontellier boys were permitting them to do so, and making their authority felt.

Music, dancing, and a recitation or two were the entertainments furnished, or rather, offered. But there was nothing systematic about the programme, no appearance of prearrangement nor even premeditation.

At an early hour in the evening the Farival twins were prevailed upon to play the piano. They were girls of fourteen, always clad in the Virgin's colors, blue and white, having been dedicated to the Blessed Virgin at their baptism. They played a duet from "Zampa," and at the earnest solicitation of every one present followed it with the overture to "The Poet and the Peasant."

"Allez vous-en! Sapristi!" shrieked the parrot outside the door. He was the only being present who possessed sufficient candor to admit that he was not listening to these gracious performances for the first time that summer. Old Monsieur Farival, grandfather of the twins, grew indignant over the interruption, and insisted upon having the bird removed and consigned to regions of darkness. Victor Lebrun objected; and his decrees were as immutable as those of Fate. The parrot fortunately offered no further interruption to the entertainment, the whole venom of his nature apparently having been cherished up and hurled against the twins in that one impetuous outburst.

41. This passage "*and his decrees were as immutable as those of Fate*" characterizes its subject, how?

A. He will not be denied

B. He is an angry man

C. He is the eldest in the family

D. He strikes fear into those around him

E. He is easily ignored

The correct answer is A.

We do not have enough information to determine the speaker's age (C), nor do we learn enough about the scene to determine if he is angry (B) or if he creates fear in others (D). A is the safest choice. (E) does not apply at all.

42. "Music, dancing, and a recitation or two were the entertainments furnished, or rather, offered." This unusual passage speaks to the proceeding's...

A. Modest entertainment

B. Banality and blandness

C. Informality and spontaneity

D. Inexpensiveness and triteness

E. Luster and joyousness

The correct answer is C.

The author's ambiguous phrasing suggests a party that was thrown together on the fly. "A recitation or two" and "furnished, or rather, offered" suggest an event that had little fore-planning.

43. **The term "prevailed upon" in paragraph five characterizes the Farival twins as...**

A. Talented

B. Reluctant

C. Timid

D. Eager

E. Popular

The correct answer is B.

One is "prevailed upon" when one takes convincing to do something. The phrase does not speak to their talent (A) or popularity (E), and it does not suggest they are eager (D) or necessarily timid (C).

44. **In context, the line "the whole venom of his nature apparently having been cherished up and hurled against the twins in that one impetuous outburst" (paragraph six) can best be paraphrased as...**

A. He calmed immediately after being chastised

B. He spent all of his pent-up rage in one interjection

C. He naturally felt himself sickened by these proceedings

D. He exposed his deep feelings for them all in out exclamation

E. He hated the twins

The correct answer is B.

The parrot "cherished" (or pent-up) his rage and then "hurled it against the twins", falling silent thereafter. (A) is close but inaccurate, the bird did not require chastisement to calm down. (C), (D), and (E) would not apply to a disruptive parrot.

45. **What aspect of imagery consistently appears in this excerpt?**

A. Odor

B. Sound

C. Tactile sensation

D. Color

E. Emotion

The correct answer is E.

The piece features descriptions of the colors of branches, the twins' outfits, the comic pages, and the curtains. Little attention is paid to describing actual sound, less so to odor or touch. Emotion (E) is not an aspect of imagery.

46. "With the material help of Madame Lebrun" (paragraph two) implies what in context?

A. Madame Lebrun barely helped

B. Madame Lebrun assisted in constructing the stage

C. Madame Lebrun provided many of the physical necessities

D. Madame Lebrun aided as best she could

E. Madame Lebrun provided only reluctant support

The correct answer is C.

"Material help" suggests she provided furniture, such as the tables and chairs later described in the paragraph.

47. The gathering depicted in the excerpt can best be described as...

A. Bland

B. Ineffective

C. Low-key

D. Snobbish

E. Enjoyable

The correct answer is E.

The gathering is depicted as lively and inexpensive, not bland (A) or snobbish (D). It is also an exciting event with many entertainments, so ineffective (B) and low-key (C) are poor descriptors.

48. Paragraph five implies the primary characteristic of the Farival twins is their...

A. Beauty

B. Skill

C. Oddness

D. Chicness

E. Purity

The correct answer is E.

The author takes great pains to describe them by their "virgin's colors" and their virgin baptism. Their physical appearance and talent is barely touched on. Their primary descriptor is their purity.

Questions 49-55. Read the following passage carefully before you decide on your answers to the questions.

O wild West Wind, thou breath of Autumn's being,
Thou, from whose unseen presence the leaves dead
Are driven, like ghosts from an enchanter fleeing,

Yellow, and black, and pale, and hectic red,
Pestilence-stricken multitudes: O thou,
Who chariotest to their dark wintry bed

The winged seeds, where they lie cold and low,
Each like a corpse within its grave, until
Thine azure sister of the Spring shall blow

Her clarion o'er the dreaming earth, and fill
(Driving sweet buds like flocks to feed in air)
With living hues and odors plain and hill:

Wild Spirit, which art moving everywhere;
Destroyer and preserver; hear, oh, hear!

Thou on whose stream, 'mid the steep sky's commotion,
Loose clouds like earth's decaying leaves are shed,
Shook from the tangled boughs of Heaven and Ocean,

Angels of rain and lightning: there are spread
On the blue surface of thine aery surge,
Like the bright hair uplifted from the head

Of some fierce Maenad, even from the dim verge
Of the horizon to the zenith's height,
The locks of the approaching storm. Thou dirge

Of the dying year, to which this closing night
Will be the dome of a vast sepulchre,
Vaulted with all thy congregated might

Of vapors, from whose solid atmosphere
Black rain, and fire, and hail will burst: oh, hear!

49. The first line of this poem exhibits what poetic devices?

I. Alliteration

II. Personification

III. Onomatopoeia

A. Only I

B. Only II

C. Only III

D. I and II

E. I, II, and III

The correct answer is D.

"Wild West wind" is an alliteration and "breath" is a personification of the wind the poem goes on to describe.

50. What best describes the final stanza of this selection?

A. Slant rhyme

B. Heroic couplet

C. Hyperbole

D. Irony

E. Blank verse

The correct answer is B.

The final line is a classic heroic couplet, it contains an AA rhyme and has ten syllables per line. "Rhyme" is too vague for this question (A), and it exhibits no hyperbole (C), irony (D), or blank verse (E).

51. **"Wild Spirit, which art moving everywhere; Destroyer and preserver; hear, oh, hear!" This passage displays a…**

A. Enjambment

B. Slant rhyme

C. Simile

D. Iamb

E. Allegory

The correct answer is B.

"Everywhere" and "hear" are not "true" rhymes, though they are close. The selection features no enjambment (A), simile (C), iamb (D), or allegory (E).

52. **This poem is written in what style?**

A. Vers libre

B. Heroic couplet

C. Epic saga

D. Imagist soliloquy

E. Iambic pentameter

The correct answer is E.

The piece features ten syllables per line divided into five iambs, suggesting similarities to a sonnet.

53. **What in the poem is compared to "Angels of rain and lightning"?**

A. The wind

B. Maenads

C. Clouds

D. Human souls

E. Autumn

The correct answer is C.

Two lines earlier the poem describes "loose clouds" which are later likened to angels of rain and lightning.

**54. "Of the dying year, to which this closing night/ Will be the dome of a vast sepulchre,/ Vaulted with all thy congregated might"
This passage exhibits…**

A. A metaphor

B. An allegory

C. A comparison

D. A consonance

E. An allusion

The correct answer is A.

A metaphor is the best way to describe this passage, as it suggests the "closing night" will be the "dome of a vast sepulcher", without a comparative term such as "like" or "as".

55. How many stanzas does this poem contain?

A. Four

B. Five

C. Eight

D. Ten

E. Twelve

The correct answer is D.

There are ten stanzas, though they are irregular in terms of line count.

Sample Test Three

Section I

Multiple Choice Questions.
Time: 60 minutes.
Percent of total grade on the exam: 45 percent.

Instructions: This section of the exam consists of selections from literary works and questions on their content, form, and style. After reading each passage and poem, choose the best answer to each question and then fill in the corresponding oval on the answer sheet.

Questions 1-8. Read the following passage carefully before you decide on your answers to the questions.

William Wordsworth — "I Wandered Lonely As A Cloud"

I wandered lonely as a cloud
That floats on high o'er vales and hills,
When all at once I saw a crowd,
A host, of golden daffodils;
Beside the lake, beneath the trees,
Fluttering and dancing in the breez(E).

Continuous as the stars that shine
And twinkle on the milky way,
They stretched in never-ending line
Along the margin of a bay:
Ten thousand saw I at a glance,
Tossing their heads in sprightly danc(E).

The waves beside them danced; but they
Out-did the sparkling waves in glee:
A poet could not but be gay,
In such a jocund company:
I gazed—and gazed—but little thought
What wealth the show to me had brought:

For oft, when on my couch I lie
In vacant or in pensive mood,
They flash upon that inward eye
Which is the bliss of solitude;
And then my heart with pleasure fills,
And dances with the daffodils.

1. **What type of passage is the above selection?**

   A. Lyrical poem

   B. Haiku poem

   C. Acrostic poem

   D. Limerick poem

   E. Cinquain poem

2. **The permanence of stars as compared with flowers emphasizes**

   A. the impermanence of life.

   B. the permanence of memory for the poet.

   C. the earlier comparison of the sky to the lake.

   D. that stars are frozen above and daffodils dance below.

   E. the similarity of the inward eye with the fleeting bliss of solitud(E)

3. **The scheme of the poem is**

   A. ballad.

   B. Scottish stanza.

   C. Spenserian stanza.

   D. quatrain-couplet.

   E. sonnet.

4. **This poem uses the ________ metric pattern.**

   A. dactylic tetrameter

   B. trochaic pentameter

   C. trochaic tetrameter

   D. iambic pentameter

   E. iambic tetrameter

5. **What is a literary device used in the last two lines of the first two stanzas?**

A. Simile.

B. Metaphor.

C. Personification.

D. Allegory.

E. Paradox.

6. **In what literary period did this author write?**

A. Edwardian Movement.

B. Romanticism.

C. Existentialism.

D. Renaissance Literature.

E. Victorian Movement.

7. **As used in this poem, the best choice for a synonym of jocund means________**

A. pleasant.

B. vapid.

C. lonely.

D. jovial.

E. sad.

8. **What literary device is used in line 9, "They stretched in never-ending line." ?**

A. hyperbole.

B. onomatopoeia.

C. epithet.

D. irony.

E. anecdote.

Questions 9-16. Read the following selection and answer the questions below, selecting the best choice of the options presented.

My Bondage and My Freedom

Disappearing from the kind reader, in a flying cloud or balloon (pardon the figure), driven by the wind, and knowing not where I should land—whether in slavery or in freedom—it is proper that I should remove, at once, all anxiety, by frankly making known where I alighted. The flight Disappearing from the kind reader, in a flying cloud or balloon (pardon the figure), driven by the wind, and knowing not where I should land--whether in slavery or in freedom--it is proper that I should remove, at once, all anxiety, by frankly making known where I alighted. The flight was a bold and perilous one; but here I am, in the great city of New York, safe and sound, without loss of blood or bone. In less than a week after leaving Baltimore, I was walking amid the hurrying throng, and gazing upon the dazzling wonders of Broadway. The dreams of my childhood and the purposes of my manhood were now fulfilled. A free state around me, and a free earth under my feet! What a moment was this to me! A whole year was pressed into a single day. A new world burst upon my agitated vision. I have often been asked, by kind friends to whom I have told my story, how I felt when first I found myself beyond the limits of slavery; and I must say here, as I have often said to them, there is scarcely anything about which I could not give a more satisfactory answer. It was a moment of joyous excitement, which no words can describe. In a letter to a friend, written soon after reaching New York. I said I felt as one might be supposed to feel, on escaping from a den of hungry lions.

9. In what literary period did this author write?

A. Transcendentalism.

B. Realism.

C. Victorian.

D. Modernism.

E. Naturalism.

10. When the author writes "escaping from a den of hungry lions," what type of literary device is he using?

A. Simile.

B. Personification.

C. Metaphor.

D. Hyperbole.

E. Irony.

11. **What is the author's theme in this passage?**

    A. Anger at being a slave.

    B. Numb, as one might be supposed to feel.

    C. Confusion at the new things he is seeing.

    D. Self-discovery after flight from slavery.

    E. None of these describe his theme.

12. **In context of the passage, the opening phrase "to the kind reader" used by the author sets what kind of opening tone?**

    A. Friendly

    B. Condescending

    C. Boisterous

    D. Prideful

    E. Meek

13. **The author of this book relays his own experiences fighting slavery? Why does he fight against it (i.e. what is the theme of the book)?**

    A. Slavery is unnatural.

    B. Slavery wasn't needed as an economic engine.

    C. Slavery was morally acceptable.

    D. Slavery enabled him to see the light of day.

    E. Slavery made time move too quickly.

14. **What does the author figuratively mean by "hurrying throng"?**

    A. The people that bump into him walking past him.

    B. His blurred vision from bright sunlight.

    C. The New York tradesmen rushing to their jobs.

    D. The busy middle class.

    E. The bustling crowd of free people.

15. What is the author's tone?

A. Cautious

B. Enlightened

C. Exuberant

D. Nervous

E. None of these apply

16. Who wrote this novel?

A. E.B. White

B. Francis Scott

C. Frederick Douglass

D. Harriet Beecher Stowe

E. Ralph Waldo Emerson

Questions 17-24. Read the following poem by Emily Dickenson and answer the questions below, selecting the best choice of the options presented.

IN THE GARDEN

A bird came down the walk:
He did not know I saw;
He bit an angle-worm in halves
And ate the fellow, raw.

And then, he drank a dew
From a convenient grass,
And then hopped sidewise to the wall
To let a beetle pass.

He glanced with rapid eyes
That hurried all abroad,—
They looked like frightened beads, I thought;
He stirred his velvet head

Like one in danger; cautious,
I offered him a crumb,
And he unrolled his feathers
And rowed him softer home

Than oars divide the ocean,

Too silver for a seam,
Or butterflies, off banks of noon,
Leap, splashless, as they swim.

17. **What type of literary device is used in the author's phrase, "drank a dew"?**

A. Allusion.

B. Foreshadowing.

C. Juxtaposition.

D. Satire.

E. Alliteration.

18. **The author describes action beginning in line 15 of the bird's flight. What type of literary device is used?**

A. Simile.

B. Metaphor.

C. Irony.

D. Satire.

E. None of these are correct.

19. **The rhyme scheme of the poem (except the final three stanzas) is**

A. XAXA or Ghazal.

B. Scottish stanza.

C. Spenserian stanza.

D. quatrain-couplet.

E. Petrarchan sonnet.

20. **This poem uses a particular metric pattern throughout the poem, except in the third line of each stanza. What is the main metric pattern?**

A. dactylic tetrameter

B. trochaic trimeter

C. trochaic tetrameter

D. iambic pentameter

E. iambic trimeter

21. **What literary device is used when the bird's eyes are compared to frightened beads?**

A. Reverse Personification.

B. Metaphor.

C. Simile.

D. Allegory.

E. Paradox.

22. **What does the dash at the end of line 12 represent?**

A. A change in focus from the bird to the water.

B. An abrupt change for the bird.

C. An emotional shift from fear to fascination.

D. It only shows the middle of the poem.

E. None of these accurately describe the meaning of the dash.

23. **What is the author's tone in this poem?**

A. She takes the perspective of the bird.

B. The author's tone is harsh toward potential prey.

C. The tone is factual, describing the actions of a bird.

D. Ornithology fascinated the author and she uses flowery language to describe it.

E. The author's tone is gentle and respectful demeanor regarding nature.

24. **What is a potential meaning of the allegory used by the author?**

A. It could reveal the author's perceptions of God.

B. The allegory could be looking at the author's view of marriage.

C. The author could reveal the hierarchy between man and beast.

D. Descriptions of the forces of nature could parallel emotions.

E. There is no allegory used as a literary device in this poem.

Questions 25-32. Read the following selection and answer the questions below, selecting the best choice of the options presented.

There is no frigate like a book
To take us lands away,
Nor any coursers like a page
Of prancing poetry;
This traverse may the poorest take
Without oppress of toll;
How frugal is the chariot
That bears the human soul!

25. **Authors use particular literary structures for descriptions. What best explains the type that Emily Dickinson employs in this poem?**

A. Connotative

B. Argumentative

C. Narrative

D. Rhetoric

E. Expository

26. **How many types of transport does the author incorporate?**

A. Two

B. Three

C. Four

D. Five

E. None

27. If the words 'frigate, coursers, and traverse' were replaced with synonyms, what would the best choice of the following options include?

A. Train, car, carriage

B. Train, horse, carriage

C. Ship, car, carriage

D. Ship, car, train

E. Ship, horse, carriage

28. Which of the following descriptions more closely describes the author's intended meaning of poem?

A. Difficulties at work

B. The importance of books

C. Confessions for the soul

D. Poverty makes things difficult

E. Describing modes of transportation

29. There are very descriptive and strong feelings conveyed by the poet. Which of the following is not the definition of what she shares?

A. Overstatement

B. Paradox

C. Understatement

D. Irony

E. Sarcasm

30. What kind of poetry form is utilized by Ms. Dickinson in this poem?

A. Alexandrine

B. Didactic poetry

C. Ballad stanza

D. Epitaph

E. Rondel

31. Who is the author of this poem?

A. Emily Dickinson

B. Emily Brontë

C. Emily Mortimer

D. Lord Byron

E. William Blake

32. When the boat is compared to a book, that is an example of:

A. a metaphor.

B. personification.

C. a simile.

D. an extended metaphor.

E. none of these.

Questions 33-40. Read the following selection and answer the questions below, selecting the best choice of the options presented.

A man is born into this world with only a tiny spark of goodness in him. The spark is God, it is the soul; the rest is ugliness and evil, a shell. The spark must be guarded like a treasure, it must be nurtured, it must be fanned into flame. It must learn to seek out other sparks, it must dominate the shell. Anything can be a shell, Reuven. Anything. Indifference, laziness, brutality, and genius. Yes, even a great mind can be a shell and choke the spark.

"Reuven, the Master of the Universe blessed me with a brilliant son. And he cursed me with all the problems of raising him. Ah, what it is to have a Daniel, whose mind is like a pearl, like a sun. Reuven, when my Daniel was four years old, I saw him reading a story from a book. And I was frightened. He did not read the story, he swallowed it, as one swallows food or water. There was no soul in my four-year-old Daniel, there was only his mind. He was a mind in a body without a soul. It was a story in a Yiddish book about a poor Jew and his struggles to get to Eretz Yisroel before he died. Ah, how that man suffered! And my Daniel *enjoyed* the story, he *enjoyed* the last terrible page, because when he finished it he realized for the first time what a memory he had. He looked at me proudly and told me back the story from memory, and I cried inside my heart. I went away and cried to the Master of the Universe, 'What have you done to me? A mind like this I need for a son? A *heart* I need for a son, a *soul* I need for a son, *compassion* I want for my son, righteousness, mercy, strength to suffer and carry pain, *that* I want from my son, not a mind without a soul!'"

Reb Saunders paused and took a deep, trembling breath. I tried to swallow; my mouth was sand-dry. Danny sat with his right hand over his eyes, his glasses pushed up on his forehead. He was crying silently, his shoulders quivering. Reb Saunders did not look at him.

33. According to the passage, what was the goal behind raising Danny in silence?

A. For the speaker to be cruel.

B. The speaker thought he was being noble.

C. The narrator believed by being harsh, he was right.

D. The speaker wanted other people to think they were normal.

E. He wanted to develop Danny's compassion and soul.

34. When the narrator describes Danny "swallowing" the story, what kind of literary device is employed?

A. A simile.

B. A metaphor.

C. An allusion.

D. Personification.

E. An alliteration.

35. What is the author doing when using italics?

A. The author is using short words to mean big things.

B. The author signifies the important things in a person's life.

C. The speaker is listing the attributes of his son.

D. The speaker shows what his son understood in the stories.

E. None of these things apply to those words.

36. When Reb's mouth went "sand-dry," this is an example of:

A. a parody.

B. an allusion.

C. a synecdoche.

D. a metaphor.

E. an oxymoron.

37. **Throughout the book, Reuven had been the peripheral narrator. Who is the narrator in this section?**

A. It is still Reuven.

B. It is Reb Saunders

C. It is Danny.

D. It is a third person narrator.

E. It is Eretz Yisroel.

38. **This passage is written as:**

A. the denouement.

B. the complication.

C. the climax.

D. the suspense.

E. the introduction.

39. **What is the theme of this passage?**

A. Recounting the last moments of an old man's life.

B. The discussion of coming marriage of Danny.

C. The symbolism of reading as an alternative for family interactions.

D. The adoption of Reuven by Reb.

E. Another example of Jews suffering to get further in life.

40. **What is the writing style used by this author in this passage?**

A. Expository

B. Didactic

C. Persuasive

D. Descriptive

E. Theatrical

Questions 41-48. Read the following selection and answer the questions below, selecting the best choice of the options presented.

Okonkwo and his fellow prisoners were set free as soon as the fine was paid. The District Commissioner spoke to them again about the great queen, and about peace and good government. But the men did not listen. They just sat and looked at him and at his interpreter. In the end they were given back their bags and sheathed machetes and told to go home. They rose and left the courthouse. They neither spoke to anyone nor among themselves.

The courthouse, like the church, was but a little way outside the village. The footpath that linked them was a very busy one because it also led to the stream, beyond the court. It was open and sandy. Footpaths were open and sandy in the dry season. But when the rains came the bush grew thick on either side and closed in on the path. It was now dry season.

As they made their way to the village the six men met women and children going to the stream with their waterpots. But them wore such heavy and fearsome looks to them, but edged out of the way to let them pass. In the village little groups of men joined them until they became a sizable company. They walked silently. As each of the six men got to his compound, he turned in, taking some of the crowd with him. The village was air in a silent, suppressed way.

Ezinma had prepared some food for her father as soon as news spread that the six men would be released. She took it to him in his obi. He ate absentmindedly. He had no appetite, he only ate to please her. His male relations and friends had gathered in his obi, and Obierika was urging him to eat. Nobody else spoke, but they noticed the log stripes on Okonkwo's back where the warder's whip had cut into his flesh.

41. Who is the protagonist of this story?

A. Obierika

B. Ezinma

C. Okonkwo

D. The District Commissioner

E. Okonkwo's wife

42. What is the name of this book?

A. Obi

B. Things Fall Apart

C. Let the Circle Be Unbroken

D. Ashes and Dust

E. The rainy season

43. What category of literature does this book represent?

A. Romantic.

B. Victorian.

C. Modernism.

D. Transcendentalism.

E. Post Colonial.

44. The main character of the book appears to have what occur throughout the book?

A. He is a champion of his village.

B. He shows that he is good provider for his family.

C. He represents the disintegration of his society against the change.

D. The village doesn't support him.

E. The courthouse is targeting him to get rid of the village.

45. The narrative structure of this passage is:

A. simple narrative.

B. cause and effect.

C. chronological.

D. inductive.

E. deductive.

46. The literary style of the book is:

A. comedy.

B. tragedy.

C. drama.

D. exploration.

E. quest.

47. How is this passage narrated?

A. First person.

B. Second person.

C. Third person.

D. Omniscient observer.

E. None of these.

48. What is the main idea of this passage?

A. The village members continue to carry out the traditions of their ancestors.

B. There is a drought affecting crops and village life.

C. The interpreter was sharing with them a new way of life.

D. The government and church were coming together for the people.

E. People are resistant to change, and the village and protagonist illustrate it.

Questions 49-55. Read the following selection and answer the questions below, selecting the best choice of the options presented.

Mornings, he likes to sit in his new leather chair by his new living room window, looking out across the rooftops and chimney pots, the clotheslines and telegraph lines and office towers. It's the first time Manhattan, from high above, hasn't crushed him with desire. On the contrary the view makes him feel smug. All those people down there, striving, hustling, pushing, shoving, busting to get what Willie's already got. In spades. He lights a cigarette, blows a jet of smoke against the window. Suckers.

49. The subject in this passage is:

A. a character, and seems to be the lead of the story.

B. a supporting character.

C. has an attitude of a criminal.

D. is female.

E. has been poor his whole life.

50. **What kind of description is the author providing of this scene?**

    A. Backstory of the character.

    B. A characterization of what the character is like.

    C. A narrative in the first person.

    D. The unreliable narrative about a character.

    E. The author is using a persuasive argument.

51. **What types of words are "striving, hustling, pushing, shoving, bustling"?**

    A. Adjectives

    B. Adverbs

    C. Nouns

    D. Gerunds

    E. Verbs

52. **If you had to explain the phrase "crushed him" in the paragraph above and context of the paragraph, what would be the best appropriate explanation?**

    A. The city sustained him with all the opportunity available.

    B. The city called to him to be part of its life.

    C. The city complimented him for everything he has achieved.

    D. The city had energized him to get what he felt he deserved.

    E. The city smothered him with all its offerings.

53. **Replacing the word "smug" with an antonym in context would have which of the following used?**

    A. Sleepy

    B. Prideful

    C. Humble

    D. Self-satisfied

    E. Elated

54. **When the author uses the phrase, "In spades," which of the following is best representing what he is referencing?**

A. The apartment where Willie is living.

B. The personal satisfaction of accumulated wealth.

C. Modern comforts in his home.

D. The loved ones surrounding him.

E. None of these is representative.

55. **By using the introductory word "Mornings," the author achieves what?**

A. An optimistic tone for the passage.

B. A simple description of time of day, or chronology for the passage.

C. It's the start of the book, so he sets the passage at "day one."

D. A and C.

E. None of these.

Free Response Essay Sample Questions

Section II

Time: 120 minutes

Percent of total grade on the exam: 55 percent.

Question 1.

(Suggested time—40 minutes. This question counts as one-third of the total essay section score.)

In the following poem, a great battle is being waged, but it is within the speaker's soul. Read the speech carefully. Then write a well-organized essay in which you analyze how Shakespeare uses elements such as allusion, figurative language, and tone to convey the speaker's complex response to the love he holds for this beauty.

Since brass, nor stone, nor earth, nor boundless sea,
But sad mortality o'ersways their power,
How with this rage shall beauty hold a plea,
Whose action is no stronger than a flower?
O how shall summer's honey breath hold out
Against the wrackful siege of batt'ring days,
When rocks impregnable are not so stout,
Nor gates of steel so strong, but Time decays?
O fearful meditation! where, alack,
Shall Time's best jewel from Time's chest lie hid?
Or what strong hand can hold his swift foot back?
Or who his spoil of beauty can forbid?
O none, unless this miracle have might,
That in black ink my love may still shine bright.

Shakespeare, 1609

Sample Test Three

Question 2.
(Suggested time—40 minutes. This question counts as one-third of the total essay section score.)

The following passage is from Moby Dick. Read the passage carefully. Then write a well-organized essay in which you analyze how literary devices dramatize the teachings of characters with more experiences to novices. Do not summarize the plot.

> "Consider the subtleness of the sea; how its most dreaded creatures glide under water, unapparent for the most part, and treacherously hidden beneath the loveliest tints of azure. Consider also the devilish brilliance and beauty of many of its most remorseless tribes, as the dainty embellished shape of many species of sharks. Consider, once more, the universal cannibalism of the sea; all whose creatures prey upon each other, carrying on eternal war since the world began.
>
> "Consider all this; and then turn to the green, gentle, and most docile earth; consider them both, the sea and the land; and do you not find a strange analogy to something in yourself? For as this appalling ocean surrounds the verdant land, so in the soul of man there lies one insular Tahiti, full of peace and joy, but encompassed by all the horrors of the half-known life. God keep thee! Push not off from that isle, thou canst never return!"

Question 3.
(Suggested time—40 minutes. This question counts as one-third of the total essay section score.)

A good author exploits the protagonist's inner struggles, developing a fatal flaw that either attracts or repulses a reader as well as the characters in the book. Using a protagonist's suffering over a perceived moral dilemma, use an example of literature to illustrate how not all is always as it appears.

Sample Test Three

Sample Test Three: ANSWER KEY

Question Number	Correct Answer	Your Answer
1.	A	
2.	B	
3.	D	
4.	E	
5.	C	
6.	B	
7.	D	
8.	A	
9.	A	
10.	C	
11.	C	
12.	B	
13.	A	
14.	E	
15.	C	
16.	C	
17.	E	
18.	B	
19.	A	
20.	E	
21.	C	
22.	B	
23.	E	
24.	A	
25.	A	
26.	B	
27.	E	
28.	B	

Question Number	Correct Answer	Your Answer
29.	E	
30.	C	
31.	A	
32.	C	
33.	E	
34.	C	
35.	B	
36.	B	
37.	B	
38.	A	
39.	A	
40.	C	
41.	C	
42.	B	
43.	C	
44.	A	
45.	C	
46.	B	
47.	D	
48.	A	
49.	A	
50.	C	
51.	C	
52.	D	
53.	C	
54.	B	
55.	A	

Answer Key and Rationale

Questions 1-8. Read the following passage carefully before you decide on your answers to the questions.

William Wordsworth — "I Wandered Lonely As A Cloud"

I wandered lonely as a cloud
That floats on high o'er vales and hills,
When all at once I saw a crowd,
A host, of golden daffodils;
Beside the lake, beneath the trees,
Fluttering and dancing in the breeze.

Continuous as the stars that shine
And twinkle on the milky way,
They stretched in never-ending line
Along the margin of a bay:
Ten thousand saw I at a glance,
Tossing their heads in sprightly dance.

The waves beside them danced; but they
Out-did the sparkling waves in glee:
A poet could not but be gay,
In such a jocund company:
I gazed—and gazed—but little thought
What wealth the show to me had brought:

For oft, when on my couch I lie
In vacant or in pensive mood,
They flash upon that inward eye
Which is the bliss of solitude;
And then my heart with pleasure fills,
And dances with the daffodils.

1. **What type of passage is the above selection?**

   A. Lyrical poem

   B. Haiku poem

   C. Acrostic poem

   D. Limerick poem

   E. Cinquain poem

   The correct answer is A.

   This is where literary terms are important. In poetry, many of the devices and nomenclature need to be memorized and understood so you can answer these questions quickly and accurate.

2. **The permanence of stars as compared with flowers emphasizes**

   A. the impermanence of life.

   B. the permanence of memory for the poet.

   C. the earlier comparison of the sky to the lake.

   D. that stars are frozen above and daffodils dance below.

   E. the similarity of the inward eye with the fleeting bliss of solitude.

   The correct answer is B.

   The key word in option A is opposite in meaning and the relationship of the verbs in (D) are not correctly aligned for the comparison. (E) is not part of the poem at all. If you don't know the answer between (B) and (C), look back at the poem - and there is no comparison of sky to lake, so that gives you the right answer.

3. The scheme of the poem is

A. ballad.

B. Scottish stanza.

C. Spenserian stanza.

D. quatrain-couplet.

E. sonnet.

The correct answer is D.

While this may not be one of the typical questions on the test, it is incorporated so you remember to look at general literary definitions. You can also figure this out by looking at quatrain, which has the base that means "four" and couplet means "two" - that is the same pattern as the poem. (E) isn't right because a sonnet is one verse of specific length; a ballad is the manner of telling a story so it isn't (A). There are particular components of (B) and (C), but if you get to this stage and use the root words, you may be able to guess the right answer if you don't know.

4. This poem uses the ________ metric pattern.

A. dactylic tetrameter

B. trochaic pentameter

C. trochaic tetrameter

D. iambic pentameter

E. iambic tetrameter

The correct answer is E.

Similar to the rationale of the first question, you need to know these terms. You can "break them down" into tetra - meaning four - and meter,or beat. Iambic is a rhythm of two, so there are four sets of two beats

5. **What is a literary device used in the last two lines of the first two stanzas?**

A. Simile.

B. Metaphor.

C. Personification.

D. Allegory.

E. Paradox.

The correct answer is C.

When an inanimate or non-human objects is given person-like traits, it's called personification. You should be familiar enough with all the other answers to know that they do not apply, since the couplets that end the first two stanzas do not include explicit comparisons between the daffodils and other things, nor do they invite an allegorical or paradoxical reading. There is always a dimension of metaphor to personification, so (B) may be hard to rule out, but on reflection you will see that (C) is the more precise answer.

6. **In what literary period did this author write?**

A. Edwardian Movement.

B. Romanticism.

C. Existentialism.

D. Renaissance Literature.

E. Victorian Movement.

The correct answer is B.

In an AP situation, your understanding of when great writers of literature wrote, and the context of their writing - when they wrote - often gives additional insights to the meaning of their work or the themes.

7. **As used in this poem, the best choice for a synonym of jocund means**

A. pleasant.

B. vapid.

C. lonely.

D. jovial.

E. sad.

The correct answer is D.

This is a question that tests vocabulary - you should be able to eliminate choices (A), (C), and (E). If you don't know what jocund means, or either vapid or jovial, this is how they are testing for reading comprehension. Jovial is happy and that fits into the structure of the passage within context.

8. **What literary device is used in line 9. "They stretched in never-ending line."**

   A. hyperbole.

   B. onomatopoeia.

   C. epithet.

   D. irony.

   E. anecdote.

The correct answer is A.

While "never-ending line" has the rhythm of a typical epithet (such as "star-cross' d lovers" or "winedark sea"), the distinctive quality of the descriptive term, "never-ending," is that it could not literally be true and so is a figure of speech. "Hyperbole" is the correct term for a figurative exaggeration. "Onomatopoeia" refers to a word that imitates a sound, while an anecdote is a brief narrative. "Irony" can be ruled out based on the context of the poem as a whole.

Questions 9-16. Read the following selection and answer the questions below, selecting the best choice of the options presented.

My Bondage and My Freedom

Disappearing from the kind reader, in a flying cloud or balloon (pardon the figure), driven by the wind, and knowing not where I should land—whether in slavery or in freedom—it is proper that I should remove, at once, all anxiety, by frankly making known where I alighted. The flight Disappearing from the kind reader, in a flying cloud or balloon (pardon the figure), driven by the wind, and knowing not where I should land--whether in slavery or in freedom--it is proper that I should remove, at once, all anxiety, by frankly making known where I alighted. The flight was a bold and perilous one; but here I am, in the great city of New York, safe and sound, without loss of blood or bone. In less than a week after leaving Baltimore, I was walking amid the hurrying throng, and gazing upon the dazzling wonders of Broadway. The dreams of my childhood and the purposes of my manhood were now fulfilled. A free state around me, and a free earth under my feet! What a moment was this to me! A whole year was pressed into a single day. A new world burst upon my agitated vision. I have often been asked, by kind friends to whom I have told my story, how I felt when first I found myself beyond the limits of slavery; and I must say here, as I have often said to them, there is scarcely anything about which I could not give a more satisfactory answer. It was a moment of joyous excitement, which no words can describe. In a letter to a friend, written soon after reaching New York. I said I felt as one might be supposed to feel, on escaping from a den of hungry lions.

9. In what literary period did this author write?

A. Transcendentalism.

B. Realism.

C. Victorian.

D. Modernism.

E. Naturalism.

The correct answer is A.

10. When the author writes "escaping from a den of hungry lions," what type of literary device is he using?

A. Simile

B. Personification.

C. Metaphor.

D. Hyperbole.

E. Irony.

The correct answer is C.

The challenge here is to differentiate between simile and metaphor. In context, the complete sentence reads, "I said I felt as one might be supposed to feel, on escaping from a den of hungry lions." The word "as" in the sentence suggests a simile. Since the question directs you to focus on the phrase, "escaping from a den of hungry lions," the more appropriate answer is the more inclusive term, "metaphor"

11. What is the author's theme in this passage?

A. Anger at being a slave.

B. Numb, as one might be supposed to feel.

C. Confusion at the new things he is seeing.

D. Self-discovery after flight from slavery.

E. None of these describe his theme.

The correct answer is C.

The author is in a storm of new sensations.

12. In context of the passage, the opening phrase "to the kind reader" used by the author sets what kind of opening tone?

A. Friendly

B. Condescending

C. Boisterous

D. Prideful

E. Meek

The correct answer is B.

If you were answering too quickly, you may think (A) is the correct answer. But look at the context. The speaker is pandering to the listener.

13. The author of this book relays his own experiences fighting slavery. Why does he fight against it (i.e. what is the theme of the book)?

A. Slavery is unnatural.

B. Slavery wasn't needed as an economic engine.

C. Slavery was morally acceptable.

D. Slavery enabled him to see the light of day.

E. Slavery made time move too quickly.

The correct answer is A.

The question expects you to make your best guess as to the theme of the book based on the passage in the test. It might also be possible for you to identify the word in question- My Bondage and my Freedom by Frederick Douglass-and base your answer on your background knowledge of the text. You have to assess these answers carefully in light of both possibilities and choose a thematic statement that is consistent with what you know about the book as a whole (if you have that kind of background knowledge) and with the passage selected for the test.

14. What does the author figuratively mean by "hurrying throng"?

A. The people that bump into him walking past him.

B. His blurred vision from bright sunlight.

C. The New York tradesmen rushing to their jobs.

D. The busy middle class.

E. The bustling crowd of free people.

The correct answer is E.

The middle three options are not correct, but (A) could possibly be accurate. However, there is nothing in the passage that should lead you to think he was bumped into by people passing him. Don't make assumptions or you won't select the right answer.

15. What is the author's tone?

A. Cautious

B. Enlightened

C. Exuberant

D. Nervous

E. None of these apply

The correct answer is C.

While the feeling of the character may be (D), there are more cues that point to (C) being the right answer.

16. Who wrote this novel?

A. E.B. White

B. Francis Scott

C. Frederick Douglass

D. Harriet Beecher Stowe

E. Ralph Waldo Emerson

The correct answer is C.

Some of the main pieces of literature are listed for you in the book, and it would be wise to know some of the main and often used authors and their high profile works.

Questions 17-24. Read the following poem by Emily Dickenson and answer the questions below, selecting the best choice of the options presented.

IN THE GARDEN

A bird came down the walk:
He did not know I saw;
He bit an angle-worm in halves
And ate the fellow, raw.

And then, he drank a dew
From a convenient grass,
And then hopped sidewise to the wall
To let a beetle pass.

He glanced with rapid eyes
That hurried all abroad,—
They looked like frightened beads, I thought;
He stirred his velvet head

Like one in danger; cautious,
I offered him a crumb,
And he unrolled his feathers
And rowed him softer home

Than oars divide the ocean,
Too silver for a seam,
Or butterflies, off banks of noon,
Leap, splashless, as they swim.

17. What type of literary device is used in the author's phrase, "drank a dew"?

A. Allusion.

B. Foreshadowing.

C. Juxtaposition.

D. Satire.

E. Alliteration.

The correct answer is E.

Clearly the phrase is alliterative, and so € is the correct answer. The fact that the phrase is so brief is helpful with regard to eliminating the other possibilities; it's difficult for a brief phrase to communicate any satirical intent, and (A), (B) and (C) are unlikely for the same reason.

18. The author describes action beginning in line 15 of the bird's flight. What type of literary device is used?

A. Simile.

B. Metaphor.

C. Irony.

D. Satire.

E. None of these are correct.

The correct answer is B.

Remember, absolute answers, such as ones that give "always" or "never" or "none" are typically incorrect. Of the remaining options, you should know these definitions, especially the difference between simile and metaphor.

19. The rhyme scheme of the poem (except the final three stanzas) is

A. XAXA or Ghazal.

B. Scottish stanza.

C. Spenserian stanza.

D. quatrain-couplet.

E. Petrarchan sonnet.

The correct answer is A.

Even if you don't know the terms (which you should have memorized for poetry), the pattern is usually listed for you. As long as you know how to use those abbreviations, you can get any poetry scheme question correct.

20. This poem uses a particular metric pattern throughout the poem, except in the third line of each stanza. What is the main metric pattern?

A. dactylic tetrameter

B. trochaic trimeter

C. trochaic tetrameter

D. iambic pentameter

E. iambic trimeter

The correct answer is E.

Using the logic explained in earlier rational, iambic is "rhythm of two and tri- means three. You should be able to get to the root of any of these words and determine the correct answer if you don't know it, so practice!

21. What literary device is used when the bird's eyes are compared to frightened beads?

A. Reverse Personification.

B. Metaphor.

C. Simile.

D. Allegory.

E. Paradox.

The correct answer is C.

While these types of questions are not likely to come back-to-back in the actual exam, they were placed in repetitive order here to show you that you need to remain focus, answer each question and move forward.

22. What does the dash at the end of line 12 represent?

A. A change in focus from the bird to the water.

B. An abrupt change for the bird.

C. An emotional shift from fear to fascination.

D. It only shows the middle of the poem.

E. None of these accurately describe the meaning of the dash.

The correct answer is B.

In context, the bird goes from drinking and allowing a beetle to pass to abruptly being wary. That is the opposite of (C), but many students who rush through the test may select that option. Literally, (D) is not accurate nor is (A).

23. What is the author's tone in this poem?

A. She takes the perspective of the bird.

B. The author's tone is harsh toward potential prey.

C. The tone is factual, describing the actions of a bird.

D. Ornithology fascinated the author and she uses flowery language to describe it.

E. The author's tone is gentle and respectful demeanor regarding nature.

The correct answer is E.

Answers (A) and (D) can be eliminated because they do not address tone, which is the subject of the question. You have to read the poem and make an educated judgment as to whether the poem is primarily factual and descriptive (C) or harsh toward potential prey (B) or gentle and respectful €. You can also bring background knowledge about Emily Dickinson to the question.

24. What is a potential meaning of the allegory used by the author?

A. It could reveal the author's perceptions of God.

B. The allegory could be looking at the author's view of marriage.

C. The author could reveal the hierarchy between man and beast.

D. Descriptions of the forces of nature could parallel emotions.

E. There is no allegory used as a literary device in this poem.

The correct answer is A.

Knowing your definitions, (E) can be removed as correct because you would have identified the allegory previously. While (D) is a fair choice, (A) is a better one - again, known the traits of the era, you would be able to most easily identify the right choice.

Questions 25-32. Read the following selection and answer the questions below, selecting the best choice of the options presented.

There is no frigate like a book
To take us lands away,
Nor any coursers like a page
Of prancing poetry;
This traverse may the poorest take
Without oppress of toll;
How frugal is the chariot
That bears the human soul!

25. Authors use particular literary structures for descriptions. What best explains the type that Emily Dickinson employs in this poem?

A. Connotative

B. Argumentative

C. Narrative

D. Rhetoric

E. Expository

The correct answer is A.

You need to know the definitions of literary terms.

26. **How many types of transport does the author incorporate?**

A. Two

B. Three

C. Four

D. Five

E. None

The correct answer is B.

You can see the next question to identify the three options.

27. **If the words 'frigate, coursers, and traverse' were replaced with synonyms, what would the best choice of the following options include?**

A. Train, car, carriage

B. Train, horse, carriage

C. Ship, car, carriage

D. Ship, car, train

E. Ship, horse, carriage

The correct answer is E.

You can see them listed in the poem.

28. **Which of the following descriptions more closely describes the author's intended meaning of poem?**

A. Difficulties at work

B. The importance of books

C. Confessions for the soul

D. Poverty makes things difficult

E. Describing modes of transportation

The correct answer is B.

The main idea of the poem is stated in the first line.

29. There are very descriptive and strong feelings conveyed by the poet. Which of the following is not the definition of what she shares?

A. Overstatement

B. Paradox

C. Understatement

D. Irony

E. Sarcasm

The correct answer is E.

The other four selections are used at various times in the poem and you must read carefully as the question asks for the one that isn't used.

30. What kind of poetry form is utilized by Ms. Dickinson in this poem?

A. Alexandrine

B. Didactic poetry

C. Ballad stanza

D. Epitaph

E. Rondel

The correct answer is C.

You should be able to eliminate (B), (D), and (E) immediately. Alexandrine is a French style that has twelve syllables. If you didn't know that, and you probably won't, a ballad stanza is four line verses - and that should be enough to get it right.

31. Who is the author of this poem?

A. Emily Dickinson

B. Emily Brontë

C. Emily Mortimer

D. Lord Byron

E. William Blake

The correct answer is A.

Sometimes they give you the answer in another question or in the passage - it checks to see if you are actually reading!

32. When the boat is compared to a book, that is an example of:

A. a metaphor.

B. personification.

C. a simile.

D. an extended metaphor.

E. none of these.

The correct answer is C.

You should know the definitions of these literary terms.

Questions 33-40. Read the following selection and answer the questions below, selecting the best choice of the options presented.

"A man is born into this world with only a tiny spark of goodness in him. The spark is God, it is the soul; the rest is ugliness and evil, a shell. The spark must be guarded like a treasure, it must be nurtured, it must be fanned into flame. It must learn to seek out other sparks, it must dominate the shell. Anything can be a shell, Reuven. Anything. Indifference, laziness, brutality, and genius. Yes, even a great mind can be a shell and choke the spark.

"Reuven, the Master of the Universe blessed me with a brilliant son. And he cursed me with all the problems of raising him. Ah, what it is to have a Daniel, whose mind is like a pearl, like a sun. Reuben, when my Daniel was four years old, I saw him reading a story from a book. And I was frightened. He did not read the story, he swallowed it, as one swallows food or water. There was no soul in my four-year-old Daniel, there was only his mind. He was a mind in a body without a soul. It was a story in a Yiddish book about a poor Jew and his struggles to get to Eretz Yisroel before he died. Ah, how that man suffered! And my Daniel *enjoyed* the story, he *enjoyed* the last terrible page, because when he finished it he realized for the first time what a memory he had. He looked at me proudly and told me back the story from memory, and I cried inside my heart. I went away and cried to the Master of the Universe, 'What have you done to me? A mind like this I need for a son? A *heart* I need for a son, a *soul* I need for a son, *compassion* I want for my son, righteousness, mercy, strength to suffer and carry pain, *that* I want from my son, not a mind without a soul!'"

Reb Saunders paused and took a deep, trembling breath. I tried to swallow; my mouth was sand-dry. Danny sat with his right hand over his eyes, his glasses pushed up on his forehead. He was crying silently, his shoulders quivering. Reb Saunders did not look at him.

33. **According to the passage, what was the goal behind raising Danny in silence?**

A. For the speaker to be cruel.

B. The speaker thought he was being noble.

C. The narrator believed by being harsh, he was right.

D. The speaker wanted other people to think they were normal.

E. He wanted to develop Danny's compassion and soul.

The correct answer is E.

The intention of the speaker wasn't to be cruel or noble, and there was no indication that the speaker wanted to appear "normal" to his neighbors. This is an example of when your ability to infer is tested. By the repetition of the italics, that should give you an indication those are the important traits that Reb wanted to develop in Danny.

34. **When the narrator describes Danny "swallowing" the story, what kind of literary device is employed?**

A. A simile.

B. A metaphor.

C. An allusion.

D. Personification.

E. An alliteration.

The correct answer is C.

Know your literary term

35. **What is the author doing when using italics?**

A. The author is using short words to mean big things.

B. The author signifies the important things in a person's life.

C. The speaker is listing the attributes of his son.

D. The speaker shows what his son understood in the stories.

E. None of these things apply to those words.

The correct answer is B.

Option (C) is not correct - it is actually the opposite. It also isn't the explanation of his son's attributes, but the ones Danny was lacking. (A) is not correct, either, and you should know by now to be skeptical of answers like (E).

36. When Reb's mouth went "sand-dry," this is an example of:

A. a parody.

B. an allusion.

C. a synecdoche.

D. a metaphor.

E. an oxymoron.

The correct answer is B.

Synecdoche is a figure of speech in which a term for a part of something refers to the whole of something or vice versa, whereas oxymoron and juxtaposition both involve taking elements that appear to be contradictory and combining them in some form. "Sand-dry," on the other hand, is metaphorical language in which the quality of Reb Saunders' mouth is compared to sand. Since there are none of the explicit comparison terms that would it a simile, the best term for this metaphor.

37. Throughout the book, Reuven had been the peripheral narrator. Who is the narrator in this section?

A. It is still Reuven.

B. It is Reb.

C. It is Danny.

D. It is a third person narrator.

E. It is Eretz Yisroel.

The correct answer is B.

This is clear in the beginning of the last paragraph.

38. This passage is written as:

A. the denouement.

B. the complication.

C. the climax.

D. the suspense.

E. the introduction.

The correct answer is A.

By knowing the stages used in literature, you should be able to answer the question. You can also infer the meaning from the poignant phrases in the passage to help you pick the right option.

39. What is the theme of this passage?

A. Recounting the last moments of an old man's life.

B. The discussion of coming marriage of Danny.

C. The symbolism of reading as an alternative for family interactions.

D. The adoption of Reuven by Reb.

E. Another example of Jews suffering to get further in life.

The correct answer is A.

This question should have been easy to answer. There is no mention of Danny's marriage. Reading was not an alternative for attributes, but Reb believed it was a replacement for personality traits. There is no discussion that supports option (D) and (E) is not correct, either.

40. What is the writing style used by this author in this passage?

A. Expository

B. Didactic

C. Persuasive

D. Descriptive

E. Theatrical

The correct answer is C.

If you can't tell from the description being given by the speaker, then if you know the basic definitions of these terms then you would be able to pick the right answer.

Questions 41-48. Read the following selection and answer the questions below, selecting the best choice of the options presented.

Okonkwo and his fellow prisoners were set free as soon as the fine was paid. The District Commissioner spoke to them again about the great queen, and about peace and good government. But the men did not listen. They just sat and looked at him and at his interpreter. In the end they were given back their bags and sheathed machetes and told to go home. They rose and left the courthouse. They neither spoke to anyone nor among themselves.

The courthouse, like the church, was but a little way outside the village. The footpath that linked them was a very busy one because it also led to the stream, beyond the court. It was open and sandy. Footpaths were open and sandy in the dry season. But when the rains came the bush grew thick on either side and closed in on the path. It was now dry season.

As they made their way to the village the six men met women and children going to the stream with their waterpots. But them wore such heavy and fearsome looks to them, but edged out of the way to let them pass. In the village little groups of men joined them until they became a sizable company. They walked silently. As each of the six men got to his compound, he turned in, taking some of the crowd with him. The village was air in a silent, suppressed way.

Ezinma had prepared some food for her father as soon as news spread that the six men would be released. She took it to him in his obi. He ate absentmindedly. He had no appetite, he only ate to please her. His male relations and friends had gathered in his obi, and Obierika was urging him to eat. Nobody else spoke, but they noticed the log stripes on Okonkwo's back where the warder's whip had cut into his flesh.

41. Who is the protagonist of this story?

A. Obierika

B. Ezinma

C. Okonkwo

D. The District Commissioner

E. Okonkwo's wife

The correct answer is C.

While multiple characters appear in the passage, the facts that the passage begins with Okonkwo, and that he is the only one named out of the six men who are released, and that the passage ends with an observation about Okonkwo's scars, suggest that Okonkwo is the focus of the narrative, or the protagonist.

42. What is the name of this book?

A. Obi

B. Things Fall Apart

C. Let the Circle Be Unbroken

D. Ashes and Dust

E. The rainy season

The correct answer is B.

We mentioned in the chapters that you should have familiarity with era and types of literature, such as some key writers and books in American, British and World Literature.

43. What category of literature does this book represent?

A. Romantic.

B. Victorian.

C. Modernism.

D. Transcendentalism.

E. Post Colonial.

The correct answer is C.

Knowing the literary eras are important. If you forget during the test, look at the keys of each word. Romantic era as well as Victorian are much older - and a book about Africa from the native resident's perspective would not likely have been widely published early in literature. Post-colonial refers to British colonies and usually Indian pieces. Narrowed down to Transcendentalism and Modernism, you may recall the first is written by American authors and in particular Ralph Waldo Emerson.

44. The main character of the book appears to have what occur throughout the book?

A. He is a champion of his village.

B. He shows that he is good provider for his family.

C. He represents the disintegration of his society against the change.

D. The village doesn't support him.

E. The courthouse is targeting him to get rid of the village.

The correct answer is A.

Neither (D) nor (E) are correct, and that can be known from the passage. He is a tragic hero, and nothing in the passage represents (C) being accurate. Of the two remaining, while both (A) and (B) are true, option (A) is supported by the characterization in the passage.

45. The narrative structure of this passage is:

A. simple narrative.

B. cause and effect.

C. chronological.

D. inductive.

E. deductive.

The correct answer is C.

While it is a narration, and yes because of their release there is food waiting at the village, it is a chronological stepwise piece and that is the best answer.

46. The literary style of the book is:

A. comedy.

B. tragedy.

C. drama.

D. exploration.

E. quest.

The correct answer is B.

It describes the downfall of the main character due to his own choices. While (C) is a tempting answer, it is not the best option.

47. How is this passage narrated?

A. First person.

B. Second person.

C. Third person.

D. Omniscient observer.

E. None of these.

The correct answer is D.

Third person may seem like a desirable option, but it only gives the point of view from one particular person and there are two "inside thoughts" here. Omniscient means they see everything. You should have been able to discount (A) and (B) quite easily.

48. What is the main idea of this passage?

A. The village members continue to carry out the traditions of their ancestors.

B. There is a drought affecting crops and village life.

C. The interpreter was sharing with them a new way of life.

D. The government and church were coming together for the people.

E. People are resistant to change, and the village and protagonist illustrate it.

The correct answer is A.

This is the best option for the passage and though (E) may be accurate for the book, you must answer according to what's in the passage.

Questions 49-55. Read the following selection and answer the questions below, selecting the best choice of the options presented.

Mornings, he likes to sit in his new leather chair by his new living room window, looking out across the rooftops and chimney pots, the clotheslines and telegraph lines and office towers. It's the first time Manhattan, from high above, hasn't crushed him with desire. On the contrary the view makes him feel smug. All those people down there, striving, hustling, pushing, shoving, busting to get what Willie's already got. In spades. He lights a cigarette, blows a jet of smoke against the window. Suckers.

49. The subject in this passage is:

A. a character, and seems to be the lead of the story.

B. a supporting character.

C. has an attitude of a criminal.

D. is female.

E. has been poor his whole life.

The correct answer is A.

The female pronoun is used, so (D) is inaccurate. (B) is not accurate as he is the focus of the passage. You can not infer (E) is correct. Of (A) and (C), there is no support for this character being a criminal. Remember not to make assumptions when you answer questions.

50. What kind of description is the author providing of this scene?

A. Backstory of the character.

B. A characterization of what the character is like.

C. A narrative in the first person.

D. The unreliable narrative about a character.

E. The author is using a persuasive argument.

The correct answer is C.

Backstory isn't accurate because a current scene is described. (B) uses the same root-word twice, which is usually an indication that it is not a correct guess. There is nothing to suggest the character is unreliable. This leaves options (C) and (E) and neither the author nor character are persuading the reader toward a conclusion.

51. **What types of words are "striving, hustling, pushing, shoving, bustling"?**

A. Adjectives

B. Adverbs

C. Nouns

D. Gerunds

E. Verbs

The correct answer is C.

Backstory isn't accurate because a current scene is described. (B) uses the same root-word twice, which is usually an indication that it is not a correct guess. There is nothing to suggest the character is unreliable. This leaves options (C) and (E) and neither the author nor character are persuading the reader toward a conclusion.

52. **If you had to explain the phrase "crushed him" in the paragraph above and context of the paragraph, what would be the best appropriate explanation?**

A. The city sustained him with all the opportunity available.

B. The city called to him to be part of its life.

C. The city complimented him for everything he has achieved.

D. The city had energized him to get what he felt he deserved.

E. The city smothered him with all its offerings.

The correct answer is E.

The key to the question is the placement of the phrase in context. The phrase is meant to refer to how the character has felt in the past, and it explicitly does not describe how he feels in the passage itself. (A) through (D), which fit the tiumphalist tone of the passage, can therefore be rejected. It's clear, then, that (E), which is the only answer describing an undesirable state, is the best answer.

53. **Replacing the word "smug" with an antonym in context would have which of the following used?**

A. Sleepy

B. Prideful

C. Humble

D. Self-satisfied

E. Elated

The correct answer is C.

This involves knowing the words meanings as well as reading carefully as the question asked for antonym.

54. When the author uses the phrase, "In spades," which of the following is best representing what he is referencing?

A. The apartment where Willie is living.

B. The personal satisfaction of accumulated wealth.

C. Modern comforts in his home.

D. The loved ones surrounding him.

E. None of these is representative.

The correct answer is B.

The context and reading comprehension bring you to the correct answer. Nothing implying loved ones, modern comforts or the mere large apartment relate to the question.

55. By using the introductory word "Mornings," the author achieves what?

A. An optimistic tone for the passage.

B. A simple description of time of day, or chronology for the passage.

C. It's the start of the book, so he sets the passage at "day one."

D. A and C.

E. None of these.

The correct answer is A.

Context of the tone of the passage shows the character speaking is in a good mood, but it does not mean that it actually is morning and there is no indication that it is the start of the book.

Sample Test Four

Section I

Multiple Choice Questions.
Time: 60 minutes.
Percent of total grade on the exam: 45 percent.

Instructions: This section of the exam consists of selections from literary works and questions on their content, form, and style. After reading each passage and poem, choose the best answer to each question and then fill in the corresponding oval on the answer sheet.

Questions 1-8. Read the following passage carefully before you decide on your answers to the questions.

"Mother," said little Pearl, "the sunshine does not love you. It runs away and hides itself, because it is afraid of something on your bosom. . . . It will not flee from me, for I wear nothing on my bosom yet!" "Nor ever will, my child, I hope," said Hester. "And why not, mother?" asked Pearl, stopping short. . . . "Will it not come of its own accord, when I am a woman grown?"

—*The Scarlett Letter*

1. Who is the author of this book?

A. William Faulkner

B. Nathaniel Hawthorne

C. William Blake

D. William Shakespeare

E. Frederick Douglass

2. What is the relationship between these two characters?

A. Mother and daughter

B. Sisters

C. Aunt and niece

D. Cousins

E. Grandmother and grandchild

3. What kind of description is the author providing of this scene?

A. A symbolic, metaphorical description that provides a backstory of the main character

B. A characterization of what the character is like

C. A narrative, with the end of the selection giving thoughts in the first person

D. The unreliable narrative about a character

E. The author is using a persuasive argument

4. What does the "sunshine" represent?

A. Light

B. Hope

C. Purity

D. Heaven

E. Good luck

5. Why doesn't Pearl have anything on her bosom?

A. Only one person in the village wears the symbol at a time.

B. The symbol is used to signify divorce, and Pearl is not yet married.

C. It represents pregnancy and she is too young to be pregnant.

D. She will inherit the symbol to wear when her mother dies.

E. It's a symbol of womanhood, and Pearl is still considered a child.

6. The author portrays the attitude of the character Pearl as:

A. condescending

B. loving

C. disrespectful

D. innocent

E. resentful

7. **"Will it not come of its own accord, when I am a woman grown?" What is the author implying that Pearl is asking for?**

   A. If the scarlet letter will be handed down to her when she becomes a woman.

   B. If she will become pregnant when she becomes mature enough.

   C. Whether or not she will get divorced when she marries.

   D. If she will find true love when she grows up.

   E. If her mother will share this symbol with her when she is old enough.

8. **Which of the following best describes the author's message?**

   A. Little girls are oblivious to the world around them.

   B. Daughters always question things that their mothers do.

   C Growing up means losing your innocence.

   D. The world will know when you have sinned.

   E. None of the above.

Questions 9-16. Read the following passage carefully before you decide on your answers to the questions.

Death, be not proud

Death, be not proud, though some have called thee
Mighty and dreadful, for thou art not so;
For those whom thou think'st thou dost overthrow
Die not, poor Death, nor yet canst thou kill me.
From rest and sleep, which but thy pictures be,
Much pleasure; then from thee much more must flow,
And soonest our best men with thee do go,
Rest of their bones, and soul's delivery.

Thou art slave to fate, chance, kings, and desperate men,
And dost with poison, war, and sickness dwell,
And poppy or charms can make us sleep as well
And better than thy stroke; why swell'st thou then?
One short sleep past, we wake eternally
And death shall be no more;
Death, thou shalt die.

9. Who wrote this poem, titled "Death, be not Proud?"

A. John Donne

B. William Shakespeare

C. Emily Dickinson

D. Edgar Allen Poe

E. William Wordsworth

10. What type of poem is this?

A. Ballad

B. Epic

C. Haiku

D. Prose

E. Sonnet

11. What is the rhyme scheme in the first stanza?

A. ABBAABBA

B. AABBABBA

C. ABCABCBC

D. AABBCCAA

E. ABBBAAAB

12. What is the author implying in the following line?
"Die not, poor Death, nor yet canst thou kill me."

A. He/She is invincible.

B. His/Her soul will go to heaven; therefore, death does not end life.

C. Death does not decide when he/she will die.

D. Poor people do not decide when they will die.

E. He/she will defend themselves against a murderer.

13. What does the following line represent?
"One short sleep past, we wake eternally"

A. Being buried

B. A coma

C. Fighting off disease

D. A dream

E. Resurrection

14. The last line of the poem tries to explain ________.

A. That heaven/the afterlife defeats death.

B. that death dies when the human body dies.

C. that death can be defeated with death.

D. that death is only a threat to those that are alive.

E. None of the above.

15. Why are poison, war, and sickness mentioned?

A. To give examples of cowardly death scenarios.

B. To show that you can be killed by others or in a passive way.

C. To provoke memories from the reader.

D. To personify death as a bully.

E. None of the above.

16. The author speaks about death as if it's a/an ______.

A. theory

B. legacy

C. person

D. threat

E. imaginary concept

Questions 17-24. Read the following passage carefully before you decide on your answers to the questions.

"You boys know what tropism is, it's what makes a plant grow toward the light. Everything aspires to the light. You don't have to chase down a fly to get rid of it —you just darken the room, leave a crack of light in a window, and out he goes. Works every time. We all have that instinct, that aspiration. Science can't — what was your word? *Dim?* — science can't dim that. All science can do is turn out the false lights so the true light can get us home."

—*Old School*

17. Who is the author of the novel *Old School***?**

A. Ernest Hemingway

B. Tobias Wolff

C. Geoffrey Chaucer

D. William Blake

E. William Wordsworth

18. Which point of view is this written in?

A. First-person

B. Second-person

C. Third-person

D. Third-person plural

E. None of the above

19. Tropism is ____.

A. photosynthesis

B. always caused by light

C. the moving of an organism in response to a stimulus

D. an imaginary concept

E. survival of the fittest

20. **Why would the author mention tropism as an instinct or aspiration?**

A. All organisms are instinctive when they are hunting.

B. All organisms use strategies like this to attract prey.

C. It represents being able to flee.

D. Everyone wants to be attractive.

E. It represents moving towards a goal.

21. **The word *dim* is significant because ____.**

A. Light is necessary for tropism to occur.

B. Bad influences

C. Dim lights

D. Lights that prompt tropism

E. Parents

22. **What do the false lights mentioned in the last line represent?**

A. Bad influences

B. Dim lights

C. Lights that prompt tropism

D. Parents

E. All great persons wear silk.

23. **What does this passage imply about the main character?**

A. He questions scientific theories.

B. He doesn't believe science has all the answers.

C. He is highly intelligent.

D. Science is his favorite subject.

E. All of the above.

24. The literal interpretation of this passage is science. The symbolic interpretation is:

A. Religion

B. Motivation

C. Instinct

D. Aspiration

E. Economics

Questions 25-32. Read the following passage carefully before you decide on your answers to the questions.

"And if she thought anything, it was No. No. Nono. Nonono. Simple. She just flew. Collected every bit of life she had made, all the parts of her that were precious and fine and beautiful, and carried, pushed, dragged them through the veil, out, away, over there where no one could hurt them. Over there. Outside this place, where they would be safe."

—*Beloved*

25. Who wrote *Beloved*?

A. Martin Luther King

B. Frederick Douglass

C. Maya Angelou

D. Toni Morrison

E. Zora Neal Hurston

26. What does "No. No. Nono. Nonono." represent?

A. Children fighting with their parents

B. Parents defending discipline

C. Teachers arguing with parents

D. Children being defiant

E. Parents defending their children

27. What are "bits of life"?

A. Children

B. Belongings

C. Crops

D. Flowers

E. Poems

28. What does the veil represent?

A. A wedding

B. A funeral

C. Birth

D. Puberty

E. None of the above

29. Where is "over there"?

A. Africa

B. The Underground Railroad

C. The slaves quarters

D. The afterlife

E. The garden

30. Where would they be safe?

A. Nowhere on this earth

B. Off the plantation

C. Back in Africa

D. In school

E. Up North

31. The author implies that the main character ______.

A. would rather see her children die than watch them suffer.

B. is trying to hide her children from the master.

C. Is planning on escaping on the Underground Railroad.

D. would like to return to Africa.

E. is hiding her belongings from fellow slaves.

32. What literary device is used in this passage?

A. Alliteration

B. Allegory

C. Analogy

D. Anecdote

E. Anagram

Questions 33-40. Read the following passage carefully before you decide on your answers to the questions.

"A Dream Within a Dream"

Take this kiss upon the brow!
And, in parting from you now,
Thus much let me avow —
You are not wrong, who deem
That my days have been a dream;
Yet if hope has flown away
In a night, or in a day,
In a vision, or in none,
Is it therefore the less gone?
All that we see or seem
Is but a dream within a dream.

I stand amid the roar
Of a surf-tormented shore,
And I hold within my hand
Grains of the golden sand —
How few! yet how they creep
Through my fingers to the deep,
While I weep — while I weep!
O God! Can I not grasp

Them with a tighter clasp?
O God! can I not save
One from the pitiless wave?
Is all that we see or seem
But a dream within a dream?

33. Who wrote *A Dream Within a Dream*?

A. Emily Dickinson

B. William Shakespeare

C. Edgar Allen Poe

D. Jamaica Kincaid

E. Robert Frost

34. What is the rhyme scheme?

A. AAABBAACCDD

B. AAABBCCDDBB

C. AABBCDCDAAB

D. ABABABABCCD

E. ABBABBACCAB

35. Why is there an exclamation point in the first line?

A. To portray an unwanted kiss

B. To demonstrate a demand

C. To show excitement

D. To explain a romantic kiss

E. To show a sense of urgency

36. What is the significance of the line "And, in parting from you now,"

A. It represents a goodbye before traveling

B. A little boy is running away from home

C. A parent is abandoning their child

D. It represents a breakup

E. It symbolizes an abortion

37. What element is described with personification?

A. Love

B. The ocean

C. Sand

D. The night

E. All of the above

38. What is the difference between the first and second stanza?

A. The first stanza describes love, and the second stanza describes hate.

B. The first stanza is calm, and the second stanza has action.

C. The first stanza has action, and the second stanza is calm.

D. The first stanza represents hope, and the second stanza represents losing hope.

E. There are no major differences.

39. What is the similarity between the ocean and his tears?

A. Salt water

B. They're both parts of nature

C. He cannot control either

D. They're both unpredictable

E. None of the above

40. What is the similarity between the sand and his love?

A. He dreams about both.

B. They are both beautiful parts of nature.

C. They are both unobtainable.

D. They both happen in waves.

E. All of the above.

Questions 41-47. Read the following passage carefully before you decide on your answers to the questions.

"Then you must tell 'em dat love ain't somethin' lak uh grindstone dat's de same thing everywhere and do de same thing tuh everything it touch. Love is lak de sea. It's uh movin' thing, but still and all, it takes its shape from de shore it meets, and it's different with every shore."

—*Their Eyes Were Watching God*

41. Who wrote this novel?

A. Toni Morrison

B. Zora Neal Hurston

C. W.E.B. Dubois

D. Maya Angelou

E. Richard Wright

42. What literary device is used to show the similarity between love and the sea?

A. Simile

B. Metaphor

C. Euphemism

D. Flashback

E. Foreshadowing

43. In what form is this written?

A. Phonetic

B. Informal

C. With an accent

D. Vernacular

E. Stream of consciousness

44. ______ is used to describe the sea.

A. Imagery

B. Alliteration

C. Action

D. Personification

E. All of the above

45. How does the author portray love?

A. It's different for each relationship.

B. It's unobtainable.

C. It causes waves in your life.

D. It comes and goes like the tide.

E. None of the above.

46. What is a grindstone?

A. A stone made of sand

B. A workday

C. A square stone used to grind sediment

D. A round stone used to sharpen tools

E. A plantation

47. What best describes love in this passage?

A. Grindstone

B. Uh movin' thing

C. Still

D. Same thing

E. Everyone

Questions 48-55. Read the following passage carefully before you decide on your answers to the questions.

"Oh, Jake," Brett said, "we could have had such a damned good time together."

Ahead was a mounted policeman in khaki directing traffic. He raised his baton. The car slowed suddenly pressing Brett against me.

"Yes," I said. "Isn't it pretty to think so?"

—*The Sun Also Rises*

48. Who wrote this novel?

A. Henry David Thoreau

B. Ernest Hemingway

C. F. Scott Fitzgerald

D. Harper Lee

E. J.R.R. Tolkien

49. What is the significance of the policeman waiting his baton?

A. It symbolizes that it's time to move along

B. Their love will never be legal

C. If they get caught they will go to jail

D. It shows their love stuck, as if in traffic

E. All of the above

50. Which is true about Brett?

A. She has always been in love with Jake.

B. She refuses to go anywhere without Jake.

C. She sees Jake in her future.

D. She regrets the past.

E. All of the above.

51. Which is true about Jake?

A. He sees Brett in his future.

B. He wants to marry Brett.

C. He doesn't think their relationship would ever work out.

D. He loves Brett as a friend.

E. He thinks Brett is pretty.

52. Which literary device would be most appropriate before this dialogue?

A. Flashforward

B. Foreshadowing

C. Backflash

D. Metaphor

E. Flashback

53. Which literary device would be most appropriate after this dialogue?

A. Flashforward

B. Foreshadowing

C. Backflash

D. Metaphor

E. Flashback

54. Which is the best description of this dialogue and its placement in the story?

A. Introduction

B. Cliffhanger

C. Frame story

D. Backstory

E. Setting

55. Why did the car slow down?

A. There was traffic.

B. The policeman waved his baton.

C. The driver needed directions.

D. The driver was picking up another passenger.

E. It was time to get out.

Free Response Essay Sample Questions

Section II

Time: 120 minutes

Percent of total grade on the exam: 55 percent.

Question 1.

(Suggested time—40 minutes. This question counts as one-third of the total essay sec-tion score.)

Read the following poems about dreams by Edgar Allen Poe. Then write a well-organized essay in which you analyze the poems' literary elements such as figurative language, parallelism and tone to compare his two poems.

Poem one

Take this kiss upon the brow!
And, in parting from you now,
Thus much let me avow--
You are not wrong, who deem
That my days have been a dream;
Yet if hope has flown away
In a night, or in a day,
In a vision, or in none,
Is it therefore the less gone?
All that we see or seem
Is but a dream within a dream.

I stand amid the roar
Of a surf-tormented shore,
And I hold within my hand
Grains of the golden sand--
How few! yet how they creep
Through my fingers to the deep,
While I weep--while I weep!
O God! can I not grasp
Them with a tighter clasp?
O God! can I not save
One from the pitiless wave?
Is all that we see or seem
But a dream within a dream?

Poem two

In visions of the dark night
I have dreamed of joy departed-
But a waking dream of life and light
Hath left me broken-hearted.

Ah! what is not a dream by day
To him whose eyes are cast
On things around him with a ray
Turned back upon the past?

That holy dream- that holy dream,
While all the world were chiding,
Hath cheered me as a lovely beam
A lonely spirit guiding.

What though that light, thro' storm and night,
So trembled from afar-
What could there be more purely bright
In Truth's day-star?

Question 2.

(Suggested time—40 minutes. This question counts as one-third of the total essay sec-tion score.)

The following passage is from Crime and Punishment. Read the passage carefully. Consider if it is better to be honest (or use candor) or to be just; or if there is a differ-ence between honesty and candor. Then write a well-organized essay in which you use examples from this work or others to argue honesty/ candor versus flattery/being just. Do not summarize the plot.

> "There is nothing in the world more difficult than candor, and nothing easier than flattery. If there is a hundredth of a fraction of a false note to candor, it immediately produces dissonance, and as a result, exposure. But in flattery, even if everything is false down to the last note, it is still pleasant, and people will listen not without pleas-ure; with coarse pleasure, perhaps, but pleasure nevertheless."

Question 3.

(Suggested time—40 minutes. This question counts as one-third of the total essay sec-tion score.)

Chose a literary work that describes a perception of utopia. In your analysis, describe impacts of that perception on a particular character and experiences or choices made because of that perception or devotion to a utopian ideal. In your essay, do not merely summarize the plot.

Sample Test Four: ANSWER KEY

Question Number	Correct Answer	Your Answer
1.	B	
2.	A	
3.	A	
4.	C	
5.	C	
6.	D	
7.	B	
8.	C	
9.	A	
10.	E	
11.	A	
12.	B	
13.	E	
14.	A	
15.	B	
16.	C	
17.	B	
18.	B	
19.	C	
20.	E	
21.	B	
22.	A	
23.	B	
24.	A	
25.	D	
26.	E	
27.	A	
28.	B	

Question Number	Correct Answer	Your Answer
29.	D	
30.	A	
31.	A	
32.	B	
33.	C	
34.	A	
35.	E	
36.	D	
37.	C	
38.	B	
39.	C	
40.	C	
41.	B	
42.	A	
43.	D	
44.	D	
45.	A	
46.	D	
47.	B	
48.	B	
49.	A	
50.	D	
51.	C	
52.	E	
53.	A	
54.	B	
55.	E	

Answer Key and Rationale

Questions 1-8. Read the following passage carefully before you decide on your answers to the questions.

"Mother," said little Pearl, "the sunshine does not love you. It runs away and hides itself, because it is afraid of something on your bosom. . . . It will not flee from me, for I wear nothing on my bosom yet!"

"Nor ever will, my child, I hope," said Hester.

"And why not, mother?" asked Pearl, stopping short. . . . "Will it not come of its own accord, when I am a woman grown?"

—*The Scarlett Letter*

1. Who is the author of this book?

A. William Faulkner

B. Nathaniel Hawthorne

C. William Blake

D. William Shakespeare

E. Frederick Douglass

The correct answer is B.

The very famous novel, *The Scarlett Letter*, was written by Nathaniel Hawthorne.

2. What is the relationship between these two characters?

A. Mother and daughter

B. Sisters

C. Aunt and niece

D. Cousins

E. Grandmother and grandchild

The correct answer is A.

For this question, the word "mother" is a dead giveaway to the characters' relationship.

3. What kind of description is the author providing of this scene?

A. A symbolic, metaphorical description that provides a backstory of the main character

B. A characterization of what the character is like

C. A narrative, with the end of the selection giving thoughts in the first person

D. The unreliable narrative about a character

E. The author is using a persuasive argument

The correct answer is A.

The author provides details through symbolism to describe the main character's past.

4. What does the "sunshine" represent?

A. Light

B. Hope

C. Purity

D. Heaven

E. Good luck

The correct answer is C.

Sunshine representing light is a literal interpretation, which can be quickly eliminated. Sunshine symbolizing hope, heaven, or good luck is possible for another passage, but the context should point to the correct answer. For this particular question, sunshine represents purity.

5. Why doesn't Pearl have anything on her bosom?

A. Only one person in the village wears the symbol at a time.

B. The symbol is used to signify divorce, and Pearl is not yet married.

C. It represents pregnancy and she is too young to be pregnant.

D. She will inherit the symbol to wear when her mother dies.

E. It's a symbol of womanhood, and Pearl is still considered a child.

The correct answer is C.

The scarlet letter on her mother's bosom represents pregnancy. The daughter is too young to be pregnant.

6. The author portrays the attitude of the character Pearl as:

A. condescending

B. loving

C. disrespectful

D. innocent

E. resentful

The correct answer is D.

Pearl is very respectful, and in no way condescending or resentful of her mother, which quickly eliminates (A), (C), and (E). While loving could be a quality used to describe Pearl, (D) is the best answer.

7. "Will it not come of its own accord, when I am a woman grown?" What is the author implying that Pearl is asking for?

A. If the scarlet letter will be handed down to her when she becomes a woman.

B. If she will become pregnant when she becomes mature enough.

C. Whether or not she will get divorced when she marries.

D. If she will find true love when she grows up.

E. If her mother will share this symbol with her when she is old enough.

The correct answer is B.

The daughter is questioning at what point she will be able to wear a similar letter on her bosom, as she wants to be like her mother. The symbolism behind this question represents her inquiry as to whether or not she'll become pregnant when she is mature enough.

8. Which of the following best describes the author's message?

A. Little girls are oblivious to the world around them.

B. Daughters always question things that their mothers do.

C Growing up means losing your innocence.

D. The world will know when you have sinned.

E. None of the above.

The correct answer is C.

(A) and (B) can be ruled out quickly, due to the deep level of symbolism in The Scarlett Letter. While it may be true that this novel represents the world recognizing sin, it's more evident that the author's intention was to portray losing innocence as one grows older.

Questions 9-16. Read the following passage carefully before you decide on your answers to the questions.

Death, be not proud

Death, be not proud, though some have called thee
Mighty and dreadful, for thou art not so;
For those whom thou think'st thou dost overthrow
Die not, poor Death, nor yet canst thou kill me.
From rest and sleep, which but thy pictures be,
Much pleasure; then from thee much more must flow,
And soonest our best men with thee do go,
Rest of their bones, and soul's delivery.

Thou art slave to fate, chance, kings, and desperate men,
And dost with poison, war, and sickness dwell,
And poppy or charms can make us sleep as well
And better than thy stroke; why swell'st thou then?
One short sleep past, we wake eternally
And death shall be no more;
Death, thou shalt die.

9. Who wrote this poem, titled "Death, be not Proud?"

A. John Donne

B. William Shakespeare

C. Emily Dickinson

D. Edgar Allen Poe

E. William Wordsworth

The correct answer is A.

John Donne is the author of this poem.

10. What type of poem is this?

A. Ballad

B. Epic

C. Haiku

D. Prose

E. Sonnet

The correct answer is E.

This poem is a sonnet. All sonnets have iambic pentameter. The Haiku is made up of a short poem with specific syllables per line. Prose is told in story form and does not always rhyme. The ballad is free verse, often set to music.

11. What is the rhyme scheme in the first stanza?

A. ABBAABBA

B. AABBABBA

C. ABCABCBC

D. AABBCCAA

E. ABBBAAAB

The correct answer is A.

By looking over the words that rhyme in the first stanza, it's easy to determine the rhyme scheme as ABBAABBA.

12. What is the author implying in the following line?
"Die not, poor Death, nor yet canst thou kill me."

A. He/She is invincible.

B. His/Her soul will go to heaven; therefore, death does not end life.

C. Death does not decide when he/she will die.

D. Poor people do not decide when they will die.

E. He/she will defend themselves against a murderer.

The correct answer is B.

The author implies that although death may be the end of their body on earth, their soul will live on in heaven. Therefore, (B) is the best option.

13. What does the following line represent?
"One short sleep past, we wake eternally"

A. Being buried

B. A coma

C. Fighting off disease

D. A dream

E. Resurrection

The correct answer is E.

This is a straightforward question: the words "wake" and "eternally" are direct connections to resurrection.

14. The last line of the poem tries to explain ________.

A. That heaven/the afterlife defeats death.

B. that death dies when the human body dies.

C. that death can be defeated with death.

D. that death is only a threat to those that are alive.

E. None of the above.

The correct answer is A.

Because we know the poem views death as inferior to the afterlife, and the author believes heaven is a place their soul will live eternally, (A) is the best answer.

15. Why are poison, war, and sickness mentioned?

A. To give examples of cowardly death scenarios.

B. To show that you can be killed by others or in a passive way.

C. To provoke memories from the reader.

D. To personify death as a bully.

E. None of the above.

The correct answer is B.

Poison, war, and sickness are all practical ways to die and mentioning them displays death as something that can happen to anyone. Each of these scenarios are nearly impossible to avoid and can be related to by the reader, regardless of their stature.

16. **The author speaks about death as if it's a/an ______.**

A. theory

B. legacy

C. person

D. threat

E. imaginary concept

The correct answer is C.

This poem uses personification to describe death. It's viewed as something that tries to take away from others. Therefore, (C) is the best answer.

Questions 17-24. Read the following passage carefully before you decide on your answers to the questions.

"You boys know what tropism is, it's what makes a plant grow toward the light. Everything aspires to the light. You don't have to chase down a fly to get rid of it —you just darken the room, leave a crack of light in a window, and out he goes. Works every time. We all have that instinct, that aspiration. Science can't — what was your word? *Dim?* — science can't dim that. All science can do is turn out the false lights so the true light can get us home."

—*Old School*

17. **Who is the author of the novel** *Old School*?

A. Ernest Hemingway

B. Tobias Wolff

C. Geoffrey Chaucer

D. William Blake

E. William Wordsworth

The correct answer is B.

The novel *Old School* was written by Tobias Wolff.

18. Which point of view is this written in?

A. First-person

B. Second-person

C. Third-person

D. Third-person plural

E. None of the above

The correct answer is B.

Throughout the poem, the author uses the word "you," which is a direct indicator of second-person point of view.

19. Tropism is ____.

A. photosynthesis

B. always caused by light

C. the moving of an organism in response to a stimulus

D. an imaginary concept

E. survival of the fittest

The correct answer is C.

Context clues are needed to determine this answer, as tropism is not a common vocabulary word. Using the first and second sentences, you can determine that (C) is the best answer.

20. Why would the author mention tropism as an instinct or aspiration?

A. All organisms are instinctive when they are hunting.

B. All organisms use strategies like this to attract prey.

C. It represents being able to flee.

D. Everyone wants to be attractive.

E. It represents moving towards a goal.

The correct answer is E.

Again, context clues are critical for zeroing in on the correct answer. Similar to moving in response to a stimulus, the author mentions tropism as an instinct or aspiration because a goal can be viewed as the stimulus.

21. The word *dim* is significant because ____.

A. Light is necessary for tropism to occur.

B. Bad influences

C. Dim lights

D. Lights that prompt tropism

E. Parents

The correct answer is B.

Symbolism is important for narrowing in on the answer for this particular question. (D) has no connection and can easily be eliminated. (A) and (C) are literal interpretations, whereas (B) connects the representation of the dimming of faith.

22. What do the false lights mentioned in the last line represent?

A. Bad influences

B. Dim lights

C. Lights that prompt tropism

D. Parents

E. All great persons wear silk.

The correct answer is A.

The best connection to the false lights in the last line is bad influences.

23. What does this passage imply about the main character?

A. He questions scientific theories.

B. He doesn't believe science has all the answers.

C. He is highly intelligent.

D. Science is his favorite subject.

E. All of the above.

The correct answer is B.

The author is very skeptical of science and its abilities. While (A), (C), and (D), may all be possible, (B) is the most apparent.

24. The literal interpretation of this passage is science. The symbolic interpretation is:

A. Religion

B. Motivation

C. Instinct

D. Aspiration

E. Economics

The correct answer is A.

The best symbolic interpretation for this passage is religion.

Questions 25-32. Read the following passage carefully before you decide on your answers to the questions.

"And if she thought anything, it was No. No. Nono. Nonono. Simple. She just flew. Collected every bit of life she had made, all the parts of her that were precious and fine and beautiful, and carried, pushed, dragged them through the veil, out, away, over there where no one could hurt them. Over there. Outside this place, where they would be safe."

—*Beloved*

25. Who wrote *Beloved*?

A. Martin Luther King

B. Frederick Douglass

C. Maya Angelou

D. Toni Morrison

E. Zora Neal Hurston

The correct answer is D.

Beloved was written by Toni Morrison.

26. What does "No. No. Nono. Nonono." represent?

A. Children fighting with their parents

B. Parents defending discipline

C. Teachers arguing with parents

D. Children being defiant

E. Parents defending their children

The correct answer is E.

The best hint for figuring out the context of this piece after the quote is the element of bringing the children somewhere that no one can hurt them. By understanding this context, it's clear that (E) is the best answer.

27. What are "bits of life"?

A. Children

B. Belongings

C. Crops

D. Flowers

E. Poems

The correct answer is A.

Again, context plays a huge role in determining the correct answer for this question. Collecting her "bits of life" represents her children, and in the former question we learned that this passage is about a parent trying to protect her children. This assists in zeroing in on (A) as the correct answer.

28. What does the veil represent?

A. A wedding

B. A funeral

C. Birth

D. Puberty

E. None of the above

The correct answer is B.

The veil represents death in this context. While a veil is most commonly representative of a wedding, this is the most literal interpretation. The symbolism in the passage makes (B) the most appropriate answer.

29. Where is "over there"?

A. Africa

B. The Underground Railroad

C. The slaves quarters

D. The afterlife

E. The garden

The correct answer is D.

Because we're aware that the veil represents death, it's easy to determine that "over there" represents the afterlife. The author would rather see her children die that continue living the way that they have been living recently. (D) is the correct answer.

30. Where would they be safe?

A. Nowhere on this earth

B. Off the plantation

C. Back in Africa

D. In school

E. Up North

The corrrect answer is A.

Again, the element of death plays a big part in this story. If the family felt safe escaping somewhere, they probably would have made a plan to go to a place they'd be accepted and wouldn't face the same adversity. (A) is the best answer.

31. The author implies that the main character ______.

A. would rather see her children die than watch them suffer.

B. is trying to hide her children from the master.

C. Is planning on escaping on the Underground Railroad.

D. would like to return to Africa.

E. is hiding her belongings from fellow slaves.

The correct answer is A.

The symbolism points to the main character considering death for her children instead of watching them go through horrid tragedies. This makes (A) the best answer.

32. What literary device is used in this passage?

A. Alliteration

B. Allegory

C. Analogy

D. Anecdote

E. Anagram

The correct answer is B.

An allegory is a literary device in stories or poetry in which the symbolism makes such a great impact that there is actually hidden meaning. This passage does not represent the literal interpretation, making (B) the best answer.

Questions 33-40. Read the following passage carefully before you decide on your answers to the questions.

"A Dream Within a Dream"

Take this kiss upon the brow!
And, in parting from you now,
Thus much let me avow —
You are not wrong, who deem
That my days have been a dream;
Yet if hope has flown away
In a night, or in a day,
In a vision, or in none,
Is it therefore the less gone?
All that we see or seem
Is but a dream within a dream.

I stand amid the roar
Of a surf-tormented shore,
And I hold within my hand
Grains of the golden sand —
How few! yet how they creep
Through my fingers to the deep,
While I weep — while I weep!
O God! Can I not grasp
Them with a tighter clasp?
O God! can I not save
One from the pitiless wave?
Is all that we see or seem
But a dream within a dream?

33. Who wrote *A Dream Within a Dream*?

A. Emily Dickinson

B. William Shakespeare

C. Edgar Allen Poe

D. Jamaica Kincaid

E. Robert Frost

The correct answer is C.

Edgar Allen Poe wrote *A Dream Within A Dream.*

34. What is the rhyme scheme?

A. AAABBAACCDD

B. AAABBCCDDBB

C. AABBCDCDAAB

D. ABABABABCCD

E. ABBABBACCAB

The correct answer is A.

Just like the other poems in this practice test, looking through the last words in each sentence can help zero in on the correct option for rhyme scheme. The correct answer for this question is (A).

35. Why is there an exclamation point in the first line?

A. To portray an unwanted kiss

B. To demonstrate a demand

C. To show excitement

D. To explain a romantic kiss

E. To show a sense of urgency

The correct answer is E.

Exclamation points are a way to represent an extreme situation. For the first line in this poem, the punctuation mark shows a sense of urgency, making (E) the best answer.

36. What is the significance of the line "And, in parting from you now,"

A. It represents a goodbye before traveling

B. A little boy is running away from home

C. A parent is abandoning their child

D. It represents a breakup

E. It symbolizes an abortion

The correct answer is D.

(D) is the best option because "parting" represents ending a relationship.

37. What element is described with personification?

A. Love

B. The ocean

C. Sand

D. The night

E. All of the above

The correct answer is C.

The word "creep" is a dead giveaway in trying to find personification. (C) is the best answer for this question.

38. What is the difference between the first and second stanza?

A. The first stanza describes love, and the second stanza describes hate.

B. The first stanza is calm, and the second stanza has action.

C. The first stanza has action, and the second stanza is calm.

D. The first stanza represents hope, and the second stanza represents losing hope.

E. There are no major differences.

The correct answer is B.

Looking at the punctuation and the action within the writing, it's easy to determine that (B) is the best answer.

39. What is the similarity between the ocean and his tears?

A. Salt water

B. They're both parts of nature

C. He cannot control either

D. They're both unpredictable

E. None of the above

The correct answer is C.

Waves are caused by the moon's pull on the earth, and his tears are caused naturally. (D) can quickly be eliminated because they are predictable. While it is true that the ocean and his tears are made of salt water and they are both parts of nature, (C) is the best answer given the context of the poem.

40. What is the similarity between the sand and his love?

A. He dreams about both.

B. They are both beautiful parts of nature.

C. They are both unobtainable.

D. They both happen in waves.

E. All of the above.

The correct answer is C.

The sand and his love are both slipping away from his fingers. (C) is the best answer because he portrays both at unobtainable.

Questions 41-47. Read the following passage carefully before you decide on your answers to the questions.

"Then you must tell 'em dat love ain't somethin' lak uh grindstone dat's de same thing everywhere and do de same thing tuh everything it touch. Love is lak de sea. It's uh movin' thing, but still and all, it takes its shape from de shore it meets, and it's different with every shore."

—*Their Eyes Were Watching God*

41. Who wrote this novel?

A. Toni Morrison

B. Zora Neal Hurston

C. W.E.B. Dubois

D. Maya Angelou

E. Richard Wright

The correct answer is B.

Zora Neal Hurston wrote *Their Eyes Were Watching God.*

42. What literary device is used to show the similarity between love and the sea?

A. Simile

B. Metaphor

C. Euphemism

D. Flashback

E. Foreshadowing

The correct answer is A.

The use of "like" is a clear indicator that the literary device used in this passage is a simile.

43. In what form is this written?

A. Phonetic

B. Informal

C. With an accent

D. Vernacular

E. Stream of consciousness

The correct answer is D.

Vernacular is a type of dialect that is commonly only used within communities. While it may seem this person has an accent, they are actually speaking in the vernacular. This makes (D) the best answer.

44. ______ is used to describe the sea.

A. Imagery

B. Alliteration

C. Action

D. Personification

E. All of the above

The correct answer is D.

Personification is used to describe the sea when the author said it was a moving thing.

45. How does the author portray love?

A. It's different for each relationship.

B. It's unobtainable.

C. It causes waves in your life.

D. It comes and goes like the tide.

E. None of the above.

The correct answer is A.

This is an easy answer- love is portrayed as a different experience for everyone, which makes A the best answer.

46. What is a grindstone?

A. A stone made of sand

B. A workday

C. A square stone used to grind sediment

D. A round stone used to sharpen tools

E. A plantation

The correct answer is D.

A grindstone is a round stone used to sharpen tools, making (D) the best answer.

47. What best describes love in this passage?

A. Grindstone

B. Uh movin' thing

C. Still

D. Same thing

E. Everyone

The correct answer is B.

Again, the author portrays love as fluid, moving thing. It's explained as a different experience for everyone, making (B) the best answer.

Questions 48-55. Read the following passage carefully before you decide on your answers to the questions.

"Oh, Jake," Brett said, "we could have had such a damned good time together."

Ahead was a mounted policeman in khaki directing traffic. He raised his baton. The car slowed suddenly pressing Brett against me.

"Yes," I said. "Isn't it pretty to think so?"

—*The Sun Also Rises*

48. Who wrote this novel?

A. Henry David Thoreau

B. Ernest Hemingway

C. F. Scott Fitzgerald

D. Harper Lee

E. J.R.R. Tolkien

The correct answer is B.

Ernest Hemmingway wrote *The Sun Also Rises.*

49. What is the significance of the policeman waiting his baton?

A. It symbolizes that it's time to move along

B. Their love will never be legal

C. If they get caught they will go to jail

D. It shows their love stuck, as if in traffic

E. All of the above

The correct answer is A.

Using the phrase "could have" shows that the characters are thinking their time is finished and their relationship will never be. The policeman raising his baton symbolizes moving along in a literal sense, which draws a strong (and deliberate from the author) connection to the situation Brett and Jake are in.

50. Which is true about Brett?

A. She has always been in love with Jake.

B. She refuses to go anywhere without Jake.

C. She sees Jake in her future.

D. She regrets the past.

E. All of the above.

The correct answer is D.

As mentioned in the previous question, this particular passage sets a scene of looking backwards. It's implied that if she really did love Jake, she would have fought harder for him instead of simply letting him go. (D) is the best answer for this question because it's most obvious that she has regrets.

51. Which is true about Jake?

A. He sees Brett in his future.

B. He wants to marry Brett.

C. He doesn't think their relationship would ever work out.

D. He loves Brett as a friend.

E. He thinks Brett is pretty.

The correct answer is C.

While Brett is thinking of the "what if" in their relationship, Jake has already come to terms with the fact that it will never work out. He may have loved her in the past, but he has accepted their relationship not moving forward. Because of this, (C) is the best answer.

52. Which literary device would be most appropriate before this dialogue?

A. Flashforward

B. Foreshadowing

C. Backflash

D. Metaphor

E. Flashback

The correct answer is E.

This passage makes the reader question what has happened in their relationship in the past to make them question why it would never work out. A flashback would be most appropriate to give the reader context and more details about what they've been through. This makes (E) the best answer for this question.

53. Which literary device would be most appropriate after this dialogue?

A. Flashforward

B. Foreshadowing

C. Backflash

D. Metaphor

E. Flashback

The correct answer is A.

It would be most appropriate to see where the two of them ended up following this conversation. A flashforward could be one, five, even fifty years later. Therefore, the best answer is (A).

54. Which is the best description of this dialogue and its placement in the story?

A. Introduction

B. Cliffhanger

C. Frame story

D. Backstory

E. Setting

The correct answer is B.

There is obvious action in this piece, and the author is trying to provoke emotion in the reader by making them think of the possible outcomes for Brett and Jake's relationship. Because of the rising action, (B) is the best answer.

55. Why did the car slow down?

A. There was traffic.

B. The policeman waved his baton.

C. The driver needed directions.

D. The driver was picking up another passenger.

E. It was time to get out.

The correct answer is E.

Just like Brett and Jake's relationship, their cab ride has come to an end. The literal interpretation of their cab ride ending ties in with the symbolism of their decision to end all thoughts of being together in the future. Knowing the context of this story, (E) is the correct answer.

Sample Test Five

Section I

Multiple Choice Questions.
Time: 60 minutes.
Percent of total grade on the exam: 45 percent.

Instructions: This section of the exam consists of selections from literary works and questions on their content, form, and style. After reading each passage and poem, choose the best answer to each question and then fill in the corresponding oval on the answer sheet

Questions 1-8. Read the passage and answer the following questions carefully.

The history of all hitherto existing society is the history of class struggles. Freeman and slave, patrician and plebeian, lord and serf, guildmaster and journeyman, in a word, oppressor and oppressed, stood in constant opposition to one another, carried on an uninterrupted, now hidden, now open fight, a fight that each time ended, either in a revolutionary reconstitution of society at large, or in the common ruin of the contending classes.

In the earlier epochs of history, we find almost everywhere a complicated arrangement of society into various orders, a manifold gradation of social rank. In ancient Rome we have patricians, knights, plebeians, slaves; in the Middle Ages, feudal lords, vassals, guild- masters, journeymen, apprentices, serfs; in almost all of these classes, again, subordinate gradations.

The modern bourgeois society that has sprouted from the ruins of feudal society, has not done away with class antagonisms. It has but established new classes, new conditions of oppression, new forms of struggle in place of the old ones.

Our epoch, the epoch of the bourgeoisie, possesses, however, this distinctive feature: It has simplified the class antagonisms. Society as a whole is more and more splitting up into two great hostile camps, into two great classes directly facing each other - bourgeoisie and proletariat...

1. **The first sentence can best be paraphrased as...**

   A. Every future societal shall deal with issues of class

   B. Education of history is essential for a society to develop

   C. Struggle between classes is the most important aspect of history

   D. In the past, class struggles were very common

   E. Society only began to exist with the invention of class

2. This piece could best be described as a…

A. Didactic

B. Allegory

C. Extended metaphor

D. Warning

E. Entreaty

3. In context, "manifold" can be assumed to mean…

A. Assertive

B. Oppressive

C. Ludicrous

D. Numerous

E. Insurmountable

4. Through repetition, this piece, particularly the second paragraph ("Freeman and slaves," etc.) makes effective use of…

A. Juxtaposition

B. Pathos

C. Appeal to authority

D. Logic

E. Rhetoric

5. What is the author's attitude towards class as a concept?

A. It is a necessary evil

B. It is an inevitability

C. It is a tool of oppression

D. It is useful, but often misused

E. It is a reward from the upper class

6. The author's prose in this piece appeals to the reader through its...

A. Factual accuracy

B. Simplicity

C. Superior tone

D. Vernacular

E Creativity

7. What can we assume will be the subject of this longer piece?

A. The volatile history of class struggle

B. The need to improve conditions for the lower class

C. The contemporary struggle of the upper and lower classes

D. The methods by which the upper class created such a dualistic society

E. The various forms in which this struggle manifests on a personal level

8. What best describes the tone of this piece?

A. Emphatic

B. Dithering

C. Scholarly

D. Fearful

E. Celebratory

Questions 9-16. Read the passage and answer the following questions carefully.

Most of the luxuries, and many of the so-called comforts of life, are not only not indispensable, but positive hindrances to the elevation of mankind. With respect to luxuries and comforts, the wisest have ever lived a more simple and meagre life than the poor. The ancient philosophers, Chinese, Hindoo, Persian, and Greek, were a class than which none has been poorer in outward riches, none so rich in inward. We know not much about them. It is remarkable that we know so much of them as we do. The same is true of the more modern reformers and benefactors of their race. None can be an impartial or wise observer of human life but from the vantage ground of what we should call voluntary poverty. Of a life of luxury the fruit is luxury, whether in agriculture, or commerce, or literature, or art. There are nowadays professors of philosophy, but not philosophers. Yet it is admirable to profess because it was once admirable to live. To be a philosopher is not merely to have subtle thoughts, nor even to found a school, but so to love wisdom as to live according to its dictates, a life of simplicity, independence, magnanimity, and trust. It is to solve some of the problems of life, not only theoretically, but practically. The success of great scholars and thinkers is commonly a courtier-like success, not kingly, not manly. They make shift to live merely by conformity, practically as their fathers did, and are in no sense the progenitors of a noble race of men. But why do men degenerate ever? What makes families run out? What is the nature of the luxury which enervates and destroys nations? Are we sure that there is none of it in our own lives? The philosopher is in advance of his age even in the outward form of his life. He is not fed, sheltered, clothed, warmed, like his contemporaries. How can a man be a philosopher and not maintain his vital heat by better methods than other men?

9. What, in context, is "voluntary poverty"?

A. A perspective, the only valid one when assessing humanity

B. A transient state of spiritual disillusionment

C. A general lack of goods and services

D. A state of being created by Hindus and Greeks

E. A positive hindrance to mankind

10. To this author, philosophers are all these things EXCEPT...

A. A lover of wisdom

B. A practical person

C. A subtle thinker

D. Aged beyond their years

E. Forebears of men

11. In the last sentence, the phrase "vital heat" is an example of a...

A. Euphemism

B. Synecdoche

C. Oxymoron

D. Innuendo

E. Allusion

12. The latter half of this selection makes frequent use of...

A. Neologism

B. Metaphor

C. Inquiry

D. Screed

E. Rhetorical questions

13. What is meant by the sentence "The success of great scholars and thinkers is commonly a courtier-like success, not kingly, not manly"?

A. Great thinkers naturally find themselves in leadership positions

B. Commoners and royalty alike often shun those who spout new ideas

C. Success is rare for a philosophe

D. Philosophers often find themselves more towards the middle of the social hierarchy

E. Without patronage, scholars do not flourish

14. What is meant by the phrase "to make shift" towards the end of the selection?

A. To go about

B. To avoid

C. To refuse

D. To mock up

E. Satirize

15. The first sentence of this piece contains what grammatical faux pas?

A. Repetition

B. Double Negative

C. Ambiguity

D. Dangling participle

E. Verb tense confusion

16. What is the best synonym for the word "enervate" in the sentence "*What is the nature of the luxury which enervates and destroys nations*"?

A. Encourages

B. Decays

C. Inhibits

D. Grows

E. Creates

Questions 17-24. Read the passage and answer the following questions carefully.

We observe today not a victory of party, but a celebration of freedom — symbolizing an end, as well as a beginning — signifying renewal, as well as change. For I have sworn before you and Almighty God the same solemn oath our forebears prescribed nearly a century and three-quarters ago.

The world is very different now. For man holds in his mortal hands the power to abolish all forms of human poverty and all forms of human life. And yet the same revolutionary beliefs for which our forebears fought are still at issue around the globe — the belief that the rights of man come not from the generosity of the state, but from the hand of God.

We dare not forget today that we are the heirs of that first revolution. Let the word go forth from this time and place, to friend and foe alike, that the torch has been passed to a new generation of Americans — born in this century, tempered by war, disciplined by a hard and bitter peace, proud of our ancient heritage, and unwilling to witness or permit the slow undoing of those human rights to which this nation has always been committed, and to which we are committed today at home and around the world.

Let every nation know, whether it wishes us well or ill, that we shall pay any price, bear any burden, meet any hardship, support any friend, oppose any foe, to assure the survival and the success of liberty.

This much we pledge — and more.

17. The second to last paragraph ("let every nation know") contains what two rhetorical devices?

A. Alliteration and asyndeton

B. Enumeration and neologism

C. Parallelism and malapropism

D. Rhetorical question and invective

E. Begging the question and ambiguity

18. "For man holds in his mortal hands the power to abolish all forms of human poverty and all forms of human life." This statement is a prime example of…

A. Irony

B. Emphasis

C. Verbosity

D. Grandiosity

E. Hyperbole

19. What can we infer is the "first revolution" that the speaker is referring to?

A. The drafting of the Constitution

B. The Cold War

C. WWII

D. American Independence

E. The Civil War

20. The piece makes frequent use of what rhetorical device evidenced by the word "not"?

A. Diction

B. Double negative

C. Antithesis

D. Hubris

E. Hamartia

21. This piece could best be characterized as…

A. A dire warning

B. A sermon

C. A call to action

D. A celebration of success

E. An apology

22. What is the tone the speaker is striving for in this piece?

A. Reassuring

B. Imperious

C. Knowledgeable

D. Pleading

E. Optimistic

23. What is meant by the sentence "the belief that the rights of man come not from the generosity of the state, but from the hand of God"?

A. Human rights must be fought for at all costs

B. Civil rights are only possible through the church

C. The clergy deserve commendation for their civil rights work

D. Every person has the right to certain liberties

E. Governments and churches struggle often for control

24. What can we infer is the speaker's attitude towards God?

A. God is a useful metaphor

B. God represents the fundamental laws of nature

C. Religion is a farce to be ignored

D. All people should accept God's love

E. There is only one true way to understand God

Questions 25-32. Read the passage and answer the following questions carefully.

Many people come to Hartford to address meetings as advocates of some reform. Tonight it is not to advocate a reform that I address a meeting in Hartford. I do not come here as an advocate, because whatever position the suffrage movement may occupy in the United States of America, in England it has passed beyond the realm of advocacy and it has entered into the sphere of practical politics. It has become the subject of revolution and civil war, and so tonight I am not here to advocate woman suffrage. American suffragists can do that very well for themselves.

I am here as a soldier who has temporarily left the field of battle in order to explain — it seems strange it should have to be explained — what civil war is like when civil war is waged by women. I am not only here as a soldier temporarily absent from the field at battle; I am here - and that, I think, is the strangest part of my coming - I am here as a person who, according to the law courts of my country, it has been decided, is of no value to the community at all: and I am adjudged because of my life to be a dangerous person, under sentence of penal servitude in a convict prison. So you see there is some special interest in hearing so unusual a person address you. I dare say, in the minds of many of you —you will perhaps forgive me this personal touch — that I do not look either very like a soldier or very like a convict, and yet I am both.

25. What was the speaker's purpose in creating this piece of oratory?

A. To explain the need for women's suffrage

B. To describe the unusual forms her struggle has taken

C. To impress upon them the value of women

D. To stress the need for temperance in the struggle for full rights

E. To ask that they join in her fight for equality

26. The final sentence contains a prime example of...

A. Hyperbole

B. Allusion

C. Irony

D. Innuendo

E Metaphor

27. The perspective of this piece is...

A. Universal

B. Detached

C. Inquiring

D. Personal

E. Scholarly

28. Who can we assume was the intended audience of this piece?

A. Undecided voters

B. Academics

C. Politicians

D. Legal professionals

E. Anti-suffragettes

29. The "field of battle" in this piece is used as a...

A. Simile

B. Allegory

C. Metaphor

D. Insinuation

E. Idiom

30. What is meant by the phrase "practical politics"?

A. Academic inquiry

B. Legal requirement

C. Day-to-day struggle

D. Unjustified strife

E. Ignorant prejudice

31. What is the relationship between the first and second paragraphs?

A. The first paragraph describes the expectations of this oratory, and the second explains how she will be subverting them

B. The first paragraph demonstrates the need for women's suffrage, and the second explains the obstacles they will encounter on the way

C. The first paragraph highlights the speaker's origin, while the second establishes her credentials

D. The first paragraph illustrates the inaction of the audience, and the second spurs them towards greater advocacy

E. The first paragraph offers a logical explanation of the speaker's politics, while the second plays more to emotion

32. The speaker mentions the struggles in England primarily to...

A. Warn the audience of what is to come

B. Detail the experiences of the speaker

C. Explain the need for revolution

D. Highlight the ineffectiveness of American suffragettes

E. Caution the audience against overt action

Questions 33-40. Read the passage and answer the following questions carefully.

The habit of reading is one of the greatest resources of mankind; and we enjoy reading books that belong to us much more than if they are borrowed. A borrowed book is like a guest in the house; it must be treated with punctiliousness, with a certain considerate formality. You must see that it sustains no damage; it must not suffer while under your roof. You cannot leave it carelessly, you cannot mark it, you cannot turn down the pages, you cannot use it familiarly. And then, some day, although this is seldom done, you really ought to return it.

But your own books belong to you; you treat them with that affectionate intimacy that annihilates formality. Books are for use, not for show; you should own no book that you are afraid to mark up, or afraid to place on the table, wide open and face down. A good reason for marking favorite passages in books is that this practice enables you to remember more easily the significant sayings, to refer to them quickly, and then in later years, it is like visiting a forest where you once blazed a trail. You have the pleasure of going over the old ground, and recalling both the intellectual scenery and your own earlier self.

Everyone should begin collecting a private library in youth; the instinct of private property, which is fundamental in human beings, can here be cultivated with every advantage and no evils. One should have one's own bookshelves, which should not have doors, glass windows, or keys; they should be free and accessible to the hand as well as to the eye. The best of mural decorations is books; they are more varied in color and appearance than any wallpaper, they are more attractive in design, and they have the prime advantage of being separate personalities, so that if you sit alone in the room in the firelight, you are surrounded with intimate friends. The knowledge that they are there in plain view is both stimulating and refreshing. You do not have to read them all. Most of my indoor life is spent in a room containing six thousand books; and I have a stock answer to the invariable question that comes from strangers. "Have you read all of these books?"

"Some of them twice." This reply is both true and unexpected.

There are of course no friends like living, breathing, corporeal men and women; my devotion to reading has never made me a recluse. How could it? Books are of the people, by the people, for the people. Literature is the immortal part of history; it is the best and most enduring part of personality. But book-friends have this advantage over living friends; you can enjoy the most truly aristocratic society in the world whenever you want it. The great dead are beyond our physical reach, and the great living are usually almost as inaccessible; as for our personal friends and acquaintances, we cannot always see them. Perchance they are asleep, or away on a journey. But in a private library, you can at any moment converse with Socrates or Shakespeare or Carlyle or Dumas or Dickens or Shaw or Barrie or Galsworthy. And there is no doubt that in these books you see these men at their best. They wrote for you. They "laid themselves out," they did their ultimate best to entertain you, to make a favorable impression. You are necessary to them as an audience is to an actor; only instead of seeing them masked, you look into their innermost heart of heart.

33. What is the best synonym for "punctiliousness" in the first paragraph?

A. Propriety

B. Specificity

C. Care

D. Morality

E. Timeliness

34. The personification of books in the first two paragraphs is established primarily through...

A. Metaphor

B. Simile

C. Allusion

D. Satire

E. Hyperbole

35. The tone of this piece could best be described as...

A. Empowering

B. Humorous

C. Caustic

D. Self-deprecating

E. Poetic

36. According to the author, what is the primary benefit of books over people?

A. Books are eternal and unchanging

B. Books can be altered to suit your needs

C. Books can be ignored more easily than living friends

D. Books take up less of your time

E. Books serve many purposes, and are attractive decorations

37. How does the author establish a close relationship with his audience?

A. Through simple language and syntax

B. Through careful repetitions and fatherly diction

C. Through intellectual queries and abstract ideas

D. Through personal pronouns and familiar tone

E. Through keen satire and witty aphorisms

38. The final paragraph contains all of these rhetorical devices EXCEPT…

A. Rhetorical question

B. Parallelism

C. Personification

D. Appeal to authority

E. Asyndeton

39. In the final few lines of the last paragraph, what does "they" refer to?

A. Books

B. Great men

C. Friends

D. Readers

E. Actors

40. "The answer is both true and unexpected" marks a shift from…

A. The more general merits of books to personal experiences of the author

B. The need for books to the methods of acquiring them

C. The merits of books to consumers, and then to those that create them

D. The superficial benefits of books to their more spiritual or intellectual uses

E. The author's history with books to the experiences of his friends

Questions 41-48. Read the passage and answer the following questions carefully.

I read the other day some verses written by an eminent painter which were original and not conventional. The soul always hears an admonition in such lines, let the subject be what it may. The sentiment they instil is of more value than any thought they may contain. To believe your own thought, to believe that what is true for you in your private heart is true for all men, — that is genius. Speak your latent conviction, and it shall be the universal sense; for the inmost in due time becomes the outmost — and our first thought is rendered back to us by the trumpets of the Last Judgment. Familiar as the voice of the mind is to each, the highest merit we ascribe to Moses, Plato, and Milton is, that they set at naught books and traditions, and spoke not what men but what they thought. A man should learn to detect and watch that gleam of light which flashes across his mind from within, more than the lustre of the firmament of bards and sages. Yet he dismisses without notice his thought, because it is his. In every work of genius we recognize our own rejected thoughts: they come back to us with a certain alienated majesty. Great works of art have no more affecting lesson for us than this. They teach us to abide by our spontaneous impression with good-humored inflexibility then most when the whole cry of voices is on the other side. Else, to-morrow a stranger will say with masterly good sense precisely what we have thought and felt all the time, and we shall be forced to take with shame our own opinion from another.

There is a time in every man's education when he arrives at the conviction that envy is ignorance; that imitation is suicide; that he must take himself for better, for worse, as his portion; that though the wide universe is full of good, no kernel of nourishing corn can come to him but through his toil bestowed on that plot of ground which is given to him to till. The power which resides in him is new in nature, and none but he knows what that is which he can do, nor does he know until he has tried. Not for nothing one face, one character, one fact, makes much impression on him, and another none. This sculpture in the memory is not without pre-established harmony. The eye was placed where one ray should fall, that it might testify of that particular ray. We but half express ourselves, and are ashamed of that divine idea which each of us represents. It may be safely trusted as proportionate and of good issues, so it be faithfully imparted, but God will not have his work made manifest by cowards. A man is relieved and gay when he has put his heart into his work and done his best; but what he has said or done otherwise, shall give him no peace. It is a deliverance which does not deliver. In the attempt his genius deserts him; no muse befriends; no invention, no hope.

41. What is the best synonym for "admonition" at the beginning of the first paragraph?

A. Strong suggestion

B. Dire warning

C. Direct insult

D. False accusation

E. Cutting remark

42. **In context, how can you best paraphrase the sentence "that he must take himself for better, for worse, as his portion"?**

A. He must accept his own limitations

B. He should forge his own identity

C. His must consider how he will be remembered

D. He must seize life by the horns

E. He must consider his own flaws

43. **This piece can best be characterized as a...**

A. Screed

B. Satire

C. Persuasive essay

D. Extended metaphor

E. Narrative essay

44. **What is meant by the phrase "envy is ignorance"?**

A. It is counterproductive to imitate

B. Ignorance comes from a place of extreme ego

C. Jealousy is a natural part of education

D. The educated possess no envy

E. Such emotions are a fancy of youth

45. **What best paraphrases the most "affecting lesson" of great art?**

A. It communicates with us across time

B. We make it for ourselves

C. It reflects our inner worlds

D. It teaches us to be spontaneous

E. It creates great profits, both physical and spiritual

46. **The central theme of this piece is…**

A. The struggle of the artist against society

B. The necessity of art in daily life

C. The need for individuality

D. The superficial nature of art

E. The need to isolate oneself from outside influences

47. **In context, what is meant by the sentence "A man is relieved and gay when he has put his heart into his work and done his best; but what he has said or done otherwise, shall give him no peace"?**

A. An artist is never satisfied with his work

B. Common people cannot understand the struggles of the artist

C. Hard work is the only freedom worth having

D. Great art comes with the terrible price of isolation

E. Only work done to one's own standards is satisfying

48. **What causes a man's "genius to desert him"?**

A. Insufficient skill

B. Lack of focus

C. Bad luck

D. Unoriginality

E. Divine will

Questions 49-55. Read the passage and answer the following questions carefully.

In the title of this study is used the somewhat pretentious phrase, the spirit of capitalism. What is to be understood by it? The attempt to give anything like a definition of it brings out certain difficulties which are in the very nature of this type of investigation.

If any object can be found to which this term can be applied with any understandable meaning, it can only be an historical individual, i.e. a complex of elements associated in historical reality which we unite into a conceptual whole from the standpoint of their cultural significance.

Such an historical concept, however, since it refers in its content to a phenomenon significant for its unique individuality, cannot be defined according to the formula genus proximum, differentia specifica, but it must be gradually put together out of the individual parts which are taken from historical reality to make it up. Thus the final and definitive concept cannot stand at the beginning of the investigation, but must come at the end. We must, in other words, work out in the course of the discussion, as its most important result, the best conceptual formulation of what we here understand by the spirit of capitalism, that is the best from the point of view which interests us here. This point of view (the one of which we shall speak later) is, further, by no means the only possible one from which the historical phenomena we are investigating can be analysed. Other standpoints would, for this as for every historical phenomenon, yield other characteristics as the essential ones. The result is that it is by no means necessary to understand by the spirit of capitalism only what it will come to mean to us for the purposes of our analysis. This is a necessary result of the nature of historical concepts which attempt for their methodological purposes not to grasp historical reality in abstract general formulae, but in concrete genetic sets of relations which are inevitably of a specifically unique and individual character.

Thus, if we try to determine the object, the analysis and historical explanation of which we are attempting, it cannot be in the form of a conceptual definition, but at least in the beginning only a provisional description of what is here meant by the spirit of capitalism. Such a description is, however, indispensable in order clearly to understand the object of the investigation. For this purpose we turn to a document of that spirit which contains what we are looking for in almost classical purity, and at the same time has the advantage of being free from all direct relationship to religion, being thus, for our purposes, free of preconceptions.

49. What is the "object" referred to throughout this piece?

A. A pretentious phrase

B. The formula

C. An historical individual

D. The analysis

E. The result of the investigation

50. What is the relationship between the first and second paragraphs?

A. The first paragraph establishes the title of the piece, the second deconstructs it

B. The first paragraph explains the value of capitalism, while the second calls its import into question

C. The first paragraph offers a rhetorical question, and the second elucidates the difficulties in answering it

D. The first paragraph illustrates the speaker's main concern, and the second establishes his credentials in addressing it

E. The first paragraph sets the tone of the piece, and the second offers a witty subversion

51. What differentiates this query into a "historical object" from other, similar inquiries?

A. It can only be ascertained at the end of the investigation, after its aspects have been examined

B. It has no physical presence and must be assessed in theoretical terms

C. It requires deep knowledge of history that is hard to obtain

D. It can be completed through assumptions rather than common facts

E. It needs a more methodical approach than other such inquiries

52. What is the author saying with the last sentence?

A. He will describe the need to divorce religion from this discussion

B. He will now discuss a document that is unprejudiced by political or religious viewpoints

C. Religion inherently taints a discussion, and must be purged from further inquiries

D. The spirit of capitalism is closely tied to religious interests, ones that must be understood

E. Societal biases have influenced our discussion, but further points of evidence will mitigate this

53. "Other standpoints would, for this as for every historical phenomenon, yield other characteristics as the essential ones. The result is that it is by no means necessary to understand by the spirit of capitalism only what it will come to mean to us for the purposes of our analysis." What is meant by this passage?

A. Our understanding of this topic is influenced by our cultural perspective, but this shall suffice for the purposes of discussion

B. Our viewpoint of this topic is woefully inadequate, and we must seek any other perspective that we can

C. Academia can only go so far, and we must make assumptions where scholarship fails us

D. The spirit of capitalism cannot be measured in such a small argument, but we must try

E. Others may disagree with our assessment here, but they are incorrect, as we will now demonstrate

54. What is the subject of the verb "yield" towards the middle of paragraph three?

A. Characteristics

B. Phenomenon

C. Historical

D. Standpoints

E. Essential ones

55. What can we assume will follow this selection?

A. A segue into the nature of capitalism

B. A piece on the author's cultural background

C. A screed against the influence of religion

D. A point of evidence offering provisional description

E. A clear description of terms

Free Response Essay Sample Questions

Section II

Time: 2 hours

Question 1

(Suggested time: 40 minutes. This question counts one-third of the total essay section score.)

The concept, creation, and construction of the American railroads were monumental tasks that gave rise to America as a true superpower. If not for the development and surge of rail lines, the United States would not be the world economic engine it is today.

Carefully read the six sources, including the introductory information for each source. Then synthesize information from at least three of the sources and incorporate it into a coherent, well-developed essay that argues a position clearly.

Make sure your argument is central; use the sources to illustrate and support your reasoning. Avoid merely summarizing the sources. Indicate clearly which sources you are referencing, whether through direct quotation, paraphrase, or summary. You may cite the sources as Source A, Source B, etc., or by using the descriptions in parentheses.

Source A (Stanford)
Source B (PBS)
Source C (Live Science)
Source D (Scientific American)
Source E (History)
Source F (Economic)

Source A, Excerpt of "Stanford's Rise of Monopolies: History of American Railroads", http://cs.stanford.edu/people/eroberts/cs181/projects/corporate-monopolies/development_rr.html

The concept of constructing a railroad in the United States was first conceived by Colonel John Stevens, in 1812. He described his theories in a collection of works called "Documents tending to prove the superior advantages of railways and steam carriages over canal navigation."

The earliest railroads constructed were horse drawn cars running on tracks, used for transporting freight. The first to be chartered and built was the Granite Railway of Massachusetts, which ran approximately three miles (1826). The first regular carrier of passengers and freight was the Baltimore and Ohio railroad, completed on February 28, 1827. It was not until Christmas Day, 1830, when the South Carolina Canal and Railroad Company completed the first mechanical passenger train, that the modern railroad industry was born. This industry would have a profound effect on the nation in the coming decades, often determining how an individual lived his life.

By 1835, dozens of local railroad networks had been put into place. Each one of these tracks went no more than a few miles, but the potential for this mode of transportation was finally being realized. With every passing year, the number of these railway systems grew exponentially. By 1850, over 9,000 miles of track had been lain. Along with the proliferation of railroads came increased standardization of the field. An ideal locomotive was developed which served as the model for all subsequent trains. Various companies began to cooperate with one another, to both maximize profits and minimize expenditures.

This interaction of various companies initiated the trend of conglomeration which would continue through the rest of the Nineteenth Century. In 1850, the New York Central Railroad Company was formed by the merging of a dozen small railroads between the Hudson River and Buffalo. Single companies had begun to extend their railway systems outside of the local domain. Between 1851 and 1857, the federal government issued land grants to Illinois to construct the Illinois Central railroad. The government set a precedent with this action, and fostered the growth of one of the largest companies in the nation.

Source B, Excerpt of PBS Timeline
http://www.pbs.org/wgbh/americanexperience/features/timeline/streamliners/

1851
Telegraphs are now used for dispatching trains.

1853
The growing railroad industry attracts energetic young employees like the Scottish immigrant Andrew Carnegie, who launches his career at the Pennsylvania Railroad as a $35-per-month telegraph operator.

1856
In England, Henry Bessemer develops the Bessemer converter, which enables steel to be manufactured inexpensively, an accomplishment for which he is knighted in 1879. The process will be introduced in Troy, New York, nine years later.

1860
There are now 30,000 miles of railroad in the United States.

1861
The Civil War begins. It will be the first war in which railroads play a significant role in transporting soldiers and equipment.

1865
The first domestic steel rails are produced. Steel rails are costly; only the lines with heavy traffic can afford to put them in place. By 1890, the majority of all railroad mileage will be laid with steel rails.
The first railroad sleeping car, designed by George Pullman, appears in the United States. When one of Pullman's cars is attached to the funeral train carrying Abraham Lincoln's body in April, demand for them skyrockets. Two years later Pullman will introduce the refrigerator car.

1879
Thomas Edison and English inventor Joseph Wilson Swan independently devise the first practical electric lights.

1880
There are now 93,000 miles of railroad in the United States.

1881
George Westinghouse perfects the first automatic electric block signal, which is designed to prevent train crashes, increase passenger safety, and move rail traffic more efficiently. Westinghouse's safety devices will have a tremendous impact on the railroad industry.

September 16, 1908
Billy Durant incorporates General Motors. Within days, GM buys Buick, and later Oldsmobile and Cadillac.

Source C, Live Science 7th most important historic invention that changed the world, list from March 6, 2012

The Printing Press

The German Johannes Gutenberg invented the printing press around 1440. Key to its development was the hand mold, a new molding technique that enabled the rapid creation of large quantities of metal movable type. Printing presses exponentially increased the speed with which book copies could be made, and thus they led to the rapid and widespread dissemination of knowledge for the first time in history. Twenty million volumes had been printed in Western Europe by 1500.

Among other things, the printing press permitted wider access to the Bible, which in turn led to alternative interpretations, including that of Martin Luther, whose "95 Theses" a document printed by the hundred-thousand sparked the Protestant Reformation.

Source D, Scientific American, Excerpt from essay contest from 1913 of the greatest invention 1888-1913

A competition sponsored in 1913 by *Scientific American* asked for essays on the 10 greatest inventions. The rules: "our time" meant the previous quarter century, 1888 to 1913; the invention had to be patentable and was considered to date from its "commercial introduction."

The first-prize essay was written by William I. Wyman, who worked in the U.S. Patent Office in Washington, D.C., and was thus well informed on the progress of inventions. His list was:

1. The electric furnace (1889) It was "the only means for commercially producing Carborundum (the hardest of all manufactured substances)." The electric furnace also converted aluminum "from a merely precious to very useful metal" (by reducing it's price 98 percent), and was "radically transforming the steel industry."
2. The steam turbine, invented by Charles Parsons in 1884 and commercially introduced over the next 10 years. A huge improvement in powering ships, the more far-reaching use of this invention was to drive generators that produced electricity.
3. The gasoline-powered automobile. Many inventors worked toward the goal of a "self-propelled" vehicle in the 19th century. Wyman gave the honor specifically to Gottleib Daimler for his 1889 engine, arguing: "a century's insistent but unsuccessful endeavor to provide a practical self-propelled car proves that the success of any type that once answered requirements would be immediate. Such success did come with the advent of the Daimler motor, and not before."
4. The moving picture. Entertainment always will be important to people. "The moving picture has transformed the amusements of the multitude." The technical pioneer he cited was Thomas Edison.
5. The airplane. For "the Realization of an age-long dream" he gave the laurels of success to the Wright brothers, but apart from its military use reserved judgment on the utility of the invention: "It presents the least commercial utility of all the inventions considered."

Source E, Ranking of Innovations that Changed History from history.com

11. The Steam Engine

Cars, airplanes, factories, trains, spacecraft—none of these transportation methods would have been possible if not for the early breakthrough of the steam engine. The first practical use of external combustion dates back to 1698, when Thomas Savery developed a steam-powered water pump. Steam engines were then perfected in the late 1700s by James Watt, and went on to fuel one of the most momentous technological leaps in human history during the Industrial Revolution. Throughout the 1800s external combustion allowed for exponential improvement in transportation, agriculture and manufacturing, and also powered the rise of world superpowers like Great Britain and the United States. Most important of all, the steam engine's basic principle of energy-into-motion set the stage for later innovations like internal combustion engines and jet turbines, which prompted the rise of cars and aircraft during the 20th century.

Source F, Summary from The Economic Impact of America's Frieght Railroads, May 2015, authored by the Association of American Railroads

From the food on our tables to the cars we drive to the shoes on our children's feet, freight railroads carry the things America depends on. Freight railroads in the United States are the best in the world. Every year, they save consumers billions of dollars while reducing energy consumption and pollution, lowering greenhouse gas emissions, cutting highway gridlock, and reducing the high costs of highway construction and maintenance. Millions of Americans work in industries that are more competitive in the tough global economy thanks to the affordability and productivity of America's freight railroads. In addition, America's freight railroads directly support 1.2 million jobs in various industries, including more than 185,000 well-paying jobs in the freight rail industry.

Question 2
(Suggested time: 40 minutes. This question counts one-third of the total essay section score.)

Read the following two quotes.

"There is no good and evil, there is only power and those too weak to seek it." —J. K. Rowling

"No matter how hard Evil tries, it can never quite match up to the power of Good, because Evil is ultimately self-destructive. Evil may set out to corrupt others, but in the process corrupts itself." —John Connolly

In a well-organized essay, take a position on the relationship between good and evil including a position if good and evil exist. Support your argument with appropriate evidence and examples.

Question 3
(Suggested time: 40 minutes. This question counts one-third of the total essay section score.)

The UK Schools Minister, Nick Gibb, made the following comment at the Education Reform Summit on July 9, 2015.

If we are to deliver a fairer society, in which opportunity is shared more widely, we must secure the highest standards of education for all young people, regardless of their background.

Using your own experience and background information, support an explanation of how the Minister's comments are true or false and what requirements need to be in place for evaluating results.

Sample Test Five: ANSWER KEY

Question Number	Correct Answer	Your Answer
1.	C	
2.	A	
3.	D	
4.	A	
5.	C	
6.	B	
7.	C	
8.	A	
9.	A	
10.	E	
11.	A	
12.	E	
13.	D	
14.	A	
15.	B	
16.	B	
17.	A	
18.	A	
19.	D	
20.	C	
21.	C	
22.	E	
23.	D	
24.	B	
25.	B	
26.	C	
27.	D	
28.	B	

Question Number	Correct Answer	Your Answer
29.	C	
30.	C	
31.	A	
32.	B	
33.	C	
34.	B	
35.	B	
36.	A	
37.	D	
38.	D	
39.	B	
40.	D	
41.	A	
42.	B	
43.	A	
44.	A	
45.	C	
46.	C	
47.	E	
48.	D	
49.	C	
50.	C	
51.	A	
52.	B	
53.	A	
54.	D	
55.	D	

Answer Key and Rationale

1. The first sentence can best be paraphrased as…

A. Every future societal shall deal with issues of class

B. Education of history is essential for a society to develop

C. Struggle between classes is the most important aspect of history

D. In the past, class struggles were very common

E. Society only began to exist with the invention of class

The correct answer is C.

With the opening line, the author is explaining that class struggles have defined history. (C) is the best answer.

2. This piece could best be described as a…

A. Didactic

B. Allegory

C. Extended metaphor

D. Warning

E. Entreaty

The correct answer is A.

The piece's main goal is to educate. It does not warn or entreat, and it does not deal with its subjects allegorically or in an extended metaphor.

3. In context, "manifold" can be assumed to mean…

A. Assertive

B. Oppressive

C. Ludicrous

D. Numerous

E. Insurmountable

The correct answer is D.

"Manifold" is a synonym for "various", "diverse" or "many".

4. **Through repetition, this piece, particularly the second paragraph ("Freeman and slaves," etc.) makes effective use of...**

A. Juxtaposition

B. Pathos

C. Appeal to authority

D. Logic

E. Rhetoric

The correct answer is A.

The repetitions, such as "freedman and slave" or "guildmaster and journeyman", create juxtapositions the author uses for rhetorical effect.

5. **What is the author's attitude towards class as a concept?**

A. It is a necessary evil

B. It is an inevitability

C. It is a tool of oppression

D. It is useful, but often misused

E. It is a reward from the upper class

The correct answer is C.

The author is primarily concerned with class hierarchies as a tool of oppression, stating how the modern era of bourgeoisie vs. proletariat struggle is simplified in its antagonism. He feels class struggle is oppressive.

6. **The author's prose in this piece appeals to the reader through its...**

A. Factual accuracy

B. Simplicity

C. Superior tone

D. Vernacular

E. Creativity

The correct answer is B.

The author uses primarily simple language in this treatise. It makes opinion-based assertions and relies less on factual accuracy, so (A) is inappropriate. Likewise, the piece does not strive to superior or overly familiar, so (C) and (D) do not apply. (E) is too vague.

7. **What can we assume will be the subject of this longer piece?**

A. The volatile history of class struggle

B. The need to improve conditions for the lower class

C. The contemporary struggle of the upper and lower classes

D. The methods by which the upper class created such a dualistic society

E. The various forms in which this struggle manifests on a personal level

The correct answer is C.

The author ends on his point about bourgeoisie vs. proletariat, suggesting that this is the topic he will pursuing for the longer essay.

8. **What best describes the tone of this piece?**

A. Emphatic

B. Dithering

C. Scholarly

D. Fearful

E. Celebratory

The correct answer is A.

The author makes many emphatic points throughout the piece, even in points that could best be characterized as opinion. He is stating things strongly, with no room for argument.

Questions 9-16. Read the passage and answer the following questions carefully.

Most of the luxuries, and many of the so-called comforts of life, are not only not indispensable, but positive hindrances to the elevation of mankind. With respect to luxuries and comforts, the wisest have ever lived a more simple and meagre life than the poor. The ancient philosophers, Chinese, Hindoo, Persian, and Greek, were a class than which none has been poorer in outward riches, none so rich in inward. We know not much about them. It is remarkable that we know so much of them as we do. The same is true of the more modern reformers and benefactors of their race. None can be an impartial or wise observer of human life but from the vantage ground of what we should call voluntary poverty. Of a life of luxury the fruit is luxury, whether in agriculture, or commerce, or literature, or art. There are nowadays professors of philosophy, but not philosophers. Yet it is admirable to profess because it was once admirable to live. To be a philosopher is not merely to have subtle thoughts, nor even to found a school, but so to love wisdom as to live according to its dictates, a life of simplicity, independence, magnanimity, and trust. It is to solve some of the problems of life, not only theoretically, but practically. The success of great scholars and thinkers is commonly a courtier-like success, not kingly, not manly. They make shift to live merely by conformity, practically as their fathers did, and are in no sense the progenitors of a noble race of men. But why do men degenerate ever? What makes families run out? What is the nature of the luxury which enervates and destroys nations? Are we sure that there is none of it in our own lives? The philosopher is in advance of his age even in the outward form of his life. He is not fed, sheltered, clothed, warmed, like his contemporaries. How can a man be a philosopher and not maintain his vital heat by better methods than other men?

9. What, in context, is "voluntary poverty"?

A. A perspective, the only valid one when assessing humanity

B. A transient state of spiritual disillusionment

C. A general lack of goods and services

D. A state of being created by Hindus and Greeks

E. A positive hindrance to mankind

The correct answer is A.

The author believes voluntary poverty is a state one achieves by shunning material wealth, and he insists the great thinkers throughout history have done likewise so as to better understand humanity.

10. To this author, philosophers are all these things EXCEPT…

A. A lover of wisdom

B. A practical person

C. A subtle thinker

D. Aged beyond their years

E. Forebears of men

The correct answer is E.

The author says philosophers are "in no way the progenitors of a noble race of men". (E) is the best answer.

11. In the last sentence, the phrase "vital heat" is an example of a…

A. Euphemism

B. Synecdoche

C. Oxymoron

D. Innuendo

E. Allusion

The correct answer is A.

"Vital heat" is a euphemism for one's life and soul.

12. **The latter half of this selection makes frequent use of…**

    A. Neologism

    B. Metaphor

    C. Inquiry

    D. Screed

    E. Rhetorical questions

    The correct answer is E.

    Almost every sentence past the halfway mark of this piece is a rhetorical question.

13. **What is meant by the sentence "The success of great scholars and thinkers is commonly a courtier-like success, not kingly, not manly"?**

    A. Great thinkers naturally find themselves in leadership positions

    B. Commoners and royalty alike often shun those who spout new ideas

    C. Success is rare for a philosophe

    D. Philosophers often find themselves more towards the middle of the social hierarchy

    E. Without patronage, scholars do not flourish

    The correct answer is D.

    "Courtier-like" suggests a space in between commoners and true royalty, which is where philosophers are best fitted, according to the author.

14. **What is meant by the phrase "to make shift" towards the end of the selection?**

    A. To go about

    B. To avoid

    C. To refuse

    D. To mock up

    E. satirize

    The correct answer is A.

    "To make shift" is an archaic term for "to go about". This

Sample Test Five

15. **The first sentence of this piece contains what grammatical faux pas?**

A. Repetition

B. Double Negative

C. Ambiguity

D. Dangling participle

E. Verb tense confusion

The correct answer is B.

"Not only not indispensable" is a double negative phrase.

16. **What is the best synonym for the word "enervate" in the sentence "*What is the nature of the luxury which enervates and destroys nations*"?**

A. Encourages

B. Decays

C. Inhibits

D. Grows

E. Creates

The correct answer is B.

"Enervate" is a synonym for decrease or decay.

Questions 17-24. Read the passage and answer the following questions carefully.

We observe today not a victory of party, but a celebration of freedom — symbolizing an end, as well as a beginning — signifying renewal, as well as change. For I have sworn before you and Almighty God the same solemn oath our forebears prescribed nearly a century and three-quarters ago.

The world is very different now. For man holds in his mortal hands the power to abolish all forms of human poverty and all forms of human life. And yet the same revolutionary beliefs for which our forebears fought are still at issue around the globe — the belief that the rights of man come not from the generosity of the state, but from the hand of God.

We dare not forget today that we are the heirs of that first revolution. Let the word go forth from this time and place, to friend and foe alike, that the torch has been passed to a new generation of Americans — born in this century, tempered by war, disciplined by a hard and bitter peace, proud of our ancient heritage, and unwilling to witness or permit the slow undoing of those human rights to which this nation has always been committed, and to which we are committed today at home and around the world.

Let every nation know, whether it wishes us well or ill, that we shall pay any price, bear any burden, meet any hardship, support any friend, oppose any foe, to assure the survival and the success of liberty.

This much we pledge — and more.

17. **The second to last paragraph ("let every nation know") contains what two rhetorical devices?**

A. Alliteration and asyndeton

B. Enumeration and neologism

C. Parallelism and malapropism

D. Rhetorical question and invective

E. Begging the question and ambiguity

The correct answer is A.

"Pay any price" and "bear any burden" are examples of alliteration, and the omission of a conjunction like "or" or "and" creates an asyndeton.

18. **"For man holds in his mortal hands the power to abolish all forms of human poverty and all forms of human life." This statement is a prime example of...**

A. Irony

B. Emphasis

C. Verbosity

D. Grandiosity

E. Hyperbole

The correct answer is A.

The speaker is creating rhetorical irony by contrasting these two concepts, wherein humans can destroy themselves or save themselves at the same time.

19. **What can we infer is the "first revolution" that the speaker is referring to?**

A. The drafting of the Constitution

B. The Cold War

C. WWII

D. American Independence

E. The Civil War

The correct answer is D.

This is a presidential address, and thus, the first revolution is likely the Revolutionary War.

20. The piece makes frequent use of what rhetorical device evidenced by the word "not"?

A. Diction

B. Double negative

C. Antithesis

D. Hubris

E. Hamartia

The correct answer is C.

"Antithesis" makes use of the word "not", as in "not a victory of party" and "not from the generosity of the state".

21. This piece could best be characterized as...

A. A dire warning

B. A sermon

C. A call to action

D. A celebration of success

E. An apology

The correct answer is C.

Phrases such as "the torch has been passed" suggest that this piece is a rallying cry for the listeners. It discusses dangers and obstacles, but is still fundamentally optimistic, so (A) is inaccurate. It's darker tones also preclude (B) and (C), and it has nothing in common with an apology (E).

22. What is the tone the speaker is striving for in this piece?

A. Reassuring

B. Imperious

C. Knowledgeable

D. Pleading

E. Optimistic

The correct answer is E.

The speaker insists that obstacles have befallen them, and more will likely accrue in the future, but they will survive through strength and perseverance.

23. What is meant by the sentence "the belief that the rights of man come not from the generosity of the state, but from the hand of God"?

A. Human rights must be fought for at all costs

B. Civil rights are only possible through the church

C. The clergy deserve commendation for their civil rights work

D. Every person has the right to certain liberties

E. Governments and churches struggle often for control

The correct answer is D.

The "hand of God" phrase suggests that these rights are inalienable, and are not granted by the whims of the state.

24. What can we infer is the speaker's attitude towards God?

A. God is a useful metaphor

B. God represents the fundamental laws of nature

C. Religion is a farce to be ignored

D. All people should accept God's love

E. There is only one true way to understand God

The correct answer is B.

The piece makes no mention of specific religious iconography, focusing instead on God as a broader, universal concept.

Questions 25-32. Read the passage and answer the following questions carefully.

Many people come to Hartford to address meetings as advocates of some reform. Tonight it is not to advocate a reform that I address a meeting in Hartford. I do not come here as an advocate, because whatever position the suffrage movement may occupy in the United States of America, in England it has passed beyond the realm of advocacy and it has entered into the sphere of practical politics. It has become the subject of revolution and civil war, and so tonight I am not here to advocate woman suffrage. American suffragists can do that very well for themselves.

I am here as a soldier who has temporarily left the field of battle in order to explain — it seems strange it should have to be explained — what civil war is like when civil war is waged by women. I am not only here as a soldier temporarily absent from the field at battle; I am here - and that, I think, is the strangest part of my coming - I am here as a person who, according to the law courts of my country, it has been decided, is of no value to the community at all: and I am adjudged because of my life to be a dangerous person, under sentence of penal servitude in a convict prison. So you see there is some special interest in hearing so unusual a person address you. I dare say, in the minds of many of you —you will perhaps forgive me this personal touch — that I do not look either very like a soldier or very like a convict, and yet I am both.

25. What was the speaker's purpose in creating this piece of oratory?

A. To explain the need for women's suffrage

B. To describe the unusual forms her struggle has taken

C. To impress upon them the value of women

D. To stress the need for temperance in the struggle for full rights

E. To ask that they join in her fight for equality

The correct answer is B.

The author's primary concern in this piece is to explain her own struggle, and how unusual it has been. She has great concern for the struggles of women overall, but this is secondary to her personal account.

26. The final sentence contains a prime example of...

A. Hyperbole

B. Allusion

C. Irony

D. Innuendo

E Metaphor

The correct answer is C.

"I do not look very like a solider or convict, yet I am both" is an ironic statement, meant to impress upon them the absurd reality of her situation.

27. The perspective of this piece is...

A. Universal

B. Detached

C. Inquiring

D. Personal

E. Scholarly

The correct answer is D.

The piece is about the speaker's opinions and experiences. It is formal in nature, but the subject matter is strictly personal.

28. Who can we assume was the intended audience of this piece?

A. Undecided voters

B. Academics

C. Politicians

D. Legal professionals

E. Anti-suffragettes

The correct answer is B.

The author mentions she is speaking at Hartford, and is talking to a crowd of advocates for reform. (B) is the safest answer with the fewest assumptions.

29. The "field of battle" in this piece is used as a...

A. Simile

B. Allegory

C. Metaphor

D. Insinuation

E. Idiom

The correct answer is C.

The "field of battle" the speaker describes is the figurative battlefield that women fight on for equality in the political and social spheres.

30. What is meant by the phrase "practical politics"?

A. Academic inquiry

B. Legal requirement

C. Day-to-day struggle

D. Unjustified strife

E. Ignorant prejudice

The correct answer is C.

"Practical politics" is understood to mean the politics of daily life for women, with all the struggles that entails.

31. What is the relationship between the first and second paragraphs?

A. The first paragraph describes the expectations of this oratory, and the second explains how she will be subverting them

B. The first paragraph demonstrates the need for women's suffrage, and the second explains the obstacles they will encounter on the way

C. The first paragraph highlights the speaker's origin, while the second establishes her credentials

D. The first paragraph illustrates the inaction of the audience, and the second spurs them towards greater advocacy

E. The first paragraph offers a logical explanation of the speaker's politics, while the second plays more to emotion

The correct answer is A.

The author is primarily concerned in the first paragraph with establishing baseline expectations about herself and the argument she is making. The second paragraph is all about subverting them for rhetorical effect.

32. The speaker mentions the struggles in England primarily to...

A. Warn the audience of what is to come

B. Detail the experiences of the speaker

C. Explain the need for revolution

D. Highlight the ineffectiveness of American suffragettes

E. Caution the audience against overt action

The correct answer is B.

Her mention of the struggles in England serve to highlight her "credentials" so to speak, and lend greater import to the rest of her arguments.

Questions 33-40. Read the passage and answer the following questions carefully.

The habit of reading is one of the greatest resources of mankind; and we enjoy reading books that belong to us much more than if they are borrowed. A borrowed book is like a guest in the house; it must be treated with punctiliousness, with a certain considerate formality. You must see that it sustains no damage; it must not suffer while under your roof. You cannot leave it carelessly, you cannot mark it, you cannot turn down the pages, you cannot use it familiarly. And then, some day, although this is seldom done, you really ought to return it.

But your own books belong to you; you treat them with that affectionate intimacy that annihilates formality. Books are for use, not for show; you should own no book that you are afraid to mark up, or afraid to place on the table, wide open and face down. A good reason for marking favorite passages in books is that this practice enables you to remember more easily the significant sayings, to refer to them quickly, and then in later years, it is like visiting a forest where you once blazed a trail. You have the pleasure of going over the old ground, and recalling both the intellectual scenery and your own earlier self.

Everyone should begin collecting a private library in youth; the instinct of private property, which is fundamental in human beings, can here be cultivated with every advantage and no evils. One should have one's own bookshelves, which should not have doors, glass windows, or keys; they should be free and accessible to the hand as well as to the eye. The best of mural decorations is books; they are more varied in color and appearance than any wallpaper, they are more attractive in design, and they have the prime advantage of being separate personalities, so that if you sit alone in the room in the firelight, you are surrounded with intimate friends. The knowledge that they are there in plain view is both stimulating and refreshing. You do not have to read them all. Most of my indoor life is spent in a room containing six thousand books; and I have a stock answer to the invariable question that comes from strangers. "Have you read all of these books?"

"Some of them twice." This reply is both true and unexpected.

There are of course no friends like living, breathing, corporeal men and women; my devotion to reading has never made me a recluse. How could it? Books are of the people, by the people, for the people. Literature is the immortal part of history; it is the best and most enduring part of personality. But book-friends have this advantage over living friends; you can enjoy the most truly aristocratic society in the world whenever you want it. The great dead are beyond our physical reach, and the great living are usually almost as inaccessible; as for our personal friends and acquaintances, we cannot always see them. Perchance they are asleep, or away on a journey. But in a private library, you can at any moment converse with Socrates or Shakespeare or Carlyle or Dumas or Dickens or Shaw or Barrie or Galsworthy. And there is no doubt that in these books you see these men at their best. They wrote for you. They "laid themselves out," they did their ultimate best to entertain you, to make a favorable impression. You are necessary to them as an audience is to an actor; only instead of seeing them masked, you look into their innermost heart of heart.

33. What is the best synonym for "punctiliousness" in the first paragraph?

A. Propriety

B. Specificity

C. Care

D. Morality

E. Timeliness

The correct answer is C.

"Punctiliousness" is a synonym for "correctness" or "attention to detail". This can be inferred from context.

34. The personification of books in the first two paragraphs is established primarily through…

A. Metaphor

B. Simile

C. Allusion

D. Satire

E. Hyperbole

The correct answer is B.

Books are personified through phrases such as "like a guest in the house" or "like visiting a forest". These phrases use "like", and thus are similes.

35. The tone of this piece could best be described as…

A. Empowering

B. Humorous

C. Caustic

D. Self-deprecating

E. Poetic

The correct answer is B.

The tone is playful and absurd, elevating books as essential creations with witty turns of phrase.

36. According to the author, what is the primary benefit of books over people?

A. Books are eternal and unchanging

B. Books can be altered to suit your needs

C. Books can be ignored more easily than living friends

D. Books take up less of your time

E. Books serve many purposes, and are attractive decorations

The correct answer is A.

The author states that "book-friends have this advantage over living friends; you can enjoy the most truly aristocratic society in the world whenever you want it."

37. How does the author establish a close relationship with his audience?

A. Through simple language and syntax

B. Through careful repetitions and fatherly diction

C. Through intellectual queries and abstract ideas

D. Through personal pronouns and familiar tone

E. Through keen satire and witty aphorisms

The correct answer is D.

The author makes frequent use of words like "you" and "I", indicating familiarity with the reader and drawing them into his rhetoric.

38. The final paragraph contains all of these rhetorical devices EXCEPT…

A. Rhetorical question

B. Parallelism

C. Personification

D. Appeal to authority

E. Asyndeton

The correct answer is D.

The author makes no appeals to authority in the final paragraph, nor anywhere else in the piece. The other poetic devices are in evidence.

39. In the final few lines of the last paragraph, what does "they" refer to?

A. Books

B. Great men

C. Friends

D. Readers

E. Actors

The correct answer is B.

The author is referring to the writers of great books, and the intimate connection they create with the reader through the act of reading.

40. "The answer is both true and unexpected" marks a shift from…

A. The more general merits of books to personal experiences of the author

B. The need for books to the methods of acquiring them

C. The merits of books to consumers, and then to those that create them

D. The superficial benefits of books to their more spiritual or intellectual uses

E. The author's history with books to the experiences of his friends

The correct answer is D.

The quoted sentence marks a shift from informal riffing on the joys of book-ownership to a more philosophical perspective on why books are essential to one's very soul.

Questions 41-48. Read the passage and answer the following questions carefully.

I read the other day some verses written by an eminent painter which were original and not conventional. The soul always hears an admonition in such lines, let the subject be what it may. The sentiment they instil is of more value than any thought they may contain. To believe your own thought, to believe that what is true for you in your private heart is true for all men, — that is genius. Speak your latent conviction, and it shall be the universal sense; for the inmost in due time becomes the outmost — and our first thought is rendered back to us by the trumpets of the Last Judgment. Familiar as the voice of the mind is to each, the highest merit we ascribe to Moses, Plato, and Milton is, that they set at naught books and traditions, and spoke not what men but what they thought. A man should learn to detect and watch that gleam of light which flashes across his mind from within, more than the lustre of the firmament of bards and sages. Yet he dismisses without notice his thought, because it is his. In every work of genius we recognize our own rejected thoughts: they come back to us with a certain alienated majesty. Great works of art have no more affecting lesson for us than this. They teach us to abide by our spontaneous impression with good-humored inflexibility then most when the whole cry of voices is on the other side. Else, to-morrow a stranger will say with masterly good sense precisely what we have thought and felt all the time, and we shall be forced to take with shame our own opinion from another.

There is a time in every man's education when he arrives at the conviction that envy is ignorance; that imitation is suicide; that he must take himself for better, for worse, as his portion; that though the wide universe is full of good, no kernel of nourishing corn can come to him but through his toil bestowed on that plot of ground which is given to him to till. The power which resides in him is new in nature, and none but he knows what that is which he can do, nor does he know until he has tried. Not for nothing one face, one character, one fact, makes much impression on him, and another none. This sculpture in the memory is not without pre-established harmony. The eye was placed where one ray should fall, that it might testify of that particular ray. We but half express ourselves, and are ashamed of that divine idea which each of us represents. It may be safely trusted as proportionate and of good issues, so it be faithfully imparted, but God will not have his work made manifest by cowards. A man is relieved and gay when he has put his heart into his work and done his best; but what he has said or done otherwise, shall give him no peace. It is a deliverance which does not deliver. In the attempt his genius deserts him; no muse befriends; no invention, no hope.

41. What is the best synonym for "admonition" at the beginning of the first paragraph?

A. Strong suggestion

B. Dire warning

C. Direct insult

D. False accusation

E. Cutting remark

The correct answer is A.

Admonition, in this context, means a strong suggestion. "Dire warning" is far too intense.

42. In context, how can you best paraphrase the sentence "that he must take himself for better, for worse, as his portion"?

A. He must accept his own limitations

B. He should forge his own identity

C. His must consider how he will be remembered

D. He must seize life by the horns

E. He must consider his own flaws

The correct answer is B.

"Take himself as his portion" means to create his best version of himself.

43. This piece can best be characterized as a...

A. Screed

B. Satire

C. Persuasive essay

D. Extended metaphor

E. Narrative essay

The correct answer is A.

The piece is emphatic, direct, and a bit caustic at times. It contains little humor or social commentary, so (B) is inappropriate. Likewise, it is not so much a persuasive essay as it does not essay a point so much as tear a point down (that of the artist assuming imitation is never justified). It contains no extended metaphor or narrative elements.

44. What is meant by the phrase "envy is ignorance"?

A. It is counterproductive to imitate

B. Ignorance comes from a place of extreme ego

C. Jealousy is a natural part of education

D. The educated possess no envy

E. Such emotions are a fancy of youth

The correct answer is A.

At this point in the essay, the author is describing how many young artists feel – that they must never imitate or else they will never become creative.

45. What best paraphrases the most "affecting lesson" of great art?

A. It communicates with us across time

B. We make it for ourselves

C. It reflects our inner worlds

D. It teaches us to be spontaneous

E. It creates great profits, both physical and spiritual

The correct answer is C.

The author says the greatest lesson of art is "In every work of genius we recognize our own rejected thoughts: they come back to us with a certain alienated majesty." This suggests art reflects our inner lives.

46. The central theme of this piece is...

A. The struggle of the artist against society

B. The necessity of art in daily life

C. The need for individuality

D. The superficial nature of art

E. The need to isolate oneself from outside influences

The correct answer is C.

This piece discusses the struggle young artists have with trying to forge their own identity while simultaneously rejecting outside influence. It also discusses how art reflects our individuality.

47. **In context, what is meant by the sentence "A man is relieved and gay when he has put his heart into his work and done his best; but what he has said or done otherwise, shall give him no peace"?**

A. An artist is never satisfied with his work

B. Common people cannot understand the struggles of the artist

C. Hard work is the only freedom worth having

D. Great art comes with the terrible price of isolation

E. Only work done to one's own standards is satisfying

The correct answer is E.

"A man is relieved and gay" when he has done his best, most personal work, but works done without these standards will gnaw at him.

48. **What causes a man's "genius to desert him"?**

A. Insufficient skill

B. Lack of focus

C. Bad luck

D. Unoriginality

E. Divine will

The correct answer is D.

The author insists that works that are not done to one's personal desires and specifications will cause the collapse of his creativity.

Questions 49-55. Read the passage and answer the following questions carefully.

In the title of this study is used the somewhat pretentious phrase, the spirit of capitalism. What is to be understood by it? The attempt to give anything like a definition of it brings out certain difficulties which are in the very nature of this type of investigation.

If any object can be found to which this term can be applied with any understandable meaning, it can only be an historical individual, i.e. a complex of elements associated in historical reality which we unite into a conceptual whole from the standpoint of their cultural significance.

Such an historical concept, however, since it refers in its content to a phenomenon significant for its unique individuality, cannot be defined according to the formula genus proximum, differentia specifica, but it must be gradually put together out of the individual parts which are taken from historical reality to make it up. Thus the final and definitive concept cannot stand at the beginning of the investigation, but must come at the end. We must, in other words, work out in the course of the discussion, as its most important result, the best conceptual formulation of what we here understand by the spirit of capitalism, that is the best from the point of view which interests us here. This point of view (the one of which we shall speak later) is, further, by no means the only possible one from which the historical phenomena we are investigating can be analysed. Other standpoints would, for this as for every historical phenomenon, yield other characteristics as the essential ones. The result is that it is by no means necessary to understand by the spirit of capitalism only what it will come to mean to us for the purposes of our analysis. This is a necessary result of the nature of historical concepts which attempt for their methodological purposes not to grasp historical reality in abstract general formulae, but in concrete genetic sets of relations which are inevitably of a specifically unique and individual character.

Thus, if we try to determine the object, the analysis and historical explanation of which we are attempting, it cannot be in the form of a conceptual definition, but at least in the beginning only a provisional description of what is here meant by the spirit of capitalism. Such a description is, however, indispensable in order clearly to understand the object of the investigation. For this purpose we turn to a document of that spirit which contains what we are looking for in almost classical purity, and at the same time has the advantage of being free from all direct relationship to religion, being thus, for our purposes, free of preconceptions.

49. What is the "object" referred to throughout this piece?

A. A pretentious phrase

B. The formula

C. An historical individual

D. The analysis

E. The result of the investigation

The correct answer is C.

The author states as much in the second paragraph.

50. What is the relationship between the first and second paragraphs?

A. The first paragraph establishes the title of the piece, the second deconstructs it

B. The first paragraph explains the value of capitalism, while the second calls its import into question

C. The first paragraph offers a rhetorical question, and the second elucidates the difficulties in answering it

D. The first paragraph illustrates the speaker's main concern, and the second establishes his credentials in addressing it

E. The first paragraph sets the tone of the piece, and the second offers a witty subversion

The correct answer is C.

The first paragraph states the ultimate question the author is seeking to answer, and the second paragraph heightens the question by explaining its intricacies and the difficulties in answering it.

51. **What differentiates this query into a "historical object" from other, similar inquiries?**

   A. It can only be ascertained at the end of the investigation, after its aspects have been examined

   B. It has no physical presence and must be assessed in theoretical terms

   C. It requires deep knowledge of history that is hard to obtain

   D. It can be completed through assumptions rather than common facts

   E. It needs a more methodical approach than other such inquiries

   The correct answer is A.

   The author explains that "the final and definitive concept cannot stand at the beginning of the investigation, but must come at the end".

52. **What is the author saying with the last sentence?**

   A. He will describe the need to divorce religion from this discussion

   B. He will now discuss a document that is unprejudiced by political or religious viewpoints

   C. Religion inherently taints a discussion, and must be purged from further inquiries

   D. The spirit of capitalism is closely tied to religious interests, ones that must be understood

   E. Societal biases have influenced our discussion, but further points of evidence will mitigate this

   The correct answer is B.

   The author states he will be reviewing a document that has "classical purity" and is free of modern preconceptions and bias.

53. **"Other standpoints would, for this as for every historical phenomenon, yield other characteristics as the essential ones. The result is that it is by no means necessary to understand by the spirit of capitalism only what it will come to mean to us for the purposes of our analysis." What is meant by this passage?**

   A. Our understanding of this topic is influenced by our cultural perspective, but this shall suffice for the purposes of discussion

   B. Our viewpoint of this topic is woefully inadequate, and we must seek any other perspective that we can

   C. Academia can only go so far, and we must make assumptions where scholarship fails us

   D. The spirit of capitalism cannot be measured in such a small argument, but we must try

   E. Others may disagree with our assessment here, but they are incorrect, as we will now demonstrate

   The correct answer is A.

The author is stating that any discussion they have will be colored by their cultural biases, but the discussion could be enlightening nonetheless.

54. What is the subject of the verb "yield" towards the middle of paragraph three?

A. Characteristics

B. Phenomenon

C. Historical

D. Standpoints

E. Essential ones

The correct answer is D.

"Standpoints" is the subject and "characteristics" is the object.

55. What can we assume will follow this selection?

A. A segue into the nature of capitalism

B. A piece on the author's cultural background

C. A screed against the influence of religion

D. A point of evidence offering provisional description

E. A clear description of terms

The correct answer is D.

The author explains he will be examining a relevant document moving forward to support his investigation.

Sample Test Six

Section I

Multiple Choice Questions.

Time: 60 minutes.

Percent of total grade on the exam: 45 percent.

Instructions: This section of the exam consists of selections from works and questions on reading comprehension and reasoning. After reading each passage, choose the best answer to each question and then fill in the corresponding oval on the answer sheet.

Questions 1-8. Read the following passage carefully before you decide on your answers to the questions.

She was forty-two, in poor health. She had recently been diagnosed with diabetes, and her doctor had urged her to get out and walk more. But her son has been shot to death a few blocks away, and Pritchett was too frightened to venture out. She spent days lying in the dark, unable to will herself to move or speak. That morning, as always, she was wearing a big loose T-shirt with Bovon's picture on it. All around her, in the tiny living room, were mementos of her murdered son. Sports trophies, photos, sympathy cards, certificates, stuffed animals.

With great care, Pritchett perched the shoebox on the arm of a vinyl armchair by the door and solely lifted one shoe. It was worn, black, dusted with red Watts dirt. It was not quite big enough to be a man's shoe, not small enough to be a child's. She leaned against the wall, pressed the open top of the shoe against her mouth and nose, and inhaled its scent with a long, deep breath. Then she closed her eyes and wept.

Skaggs stood back. Ptitchett's knees gave out. Skaggs watched her side down the wall in slow motion, her face still pressed into the shoe. She landed with a thump on the green carper. One of her orange slippers came off. On the TV across the room, the FOX 11 morning anchored pattered brightly over the sound of her sobs.

Skaggs had been a homicide detective for twenty years. In that time, he had been in a thousand living rooms like this one- each with its large TV, Afrocentric knickknacks, and imponderable grief.

—*Ghettoside* by Jill Leovy

1. What is the intended audience for this text?

A. The African-American community

B. White police officers

C. The lower class

D. Affluent communities

E. All classes and races

2. **How does the author appeal to the emotions of the audience?**

A. Including a detailed scene, including memorabilia and Pritchett's physical and emotional response to the situation

B. Opening the scene with a description of Pritchett's poor health

C. Implying that this is a very common scene to this detective

D. Mentioning things the audience can relate to, such as watching the morning news

E. Mentioning an item that the audience is familiar with, a shoe

3. **What is the major difference between Skaggs and Pritchett?**

A. Gender

B. Race

C. Professional experience

D. Health condition

E. Age

4. **Why is Pritchett wearing a T-shirt with her son's picture on it?**

A. She is unemployed and does not wear professional clothing anymore.

B. She is in terrible health and wants to stay comfortable.

C. She is advocating for change.

D. She is reminding herself what he looked like.

E. All of the above.

5. **What does the shoe represent?**

A. The last piece of evidence from the murder case.

B. A piece of her son that was murdered.

C. The detective trying to walk a mile in the victim's shoe.

D. The age of the victim.

E. The mother not being able to let go of her son's death.

6. Why is the news station in the background significant?

A. The news represents the media downplaying or silencing terrible crimes.

B. The news shows how quiet she was crying.

C. The news represents another day moving forward.

D. The news represents a woman watching television at a high volume.

E. The news represents a distraction.

7. Why was it important to mention that Skaggs has been to "a thousand living rooms like this one"?

A. He has visited every house in this neighborhood

B. Most houses in this city have the same layout

C. There is a cycle in his field of work, and he has had to deal with many murders in his twenty years as a detective

D. All African-American families decorate in the same manner

E. Grieving families always hold on to memories through pictures, teddy bears, and sympathy cards

8. Why would the author describe the woman's grief as imponderable?

A. It's not something he thought about before arriving at her house

B. Her grief was not apparent until he gave her the shoe

C. He is not sure how to console her

D. Skaggs cannot relate to the grief of a murdered child

E. This is something he's witnessed many times

Questions 9-16. Read the following passage carefully before you decide on your answers to the questions.

In the South every single thing was segregated: water fountains, public toilets and hotels and restaurants, but in "Greater Israel" i.e. the Occupied Territories, there's even segregation of the roads! Our Palestinian taxi driver tried hard to stay on the Arab only roads but one of them was blocked. He then, with great trepidation, got onto the big Jewish Settler only highway. This was simply amazing to experience. As was the realization that Palestinians have different colored license plates and that one of our group of artists and writers, a Palestinian man, had to leave our van because even inside a van he's not permitted to enter Jerusalem.

The way Palestinians are shot and killed, or arrested and beaten, as if they are not human beings, also reminds me of growing up in the South, where we were made to feel that Black life had no value. Also, the use of prison to keep politically conscious and active people out of the population. At this moment there are Palestinians in Israeli jails and prisons on a hunger strike because the majority of them were arrested without ever having been charged with anything. In the South too black people were often beaten and jailed and never given a fair trial, or sometimes never even told what they were arrested for. They were often put to work on plantations owned by the prison and by other plantation owners in the area. It was a way to re-enslave black people. After demolishing their houses and taking their land Israel has made use of workers in the Palestinian communities to build their Jewish only settlements.

-an interview with Alice Walker

9. Why is the exclamation point important in the opening sentence?

A. Segregation on the roads is not the norm

B. The author wanted to represent a loud voice

C. It sets the tone for the disgust that the author had for this place

D. It represents happiness that the roads were not segregated in the South

E. All of the above

10. What is a synonym for *trepidation*?

A. Confidence

B. Apprehension

C. Slow movement

D. Fast movement

E. Stop and go movement

11. How does the author's relationship with the South shape her message?

A. She has first-hand experience with overt racism

B. She lived in the South and now lives in the Middle East

C. She wrote about the culture of the South and the Middle East

D. She is not accepting of other cultures

E. She is surprised at the transportation systems

12. How does the author connect the past to present day?

A. She explains that jails were used for American slaves more than Palestinians

B. She gives details of the transportation systems

C. She explains language differences

D. She gives an account of how lives are made not to matter for present Palestinians, in the same manner of American slaves

E. She notes that the Palestinian had to get out of the van

13. How were black people re-enslaved?

A. They went to prison

B. They were sold back to prison-owned plantations

C. They were caught after escaping prison

D. They were caught after escaping to the North

E. They were bought and re-sold

14. Why did the Palestinians have different colored license plates?

A. To segregate the roadways

B. To represent the regions they lived in

C. To represent their religion

D. To identify who could/could not enter Israel

E. All of the above

15. How does the author defend her perspective?

A. She includes personal memories of growing up in the South

B. She quotes her parents

C. She explains that she's witnessed murder

D. She cites famous authors

E. None of the above

16. What word best describes the tone used in this passage?

A. Sarcastic

B. Anxious

C. Guilty

D. Peaceful

E. Aggressive

Questions 17-24. Read the following passage carefully before you decide on your answers to the questions.

Ladies and Gentlemen, I'd planned to speak to you tonight to report on the state of the Union, but the events of earlier today have led me to change those plans. Today is a day for mourning and remembering. Nancy and I are pained to the core by the tragedy of the shuttle Challenger. We know we share this pain with all of the people of our country. This is truly a national loss.

Nineteen years ago, almost to the day, we lost three astronauts in a terrible accident on the ground. But we've never lost an astronaut in flight. We've never had a tragedy like this.

And perhaps we've forgotten the courage it took for the crew of the shuttle. But they, the Challenger Seven, were aware of the dangers, but overcame them and did their jobs brilliantly. We mourn seven heroes: Michael Smith, Dick Scobee, Judith Resnik, Ronald McNair, Ellison Onizuka, Gregory Jarvis, and Christa McAuliffe.

We mourn their loss as a nation together.

And I want to say something to the schoolchildren of America who were watching the live coverage of the shuttle's take-off. I know it's hard to understand, but sometimes painful things like this happen. It's all part of the process of exploration and discovery. It's all part of taking a chance and expanding man's horizons. The future doesn't belong to the fainthearted; it belongs to the brave. The Challenger crew was pulling us into the future, and we'll continue to follow them.

I've always had great faith in and respect for our space program. And what happened today does nothing to diminish it. We don't hide our space program. We don't keep secrets and cover things up. We do it all up front and in public. That's the way freedom is, and we wouldn't change it for a minute.

We'll continue our quest in space. There will be more shuttle flights and more shuttle crews and, yes, more volunteers, more civilians, more teachers in space. Nothing ends here; our hopes and our journeys continue.

I want to add that I wish I could talk to every man and woman who works for NASA, or who worked on this mission and tell them: "Your dedication and professionalism have moved and impressed us for decades. And we know of your anguish. We share it."

There's a coincidence today. On this day three hundred and ninety years ago, the great explorer Sir Francis Drake died aboard ship off the coast of Panama. In his lifetime the great frontiers were the oceans, and a historian later said, "He lived by the sea, died on it, and was buried in it." Well, today, we can say of the Challenger crew: Their dedication was, like Drake's, complete.

The crew of the space shuttle Challenger honored us by the manner in which they lived their lives. We will never forget them, nor the last time we saw them, this morning, as they prepared for their journey and waved goodbye and "slipped the surly bonds of earth" to "touch the face of God." Thank you.

—*Ronald Reagan, Challenger Address*

17. What emotion does this speech portray?

A. Empathy

B. Apathy

C. Concern

D. Grief

E. Displeasure

18. Why does the speaker say "we"?

A. He is talking about himself and his wife

B. He is talking about himself and the American school children

C. He is including all Americans

D. He is including everyone in his political party

E. It represents his entire staff

19. What does the following line represent?

"The future doesn't belong to the fainthearted; it belongs to the brave."

A. A push for the school children to stay brave

B. Encouragement for school children to believe in future space exploration

C. A representation of people that fight for our country

D. Encouragement for Americans to curb their emotions

E. A note to let everyone know that only the heroic are successful

20. Why does the speaker mention the anguish for the people of NASA?

A. They've all had a role in this mission

B. They personally knew each astronaut that died

C. Each staff member worked on the spaceship

D. They know it could have been them that died

E. It was their fault that the spaceship malfunctioned

21. How does the speaker connect to their audience?

A. He mentions his wife and their emotional connection

B. He speaks loudly and clearly

C. He uses simple vocabulary

D. He mentions the names of the people that lost their lives

E. He references school children

22. Why does the speaker reference Sir Francis Drake?

A. The astronauts died supporting the school children

B. The astronauts died doing what they loved

C. He was an important historical figure of their time

D. He represents the sea, and they crashed into the sea

E. It is unclear why he mentions Sir Francis Drake

23. What is a synonym for *surly*?

A. Curly

B. Sullen

C. Large

D. Unruly

E. Unfair

24. **What is the most appropriate word to describe this speech?**

A. Hopeful

B. Mournful

C. Inspiring

D. Regretful

E. Vengeful

Questions 25-32. Read the following passage carefully before you decide on your answers to the questions.

Photo credit: Karl Merton Ferron / Baltimore Sun

"City police are mainly concerned about outsiders who do not have a stake in the community," Howard County Police Chief Gary L. Gardner, who attended the meeting, said in a memo to officials in his county. "Also, they are receiving some information that there will be attempts to disrupt the Oriole game Saturday or the Inner Harbor area — disrupt commerce."

On Friday night, Baltimore police emailed Conaway, asking for 20 extra bike racks for the Sports Legends Museum and the nearby ballpark plaza, in case they were needed as barriers against protesters. Conaway also planned to open an Emergency Operations Center at the warehouse for Saturday's game, according to another email, with "the new stadium cameras plus city watch cameras available."

On Saturday, protesters and fans at the stadium and nearby sports pubs taunted one another, and some of those bike racks were among the projectiles thrown as the demonstration turned violent. Young men jumped atop police cars and used traffic cones to smash their windshields. At the park and elsewhere downtown, storefront windows were shattered.

As the mayhem continued, fans were kept inside Camden Yards for about 30 minutes, until officials thought it was safe for them to leave.

Still, the complex sustained what the stadium authority considered fairly minor damage — broken windows at Dempsey's restaurant and Geppi's Entertainment Museum.

"This one may have to wait until the morning to get boarded up," Matthew Kastel, facilities group director for Camden Yards, emailed colleagues regarding the museum damage. "I'm not sure it would be safe to send out one of my guys at the present moment to do this."

Around 10 p.m., Freddie Gray's twin sister, Fredericka Gray, joined Mayor Stephanie Rawlings-Blake at a news conference to plead, "Can y'all please, please stop the violence?"

In the end, 31 adults and four juveniles were arrested in Saturday's unrest — among them, Wayne Gray, 47, from Baltimore's east side.

"I've been in trouble before in my life, but I had a different feeling about what I got myself into this time," Gray, says now, reflecting on his arrest that night for disorderly conduct and failure to obey a police order to leave the area of Howard and Pratt streets. "I stood up for what I believe in. I feel like I stood up for what was right."

—*The Baltimore Sun,* October 23, 2015

25. What rhetoric does the brick in the image provoke?

A. Broken pieces of the city of Baltimore

B. Rebellion against police

C. Anticipation of a riot

D. Solidarity against brutality

E. All of the above

26. Why was the image included?

A. To show the anticipation of what was about to happen

B. As evidence

C. To warn rioters of the riot gear that police would be wearin

D. To support rioters in throwing bricks

E. All of the above

27. How does the image portray police officers?

A. In unison

B. Blurred

C. Caucasian

D. Powerful

E. Large in number

28. How does the article portray police officers?

A. Defenseless

B. Powerful

C. Regal

D. Intimidated

E. Caucasian

29. Who was Fredericka Gray addressing when she said, "Can y'all please, please stop the violence?"

A. The police

B. The people of Baltimore

C. All Americans

D. Her family

E. Her friends

30. _____ is a synonym for *unrest.*

A. Sleeplessness

B. Disturbance

C. Communication

D. Meeting

E. Funeral

31. Why did Wayne Gray have a *different feeling* about being arrested?

A. He didn't feel as if what he did was wrong

B. He felt sick

C. He did not expect to be arrested

D. His other arrests were far more serious crimes

E. All of the above

32. **How does the 20 extra bike racks help to explain the situation?**

A. The Orioles game wanted to accommodate their fans

B. 20 racks were needed because of the high number of anticipated protesters

C. 20 racks were needed to accommodate the number of police officers on bicycles

D. The Orioles game wanted to use them as a barricade to keep their fans inside the stadium

E. They were all used to damage Dempsey's restaurant

Questions 33-40. Read the following passage carefully before you decide on your answers to the questions.

Two years have passed since my book came out, and three years since the October morning when I was shot by the Taliban on a school bus on my way home from class. My family has been through many changes. We were plucked from our mountain valley in Swat, Pakistan, and transported to a brick house in Birmingham, England's second-biggest city. Sometimes it seems so strange that I want to pinch myself. I'm seventeen now and one thing that has not changed is that I still don't like getting up in the morning. The most astonishing thing is that it's my father whose voice wakes me up now. He gets up first every day and prepares breakfast for me, my mother, and my brothers, Atal and Khushal. He doesn't let his work go unnoticed, of course, going on about how he squeezes fresh juice, fries eggs, heats flat bread, and takes the honey out of the cupboard. "It's only breakfast!" I tease. For the first time in his life, he also does the shopping, although he hates doing it. The man who didn't even know the price of a pint of milk is such a frequent visitor to the supermarket that he knows where everything is on the shelves! "I've become like a woman, a true feminist!" he says, and I jokingly throw things at him.

My brothers and I then all rush off to our different schools. And so does out mother, Toor Pekai, which is truly one of the biggest changes of all. She is attending a language center five days a week to learn how to read and write and also to speak English. My mother had no education and perhaps that was the reason that she always encouraged us to go to school. "Don't wake up like me and realize what you missed years later," she says. She faces so many challenges in her daily life because up until now she's had difficulty communicating when she's gone shopping, or to the doctor or the bank. Getting an education is helping her become more confident, so that she can speak up outside the home, not just inside it with us.

—*I Am Malala* by Malala Yousafzai

33. **What elements of cultural context help to explain the author's background?**

A. The explanation of her family being plucked from their mountain valley in Swat, Pakistan

B. Her fascination of her new brick home in Birmingham, England

C. The explanation of her brothers gong to different schools

D. The inclusion of juice, eggs, bread, and honey

E. All of the above

34. Why is it *astonishing* that her father wakes her up?

A. She has never met her father

B. She thought he died

C. She's not used to seeing him in the house

D. She's used to hearing an alarm clock

E. She's normally the first person awake

35. Why didn't her father go shopping before now?

A. Her mother did all the cooking, cleaning, and shopping

B. The marketplace is new

C. He didn't speak the language

D. They didn't have enough money

E. It was too dangerous to go shopping

36. How does the mother's quote, "Don't wake up like me and realize what you missed years later" influence the audience?

A. It's a reminder of oppression across the globe

B. It represents female rights being taken away

C. It represents opportunity in England

D. It's encouraging to get out and accomplish as much as you can so that you don't have regrets in the future

E. It makes the reader reflect on the last time they woke up

37. How did the author include multiple definitions with the phrase *speak up*?

A. It also represents raising her voice

B. It also means to challenge authority

C. It also means fighting for women's rights

D. It will also help her raise her children

E. All of the above

38. **What does this passage say about education?**

A. It's very important for a successful future

B. You can get shot on your way home from school

C. There are different schools for adults and children

D. It will help you with shopping and going to the doctor

E. England has great schools

39. **How does this passage portray differences in education in Pakistan and England?**

A. Men are able to go to school in both places

B. Women typically do not attend school in Pakistan

C. Women are more likely to attend school in England

D. Schools are safer in England

E. All of the above

40. **How does this passage define gender roles?**

A. It breaks gender roles because the father does the cooking and shopping

B. It follows gender roles because the mother is in school

C. It breaks gender roles because the father didn't know how much a pint of milk costs

D. It follows gender roles because the father is familiar with the supermarket

E. Gender roles are not defined

Questions 41-48. Read the following passage carefully before you decide on your answers to the questions.

International baggage claim in the Brussels airport was large and airy, with multiple carousels circling endlessly. I scurried from one to another, desperately trying to find my black suitcase. Because it was stuffed with drug money, I was more concerned than one might normally be about lost luggage.

I was twenty-four in 1993 and probably looked like just another anxious young professional woman. My Doc Martens had ben jettisoned in favor of my beautiful handmade black suede heels. I wore black silk pants and a beige jacket, a typical *jeune fille*, not a big counterculture, unless you spotted the tattoo on my neck. I had done exactly as I had been instructed, checking my bag Chicago through Paris, where I had to switch planes to take a short flight to Brussels.

When I arrived in Belgium, I looked for my black rollie at the baggage claim. It was no where to be seen. Fighting a rushing tide of panic, I asked in my mangled high school French what had become of my suitcase. "Bags don't make it onto the right flight sometimes," said the big lug working in baggage handling. "Wait for the next shuttle from Paris— It's probably on that plane."

Had my bag been detected? I knew that carrying more than $10,000 undeclared was illegal, let alone carrying it for a West African drug lord. Were the authorities closing in on me? Maybe I should try to get through customs and run? Or perhaps the bag really was just delayed, and I would be abandoning a large some of money that belonged to someone who could probably have killed me with a simple phone call. I decided that the later choice was slightly more terrifying. So I waited.

The next flight from Paris finally arrived. I sidled over to my new "friend" in baggage handling, who was sorting things out. It is hard to flirt when you're frightened. I spotted the suitcase. "Mon bag!" I exclaimed in ecstasy, seizing the Tumi. I thanked him effusively, waiving with giddy affection as I sailed through one of the unmanned doors into the terminal, where I spotted my friend Billy waiting for me. I had inadvertently skipped customs.

"I was worried. What happened?" Billy asked.

"Get me into a cab!" I hissed.

I didn't breathe until we had pulled away from the airport and were halfway across Brussels.

—*Orange is the New Black*. Piper Kerman

41. Why did the author explain her attire?

A. She wanted the audience to know how much she stood out in Europe

B. She used her clothing to try to fit in with the culture she was immersed in

C. She wanted to explain that she was a young, hip woman

D. She explained how difficult it was to wait around for her bag in heels

E. She won the bag handler over because she looked beautiful that day

Sample Test Six

42. How is stream of consciousness included in this passage?

A. It includes the author's thoughts and emotions

B. She uses the term "I"

C. The narrator is the main character

D. It includes dialogue

E. It describes her experience with luggage

43. How does the author use punctuation to express herself?

A. Question marks

B. An ellipses

C. Exclamation points

D. Quotation marks

E. All of the above

44. What is a synonym for mangled in the following line: "I asked in my *mangled* high school French"

A. Simple

B. Terrible

C. Elementary

D. Perfect

E. Accentuated

45. What part of the plot does "Mon bag!" represent?

A. Climax

B. Rising action

C. Exposition

D. Falling action

E. Resolution

46. How did she avoid going through customs?

A. She flirted with the luggage man

B. Her friend Billy came to get her

C. She slipped through an unmanned door

D. She went through customs in Paris and Chicago, so it wasn't required

E. She went through customs in Brussels

47. Why didn't she breathe until pulling away from the airport?

A. Adrenaline

B. Sadness

C. Health issues

D. She was talking to Billy

E. She was in awe of the airport

48. What is the overall message of this passage?

A. Airports often lose bags

B. Security guards are not always watching every door in the airport

C. It's helpful to have a friend pick you up from the airport

D. Doing illegal things in the airport is scary, and there's always a chance of getting caught

E. Young professional women get away with everything

Questions 49-55. Read the following passage carefully before you decide on your answers to the questions.

It is impossible for any man, when the most favourable circumstances concur, to acquire sufficient knowledge and strength of mind to discharge the duties of a king, entrusted with uncontrouled power; how then must they be violated when his very elevation is an insuperable bar to the attainment of either wisdom or virtue; when all the feelings of a man are stifled by flattery, and reflection shut out by pleasure! Surely it is madness to make the fate of thousands depend on the caprice of a weak fellow creature, whose very station sinks him necessarily below the meanest of his subjects! But one power should not be thrown down to exalt another—for all power intoxicates weak man; and its abuse proves, that the more equality there is established among men, the more virtue and happiness will reign in society. But this, and any similar maxim deduced from simple reason, raises an outcry—the church or the state is in danger, if faith in the wisdom of antiquity is not implicit; and they who, roused by the sight of human calamity, dare to attack human authority, are reviled as despisers of God, and enemies of man. These are bitter calumnies, yet they reached one of the best of men, whose ashes still preach peace, and whose memory demands a respectful pause, when subjects are discussed that lay so near his heart.

After attacking the sacred majesty of Kings, I shall scarcely excite surprise by adding my firm persuasion that every profession, in which great subordination of rank constitutes its power, is highly injurious to morality.

A standing army, for instance, is incompatible with freedom; because subordination and rigour are the very sinews of military discipline; and despotism is necessary to give vigour to enterprizes that one will directs. A spirit inspired by romantic notions of honour, a kind of morality founded on the fashion of the age, can only be felt by a few officers, whilst the main body must be moved by command, like the waves of the sea; for the strong wind of authority pushes the crowd of subalterns forward, they scarcely know or care why, with headlong fury.

—Mary Wollstonecraft *A Vindication of the Rights of Woman.* 1792

49. What type of essay is this?

A. Argumentative

B. Persuasive

C. Narrative

D. Descriptive

E. Expository

50. What is the author's tone?

A. Formal

B. Informal

C. Comic

D. Sarcastic

E. Serious

51. What does the term *sinews* represent?

A. Strength

B. Organization

C. Discipline

D. Grace

E. Downfall

52. Because of the spelling of favourable, rigour, vigour, and honour, we can assume this author was most likely from:

A. America

B. Canada

C. England

D. France

E. Ireland

53. In the phrase romantic notions of *honour*, romantic represents _____.

A. Love

B. Inspiration

C. Hope

D. Radicalism

E. Promotion

54. ***Subalterns* is a synonym for _____.**

A. Antlers

B. Waves

C. Officers

D. Submarine

E. Captains

55. **What impact on the reader does the author have in mentioning kings and common officers?**

A. She shows that regardless of rank, every profession has downfalls

B. She explains the divide between the two classes

C. She amplifies the importance of royalty

D. She demonstrates the level of respect officers have for their king

E. She questions gender roles in professional settings

Free Response Essay Sample Questions

Section II

Time: 2 hours

Question 1

(Suggested time: 40 minutes. This question counts one-third of the total essay section score.)

Climate change has been prominent in the news, though some people are not certain that it is a scientific phenomenon that it would impact large portions of the population.

Carefully read the six sources, including the introductory information for each source. Then synthesize information from at least three of the sources and incorporate it into a coherent, well-developed essay that argues a position clearly.

Make sure your argument is central; use the sources to illustrate and support your reasoning. Avoid merely summarizing the sources. Indicate clearly which sources you are referencing, whether through direct quotation, paraphrase, or summary. You may cite the sources as Source A, Source B, etc., or by using the descriptions in parentheses.

Source A (World Bank)
Source B (Humanitarian)
Source C (UNESCO)
Source D (NASA)
Source E (IPCC)
Source F (Policy)

Source A, Excerpt of World Bank Group GFDRR (Global Facility for Disaster Reduction and Recovery) Report, "Managing Disaster Risks for a Resilient Future, A Work Plan for the Global Facility for Disaster Reduction and Recovery 2016-2018."

Building on the Hydromet Program, GFDRR has established the Resilience to Climate Change thematic initiative to respond to increasing demand from countries for technical assistance to help them formulate enabling policies and investment programs for integrating climate and disaster risk into their development strategies. The program focuses specifically on resilience to hydro-meteorological disaster risks, adaptation to climate change, and management of the residual risk of climate-related disasters.

The funded activities help strengthen institutional and capacity building of partner stakeholders, to ensure that they are ready and capable of implementing long-term investment programs.

Activities are positioned to influence policymaking and investment in measures at the required scale, by leveraging both World Bank resources and those of national governments and other partners. It will also develop and test innovative approaches to disaster risk reduction to provide proven and potentially transformative solutions to the challenge of climate and disaster risk management.

Just-in-time technical assistance under this program supports highly-specialized capacity building and advice in response to country demand. Activities address specific issues related to climate resilience or weather-related disaster risk management. This rapid assistance is requested in response to a window of opportunity for critical policy reforms, or where waiting for normal processing of technical assistance grants would not be feasible. The program is already supporting Morocco in its design of a resilience fund and is expected to build capacity with Central Asian national meteorological and hydrological services…

Between 1980 and 2012, weather- related disasters accounted for 87% of total disasters recorded; they led to reported losses of $2.6 trillion and 1.4 million lives lost.

Source B, Alice Min Soo Chun and Irene E. Brisson. "Ground Rules in Humanitarian Design." 2015.

Coastal cities are by far the most developed of Africa's urban areas, and by implication have a high concentration of residential, industrial, commercial, educational and military facilities. One such coastal city is Lagos, the foremost manufacturing and port city in West Africa. Lagos is the hub of business and economic development in Nigeria, housing around 65 percent of the country's industrial establishments, more than 65 percent of all commercial activities and around 60 percent of Nigeria's non-oil economy; it is also home to four of the country's eight seaports. However, indications point to urban development as being a large creator of risk for much of the urban population, most especially the urban poor who live in more hazardous physical and human environments along the coast. Rising seas levels consequent to climate change pose real threats to coastal populations along low-lying coastal sites because of the increased likelihood of flood events; furthermore, the frequency of storm surges may also exacerbated by sea-level rise.

Source C, [11] UNESCO. "Indigenous Knowledge and Sustainability." 2000

Sophisticated knowledge of the natural world is not confined to science. Human societies all across the globe have developed rich sets of experiences and explanations relating to the environments they live in. These 'other knowledge systems' are today often referred to as traditional ecological knowledge or indigenous or local knowledge. They encompass the sophisticated arrays of information, understandings and interpretations that guide human societies around the globe in their innumerable interactions with the natural milieu: in agriculture and animal husbandry; hunting, fishing and gathering; struggles against disease and injury; naming and explanation of natural phenomena; and strategies to cope with fluctuating environments.

Source D, NASA, "Scientific consensus: Earth's climate is warming"

Multiple studies published in peer-reviewed scientific journals1 show that 97 percent or more of actively publishing climate scientists agree: Climate-warming trends over the past century are very likely due to human activities. In addition, most of the leading scientific organizations worldwide have issued public statements endorsing this position. The following is a partial list of these organizations, along with links to their published statements and a selection of related resources.

American Association for the Advancement of Science

"The scientific evidence is clear: global climate change caused by human activities is occurring now, and it is a growing threat to society." (2006)American Chemical Society

"Comprehensive scientific assessments of our current and potential future climates clearly indicate that climate change is real, largely attributable to emissions from human activities, and potentially a very serious problem." (2004)

American Medical Association

"Our AMA ... supports the findings of the Intergovernmental Panel on Climate Change's fourth assessment report and concurs with the scientific consensus that the Earth is undergoing adverse global climate change and that anthropogenic contributions are significant." (2013)

The Geological Society of America

"The Geological Society of America (GSA) concurs with assessments by the National Academies of Science (2005), the National Research Council (2006), and the Intergovernmental Panel on Climate Change (IPCC, 2007) that global climate has warmed and that human activities (mainly greenhouse-gas emissions) account for most of the warming since the middle 1900s." (2006; revised 2010)

Source E, Intergovernmental Panel on Climate Change, Excerpts from Climate Change 2014 Synthesis Report

SPM 1. Observed Changes and their Causes

Human influence on the climate system is clear, and recent anthropogenic emissions of green- house gases are the highest in history. Recent climate changes have had widespread impacts on human and natural systems.

SPM 1.1 Observed changes in the climate system

Warming of the climate system is unequivocal, and since the 1950s, many of the observed changes are unprecedented over decades to millennia. The atmosphere and ocean have warmed, the amounts of snow and ice have diminished, and sea level has risen.

SPM 1.2 Causes of climate change

Anthropogenic greenhouse gas emissions have increased since the pre-industrial era, driven largely by economic and population growth, and are now higher than ever. This has led to atmospheric concentrations of carbon dioxide, methane and nitrous oxide that are unprecedented in at least the last 800,000 years. Their effects, together with those of other anthropogenic drivers, have been detected throughout the climate system and are extremely likely to have been the dominant cause of the observed warming since the mid-20th century.

SPM 1.3 Impacts of climate change

In recent decades, changes in climate have caused impacts on natural and human systems on all continents and across the oceans. Impacts are due to observed climate change, irrespective of its cause, indicating the sensitivity of natural and human systems to changing climate.

Source F, Excerpts from the American Policy Roundtable "The Great Global Warm Up"

1. Most scientists do not believe human activities threaten to disrupt the Earth's climate. More than 17,000 scientists have signed a petition circulated by the Oregon Institute of Science and Medicine saying, in part, "there is no convincing scientific evidence that human release of carbon dioxide, methane, or other greenhouse gases is causing or will, in the foreseeable future, cause catastrophic heating of the Earth's atmosphere and disruption of the Earth's climate."
2. Our most reliable sources of temperature data show no global warming trend. Satellite readings of temperatures in the lower troposphere (an area scientists predict would immediately reflect any global warming) show no warming since readings began 23 years ago. These readings are accurate to within 0.01 degrees Celsius, and are consistent with data from weather balloons. Only land-based temperature stations show a warming trend, and these stations do not cover the entire globe, are often contaminated by heat generated by nearby urban development, and are subject to human error.

Question 2
(Suggested time: 40 minutes. This question counts one-third of the total essay section score.)

Read the following two quotes.

"I was bold in the pursuit of knowledge, never fearing to follow truth and reason to whatever results they led."

— Thomas Jefferson (Third President of the United States)

"I believe in everything until it's disproved. So I believe in fairies, the myths, dragons. It all exists, even if it's in your mind. Who's to say that dreams and nightmares aren't as real as the here and now?"

— John Lennon (artist, singer, songwriter)

In a well-organized essay, define success built on knowledge (or fact) versus dreams, and which is the better route. Support your argument with appropriate evidence and examples.

Question 3
(Suggested time: 40 minutes. This question counts one-third of the total essay section score.)

Mahatma Gandhi once said, "The best way to find yourself is to lose yourself in the service of others."

Using your own experience and background information, support an explanation of how Gandhi's comments are reflected successfully or unsuccessfully in today's society as demonstrated in literature, news reports, or other information streams.

Sample Test Six: ANSWER KEY

Question Number	Correct Answer	Your Answer
1.	E	
2.	A	
3.	B	
4.	C	
5.	A	
6.	A	
7.	C	
8.	D	
9.	A	
10.	B	
11.	A	
12.	D	
13.	B	
14.	E	
15.	A	
16.	E	
17.	A	
18.	C	
19.	B	
20.	A	
21.	A	
22.	B	
23.	B	
24.	C	
25.	E	
26.	A	
27.	A	
28.	D	

Question Number	Correct Answer	Your Answer
29.	B	
30.	B	
31.	A	
32.	B	
33.	A	
34.	C	
35.	A	
36.	D	
37.	C	
38.	A	
39.	E	
40.	A	
41.	B	
42.	A	
43.	C	
44.	B	
45.	A	
46.	C	
47.	A	
48.	D	
49.	B	
50.	E	
51.	A	
52.	C	
53.	D	
54.	C	
55.	A	

Answer Key and Rationale

Questions 1-8. Read the following passage carefully before you decide on your answers to the questions.

She was forty-two, in poor health. She had recently been diagnosed with diabetes, and her doctor had urged her to get out and walk more. But her son has been shot to death a few blocks away, and Pritchett was too frightened to venture out. She spent days lying in the dark, unable to will herself to move or speak. That morning, as always, she was wearing a big loose T-shirt with Bovon's picture on it. All around her, in the tiny living room, were mementos of her murdered son. Sports trophies, photos, sympathy cards, certificates, stuffed animals.

With great care, Pritchett perched the shoebox on the arm of a vinyl armchair by the door and solely lifted one shoe. It was worn, black, dusted with red Watts dirt. It was not quite big enough to be a man's shoe, not small enough to be a child's. She leaned against the wall, pressed the open top of the shoe against her mouth and nose, and inhaled its scent with a long, deep breath. Then she closed her eyes and wept.

Skaggs stood back. Ptitchett's knees gave out. Skaggs watched her side down the wall in slow motion, her face still pressed into the shoe. She landed with a thump on the green carper. One of her orange slippers came off. On the TV across the room, the FOX 11 morning anchored pattered brightly over the sound of her sobs.

Skaggs had been a homicide detective for twenty years. In that time, he had been in a thousand living rooms like this one- each with its large TV, Afrocentric knickknacks, and imponderable grief.

—*Ghettoside* by Jill Leovy

1. **What is the intended audience for this text?**

   A. The African-American community

   B. White police officers

   C. The lower class

   D. Affluent communities

   E. All classes and races

   The correct answer is E.

   This passage gives the perspective of a white police officer and an African American mother who is grieving over the loss of a child. The message intends to give insight on a variety of classes and races; everyone that reads it can learn from it, regardless of their background. Therefore, (E) is the best answer.

2. How does the author appeal to the emotions of the audience?

A. Including a detailed scene, including memorabilia and Pritchett's physical and emotional response to the situation

B. Opening the scene with a description of Pritchett's poor health

C. Implying that this is a very common scene to this detective

D. Mentioning things the audience can relate to, such as watching the morning news

E. Mentioning an item that the audience is familiar with, a shoe

The correct answer is A.

The author appeals to the emotions of the audience by including things that elicit an emotional response. While options (B)-(E) may have some truth, the best answer is (A).

3. What is the major difference between Skaggs and Pritchett?

A. Gender

B. Race

C. Professional experience

D. Health condition

E. Age

The correct answer is B.

This is a tricky question, as all options are true. The best answer is (B) because the passage is a representation of the difference between their race.

4. Why is Pritchett wearing a T-shirt with her son's picture on it?

A. She is unemployed and does not wear professional clothing anymore.

B. She is in terrible health and wants to stay comfortable.

C. She is advocating for change.

D. She is reminding herself what he looked like.

E. All of the above.

The correct answer is C.

This is an obvious answer- the mother would not have forgotten what her son looked like. Although she may be in terrible health, that is not a reason that she'd be wearing a tee shirt with her son's image on it. Also, professional clothing has nothing to do with this passage, nor her employment status. (C) is the only viable answer.

5. **What does the shoe represent?**

   A. The last piece of evidence from the murder case.

   B. A piece of her son that was murdered.

   C. The detective trying to walk a mile in the victim's shoe.

   D. The age of the victim.

   E. The mother not being able to let go of her son's death.

   The correct answer is A.

   The shoe was brought to the mother by the police officer to bring a sense of closure to the case. He wanted to return it to her because it was the last piece of evidence that he had in his possession. Therefore, (A) is the correct answer.

6. **Why is the news station in the background significant?**

   A. The news represents the media downplaying or silencing terrible crimes.

   B. The news shows how quiet she was crying.

   C. The news represents another day moving forward.

   D. The news represents a woman watching television at a high volume.

   E. The news represents a distraction.

   The correct answer is A.

   The news playing in the background is symbolic to the conversation that the mother and police officer are having. It is played at a low volume and although there are terrible crimes being discussed, no one seems to notice. (A) is the best answer.

7. **Why was it important to mention that Skaggs has been to "a thousand living rooms like this one"?**

   A. He has visited every house in this neighborhood

   B. Most houses in this city have the same layout

   C. There is a cycle in his field of work, and he has had to deal with many murders in his twenty years as a detective

   D. All African-American families decorate in the same manner

   E. Grieving families always hold on to memories through pictures, teddy bears, and sympathy cards

   The correct answer is C.

   (A), (B), and (D) can easily be eliminated. Because (E) represents a literal interpretation and (C) defines the symbolism within the passage, (C) is the best answer.

8. **Why would the author describe the woman's grief as imponderable?**

A. It's not something he thought about before arriving at her house

B. Her grief was not apparent until he gave her the shoe

C. He is not sure how to console her

D. Skaggs cannot relate to the grief of a murdered child

E. This is something he's witnessed many times

The correct answer is D.

This is another easy question. The officer cannot relate to the grief that the mother is feeling, and although he's seen this situation many times before, it's still an unthinkable grief that he is witnessing.

Questions 9-16. Read the following passage carefully before you decide on your answers to the questions.

In the South every single thing was segregated: water fountains, public toilets and hotels and restaurants, but in "Greater Israel" i.e. the Occupied Territories, there's even segregation of the roads! Our Palestinian taxi driver tried hard to stay on the Arab only roads but one of them was blocked. He then, with great trepidation, got onto the big Jewish Settler only highway. This was simply amazing to experience. As was the realization that Palestinians have different colored license plates and that one of our group of artists and writers, a Palestinian man, had to leave our van because even inside a van he's not permitted to enter Jerusalem.

The way Palestinians are shot and killed, or arrested and beaten, as if they are not human beings, also reminds me of growing up in the South, where we were made to feel that Black life had no value. Also, the use of prison to keep politically conscious and active people out of the population. At this moment there are Palestinians in Israeli jails and prisons on a hunger strike because the majority of them were arrested without ever having been charged with anything. In the South too black people were often beaten and jailed and never given a fair trial, or sometimes never even told what they were arrested for. They were often put to work on plantations owned by the prison and by other plantation owners in the area. It was a way to re-enslave black people. After demolishing their houses and taking their land Israel has made use of workers in the Palestinian communities to build their Jewish only settlements.

-an interview with Alice Walker

9. **Why is the exclamation point important in the opening sentence?**

A. Segregation on the roads is not the norm

B. The author wanted to represent a loud voice

C. It sets the tone for the disgust that the author had for this place

D. It represents happiness that the roads were not segregated in the South

E. All of the above

The correct answer is A.

Sample Test Six

The author used extreme punctuation as a way to voice how uncommon it was to see segregation on the roads. Although she had experienced racism and different methods of segregation, she had never seen anything quite like this before.

10. What is a synonym for *trepidation*?

A. Confidence

B. Apprehension

C. Slow movement

D. Fast movement

E. Stop and go movement

The correct answer is B.

Using context clues, it's easy to determine that apprehension is a synonym for trepidation.

11. How does the author's relationship with the South shape her message?

A. She has first-hand experience with overt racism

B. She lived in the South and now lives in the Middle East

C. She wrote about the culture of the South and the Middle East

D. She is not accepting of other cultures

E. She is surprised at the transportation systems

The correct answer is A.

The author has an obvious connection to segregation and racism from living in the South.

12. How does the author connect the past to present day?

A. She explains that jails were used for American slaves more than Palestinians

B. She gives details of the transportation systems

C. She explains language differences

D. She gives an account of how lives are made not to matter for present Palestinians, in the same manner of American slaves

E. She notes that the Palestinian had to get out of the van

The correct answer is D.

This is an account of history repeating itself. The author gives details of racism that has happened in the past in the United States and ties it in with present day Palestinian issues with racism. There's quite an overlap in her eyes. Therefore, (D) is the correct answer.

13. How were black people re-enslaved?

A. They went to prison

B. They were sold back to prison-owned plantations

C. They were caught after escaping prison

D. They were caught after escaping to the North

E. They were bought and re-sold

The correct answer is B.

The author describes the crooked system that was in place during the time of slavery. Black people were sold back to prison-owned plantation owners, making a cycle that was very difficult to break. This makes (B) the best answer.

14. Why did the Palestinians have different colored license plates?

A. To segregate the roadways

B. To represent the regions they lived in

C. To represent their religion

D. To identify who could/could not enter Israel

E. All of the above

The correct answer is E.

Each of the options are true in regard to the variations of colored license plates.

15. How does the author defend her perspective?

A. She includes personal memories of growing up in the South

B. She quotes her parents

C. She explains that she's witnessed murder

D. She cites famous authors

E. None of the above

The correct answer is A.

The author gains credibility in what she's speaking about because she has lived through a similar experience with racism and segregation. The only option that works for this question is (A).

16. **What word best describes the tone used in this passage?**

A. Sarcastic

B. Anxious

C. Guilty

D. Peaceful

E. Aggressive

The correct answer is E.

Starting with the first sentence, the author uses punctuation to express her shock and disgust with the situation that she has witnessed. Aggressive is the best word to describe the tone in this passage, making (E) the correct answer.

Questions 17-24. Read the following passage carefully before you decide on your answers to the questions.

Ladies and Gentlemen, I'd planned to speak to you tonight to report on the state of the Union, but the events of earlier today have led me to change those plans. Today is a day for mourning and remembering. Nancy and I are pained to the core by the tragedy of the shuttle Challenger. We know we share this pain with all of the people of our country. This is truly a national loss.

Nineteen years ago, almost to the day, we lost three astronauts in a terrible accident on the ground. But we've never lost an astronaut in flight. We've never had a tragedy like this.

And perhaps we've forgotten the courage it took for the crew of the shuttle. But they, the Challenger Seven, were aware of the dangers, but overcame them and did their jobs brilliantly. We mourn seven heroes: Michael Smith, Dick Scobee, Judith Resnik, Ronald McNair, Ellison Onizuka, Gregory Jarvis, and Christa McAuliffe.

We mourn their loss as a nation together.

And I want to say something to the schoolchildren of America who were watching the live coverage of the shuttle's take-off. I know it's hard to understand, but sometimes painful things like this happen. It's all part of the process of exploration and discovery. It's all part of taking a chance and expanding man's horizons. The future doesn't belong to the fainthearted; it belongs to the brave. The Challenger crew was pulling us into the future, and we'll continue to follow them.

I've always had great faith in and respect for our space program. And what happened today does nothing to diminish it. We don't hide our space program. We don't keep secrets and cover things up. We do it all up front and in public. That's the way freedom is, and we wouldn't change it for a minute.

We'll continue our quest in space. There will be more shuttle flights and more shuttle crews and, yes, more volunteers, more civilians, more teachers in space. Nothing ends here; our hopes and our journeys continue.

I want to add that I wish I could talk to every man and woman who works for NASA, or who worked on this mission and tell them: "Your dedication and professionalism have moved and impressed us for decades. And we know of your anguish. We share it."

There's a coincidence today. On this day three hundred and ninety years ago, the great explorer Sir Francis Drake died aboard ship off the coast of Panama. In his lifetime the great frontiers were the oceans, and a historian later said, "He lived by the sea, died on it, and was buried in it." Well, today, we can say of the Challenger crew: Their dedication was, like Drake's, complete.

The crew of the space shuttle Challenger honored us by the manner in which they lived their lives. We will never forget them, nor the last time we saw them, this morning, as they prepared for their journey and waved goodbye and "slipped the surly bonds of earth" to "touch the face of God." Thank you.

—*Ronald Reagan, Challenger Address*

17. What emotion does this speech portray?

A. Empathy

B. Apathy

C. Concern

D. Grief

E. Displeasure

The correct answer is A.

Although the president may not fully understand the grief that families are feeling over the loss of a loved one, he displays a great deal of empathy in this speech. Therefore, (A) is the best answer.

18. Why does the speaker say "we"?

A. He is talking about himself and his wife

B. He is talking about himself and the American school children

C. He is including all Americans

D. He is including everyone in his political party

E. It represents his entire staff

The correct answer is C.

Again, he is showing empathy. He wants to include himself, his wife, and all Americans in his speech. He's showing unity by saying "we," and encourages others to show empathy for the families that have just lost a loved one. (C) is the best answer for this question.

19. What does the following line represent?

"The future doesn't belong to the fainthearted; it belongs to the brave."

A. A push for the school children to stay brave

B. Encouragement for school children to believe in future space exploration

C. A representation of people that fight for our country

D. Encouragement for Americans to curb their emotions

E. A note to let everyone know that only the heroic are successful

The correct answer is B.

The president does not want the school children to be traumatized by this situation. He explains that the astronauts that passed away in this tragic accident died because of an accident- that they were extremely brave in going into this expedition. He encourages school children to think of them as brave, which could result in their interest in space exploration.

20. Why does the speaker mention the anguish for the people of NASA?

A. They've all had a role in this mission

B. They personally knew each astronaut that died

C. Each staff member worked on the spaceship

D. They know it could have been them that died

E. It was their fault that the spaceship malfunctioned

The correct answer is A.

Although the astronauts where the ones that lost their lives, there were many other staff members that were involved in the mission. They may have worked on the radios, helped set up equipment, helped with training, etc. He mentions the people of NASA to give them credit, and again express empathy, for their role in this mission.

21. How does the speaker connect to their audience?

A. He mentions his wife and their emotional connection

B. He speaks loudly and clearly

C. He uses simple vocabulary

D. He mentions the names of the people that lost their lives

E. He references school children

The correct answer is A.

The use of "we" in the previous question should hint towards the correct answer here. By mentioning his wife and their emotional connection, the speaker is trying to connect with the audience as best he can.

22. Why does the speaker reference Sir Francis Drake?

A. The astronauts died supporting the school children

B. The astronauts died doing what they loved

C. He was an important historical figure of their time

D. He represents the sea, and they crashed into the sea

E. It is unclear why he mentions Sir Francis Drake

The correct answer is B.

Using the context of the situation, the brave astronauts died doing what they love.

23. What is a synonym for *surly*?

A. Curly

B. Sullen

C. Large

D. Unruly

E. Unfair

The correct answer is B.

Context clues help to zero in on sullen as the correct answer for this question.

24. What is the most appropriate word to describe this speech?

A. Hopeful

B. Mournful

C. Inspiring

D. Regretful

E. Vengeful

The correct answer is C.

Calling the astronauts brave and trying to encourage school children should help in finding the correct answer. (D) and (E) are easy to eliminate, and while (A) and (B) may have some truth, (C) is the best answer for this question.

Questions 25-32. Read the following passage carefully before you decide on your answers to the questions.

Photo credit: Karl Merton Ferron / Baltimore Sun

"City police are mainly concerned about outsiders who do not have a stake in the community," Howard County Police Chief Gary L. Gardner, who attended the meeting, said in a memo to officials in his county. "Also, they are receiving some information that there will be attempts to disrupt the Oriole game Saturday or the Inner Harbor area — disrupt commerce."

On Friday night, Baltimore police emailed Conaway, asking for 20 extra bike racks for the Sports Legends Museum and the nearby ballpark plaza, in case they were needed as barriers against protesters. Conaway also planned to open an Emergency Operations Center at the warehouse for Saturday's game, according to another email, with "the new stadium cameras plus city watch cameras available."

On Saturday, protesters and fans at the stadium and nearby sports pubs taunted one another, and some of those bike racks were among the projectiles thrown as the demonstration turned violent. Young men jumped atop police cars and used traffic cones to smash their windshields. At the park and elsewhere downtown, storefront windows were shattered.

As the mayhem continued, fans were kept inside Camden Yards for about 30 minutes, until officials thought it was safe for them to leave.

Still, the complex sustained what the stadium authority considered fairly minor damage — broken windows at Dempsey's restaurant and Geppi's Entertainment Museum.

"This one may have to wait until the morning to get boarded up," Matthew Kastel, facilities group director for Camden Yards, emailed colleagues regarding the museum damage. "I'm not sure it would be safe to send out one of my guys at the present moment to do this."

Around 10 p.m., Freddie Gray's twin sister, Fredericka Gray, joined Mayor Stephanie Rawlings-Blake at a news conference to plead, "Can y'all please, please stop the violence?"

In the end, 31 adults and four juveniles were arrested in Saturday's unrest — among them, Wayne Gray, 47, from Baltimore's east side.

"I've been in trouble before in my life, but I had a different feeling about what I got myself into this time," Gray, says now, reflecting on his arrest that night for disorderly conduct and failure to obey a police order to leave the area of Howard and Pratt streets. "I stood up for what I believe in. I feel like I stood up for what was right."

—*The Baltimore Sun,* October 23, 2015

25. What rhetoric does the brick in the image provoke?

A. Broken pieces of the city of Baltimore

B. Rebellion against police

C. Anticipation of a riot

D. Solidarity against brutality

E. All of the above

The correct answer is E.

The brick has powerful meaning behind it. It represents a weapon used against the police, which is waiting in the street for a rebellious riot. It also symbolizes pushback to police brutality. The fact that it's just a piece of a brick represents the broken piece of the city of Baltimore. Each of the options can be found in the image; therefore, (E) is the best answer.

26. Why was the image included?

A. To show the anticipation of what was about to happen

B. As evidence

C. To warn rioters of the riot gear that police would be wearin

D. To support rioters in throwing bricks

E. All of the above

The correct answer is A.

It's easy to eliminate (B) and (C) for this question. Although the image does represent the riot gear that police would be wearing, the best answer for this question is (A). It clearly represents the anticipation of what may happen in the riots that were happening on the streets of Baltimore.

27. **How does the image portray police officers?**

A. In unison

B. Blurred

C. Caucasian

D. Powerful

E. Large in number

The correct answer is A.

This is a tricky question. Because we know the brick represents the people of Baltimore, we can infer that the police represent the opposing side of the riot. While they are large in number and look powerful, the best answer is (A). Their unison is a representation of the two sides of the race argument.

28. **How does the article portray police officers?**

A. Defenseless

B. Powerful

C. Regal

D. Intimidated

E. Caucasian

The correct answer is D.

Because the brick is shown as an act of defense against the police, this image represents the intimidation the people of Baltimore had on them. They are dressed in riot gear and trying to portray themselves as powerful as possible, but they would not have dressed in such attire unless they felt intimidated. The best answer for this question is (D).

29. **Who was Fredericka Gray addressing when she said, "Can y'all please, please stop the violence?"**

A. The police

B. The people of Baltimore

C. All Americans

D. Her family

E. Her friends

The correct answer is B.

Given the context of the Baltimore riots, Fredericka Gray was addressing the people of Baltimore to try to reduce the amount of violence that was happening at that time. She was aware that more rioting had been planned for that evening, and she was trying to avoid an ongoing war between the people and the police.

30. _____ is a synonym for *unrest.*

A. Sleeplessness

B. Disturbance

C. Communication

D. Meeting

E. Funeral

The correct answer is B.

Using the context clues in the article, it's easy to determine that disturbance is a synonym for unrest.

31. Why did Wayne Gray have a *different feeling* about being arrested?

A. He didn't feel as if what he did was wrong

B. He felt sick

C. He did not expect to be arrested

D. His other arrests were far more serious crimes

E. All of the above

The correct answer is A.

This was not a typical arrest. Wayne was not being arrested for an obvious crime. Instead, he felt as though he was standing up for something he believed in. Because he didn't feel as if what he did was wrong, (A) is the best answer.

32. How does the 20 extra bike racks help to explain the situation?

A. The Orioles game wanted to accommodate their fans

B. 20 racks were needed because of the high number of anticipated protesters

C. 20 racks were needed to accommodate the number of police officers on bicycles

D. The Orioles game wanted to use them as a barricade to keep their fans inside the stadium

E. They were all used to damage Dempsey's restaurant

The correct answer is B.

There was an extremely large number of protesters projected for that evening. The 20 extra bike racks were needed as barriers for the protesters, making (B) the best answer.

Questions 33-40. Read the following passage carefully before you decide on your answers to the questions.

Two years have passed since my book came out, and three years since the October morning when I was shot by the Taliban on a school bus on my way home from class. My family has been through many changes. We were plucked from our mountain valley in Swat, Pakistan, and transported to a brick house in Birmingham, England's second-biggest city. Sometimes it seems so strange that I want to pinch myself. I'm seventeen now and one thing that has not changed is that I still don't like getting up in the morning. The most astonishing thing is that it's my father whose voice wakes me up now. He gets up first every day and prepares breakfast for me, my mother, and my brothers, Atal and Khushal. He doesn't let his work go unnoticed, of course, going on about how he squeezes fresh juice, fries eggs, heats flat bread, and takes the honey out of the cupboard. "It's only breakfast!" I tease. For the first time in his life, he also does the shopping, although he hates doing it. The man who didn't even know the price of a pint of milk is such a frequent visitor to the supermarket that he knows where everything is on the shelves! "I've become like a woman, a true feminist!" he says, and I jokingly throw things at him.

My brothers and I then all rush off to our different schools. And so does out mother, Toor Pekai, which is truly one of the biggest changes of all. She is attending a language center five days a week to learn how to read and write and also to speak English. My mother had no education and perhaps that was the reason that she always encouraged us to go to school. "Don't wake up like me and realize what you missed years later," she says. She faces so many challenges in her daily life because up until now she's had difficulty communicating when she's gone shopping, or to the doctor or the bank. Getting an education is helping her become more confident, so that she can speak up outside the home, not just inside it with us.

—*I Am Malala* by Malala Yousafzai

33. What elements of cultural context help to explain the author's background?

A. The explanation of her family being plucked from their mountain valley in Swat, Pakistan

B. Her fascination of her new brick home in Birmingham, England

C. The explanation of her brothers gong to different schools

D. The inclusion of juice, eggs, bread, and honey

E. All of the above

The correct answer is A.

The only option here that points to the author's background is the mention of her former mountain valley home.

34. Why is it *astonishing* that her father wakes her up?

A. She has never met her father

B. She thought he died

C. She's not used to seeing him in the house

D. She's used to hearing an alarm clock

E. She's normally the first person awake

The correct answer is C.

The author was blown away that she was able to see her father each morning because she was not used to seeing him in the house. He had been hard at work each day before moving to England. Because of this, (C) is the best answer.

35. Why didn't her father go shopping before now?

A. Her mother did all the cooking, cleaning, and shopping

B. The marketplace is new

C. He didn't speak the language

D. They didn't have enough money

E. It was too dangerous to go shopping

The correct answer is A.

Again, her father was always working before moving to England. Her mother is now in class to learn English, and her father has taken over some of the household duties. It's easy to determine that (A) is the best answer.

36. How does the mother's quote, "Don't wake up like me and realize what you missed years later" influence the audience?

A. It's a reminder of oppression across the globe

B. It represents female rights being taken away

C. It represents opportunity in England

D. It's encouraging to get out and accomplish as much as you can so that you don't have regrets in the future

E. It makes the reader reflect on the last time they woke up

The correct answer is D.

This is an easy question. (D) is the only option that represents the mother's quote.

37. How did the author include multiple definitions with the phrase *speak up*?

A. It also represents raising her voice

B. It also means to challenge authority

C. It also means fighting for women's rights

D. It will also help her raise her children

E. All of the above

The correct answer is C.

Speaking up has multiple meanings in this passage. It does not represent raising one's voice, the most literal representation. It best represents fighting for women's rights, making (C) the best answer.

38. What does this passage say about education?

A. It's very important for a successful future

B. You can get shot on your way home from school

C. There are different schools for adults and children

D. It will help you with shopping and going to the doctor

E. England has great schools

The correct answer is A.

Education is held at a very high standard in this passage. The mother did not have an education and was extremely supportive in getting her children an educational experience.

39. How does this passage portray differences in education in Pakistan and England?

A. Men are able to go to school in both places

B. Women typically do not attend school in Pakistan

C. Women are more likely to attend school in England

D. Schools are safer in England

E. All of the above

The correct answer is E.

Each of the options are included in this passage. Men have more rights in Pakistan, and they're able to go to school in each country. It's mentioned that women do not typically attend school in Pakistan. Safety concerns were only mentioned in the mention of a Pakistan school. Because of this, (E) is the correct answer.

40. How does this passage define gender roles?

A. It breaks gender roles because the father does the cooking and shopping

B. It follows gender roles because the mother is in school

C. It breaks gender roles because the father didn't know how much a pint of milk costs

D. It follows gender roles because the father is familiar with the supermarket

E. Gender roles are not defined

The correct answer is A.

Typical gender roles were not followed in this passage due to the fact the father was the one that did the cooking and shopping. Therefore, (A) is the best answer.

Questions 41-48. Read the following passage carefully before you decide on your answers to the questions.

International baggage claim in the Brussels airport was large and airy, with multiple carousels circling endlessly. I scurried from one to another, desperately trying to find my black suitcase. Because it was stuffed with drug money, I was more concerned than one might normally be about lost luggage.

I was twenty-four in 1993 and probably looked like just another anxious young professional woman. My Doc Martens had ben jettisoned in favor of my beautiful handmade black suede heels. I wore black silk pants and a beige jacket, a typical *jeune fille*, not a big counterculture, unless you spotted the tattoo on my neck. I had done exactly as I had been instructed, checking my bag Chicago through Paris, where I had to switch planes to take a short flight to Brussels.

When I arrived in Belgium, I looked for my black rollie at the baggage claim. It was no where to be seen. Fighting a rushing tide of panic, I asked in my mangled high school French what had become of my suitcase. "Bags don't make it onto the right flight sometimes," said the big lug working in baggage handling. "Wait for the next shuttle from Paris— It's probably on that plane."

Had my bag been detected? I knew that carrying more than $10,000 undeclared was illegal, let alone carrying it for a West African drug lord. Were the authorities closing in on me? Maybe I should try to get through customs and run? Or perhaps the bag really was just delayed, and I would be abandoning a large some of money that belonged to someone who could probably have killed me with a simple phone call. I decided that the later choice was slightly more terrifying. So I waited.

The next flight from Paris finally arrived. I sidled over to my new "friend" in baggage handling, who was sorting things out. It is hard to flirt when you're frightened. I spotted the suitcase. "Mon bag!" I exclaimed in ecstasy, seizing the Tumi. I thanked him effusively, waiving with giddy affection as I sailed through one of the unmanned doors into the terminal, where I spotted my friend Billy waiting for me. I had inadvertently skipped customs.

"I was worried. What happened?" Billy asked.

"Get me into a cab!" I hissed.

I didn't breathe until we had pulled away from the airport and were halfway across Brussels.

—*Orange is the New Black*. Piper Kerman

41. Why did the author explain her attire?

A. She wanted the audience to know how much she stood out in Europe

B. She used her clothing to try to fit in with the culture she was immersed in

C. She wanted to explain that she was a young, hip woman

D. She explained how difficult it was to wait around for her bag in heels

E. She won the bag handler over because she looked beautiful that day

The correct answer is B.

The author used her attire to make herself mesh with the setting that she was immersed in. She was out of the country and trying her best to fit in, particularly because she was involved in illegal activity. Because she was trying to use her clothing to fit in, (B) is the best answer.

42. How is stream of consciousness included in this passage?

A. It includes the author's thoughts and emotions

B. She uses the term "I"

C. The narrator is the main character

D. It includes dialogue

E. It describes her experience with luggage

The correct answer is A.

Steam of consciousness includes the thoughts, actions, and emotions of the main character. The author included her thoughts and the emotions that she was feeling at the time, making (A) the best answer.

43. How does the author use punctuation to express herself?

A. Question marks

B. An ellipses

C. Exclamation points

D. Quotation marks

E. All of the above

The correct answer is C.

Of the punctuation marks included in the options for this question, exclamation points is the best answer for what the author used to express herself.

44. What is a synonym for mangled in the following line: "I asked in my *mangled* high school French"

A. Simple

B. Terrible

C. Elementary

D. Perfect

E. Accentuated

The correct answer is B.

Mangled is used as an informal way of describing her language abilities as terrible.

45. What part of the plot does "Mon bag!" represent?

A. Climax

B. Rising action

C. Exposition

D. Falling action

E. Resolution

The correct answer is A.

This statement represents the main character getting away with the crime that she was committing, making it the climax.

46. How did she avoid going through customs?

A. She flirted with the luggage man

B. Her friend Billy came to get her

C. She slipped through an unmanned door

D. She went through customs in Paris and Chicago, so it wasn't required

E. She went through customs in Brussels

The correct answer is C.

Using the details in the passage, it's easy to zero in on (C) as the correct answer.

47. Why didn't she breathe until pulling away from the airport?

A. Adrenaline

B. Sadness

C. Health issues

D. She was talking to Billy

E. She was in awe of the airport

The correct answer is A.

She had just gotten away with illegal activity, making her adrenaline at an all-time high. It's clear that she was not sad, and there's no mention of health issues in this passage. A is the best answer.

48. What is the overall message of this passage?

A. Airports often lose bags

B. Security guards are not always watching every door in the airport

C. It's helpful to have a friend pick you up from the airport

D. Doing illegal things in the airport is scary, and there's always a chance of getting caught

E. Young professional women get away with everything

The correct answer is D.

The author left plenty of room in the passage for the reader to think she might get caught. Because she portrays the emotions involved in doing something illegal in the airport, and her thoughts of how she might get caught, (D) is the best answer.

Questions 49-55. Read the following passage carefully before you decide on your answers to the questions.

It is impossible for any man, when the most favourable circumstances concur, to acquire sufficient knowledge and strength of mind to discharge the duties of a king, entrusted with uncontrouled power; how then must they be violated when his very elevation is an insuperable bar to the attainment of either wisdom or virtue; when all the feelings of a man are stifled by flattery, and reflection shut out by pleasure! Surely it is madness to make the fate of thousands depend on the caprice of a weak fellow creature, whose very station sinks him necessarily below the meanest of his subjects! But one power should not be thrown down to exalt another—for all power intoxicates weak man; and its abuse proves, that the more equality there is established among men, the more virtue and happiness will reign in society. But this, and any similar maxim deduced from simple reason, raises an outcry—the church or the state is in danger, if faith in the wisdom of antiquity is not implicit; and they who, roused by the sight of human calamity, dare to attack human authority, are reviled as despisers of God, and enemies of man. These are bitter calumnies, yet they reached one of the best of men, whose ashes still preach peace, and whose memory demands a respectful pause, when subjects are discussed that lay so near his heart.

After attacking the sacred majesty of Kings, I shall scarcely excite surprise by adding my firm persuasion that every profession, in which great subordination of rank constitutes its power, is highly injurious to morality.

A standing army, for instance, is incompatible with freedom; because subordination and rigour are the very sinews of military discipline; and despotism is necessary to give vigour to enterprizes that one will directs. A spirit inspired by romantic notions of honour, a kind of morality founded on the fashion of the age, can only be felt by a few officers, whilst the main body must be moved by command, like the waves of the sea; for the strong wind of authority pushes the crowd of subalterns forward, they scarcely know or care why, with headlong fury.

—Mary Wollstonecraft *A Vindication of the Rights of Woman.* 1792

49. What type of essay is this?

A. Argumentative

B. Persuasive

C. Narrative

D. Descriptive

E. Expository

The correct answer is B.

This essay was written with the intention of being persuasive, making (B) the best answer.

50. What is the author's tone?

A. Formal

B. Informal

C. Comic

D. Sarcastic

E. Serious

The correct answer is E.

The author's tone was very serious in describing power structures, which makes (E) the best answer.

51. **What does the term *sinews* represent?**

A. Strength

B. Organization

C. Discipline

D. Grace

E. Downfall

The correct answer is A.

The mention of sinews and this word's relationship to the military should be a good indicator of the correct answer for this question.

52. **Because of the spelling of favourable, rigour, vigour, and honour, we can assume this author was most likely from:**

A. America

B. Canada

C. England

D. France

E. Ireland

The correct answer is C.

This spelling was common in Old English, which stems back to England.

53. In the phrase romantic notions of *honour*, romantic represents _____.

A. Love

B. Inspiration

C. Hope

D. Radicalism

E. Promotion

The correct answer is D.

Radicalism represents the change of social structures, even if it came to a revolution. This phrase best represents the radicalism that the author has projected throughout the passage, making (D) the best answer.

54. *Subalterns* is a synonym for _____.

A. Antlers

B. Waves

C. Officers

D. Submarine

E. Captains

The correct answer is C.

It's easy to use context clues to determine that subalterns is a synonym for officers.

55. What impact on the reader does the author have in mentioning kings and common officers?

A. She shows that regardless of rank, every profession has downfalls

B. She explains the divide between the two classes

C. She amplifies the importance of royalty

D. She demonstrates the level of respect officers have for their king

E. She questions gender roles in professional settings

The correct answer is A.

Many of the options in this question go against the message that's being portrayed in this passage. She does not mention respect that officers have for their king, and the importance of royalty is questioned more than supported. While she does give examples of the divisions of classes and questions gender roles, the intention behind mentioning of kinds and common officers was to display the downfalls that each profession has, regardless of rank.

Sample Test Six

Sample Test Seven

Section I

Multiple Choice Questions.
Time: 60 minutes.
Percent of total grade on the exam: 45 percent.

Instructions: This section of the exam consists of selections from literary works and questions on their content, form, and style. After reading each passage and poem, choose the best answer to each question and then fill in the corresponding oval on the answer sheet.

Questions 1-8. Read the passage and answer the following questions carefully.

When rays of light pass through a prism, they undergo a change of direction: they are always deflected away from the refractive edge. It is possible to conceive an assembly of prisms whose refractive surfaces progressively become more nearly parallel to each other towards the middle: light rays passing through the outer prisms will undergo the greatest amount of refraction, with consequent deflection of their path towards the center, whereas the middle prism with its two parallel surfaces causes no deflection at all. When a beam of parallel rays passes through these prisms, the rays are all deflected towards the axis and converge at one point. Rays emerging from a point are also deflected by the prisms that they converge. A lens can be conceived as consisting of a large number of such prisms placed close up against one another, so that their surfaces merge into a continuous spherical surface. A lens of this kind, which collects the rays and concentrates them at one point, is called a convergent lens. Since it is thicker in the middle than at the edge, it is known as a convex lens.

In the case of a concave lens, which is thinner in the middle than at the edge, similar considerations show that all rays diverge from the center. Hence such a lens is called a divergent lens. After undergoing refraction, parallel rays appear to come from one point, while rays remerging from a point will, after passing through the lens, appear to emerge from another point. Lenses have surfaces in the same direction but having a different radii of curvature, these are known as meniscus lenses and are used more particularly in spectacles.

1. **Light rays hit convex mirror and :**

   A. the rays pass straight through.

   B. the rays bounce only straight back to the light source.

   C. bend together to cross at a single point on the other side.

   D. are refracted to open outward on the other side.

   E. are reflected outward at angles back toward the light source.

2. Light rays hit a concave surface. Light:

A. travels through the prism's surface, angling together to a point.

B. moves in the same direction but has a different radii of curvature.

C. the light merges to a point on the continuous spherical surface.

D. are always reflected away from the refractive edge.

E. experiences no deflection.

3. Spectacles use meniscus lenses, which are:

A. flat

B. varying radii of concave lenses

C. varying radii of convex lenses

D. round on both sides of the lens, meaning they have double refraction.

E. always convergent lenses

4. According to the author, a lens is made of:

A. Glass

B. Refractive edges

C. Prisms

D. Spheres

E. Radii

5. Refraction" can be taken to mean:

A. Deflection

B. Reflection

C. Redirection

D. Alteration

E. Manipulation

6. Parallel surfaces in prisms cause:

A. Very little refraction

B. Divergence of light rays

C. No refraction

D. Radii to vary

E. Reflection of light waves

7. Which of the following is NOT true of convergent lenses?

A. They are concave

B. They are made of prisms

C. They can refract light

D. They have different radii

E. They deflect light away from the refractive edge

8. What is the subject of the verb "collects" in this sentence: "A lens of this kind, which collects the rays and concentrates them at one point, is called a convergent lens"?

A. Kind

B. Lens

C. Concentrates

D. Point

E. Convergent

Questions 9-16. Read the passage and answer the following questions carefully.

It was about this time I conceived the bold and arduous project of arriving at moral perfection. I wished to live without committing any fault at any time; I would conquer all that either natural inclination, custom, or company might lead me into. As I knew, or thought I knew, what was right and wrong, I did not see why I might not always do the one and avoid the other. But I soon found I had undertaken a task of more difficulty than I had imagined. While my care was employed in guarding against one fault, I was often surprised by another; habit took the advantage of inattention; inclination was sometimes too strong for reason. I concluded, at length, that the mere speculative conviction that it was our interest to be completely virtuous was not sufficient to prevent our slipping, and that the contrary habits must be broken, and good ones acquired and established, before we can have any dependence on a steady, uniform rectitude of conduct. For this purpose I therefore contrived the following method.

In the various enumerations of the moral virtues I met in my reading, I found the catalogue more or less numerous, as different writers included more or fewer ideas under the same name. Temperance, for example, was by some confined to eating and drinking, while by others it was extended to mean the moderating every other pleasure, appetite, inclination, or passion, bodily or mental, even to our avarice and ambition. I proposed to myself, for the sake of clearness, to use rather more names, with fewer ideas annexed to each, than a few names with more ideas; and I included under thirteen names of virtues all that at that time occurred to me as necessary or desirable, and annexed to each a short precept, which fully expressed the extent I gave to its meaning.

9. What is the relationship between the first and second paragraphs?

A. The first illustrates the author's confusion at living a moral life, and the second illustrates his approach to clarifying the issue

B. The first enumerates the author's past attempts at living morally, and the second explores his more recent attempts

C. The first establishes the author as amoral, and the second describes his growth towards morality

D. The first finds humor in the author's quest for moral superiority, whereas the second is more serious by contrast

E. The first elevates the author's project as an incredible ordeal, and the second explores its value to the common man

10. In context, what is meant by "and annexed to each a short precept, which fully expressed the extent I gave to its meaning"?

A. The author made certain to avoid indulging in such excesses

B. The author reveled in his own progress towards morality

C. The author cordoned off problematic areas of his life to better study them

D. The author clarified desirable virtues with an appropriate name

E. The author became confused at his own inability to be moral

11. What is the best synonym for "enumerations" in the second paragraph?

A. Items

B. Books

C. Scholars

D. Lists

E. Virtues

12. What has the author discovered other writers feel about temperance?

A. It is an essential quality

B. It is difficult to define

C. It requires an absence of all pleasures

D. It is impossible to obtain

E. It is ultimately unnecessary

13. What best paraphrases the sentence in the first paragraph beginning with "I concluded, at length, that the mere…"?

A. Intentions are not sufficient to create a moral life if they are not followed by a change in lifestyle

B. One cannot go about the process of creating a moral life if they do not plan things out ahead of time

C. A person will inevitably slide back into bad habits and there is little that can be done about it

D. One is free to imagine themselves living a moral life, even if the possibility of living one is remote due to outside circumstances

E. The primary hindrance towards moral living is the development of bad habits, which inevitably accrue as one becomes more moral

14. What can we assume will follow this selection?

A. An explanation of the numerous ways other authors have misinterpreted morality

B. A lecture on the need for temperance in moral living

C. A list of the virtues the author has sought to acquire

D. Further description of the author's research into the topic of morality

E. Further difficulties the author has encountered on his quest

15. What is the subject of the verb "annexed" in paragraph two?

A. I

B. Fewer

C. Each

D. Myself

E. Names

16. In the final sentence of the first paragraph, what is the best synonym for "contrived"?

A. Mocked

B. Explored

C. Indicated

D. Lied

E. Created

Questions 17-24. Read the passage and answer the following questions carefully.

When it was first perceived, in early times, that no middle course for America remained between unlimited submission to a foreign legislature and a total independence of its claims, men of reflection were less apprehensive of danger from the formidable power of fleets and armies they must determine to resist than from those contests and dissensions which would certainly arise concerning the forms of government to be instituted over the whole and over the parts of this extensive country. Relying, however, on the purity of their intentions, the justice of their cause, and the integrity and intelligence of the people, under an overruling Providence which had so signally protected this country from the first, the representatives of this nation, then consisting of little more than half its present number, not only broke to pieces the chains which were forging and the rod of iron that was lifted up, but frankly cut asunder the ties which had bound them, and launched into an ocean of uncertainty.

The zeal and ardor of the people during the Revolutionary war, supplying the place of government, commanded a degree of order sufficient at least for the temporary preservation of society. The

Confederation which was early felt to be necessary was prepared from the models of the Batavian and Helvetic confederacies, the only examples which remain with any detail and precision in history, and certainly the only ones which the people at large had ever considered. But reflecting on the striking difference in so many particulars between this country and those where a courier may go from the seat of government to the frontier in a single day, it was then certainly foreseen by some who assisted in Congress at the formation of it that it could not be durable.

Negligence of its regulations, inattention to its recommendations, if not disobedience to its authority, not only in individuals but in States, soon appeared with their melancholy consequences—universal languor, jealousies and rivalries of States, decline of navigation and commerce, discouragement of necessary manufactures, universal fall in the value of lands and their produce, contempt of public and private faith, loss of consideration and credit with foreign nations, and at length in discontents, animosities, combinations, partial conventions, and insurrection, threatening some great national calamity.

17. What best summarizes the first sentence of this piece?

A. When we first realize there was no middle ground between subservience and independence, intelligent men were less afraid of war than they were of deciding how to govern our new nation

B. When our ancestors first realized they must be free instead of obedient, they realized that combat was far less challenging than the bureaucracy that would follow

C. When men realized, in the past, that freedom would be hard to win, they decided to craft a new form of government to aid in this process

D. When our new nation first achieved independence, the true struggle was not the war that followed, but the arguments between learned me who could not agree on anything

E. When men first decided independence was necessary, they could not agree who should lead them, or how

18. The phrase "ocean of uncertainty" is a...

A. Allusion

B. Metaphor

C. Allegory

D. Simile

E. Personification

19. In the last sentence of the third paragraph, what does "durable" refer to?

A. Striking

B. Courier

C. Country

D. Congress

E. Formation

20. What does the author identify as a problem in the second paragraph?

A. The similarities between his new nation and the Batavian and Helvetic confederacies

B. The ignorance of the common people

C. The unrestrained zeal of common citizens

D. The vast size of this new country

E. The brewing revolution that approaches

21. What word does "frankly" modify in the last sentence of the first paragraph?

A. Cut

B. Asunder

C. Ties

D. Representatives

E. Bound

22. The author identifies all of these as problems in the third paragraph EXCEPT:

A. Laziness

B. Envy

C. Poor trade

D. Religious intolerance

E. Increased dependence on foreign powers

23. What is "it" the first sentence of the third paragraph refers to?

A. The new nation

B. The Revolutionary War

C. Congress

D. The presidency

E. The States

24. In the first paragraph, what does the author NOT credit with aiding the representatives?

A. Providence

B. Intelligence

C. Integrity

D. The Nation

E. Purity

Questions 25-32. Read the passage and answer the following questions carefully.

No American historian, so far as I know, has ever tried to work out the probable consequences if Grant instead of Lee had been on the hot spot at Appamattox. How long would the victorious Confederacy have endured? Could it have surmounted the difficulties inherent in the doctrine of States' Rights, so often inconvenient and even paralyzing to it during the war? Could it have remedied its plain economic deficiencies, and become a self-sustaining nation? How would it have protected itself against such war heroes as Beauregard and Longstreet, Joe Wheeler and Nathan D. Forrest? And what would have been its relations to the United States, socially, economically, spiritually and politically?

I am inclined, on all these counts, to be optimistic. The chief evils in the Federal victory lay in the fact, from which we still suffer abominably, that it was a victory of what we now call Babbitts over what used to be called gentlemen. I am not arguing here, of course, that the whole Confederate army was composed of gentlemen; on the contrary, it was chiefly made up, like the Federal army, of innocent and unwashed peasants, and not a few of them got into its corps of officers. But the impulse behind it, as everyone knows, was essentially aristocratic, and that aristocratic impulse would have fashioned the Confederacy if the fortunes of war had run the other way. Whatever the defects of the new commonwealth below the Potomac, it would have at least been a commonwealth founded upon a concept of human inequality, and with a superior minority at the helm. It might not have produced any more Washingtons, Madisons, Jeffersons, Calhouns and Randolphs of Roanoke, but it would certainly not have yielded itself to the Heflins, Caraways, Bilbos and Tillmans.

The rise of such bounders was a natural and inevitable consequence of the military disaster. That disaster left the Southern gentry deflated and almost helpless. Thousands of the best young men among them had been killed, and thousands of those who survived came North. They commonly did well in the North, and were good citizens. My own native town of Baltimore was greatly enriched by their immigration, both culturally and materially; if it is less corrupt today than most other large American cities, then the credit belongs largely to Virginians, many of whom arrived with no baggage save good manners and empty bellies. Back home they were sorely missed. First the carpetbaggers ravaged the land, and then it fell into the hands of the native white trash, already so poor that war and Reconstruction could not make them any poorer. When things began to improve they seized whatever was seizable, and their heirs and assigns, now poor no longer, hold it to this day. A raw plutocracy owns and operates the New South, with no challenge save from a proletariat, white and black, that is still three-fourths peasant, and hence too stupid to be dangerous. The aristocracy is almost extinct, at least as a force in government. It may survive in backwaters and on puerile levels, but of the men who run the South today, and represent it at Washington, not 5%, by any Southern standard, are gentlemen.

25. The term "hot spot" from the first sentence is an example of a:

A. Metaphor

B. Simile

C. Allusion

D. Synecdoche

E. Neologism

26. What is this author's attitude towards the Confederacy?

A. They were pure evil

B. They were deeply flawed

C. They had a righteous cause

D. They had no chance from the beginning

E. They lacked resources to win

27. What is the author "optimistic" about, as mentioned in the second paragraph?

A. He is sure the Confederacy would have succeeded

B. He is certain the Confederacy would have failed

C. He is certain the Confederacy will rise again

D. He's confident the Confederate army could have done more

E. He believes the North won by luck

28. Which best describes the author's attitude?

A. The author is unaware of who would have won if Grant and Lee had battled

B. The author knows of no theories on what would have followed if Lee had defeated Grant

C. The author does not know any American historian who has correctly assessed the American Civil War

D. The author strongly disagrees with what occurred at Appamattox

E. The author believes the South should have been successful at Appamattox, if not for Grant

29. What are the "bounders" the author describes in paragraph three?

A. The boundaries between North and South

B. The boundaries between the Confederacy and its citizens

C. The boundaries between the aristocracy and the commoners

D. The boundaries between morality and slavery

E. The boundaries between those who died and those who fled north

30. Who is the "superior minority" mentioned in the second paragraph?

A. The North

B. Slaves

C. The peasantry

D. The gentry

E. The Confederacy

31. What is the author's attitude towards the post-Civil War migrants?

A. They were unwashed peasants

B. They were uneducated

C. They were victims

D. They were a necessary side effect

E. They were good citizens

32. The author uses the term "gentlemen" to describe:

A. Confederate officers

B. Migrants

C. Southerners in general

D. Northern elites

E. Southern aristocrats

Questions 33-40. Read the passage and answer the following questions carefully.

Most people who bother with the matter at all would admit that the English language is in a bad way, but it is generally assumed that we cannot by conscious action do anything about it. Our civilization is decadent and our language — so the argument runs — must inevitably share in the general collapse. It follows that any struggle against the abuse of language is a sentimental archaism, like preferring candles to electric light or hansom cabs to aeroplanes. Underneath this lies the half-conscious belief that language is a natural growth and not an instrument which we shape for our own purposes.

Now, it is clear that the decline of a language must ultimately have political and economic causes: it is not due simply to the bad influence of this or that individual writer. But an effect can become a cause, reinforcing the original cause and producing the same effect in an intensified form, and so on indefinitely. A man may take to drink because he feels himself to be a failure, and then fail all the more completely because he drinks. It is rather the same thing that is happening to the English language. It becomes ugly and inaccurate because our thoughts are foolish, but the slovenliness of our language makes it easier for us to have foolish thoughts. The point is that the process is reversible. Modern English, especially written English, is full of bad habits which spread by imitation and which can be avoided if one is willing to take the necessary trouble. If one gets rid of these habits one can think more clearly, and to think clearly is a necessary first step toward political regeneration: so that the fight against bad English is not frivolous and is not the exclusive concern of professional writers. I will come back to this presently, and I hope that by that time the meaning of what I have said here will have become clearer. Meanwhile, here are five specimens of the English language as it is now habitually written.

33. What does the author mean by "archaism"?

A. Mystery

B. Misidentification

C. Anachronism

D. Ignorance

E. Affectation

34. "A man may take to drink because he feels himself to be a failure, and then fail all the more completely because he drinks." In context, this sentence is best described as a:

A. Analogy

B. Metaphor

C. Simile

D. Allusion

E. Conceit

35. What does this author think of the English language?

A. It is in unavoidable decline

B. It should not be altered

C. Its rules are subject to the whims of speakers

D. It can be improved through good habits

E. Only professionals should dictate its rules

36. What can we assume will follow this passage?

A. A screed on the decline of English

B. Further evidence that English is being destroyed

C. Names of authors who have contributed to the decline of English

D. Specific examples of bad English in use

E. An illustration of how to use English properly

37. What is the subject of the verb "lies" in the last sentence of the first paragraph?

A. Language

B. Growth

C. This

D. Underneath

E. Belief

38. The author believes the decline of English is due to:

A. The imitation of bad habits

B. Societal decadence

C. People preferring what is simple

D. Political quibbling

E. Foolish thoughts

39. By characterizing language as a "natural growth", the author emphasizes its:

A. Personified qualities

B. Duplicitous nature

C. Inconsistency

D. Changeability

E. Ignorance

40. What tone is the author striving for in this piece?

A. Humorous

B. Academic

C. Angry

D. Disappointed

E. Superior

Questions 41-48. Read the passage and answer the following questions carefully.

On the domestic front, life was not easy. England was not a wealthy country and its people endured relatively poor living standards. The landed classes — many of them enriched by the confiscated wealth of former monasteries — were determined in the interests of profile to convert their arable land into pasture for sheep, so as to produce the wool that supported the country's chief economic asset, the woolen cloth trade. But the enclosing of the land only added to the misery of the poor, many of whom, evicted and displaced, left their decaying villages and gravitated to the towns where they joined the growing army of beggars and vagabonds that would become such a feature of Elizabethan life. Once, the religious houses would have dispensed charity to the destitute, but Henry VIII had dissolved them all in the 1530s, and many former monks and nuns were now themselves beggars. Nor did the civic authorities help: they passed laws in an attempt to ban the poor from towns and cities, but to little avail. It was a common sight to see men and women lying in the dusty streets, often dying in the dirt like dogs or beasts, without human compassion being shown to them. 'Certainly, wrote a Spanish observer in 1558', 'the state of England lay now most afflicted.'

And although people looked to the new Queen Elizabeth to put matters right, there were so many who doubted if she could overcome the seemingly insurmountable problems she faced, or even remain queen long enough to begin tacking them. Some, both at home and abroad, were the opinion that her title to the throne rested on very precarious foundations. Many regarded the daughter of Henry VII and Anne Boleyn as a bastard from the time of her birth on 7 September 1533, although, ignoring such slurs on the validity of his second marriage, Henry had declared Elizabeth his heir.

41. Why was land confiscated from the poor?

A. The town wanted to build a new monastery.

B. To create pastures for sheep, ultimately increasing the export of wool.

C. The town wanted to create housing for monks and nuns.

D. Queen Elizabeth wanted to expand her property.

E. The poor did not pay their taxes.

42. A vagabond is a _____.

A. Wanderer

B. Prisoner

C. Poor person

D. Rich person

E. Fighter

43. Why didn't the poor have shelter with the churches?

A. They were already filled with beggars.

B. Religious houses have never offered shelter to the poor.

C. They were also being used to raise sheep.

D. Henry VIII had dissolved them all in the 1530s.

E. Queen Elizabeth dissolved them all in the 1530s.

44. How were civic authorities unsuccessful?

A. Poor people remained within city limits

B. Public service funds ran out

C. Public housing plans extended deadlines

D. Churches did not open their doors to the poor

E. The poor overthrew them to gain their land back

45. What is a synonym for precarious?

A. Strong

B. Careful

C. Risky

D. Determined

E. Ilegimat

46. What is the author's view towards Queen Elizabeth?

A. Doubtful

B. Vengeful

C. Resentful

D. Supportive

E. Confident

47. How is the English culture portrayed in this passage?

A. Religious

B. Elitist

C. Racist

D. Diverse

E. Spiritual

48. What is Elizabeth's relationship to Henry?

A. Wife

B. Cousin

C. Lover

D. Daughter

E. Niece

Questions 49-55 Read the passage and answer the following questions carefully.

I have often thought of it as one of the most barbarous customs in the world, considering us as a civilized and a Christian country, that we deny the advantages of learning to women. We reproach the sex every day with folly and impertinence; while I am confident, had they the advantages of education equal to us, they would be guilty of less than ourselves.

One would wonder, indeed, how it should happen that women are conversible at all; since they are only beholden to natural parts, for all their knowledge. Their youth is spent to teach them to stitch and sew or make baubles. They are taught to read, indeed, and perhaps to write their names, or so; and that is the height of a woman's education. And I would but ask any who slight the sex for their understanding, what is a man (a gentleman, I mean) good for, that is taught no more? I need not give instances, or examine the character of a gentleman, with a good estate, or a good family, and with tolerable parts; and examine what figure he makes for want of education.

The soul is placed in the body like a rough diamond; and must be polished, or the luster of it will never appear. And 'tis manifest, that as the rational soul distinguishes us from brutes; so education carries on the distinction, and makes some less brutish than others. This is too evident to need any demonstration. But why then should women be denied the benefit of instruction? If knowledge and understanding had been useless additions to the sex, GOD Almighty would never have given them capacities; for he made nothing needless. Besides, I would ask such, What they can see in ignorance, that they should think it a necessary ornament to a woman?

49. What is the best synonym for "reproach" in the second sentence of this piece?

A. Attack

B. Demean

C. Move toward

D. Ignore

E. Deny

50. What is the author saying with the second sentence of the first paragraph?

A. Education for women is a necessity, and the fact that we deny it to them is a national disgrace

B. If women possessed education, they would be able to give men a taste of their own medicine

C. Men often oppress women, and if women were educated, they likely would not do the same

D. Education is a privilege, one that women must earn for themselves

E. Society is designed to oppress women, and they would likely crumble under the pressure

51. "The soul is placed in the body like a rough diamond". This is an example of a:

A. Simile

B. Metaphor

C. Analogy

D. Juxtaposition

E. Correlation

52. With the last sentence of paragraph two, the author is implying that:

A. A man with no education is hardly impressive, even if he has other advantages

B. Certain qualities of upbringing handily offset the downsides of no education

C. Upper class men have little need for education

D. Men of good stature do not appreciate education as they should

E. Education is only one facet of many that makes a man worthy

53. What is the best synonym for "manifest" in paragraph three?

A. Presumable

B. Revealed

C. Thinkable

D. Worth considering

E. Obvious

54. The author primarily supports his argument with:

A. Citations

B. Direct observation

C. Common sense

D. Examples

E. Hypotheticals

55. Throughout the piece, the author makes frequent use of:

A. Rhetorical questions

B. Hyperbole

C. Direct quotation

D. Appeals to authority

E. Satire

Free Response Essay Sample Questions

Section II

Time: 2 hours

Question 1

(Suggested time—40 minutes. This question counts as one-third of the total essay section score.)

The foundations of private property and self-determination are interlaced with the duty of individuals to respect the equal rights of others; it is the only way that a nation can be successful, or else it always leads to war. Using the following passages, support a hypothesis of how this is true or false.

Carefully read the seven sources, including the introductory information for each source. Then synthesize information from at least three of the sources and incorporate it into a coherent, well-developed essay that argues a position clearly.

Make sure your argument is central; use the sources to illustrate and support your reasoning. Avoid merely summarizing the sources. Indicate clearly which sources you are referencing, whether through direct quotation, paraphrase, or summary. You may cite the sources as Source A, Source B, etc., or by using the descriptions in parentheses.

Source A (Locke)
Source B (Lincoln)
Source C (Churchill)
Source D (Roosevelt)
Source E (Khrushchev)
Source F (Blair)
Source G (Awaluddin)

Source A, Excerpt From The Two Treatises of Civil Government, John Locke, 1689

"The state of nature has a law of nature to govern it, which obliges every one: and reason, which is that law, teaches all mankind, who will but consult it, that being all equal and independent, no one ought to harm another in his life, health, liberty, or possessions… (and) when his own preservation comes not in competition, ought he, as much as he can, to preserve the rest of mankind, and may not, unless it be to do justice on an offender, take away, or impair the life, or what tends to the preservation of the life, the liberty, health, limb, or goods of another."

Source B, Excerpt From "The Gettysburg Address", Abraham Lincoln, 1864

Four score and seven years ago our fathers brought forth on this continent, a new nation, conceived in Liberty, and dedicated to the proposition that all men are created equal.

Now we are engaged in a great civil war, testing whether that nation, or any nation so conceived and so dedicated, can long endure. We are met on a great battle-field of that war. We have come to dedicate a portion of that field, as a final resting place for those who here gave their lives that that nation might live. It is altogether fitting and proper that we should do this.

But, in a larger sense, we can not dedicate -- we can not consecrate -- we can not hallow -- this ground. The brave men, living and dead, who struggled here, have consecrated it, far above our poor power to add or detract.

The world will little note, nor long remember what we say here, but it can never forget what they did here. It is for us the living, rather, to be dedicated here to the unfinished work which they who fought here have thus far so nobly advanced. It is rather for us to be here dedicated to the great task remaining before us -- that from these honored dead we take increased devotion to that cause for which they gave the last full measure of devotion -- that we here highly resolve that these dead shall not have died in vain -- that this nation, under God, shall have a new birth of freedom -- and that government of the people, by the people, for the people, shall not perish from the earth.

Source C, Excerpt From Their Finest Hour: The Second World War (Vol 2), Winston Churchill 1949

In my long political experience I had held most of the great offices of State, but I readily admit that the post which had now fallen to me was the one I liked the best. Power, for the sake of lording it over fellow-creatures or adding to personal pomp, is rightly judged base. But power in a national iris, when a man believes he knows what orders should be given is a blessing. In any sphere of action there can be no comparison between the positions of number one and numbers two, three, or four. The duties and the problems of all persons other than number one are quite different and in many ways more difficult. It is always a misfortune when number two or three has to initiate a dominant plan or policy. He has to consider not only the merits of the policy, but the mind of his chief; not only what to advise, but what i proper for him in his station to advise; not only what to do, but how to get it agreed, and how to get it done. Moreover, number two or three will have to reckon with numbers four, five, and six, or maybe some bright outsider, number twenty. Ambition, not so much for vulgar ends, but for fame, glints in every mind. There are always several points of view which may be right, and many which are plausible. I was ruined for the time being in 1915 over the Dardanelles, and a supreme enterprise was cast away, through my trying to carry out a major and cardinal operation of war from a subordinate position. Men are ill-advised to try such ventures. This lesson had sunk into my nature.

Source D, Excerpt From "The Great Arsenal of Democracy", Franklin Delano Roosevelt December 29, 1940

The Nazi masters of Germany have made it clear that they intend not only to dominate all life and thought in their own country, but also to enslave the whole of Europe, and then to use the resources of Europe to dominate the rest of the world. It was only three weeks ago that their leader stated this: "There are two worlds that stand opposed to each other." And then in defiant reply to his opponents he said this: "Others are correct when they say: 'With this world we cannot ever reconcile ourselves.'" I can beat any other power in the world." So said the leader of the Nazis.

In other words, the Axis not merely admits but the Axis proclaims that there can be no ultimate peace between their philosophy -- their philosophy of government -- and our philosophy of government. In view of the nature of this undeniable threat, it can be asserted, properly and categorically, that the United States has no right or reason to encourage talk of peace until the day shall come when there is a clear intention on the part of the aggressor nations to abandon all thought of dominating or conquering the world.

At this moment the forces of the States that are leagued against all peoples who live in freedom are being held away from our shores. The Germans and the Italians are being blocked on the other side of the Atlantic by the British and by the Greeks, and by thousands of soldiers and sailors who were able to escape from subjugated countries. In Asia the Japanese are being engaged by the Chinese nation in another great defense. In the Pacific Ocean is our fleet.

Some of our people like to believe that wars in Europe and in Asia are of no concern to us. But it is a matter of most vital concern to us that European and Asiatic war-makers should not gain control of the oceans which lead to this hemisphere. One hundred and seventeen years ago the Monroe Doctrine was conceived by our government as a measure of defense in the face of a threat against this hemisphere by an alliance in Continental Europe. Thereafter, we stood guard in the Atlantic, with the British as neighbors. There was no treaty. There was no "unwritten agreement." And yet there was the feeling, proven correct by history, that we as neighbors could settle any disputes in peaceful fashion. And the fact is that during the whole of this time the Western Hemisphere has remained free from aggression from Europe or from Asia.

Source E, Excerpt From "The Secret Speech - On the Cult of Personality", Nikita S. Khrushchev, 1956

Marxism does not negate the role of the leaders of the workers' class in directing the revolutionary liberation movement.

While ascribing great importance to the role of the leaders and organizers of the masses, Lenin at the same time mercilessly stigmatized every manifestation of the cult of the individual, inexorably combated the foreign-to-Marxism views about a "hero" and a "crowd" and countered all efforts to oppose a "hero" to the masses and to the people.

Lenin taught that the party's strength depends on its indissoluble unity with the masses, on the fact that behind the party follow the people - workers, peasants and intelligentsia. "Only lie will win and retain the power," said Lenin, "who believes in the people, who submerges himself in the fountain of the living creativeness of the people.". . .

Stalin acted not through persuasion, explanation, and patient cooperation with people, but by imposing his concepts and demanding absolute submission to his opinion. Whoever opposed this concept or tried to prove his viewpoint, and the correctness of his position-was doomed to removal from the leading collective and to subsequent moral and physical annihilation. This was especially true during the period following the 17th party congress, when many prominent party leaders and rank-and-file party workers, honest and dedicated to the cause of communism, fell victim to Stalin's despotism. . . .

Stalin originated the concept enemy of the people. This term automatically rendered it unnecessary that the ideological errors of a man or men engaged in a controversy be proven; this term made possible the usage of the most cruel repression, violating all norms of revolutionary legality, against anyone who in any way disagreed with Stalin, against those who were only suspected of hostile intent, against those who had bad reputations. This concept, enemy of the people, actually eliminated the possibility of any kind of ideological fight or the making of one's views known on this or that issue, even those of a practical character. In the main, and in actuality, the only proof of guilt used, against all norms of current legal science, was the confession of the accused himself, and, as subsequent probing proved, confessions were acquired through physical pressures against the accused. . . .

Lenin used severe methods only in the most necessary cases, when the exploiting classes were still in existence and were vigorously opposing the revolution, when the struggle for survival was decidedly assuming the sharpest forms, even including a civil war.

Source F, Excerpt From Speech to the Council on Foreign Relations, Tony Blair, December 3, 2008

The past 40 years are littered with initiatives, signposts to various potential breakthroughs, unsatisfactory compromises, new dawns that swiftly turned to dusk and failed negotiations. Along the way, there have been immense gains that sometimes are obscured by the central impasse. Egypt and Jordan are at peace with Israel. The Arab Peace Initiative of the then Crown Prince Abdullah in 2002 signalled a new pan-Arab approach. The contours of the final status issues, if not their outcomes, have been clarified.

The Annapolis process and the limited but, nonetheless, real change on the West Bank during the past year - for which the President and Secretary Rice deserve much credit - have yielded a genuine platform for the future.

But the central impasse does indeed remain. My view - formed since I came to Jerusalem and refining much of what I thought when I tussled intermittently with the issue for 10 years as British Prime Minister - is that it remains because the reality on the ground does not, as yet, sufficiently support the compromises necessary to secure a final, negotiated settlement. In other words, we have tended to proceed on the basis that if we could only agree the terms of the two state solution - territory, refugees, Jerusalem - i.e. the theory, we would then be able to change the reality of what was happening on the ground i.e. the practice. In my view, it is as much the other way around. The political process and changing the reality have to march in lock-step. Until recently, they haven't.

The reason this is critical to resolving this dispute is as follows. The problem is not that reasonable people do not agree, roughly, what the two states look like. I don't minimize the negotiation challenge. But listen to sensible Palestinians and sensible Israelis and you will quickly find the gaps are not that big; certainly are not unbridgeable.

Source G, Excerpt from Speech "Why is peach in Aceh successful?", Hamid Awaluddin, 2008

Aceh today is a place of peace. Guns are silent. Women no longer become widows because of political violence. Children freely develop their dreams to have a brighter future because they can attend schools. The economy is running well. Social interactions are uninterrupted. The people of Aceh have already elected their own leaders through here, democratic and fair local elections. The clear line between 'we' and 'they' has already been deleted - we have only one clear line, 'we'. These realities were empty dreams during the three decades of bloody conflict. They became possible in August 2005 in Helsinki with the peace accord signed by the Government of Indonesia and the leaders of the Free Aceh Movement (GAM). In short, past differences had already been overcome to achieve a suitable future dispensation.

Question 2.
(Suggested time—40 minutes. This question counts as one-third of the total essay sec-tion score.)

The following passage comes from "Cross of Gold", delivered by William Jennings Bryan on July 9, 1896 at the Democratic National Convention in Chicago. Read the passage carefully and then write an essay that defends, challenges or qualifies Bryan's ideas about the principles of democracy. Use specific evidence to support your position.

> "They tell us that this platform was made to catch votes. We reply to them that changing conditions make new issues; that the principles upon which rest Democracy are as everlasting as the hills; but that they must be applied to new conditions as they arise. Conditions have arisen and we are attempting to meet those conditions. They tell us that the income tax ought not to be brought in here; that is not a new idea. They criticize us for our criticism of the Supreme Court of the United States. My friends, we have made no criticism. We have simply called attention to what you know. If you want criticisms, read the dissenting opinions of the Court. That will give you criticisms."

Question 3.
(Suggested time—40 minutes. This question counts as one-third of the total essay sec-tion score.)

The following quote was made by Mahatma Gandhi.

Freedom is not worth having if it does not include the freedom to make mistakes.

Consider how freedom impacts an individual's identity. Then write a carefully reasoned essay that examines the relationship between unspoken freedom and formal constraints. Use specific examples to develop your position.

Sample Test Seven: ANSWER KEY

Question Number	Correct Answer	Your Answer
1.	E	
2.	A	
3.	B	
4.	C	
5.	C	
6.	C	
7.	A	
8.	B	
9.	A	
10.	D	
11.	D	
12.	B	
13.	A	
14.	C	
15.	A	
16.	E	
17.	A	
18.	B	
19.	C	
20.	D	
21.	A	
22.	E	
23.	C	
24.	D	
25.	A	
26.	B	
27.	B	
28.	B	

Question Number	Correct Answer	Your Answer
29.	C	
30.	D	
31.	E	
32.	E	
33.	C	
34.	A	
35.	D	
36.	D	
37.	C	
38.	A	
39.	D	
40.	B	
41.	B	
42.	A	
43.	D	
44.	A	
45.	C	
46.	A	
47.	B	
48.	D	
49.	B	
50.	C	
51.	A	
52.	A	
53.	E	
54.	C	
55.	A	

Answer Key and Rationale

Questions 1-8. Read the passage and answer the following questions carefully.

When rays of light pass through a prism, they undergo a change of direction: they are always deflected away from the refractive edge. It is possible to conceive an assembly of prisms whose refractive surfaces progressively become more nearly parallel to each other towards the middle: light rays passing through the outer prisms will undergo the greatest amount of refraction, with consequent deflection of their path towards the center, whereas the middle prism with its two parallel surfaces causes no deflection at all. When a beam of parallel rays passes through these prisms, the rays are all deflected towards the axis and converge at one point. Rays emerging from a point are also deflected by the prisms that they converge. A lens can be conceived as consisting of a large number of such prisms placed close up against one another, so that their surfaces merge into a continuous spherical surface. A lens of this kind, which collects the rays and concentrates them at one point, is called a convergent lens. Since it is thicker in the middle than at the edge, it is known as a convex lens.

In the case of a concave lens, which is thinner in the middle than at the edge, similar considerations show that all rays diverge from the center. Hence such a lens is called a divergent lens. After undergoing refraction, parallel rays appear to come from one point, while rays remerging from a point will, after passing through the lens, appear to emerge from another point. Lenses have surfaces in the same direction but having a different radii of curvature, these are known as meniscus lenses and are used more particularly in spectacles.

1. Light rays hit convex mirror and :

A. the rays pass straight through.

B. the rays bounce only straight back to the light source.

C. bend together to cross at a single point on the other side.

D. are refracted to open outward on the other side.

E. are reflected outward at angles back toward the light source.

The correct answer is E.

The text states the light angles are reflected backwards by such a mirror, rather than refracted (passing through).

2. Light rays hit a concave surface. Light:

A. travels through the prism's surface, angling together to a point.

B. moves in the same direction but has a different radii of curvature.

C. the light merges to a point on the continuous spherical surface.

D. are always reflected away from the refractive edge.

E. experiences no deflection.

The correct answer is A.

The text states that a convex prisms create a point of light by angling light beams together.

3. Spectacles use meniscus lenses, which are:

A. flat

B. varying radii of concave lenses

C. varying radii of convex lenses

D. round on both sides of the lens, meaning they have double refraction.

E. always convergent lenses

The correct answer is B.

This is indicated in the last sentence of the selection.

4. According to the author, a lens is made of:

A. Glass

B. Refractive edges

C. Prisms

D. Spheres

E. Radii

The correct answer is C.

The author describes how lenses are an array of prisms, with the middle one causing the least refraction.

5. Refraction" can be taken to mean:

A. Deflection

B. Reflection

C. Redirection

D. Alteration

E. Manipulation

The correct answer is C.

The text describes how refracted light is redirected, not reflected or otherwise altered.

6. Parallel surfaces in prisms cause:

A. Very little refraction

B. Divergence of light rays

C. No refraction

D. Radii to vary

E. Reflection of light waves

The correct answer is C.

The answer is in the first paragraph: "whereas parallel surfaces cause no deflection at all".

7. Which of the following is NOT true of convergent lenses?

A. They are concave

B. They are made of prisms

C. They can refract light

D. They have different radii

E. They deflect light away from the refractive edge

The correct answer is A.

Convergent lenses are stated to be convex, not concave.

8. **What is the subject of the verb "collects" in this sentence: "A lens of this kind, which collects the rays and concentrates them at one point, is called a convergent lens"?**

   A. Kind

   B. Lens

   C. Concentrates

   D. Point

   E. Convergent

   The correct answer is B.

   "Lens" is the subject and "rays" is the object.

Questions 9-16. Read the passage and answer the following questions carefully.

It was about this time I conceived the bold and arduous project of arriving at moral perfection. I wished to live without committing any fault at any time; I would conquer all that either natural inclination, custom, or company might lead me into. As I knew, or thought I knew, what was right and wrong, I did not see why I might not always do the one and avoid the other. But I soon found I had undertaken a task of more difficulty than I had imagined. While my care was employed in guarding against one fault, I was often surprised by another; habit took the advantage of inattention; inclination was sometimes too strong for reason. I concluded, at length, that the mere speculative conviction that it was our interest to be completely virtuous was not sufficient to prevent our slipping, and that the contrary habits must be broken, and good ones acquired and established, before we can have any dependence on a steady, uniform rectitude of conduct. For this purpose I therefore contrived the following method.

In the various enumerations of the moral virtues I met in my reading, I found the catalogue more or less numerous, as different writers included more or fewer ideas under the same name. Temperance, for example, was by some confined to eating and drinking, while by others it was extended to mean the moderating every other pleasure, appetite, inclination, or passion, bodily or mental, even to our avarice and ambition. I proposed to myself, for the sake of clearness, to use rather more names, with fewer ideas annexed to each, than a few names with more ideas; and I included under thirteen names of virtues all that at that time occurred to me as necessary or desirable, and annexed to each a short precept, which fully expressed the extent I gave to its meaning.

9. **What is the relationship between the first and second paragraphs?**

 A. The first illustrates the author's confusion at living a moral life, and the second illustrates his approach to clarifying the issue

 B. The first enumerates the author's past attempts at living morally, and the second explores his more recent attempts

 C. The first establishes the author as amoral, and the second describes his growth towards morality

 D. The first finds humor in the author's quest for moral superiority, whereas the second is more serious by contrast

 E. The first elevates the author's project as an incredible ordeal, and the second explores its value to the common man

 The correct answer is A.

 The first paragraph is primarily concerned with the author's confusion at the concept of moral living, and the second is more methodological, detailing his exploits in this pursuit.

10. **In context, what is meant by "and annexed to each a short precept, which fully expressed the extent I gave to its meaning"?**

 A. The author made certain to avoid indulging in such excesses

 B. The author reveled in his own progress towards morality

 C. The author cordoned off problematic areas of his life to better study them

 D. The author clarified desirable virtues with an appropriate name

 E. The author became confused at his own inability to be moral

 The correct answer is D.

 The author is being methodical at this point in the essay, listing his virtues and giving them appropriate labels.

11. **What is the best synonym for "enumerations" in the second paragraph?**

 A. Items

 B. Books

 C. Scholars

 D. Lists

 E. Virtues

 The correct answer is D.

 "Enumerations" can be inferred to mean "lists", as the author is still describing his method and labeling process at this point.

12. What has the author discovered other writers feel about temperance?

A. It is an essential quality

B. It is difficult to define

C. It requires an absence of all pleasures

D. It is impossible to obtain

E. It is ultimately unnecessary

The correct answer is B.

The author states that many writers have different conceptions of temperance, and thus it is very difficult to define as a concept. He sets out to establish his own definitions.

13. What best paraphrases the sentence in the first paragraph beginning with "I concluded, at length, that the mere…"?

A. Intentions are not sufficient to create a moral life if they are not followed by a change in lifestyle

B. One cannot go about the process of creating a moral life if they do not plan things out ahead of time

C. A person will inevitably slide back into bad habits and there is little that can be done about it

D. One is free to imagine themselves living a moral life, even if the possibility of living one is remote due to outside circumstances

E. The primary hindrance towards moral living is the development of bad habits, which inevitably accrue as one becomes more moral

The correct answer is A.

This is the point in the essay where the author begins to describe actions, rather than confusion or methodology.

14. What can we assume will follow this selection?

A. An explanation of the numerous ways other authors have misinterpreted morality

B. A lecture on the need for temperance in moral living

C. A list of the virtues the author has sought to acquire

D. Further description of the author's research into the topic of morality

E. Further difficulties the author has encountered on his quest

The correct answer is C.

The last sentence describes the concepts that the author has identified as virtuous, and labeled as such. It follows that he will go on to list some of them.

15. What is the subject of the verb "annexed" in paragraph two?

A. I

B. Fewer

C. Each

D. Myself

E. Names

The correct answer is A.

The subject of "annexed" is "I" and the object is "precept".

16. In the final sentence of the first paragraph, what is the best synonym for "contrived"?

A. Mocked

B. Explored

C. Indicated

D. Lied

E. Created

The correct answer is E.

The best synonym is "created", as in "I created the following method".

Questions 17-24. Read the passage and answer the following questions carefully.

When it was first perceived, in early times, that no middle course for America remained between unlimited submission to a foreign legislature and a total independence of its claims, men of reflection were less apprehensive of danger from the formidable power of fleets and armies they must determine to resist than from those contests and dissensions which would certainly arise concerning the forms of government to be instituted over the whole and over the parts of this extensive country. Relying, however, on the purity of their intentions, the justice of their cause, and the integrity and intelligence of the people, under an overruling Providence which had so signally protected this country from the first, the representatives of this nation, then consisting of little more than half its present number, not only broke to pieces the chains which were forging and the rod of iron that was lifted up, but frankly cut asunder the ties which had bound them, and launched into an ocean of uncertainty.

The zeal and ardor of the people during the Revolutionary war, supplying the place of government, commanded a degree of order sufficient at least for the temporary preservation of society. The Confederation which was early felt to be necessary was prepared from the models of the Batavian and Helvetic confederacies, the only examples which remain with any detail and precision in history, and certainly the only ones which the people at large had ever considered. But reflecting on the striking difference in so many particulars between this country and those where a courier may go from the seat of government to the frontier in a single day, it was then certainly foreseen by some who assisted in Congress at the formation of it that it could not be durable.

Negligence of its regulations, inattention to its recommendations, if not disobedience to its authority, not only in individuals but in States, soon appeared with their melancholy consequences—universal languor, jealousies and rivalries of States, decline of navigation and commerce, discouragement of necessary manufactures, universal fall in the value of lands and their produce, contempt of public and private faith, loss of consideration and credit with foreign nations, and at length in discontents, animosities, combinations, partial conventions, and insurrection, threatening some great national calamity.

17. What best summarizes the first sentence of this piece?

A. When we first realize there was no middle ground between subservience and independence, intelligent men were less afraid of war than they were of deciding how to govern our new nation

B. When our ancestors first realized they must be free instead of obedient, they realized that combat was far less challenging than the bureaucracy that would follow

C. When men realized, in the past, that freedom would be hard to win, they decided to craft a new form of government to aid in this process

D. When our new nation first achieved independence, the true struggle was not the war that followed, but the arguments between learned me who could not agree on anything

E. When men first decided independence was necessary, they could not agree who should lead them, or how

The correct answer is A.

The first sentence illustrates the author's belief that the true obstacle for early Americans was not the war itself, but the idea of how to govern such a massive and unruly nation after the war was won.

18. The phrase "ocean of uncertainty" is a…

A. Allusion

B. Metaphor

C. Allegory

D. Simile

E. Personification

The correct answer is B.

"Ocean of uncertainty" is a metaphor, a poetic comparison that does not use "like" or "as".

19. In the last sentence of the third paragraph, what does "durable" refer to?

A. Striking

B. Courier

C. Country

D. Congress

E. Formation

The correct answer is C.

The sentence refers to the perceived flimsiness of the new nation and the Congress that governs it. In context, "durable" clearly refers to the nation.

20. What does the author identify as a problem in the second paragraph?

A. The similarities between his new nation and the Batavian and Helvetic confederacies

B. The ignorance of the common people

C. The unrestrained zeal of common citizens

D. The vast size of this new country

E. The brewing revolution that approaches

The correct answer is D.

In the second paragraph, the author states the massive size of the new nation is a major obstacle, explaining that it would be difficult to govern a nation that couriers could not easily cross.

21. What word does "frankly" modify in the last sentence of the first paragraph?

A. Cut

B. Asunder

C. Ties

D. Representatives

E. Bound

The correct answer is A.

"Frankly" is an adverb modifying the word "cut" which comes after it.

22. The author identifies all of these as problems in the third paragraph EXCEPT:

A. Laziness

B. Envy

C. Poor trade

D. Religious intolerance

E. Increased dependence on foreign powers

The correct answer is E.

The author describes all of the stated obstacles except E, dependence on foreign powers.

23. What is "it" the first sentence of the third paragraph refers to?

A. The new nation

B. The Revolutionary War

C. Congress

D. The presidency

E. The States

The correct answer is C.

The "it" in the third paragraph refers to Congress, described in the previous sentence. The author laments the fracturing of their newly born country as more and more people began to ignore Congress's dictums.

24. In the first paragraph, what does the author NOT credit with aiding the representatives?

A. Providence

B. Intelligence

C. Integrity

D. The Nation

E. Purity

The correct answer is D.

Since the author is referring to the founding of the nation, citing "the nation" as an aid in this process makes no sense. All of the other questions are mentioned in some form in the first paragraph.

Questions 25-32. Read the passage and answer the following questions carefully.

No American historian, so far as I know, has ever tried to work out the probable consequences if Grant instead of Lee had been on the hot spot at Appamattox. How long would the victorious Confederacy have endured? Could it have surmounted the difficulties inherent in the doctrine of States' Rights, so often inconvenient and even paralyzing to it during the war? Could it have remedied its plain economic deficiencies, and become a self-sustaining nation? How would it have protected itself against such war heroes as Beauregard and Longstreet, Joe Wheeler and Nathan D. Forrest? And what would have been its relations to the United States, socially, economically, spiritually and politically?

I am inclined, on all these counts, to be optimistic. The chief evils in the Federal victory lay in the fact, from which we still suffer abominably, that it was a victory of what we now call Babbitts over what used to be called gentlemen. I am not arguing here, of course, that the whole Confederate army was composed of gentlemen; on the contrary, it was chiefly made up, like the Federal army, of innocent and unwashed peasants, and not a few of them got into its corps of officers. But the impulse behind it, as everyone knows, was essentially aristocratic, and that aristocratic impulse would have fashioned the Confederacy if the fortunes of war had run the other way. Whatever the defects of the new commonwealth below the Potomac, it would have at least been a commonwealth founded upon a concept of human inequality, and with a superior minority at the helm. It might not have produced any more Washingtons, Madisons, Jeffersons, Calhouns and Randolphs of Roanoke, but it would certainly not have yielded itself to the Heflins, Caraways, Bilbos and Tillmans.

The rise of such bounders was a natural and inevitable consequence of the military disaster. That disaster left the Southern gentry deflated and almost helpless. Thousands of the best young men among them had been killed, and thousands of those who survived came North. They commonly did well in the North, and were good citizens. My own native town of Baltimore was greatly enriched by their immigration, both culturally and materially; if it is less corrupt today than most other large American cities, then the credit belongs largely to Virginians, many of whom arrived with no baggage save good manners and empty bellies. Back home they were sorely missed. First the carpetbaggers ravaged the land, and then it fell into the hands of the native white trash, already so poor that war and Reconstruction could not make them any poorer. When things began to improve they seized whatever was seizable, and their heirs and assigns, now poor no longer, hold it to this day. A raw plutocracy owns and operates the New South, with no challenge save from a proletariat, white and black, that is still three-fourths peasant, and hence too stupid to be dangerous. The aristocracy is almost extinct, at least as a force in government. It may survive in backwaters and on puerile levels, but of the men who run the South today, and represent it at Washington, not 5%, by any Southern standard, are gentlemen.

25. The term "hot spot" from the first sentence is an example of a:

A. Metaphor

B. Simile

C. Allusion

D. Synecdoche

E. Neologism

The correct answer is A.

The term "hot spot" is a metaphor, suggesting a place of trouble or tension. (B), (C), and (D) could not apply, and (E) would only apply if "hot spot" were a new phrase being coined in this writing.

26. What is this author's attitude towards the Confederacy?

A. They were pure evil

B. They were deeply flawed

C. They has a righteous cause

D. They had no chance from the beginning

E. They lacked resources to win

The correct answer is B.

The author takes an academic and critical stance of the Confederacy, but he does not go so far as to say they are evil (A), nor does he support their cause in any way (C). (D) and (E) rely on assumptions not present in the text.

27. What is the author "optimistic" about, as mentioned in the second paragraph?

A. He is sure the Confederacy would have succeeded

B. He is certain the Confederacy would have failed

C. He is certain the Confederacy will rise again

D. He's confident the Confederate army could have done more

E. He believes the North won by luck

The correct answer is B.

The author takes on a sardonic tone in the second paragraph, describing how even if the Confederacy had won the Civil War, they still would have floundered due to the entrenched aristocracy taking control.

28. Which best describes the author's attitude?

A. The author is unaware of who would have won if Grant and Lee had battled

B. The author knows of no theories on what would have followed if Lee had defeated Grant

C. The author does not know any American historian who has correctly assessed the American Civil War

D. The author strongly disagrees with what occurred at Appamattox

E. The author believes the South should have been successful at Appamattox, if not for Grant

The correct answer is B.

The author has no knowledge of any specific theories regarding what would have happened if the South had triumphed.

29. What are the "bounders" the author describes in paragraph three?

A. The boundaries between North and South

B. The boundaries between the Confederacy and its citizens

C. The boundaries between the aristocracy and the commoners

D. The boundaries between morality and slavery

E. The boundaries between those who died and those who fled north

The correct answer is C.

The author laments the arrival of these "bounders" (or boundaries) between classes that resulted from the South's defeat in the Civil War.

30. Who is the "superior minority" mentioned in the second paragraph?

A. The North

B. Slaves

C. The peasantry

D. The gentry

E. The Confederacy

The correct answer is D.

In the second paragraph, the author discusses at length the idea that the South would have suffered under an aristocratic "superior minority" if they had achieved freedom. The entire subject of this paragraph is the rise of this hypothetical aristocracy.

31. What is the author's attitude towards the post-Civil War migrants?

A. They were unwashed peasants

B. They were uneducated

C. They were victims

D. They were a necessary side effect

E. They were good citizens

The correct answer is E.

The author makes it clear that most of the Southern soldiers and immigrants who moved elsewhere were good people, who aided the communities they settled in. His vitriol is aimed largely at the aristocracy.

32. The author uses the term "gentlemen" to describe:

A. Confederate officers

B. Migrants

C. Southerners in general

D. Northern elites

E. Southern aristocrats

The correct answer is E.

"Gentlemen" refers to the upper class people who commanded the war, not the lower classes who served under them.

Questions 33-40. Read the passage and answer the following questions carefully.

Most people who bother with the matter at all would admit that the English language is in a bad way, but it is generally assumed that we cannot by conscious action do anything about it. Our civilization is decadent and our language — so the argument runs — must inevitably share in the general collapse. It follows that any struggle against the abuse of language is a sentimental archaism, like preferring candles to electric light or hansom cabs to aeroplanes. Underneath this lies the half-conscious belief that language is a natural growth and not an instrument which we shape for our own purposes.

Now, it is clear that the decline of a language must ultimately have political and economic causes: it is not due simply to the bad influence of this or that individual writer. But an effect can become a cause, reinforcing the original cause and producing the same effect in an intensified form, and so on indefinitely. A man may take to drink because he feels himself to be a failure, and then fail all the more completely because he drinks. It is rather the same thing that is happening to the English language. It becomes ugly and inaccurate because our thoughts are foolish, but the slovenliness of our language makes it easier for us to have foolish thoughts. The point is that the process is reversible. Modern English, especially written English, is full of bad habits which spread by imitation and which can be avoided if one is willing to take the necessary trouble. If one gets rid of these habits one can think more clearly, and to think clearly is a necessary first step toward political regeneration: so that the fight against bad English is not frivolous and is not the exclusive concern of professional writers. I will come back to this presently, and I hope that by that time the meaning of what I have said here will have become clearer. Meanwhile, here are five specimens of the English language as it is now habitually written.

33. What does the author mean by "archaism"?

A. Mystery

B. Misidentification

C. Anachronism

D. Ignorance

E. Affectation

The correct answer is C.

An archaism is an outdated term or phrase, a synonym of "anachronism".

34. "A man may take to drink because he feels himself to be a failure, and then fail all the more completely because he drinks." In context, this sentence is best described as a:

A. Analogy

B. Metaphor

C. Simile

D. Allusion

E. Conceit

The correct answer is A.

The idiom is used by the author to describe the degradation of the English language. He goes onto explain this more explicitly in the next sentence.

35. What does this author think of the English language?

A. It is in unavoidable decline

B. It should not be altered

C. Its rules are subject to the whims of speakers

D. It can be improved through good habits

E. Only professionals should dictate its rules

The correct answer is D.

The author states that English can be improved through positive action. He states the direct opposite of the other answers in the selection.

36. What can we assume will follow this passage?

A. A screed on the decline of English

B. Further evidence that English is being destroyed

C. Names of authors who have contributed to the decline of English

D. Specific examples of bad English in use

E. An illustration of how to use English properly

The correct answer is D.

The last sentence states the author's intention to illustrate some examples of misused English.

37. What is the subject of the verb "lies" in the last sentence of the first paragraph?

A. Language

B. Growth

C. This

D. Underneath

E. Belief

The correct answer is C.

"This" is the subject of "lies" and "belief" is the object.

38. The author believes the decline of English is due to:

A. The imitation of bad habits

B. Societal decadence

C. People preferring what is simple

D. Political quibbling

E. Foolish thoughts

The correct answer is A.

The author takes great pains to explain that bad English is the result of bad habits which have been allowed to grow and spread without care.

39. By characterizing language as a "natural growth", the author emphasizes its:

A. Personified qualities

B. Duplicitous nature

C. Inconsistency

D. Changeability

E. Ignorance

The correct answer is D.

The author believes language grows naturally, and thus can be corrupted or corrected. This is the central understanding of this piece.

40. What tone is the author striving for in this piece?

A. Humorous

B. Academic

C. Angry

D. Disappointed

E. Superior

The correct answer is B.

The author is discussing English, specifically its defects and methods to improve them. This is a topic of academic interest, and the author explores it with a professional, scholarly tone.

Questions 41-48. Read the passage and answer the following questions carefully.

On the domestic front, life was not easy. England was not a wealthy country and its people endured relatively poor living standards. The landed classes — many of them enriched by the confiscated wealth of former monasteries — were determined in the interests of profile to convert their arable land into pasture for sheep, so as to produce the wool that supported the country's chief economic asset, the woolen cloth trade. But the enclosing of the land only added to the misery of the poor, many of whom, evicted and displaced, left their decaying villages and gravitated to the towns where they joined the growing army of beggars and vagabonds that would become such a feature of Elizabethan life. Once, the religious houses would have dispensed charity to the destitute, but Henry VIII had dissolved them all in the 1530s, and many former monks and nuns were now themselves beggars. Nor did the civic authorities help: they passed laws in an attempt to ban the poor from towns and cities, but to little avail. It was a common sight to see men and women lying in the dusty streets, often dying in the dirt like dogs or beasts, without human compassion being shown to them. 'Certainly, wrote a Spanish observer in 1558, 'the state of England lay now most afflicted.' And although people looked to the new Queen Elizabeth to put matters right, there were so many who doubted if she could overcome the seemingly insurmountable problems she faced, or even remain queen long enough to begin tacking them. Some, both at home and abroad, were the opinion that her title to the throne rested on very precarious foundations. Many regarded the daughter of Henry VII and Anne Boleyn as a bastard from the time of her birth on 7 September 1533, although, ignoring such slurs on the validity of his second marriage, Henry had declared Elizabeth his heir.

41. Why was land confiscated from the poor?

A. The town wanted to build a new monastery.

B. To create pastures for sheep, ultimately increasing the export of wool.

C. The town wanted to create housing for monks and nuns.

D. Queen Elizabeth wanted to expand her property.

E. The poor did not pay their taxes.

The correct answer is B.

The landed classes are stated to have confiscated the lands of the poor, and sometimes abandoned monasteries, in order to convert their "arable land" into grazing fields for sheep.

42. A vagabond is a _____.

A. Wanderer

B. Prisoner

C. Poor person

D. Rich person

E. Fighter

The correct answer is A.

The root "vagari" of the word "vagabond" might remind you of "vague" and "vagaries" and suggest the root meaning of "wandering." You can also look at the word in context and see that only (A) and (C) are likely answers, and that (C) would ultimately be redundant.

43. Why didn't the poor have shelter with the churches?

A. They were already filled with beggars.

B. Religious houses have never offered shelter to the poor.

C. They were also being used to raise sheep.

D. Henry VIII had dissolved them all in the 1530s.

E. Queen Elizabeth dissolved them all in the 1530s.

The correct answer is D.

The text states that Henry dissolved houses of worship that could have housed peasants, thus turning many of the clergy into beggars.

44. How were civic authorities unsuccessful?

A. Poor people remained within city limits

B. Public service funds ran out

C. Public housing plans extended deadlines

D. Churches did not open their doors to the poor

E. The poor overthrew them to gain their land back

The correct answer is A.

The text states that civic authorities attempted to ban the poor, but it did little to stem the tide of beggars.

45. What is a synonym for precarious?

A. Strong

B. Careful

C. Risky

D. Determined

E. Ilegimat

The correct answer is C.

While "illegitimate" might remind you of the questions of legitimacy hovering around Elizabeth's birth, and so seem to fit the context, originally the word "precarious" meant "depending on another person's favor" and in the 20th century its meaning shifted to suggest physical instability. "Risky" is not a perfect synonym but is the best answer out of the group.

46. What is the author's view towards Queen Elizabeth?

A. Doubtful

B. Vengeful

C. Resentful

D. Supportive

E. Confident

The correct answer is A.

The author states that it was widely understood that the throne's position was precarious, and Elizabeth was considered unlikely to retain it.

47. How is the English culture portrayed in this passage?

A. Religious

B. Elitist

C. Racist

D. Diverse

E. Spiritual

The correct answer is B.

The primary characteristic of English culture in this passage is its elitism and hierarchy. The poor are described as a nuisance with few rights, having their lands stripped from them and then being barred from entering villages or receiving charity.

48. What is Elizabeth's relationship to Henry?

A. Wife

B. Cousin

C. Lover

D. Daughter

E. Niece

The correct answer is D.

The text states "many regarded the daughter of Henry and Anne Boleyn to be a bastard", indicating that Elizabeth is Henry's daughter.

Questions 49-55 Read the passage and answer the following questions carefully.

I have often thought of it as one of the most barbarous customs in the world, considering us as a civilized and a Christian country, that we deny the advantages of learning to women. We reproach the sex every day with folly and impertinence; while I am confident, had they the advantages of education equal to us, they would be guilty of less than ourselves.

One would wonder, indeed, how it should happen that women are conversible at all; since they are only beholden to natural parts, for all their knowledge. Their youth is spent to teach them to stitch and sew or make baubles. They are taught to read, indeed, and perhaps to write their names, or so; and that is the height of a woman's education. And I would but ask any who slight the sex for their understanding, what is a man (a gentleman, I mean) good for, that is taught no more? I need not give instances, or examine the character of a gentleman, with a good estate, or a good family, and with tolerable parts; and examine what figure he makes for want of education.

The soul is placed in the body like a rough diamond; and must be polished, or the luster of it will never appear. And 'tis manifest, that as the rational soul distinguishes us from brutes; so education carries on the distinction, and makes some less brutish than others. This is too evident to need any demonstration. But why then should women be denied the benefit of instruction? If knowledge and understanding had been useless additions to the sex, GOD Almighty would never have given them capacities; for he made nothing needless. Besides, I would ask such, What they can see in ignorance, that they should think it a necessary ornament to a woman?

49. What is the best synonym for "reproach" in the second sentence of this piece?

A. Attack

B. Demean

C. Move toward

D. Ignore

E. Deny

The correct answer is B.

"Attack" is too strong a term, and the other answers could not apply. "Reproach" and "demean" are synonymous.

50. What is the author saying with the second sentence of the first paragraph?

A. Education for women is a necessity, and the fact that we deny it to them is a national disgrace

B. If women possessed education, they would be able to give men a taste of their own medicine

C. Men often oppress women, and if women were educated, they likely would not do the same

D. Education is a privilege, one that women must earn for themselves

E. Society is designed to oppress women, and they would likely crumble under the pressure

The correct answer is C.

The author is espousing the virtues of women with that sentence, claiming that educated women likely would not be as petty as men are.

51. "The soul is placed in the body like a rough diamond". This is an example of a:

A. Simile

B. Metaphor

C. Analogy

D. Juxtaposition

E. Correlation

The correct answer is A.

"The soul is placed in the body like a rough diamond" is a simile, using the word "like" to draw a comparison between the soul and a rough diamond.

52. With the last sentence of paragraph two, the author is implying that:

A. A man with no education is hardly impressive, even if he has other advantages

B. Certain qualities of upbringing handily offset the downsides of no education

C. Upper class men have little need for education

D. Men of good stature do not appreciate education as they should

E. Education is only one facet of many that makes a man worthy

The correct answer is A.

"Examine what figure he makes for want of education" suggests that a man who lacks education still has very little to offer, even if he is rich and well-raised.

53. What is the best synonym for "manifest" in paragraph three?

A. Presumable

B. Revealed

C. Thinkable

D. Worth considering

E. Obvious

The correct answer is E.

The author is making an emphatic point by using the word "manifest". He suggests that it is obvious that a soul separates us from lesser beings, and that education is the extension of that separation.

54. The author primarily supports his argument with:

A. Citations

B. Direct observation

C. Common sense

D. Examples

E. Hypotheticals

The correct answer is C.

The author primarily supports his argument with assertions that he insists should be obvious. It is "manifest" that education is a necessity, and it is likewise obvious that women being denied it is a travesty. He also insists, based on his own common sense, that if women were educated as men are, they likely would not be as oppressive.

55. Throughout the piece, the author makes frequent use of:

A. Rhetorical questions

B. Hyperbole

C. Direct quotation

D. Appeals to authority

E. Satire

The correct answer is A.

The piece contains many rhetorical questions throughout, and makes less use of hyperbole, and no uses of satire or appeal to authority.

Sample Test Seven

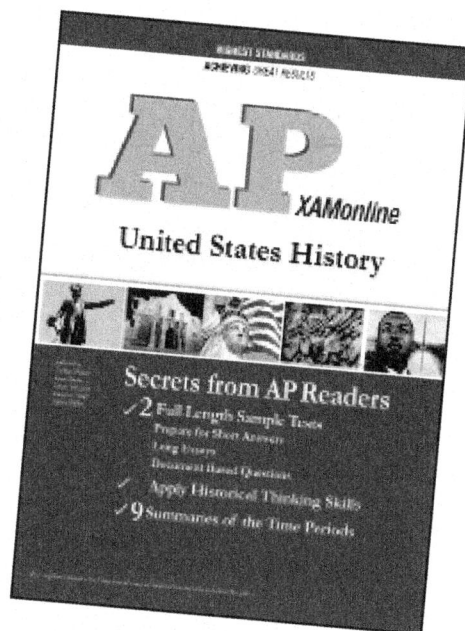

CPSIA information can be obtained
at www.ICGtesting.com
Printed in the USA
BVOW04s2028120817
491833BV00006B/13/P

9 781607 876328